Radical Right
Voters and Parties in the Electoral Market

During recent decades, radical right parties have been surging in popularity in many nations, gaining legislative seats, enjoying the legitimacy endowed by ministerial office, and striding the corridors of government power. The popularity of leaders such as Le Pen, Haider, and Fortuyn has aroused widespread popular concern and a burgeoning scholarly literature. Despite the interest, little consensus has emerged about the primary factors driving this phenomenon. The core puzzle is to explain why radical right parties have advanced in a diverse array of democracies – including Austria, Canada, Norway, France, Italy, New Zealand, Switzerland, Israel, Romania, Russia, and Chile – while failing to make comparable gains in similar societies elsewhere, such as Sweden, Britain, and the United States.

This book expands our understanding of support for radical right parties by presenting and systematically testing an integrated new theory. The wealth of cross-national survey evidence used covers almost forty countries, facilitating a broader perspective than ever seen before.

Pippa Norris is the McGuire Lecturer in Comparative Politics at the John F. Kennedy School of Government, Harvard University. Her work compares elections and public opinion, gender politics, and political communications. Companion volumes by this author, also published by Cambridge University Press, include *A Virtuous Circle* (2000), *Digital Divide* (2001), *Democratic Phoenix* (2002), *Rising Tide* (2003), *Electoral Engineering* (2004), and *Sacred and Secular* (2004).

Radical Right

Voters and Parties in the Electoral Market

PIPPA NORRIS
Harvard University

CAMBRIDGE
UNIVERSITY PRESS

CAMBRIDGE UNIVERSITY PRESS
Cambridge, New York, Melbourne, Madrid, Cape Town, Singapore, São Paulo

Cambridge University Press
40 West 20th Street, New York, NY 10011-4211, USA

www.cambridge.org
Information on this title: www.cambridge.org/9780521849142

First published 2005

Printed in the United States of America

A catalog record for this publication is available from the British Library.

Library of Congress Cataloging in Publication Data

Norris, Pippa.
Radical right : voters and parties in the electoral market / Pippa Norris.
   p. cm.
Includes bibliographical references and index.
ISBN 0-521-84914-4 (hardcover) – ISBN 0-521-61385-X (pbk.)
  1. Conservatism – Cross-cultural studies. 2. Right-wing extremists – Cross-cultural
studies. 3. Radicalism – Cross-cultural studies. 4. Political parties – Cross-cultural
studies. 5. Political culture – Cross-cultural studies. 6. Right and Left
(Political science) – Cross-cultural studies. I. Title.
JC573.N67 2005
320.53′09′0511 – dc22   2004027504

ISBN-13 978-0-521-84914-2 hardback
ISBN-10 0-521-84914-4 hardback

ISBN-13 978-0-521-61385-9 paperback
ISBN-10 0-521-61385-X paperback

Contents

Tables

Figures

Preface and Acknowledgments

In considering the explanation for the varying fortunes of contemporary radical right parties, my thoughts turned to my previous book, *Electoral Engineering* (2004), which had developed a set of propositions about how the institutional context of the formal electoral rules could shape the strategic behavior of parties and how, in turn, these actions could have a systematic impact upon patterns of voting behavior in the mass electorate. The simple idea was that richer insights could be derived if the comparative study of electoral systems, parties, and voters could be reintegrated, rather than treating each of these as distinct subdisciplines. *Electoral Engineering* examined many dimensions of voting behavior and political representation, including patterns of turnout, the impact of social cleavages, and the inclusion of women in parliament, but it did not seek to apply the theory to understanding the electoral fortunes of any particular party family. Building upon the approach developed earlier, this book focuses upon the puzzling advance of the radical right, to see how far the general theory could provide valuable insights into the roots of the popular support mobilized by parties such as Haider's FPÖ, Le Pen's Front National, and Bossi's Lega Nord.

The argument developed here suggests that the rules determining ballot nomination, campaigning, and election are important, not just for the share of seats which are awarded mechanically to radical right challengers, but also for the effectiveness of the ideological strategies they adopt. What matters for their enduring success is less the underlying conditions in mass society, exemplified by levels of unemployment, patterns of population migration, or the growth of new social risks, than how radical right parties craft their values and build their organizations to fit the broader structural constraints set by electoral rules. In this regard, parties do not work under conditions of perfect competition; instead, their actions are constrained in a regulated marketplace by the broader institutional context.

In developing this argument, the book, as ever, owes multiple debts to many friends and colleagues. The book originated during a visit to the Research School in the Social Sciences, Australian National University, and I greatly appreciate all the warm hospitality and exceptional collegiality received there. The theme of the book received encouragement in conversations over the years with many colleagues, and I am most grateful to all those who went out of their way to provide feedback on initial ideas, to send me advance proofs of forthcoming publications, to advise me about contemporary developments in their country, or to read through draft chapters and provide chapter-and-verse comments. Among others, particular thanks are due to Tim Bale, André Blais, Shaun Bowler, Wouter van der Brug, Liz Carter, Ivor Crewe, Cees van der Eijk, Lynda Erickson, David Farrell, Mark Franklin, Rachel Gibson, Elisabeth Gidengil, Jim Jupp, Jenny Mansbridge, Dave Marsh, Ian Marsh, Ian McAllister, Cas Mudde, Fritz Plasser, Marian Sawer, Pat Seyd, Stefaan Walgrave, and Chris Wlezien.

The book could not have been written without the evidence collected by collaboration among many colleagues. The study owes a large debt of gratitude to all who conducted the surveys and assembled the datasets, especially the principal investigators, as well as the funding agencies which generously supported the cross-national survey research. The primary datasets used in this book include the European Social Survey 2002 (ESS), the Comparative Study of Electoral Systems 1996–2001 (CSES), the *Expert Judgment Survey of Western European Political Parties 2000*, the Manifesto Research Group, and International IDEA's *Handbook on Funding of Political Parties and Election Campaigns*, as well as selected case studies. The surveys provide data from countries ranging from long-established democracies with market economies to authoritarian states and post-Communist societies.

The *Comparative Study of Electoral Systems* is a collaborative program of cross-national research among election study teams in more than fifty countries, with core funding provided by the National Science Foundation under grant nos. SES-9977967 and SBR-9317631. The survey data is integrated, cleaned, and released by the CSES secretariat, directed by David Howell assisted by Karen Long, based at the Center for Political Studies, Institute for Social Research, University of Michigan.

The *European Social Survey 2002* is an innovative, academically driven social survey designed to chart and explain the interaction between Europe's changing institutions and the attitudes, beliefs, and behavior patterns of its diverse populations. The survey covers more than twenty nations and employs the most rigorous methodologies. It is funded via the European Commission's Fifth Framework Programme, with supplementary funds from the European Science Foundation, which also sponsored the development of the study over a number of years. The project is directed by a Central Coordinating Team led by Roger Jowell at the Centre for Comparative Social Surveys, City University. The five other partners are Bjorn Henrichsen at NSD Norway, Ineke Stoop at SCP Netherlands, Willem Saris at the University of Amsterdam, Jack Billiet at the University of Leuven, and Peter Mohler at ZUMA Germany.

The *Expert Judgment Survey of Western European Political Parties 2000* was conducted by Marcel Lubbers at the Department of Sociology, University of Nijmegen, and the data was distributed via the Steinmetz Archive in Amsterdam.

The *Manifesto Research Group/Comparative Manifestos Project*, formed in 1979, has content analyzed party platforms since 1945 in twenty-five nations. The data was collected by a collaborative team led by Ian Budge, Hans-Dieter Klingemann, Andrea Volkens, Judith Bara, and Eric Tanenbaum.

International IDEA's *Handbook on Funding of Political Parties and Election Campaigns*, edited by Reginald Austin and Maja Tjernström and published in 2003, is an invaluable compilation of the regulations governing party and election funding. I am grateful, in particular, to Julie Ballington at IDEA for making the data available in electronic format.

Draft chapters from this book have been presented at various professional venues, providing invaluable feedback and comments, including the annual meeting of the American Political Science Association in Chicago, the annual conference of the Elections, Parties and Public Opinion (EPOP) group at Nuffield College, Oxford, and the plenary lecture of the European Consortium of Political Research at Budapest.

I also greatly appreciate the generous financial assistance provided for the book's research by the Weatherhead Center for International Affairs at Harvard University and the warm encouragement of the Director, Jorge Dominguez, as well as the stimulating collegiality provided by the Minda de Gunzburg Center for European Studies at Harvard. The support of Cambridge University Press has been invaluable, particularly the efficient assistance and continuous enthusiasm of my editor, Lew Bateman, as well as the comments of the anonymous book reviewers. Lastly, this book would not have been possible without the encouragement and stimulation provided by many colleagues and students at the John F. Kennedy School of Government and the Department of Government, Harvard University.

Cambridge, Massachusetts

Radical Right

Voters and Parties in the Electoral Market

PART I

UNDERSTANDING THE RADICAL RIGHT

I

Understanding the Rise of the Radical Right

On 21 April 2002, the defeat of the Socialist Prime Minister, Lionel Jospin, by Jean-Marie Le Pen in the first round of the French presidential elections, sent a profound shock wave throughout Europe. The result galvanized massive anti–Front National demonstrations by millions of protestors all over France. One of the best-known leaders on the radical right, Le Pen dismissed the Holocaust as a 'detail of history,' and he continues to voice anti-Semitic, racist views. These events were rapidly followed in the Netherlands by the assassination on 6 May 2002 of Pym Fortuyn, a flamboyant and controversial figure, leading to a sudden surge of support for his party in the general election. The anti-immigrant Lijst Pym Fortuyn (LPF), formed just three months before the election, suddenly became the second largest party in the Dutch Parliament and part of the governing coalition. Nor are these isolated gains; during the last two decades, radical right parties have been surging in popularity in many nations, gaining legislative seats, enjoying the legitimacy endowed by ministerial office, and entering the corridors of government power. Some have proved temporary 'flash' parties while others have experienced more enduring success across a series of contests. The popularity of figures such as Jean-Marie Le Pen, Jörg Haider, Umberto Bossi, Carl Hagen, and Pym Fortuyn has aroused widespread popular concern and a burgeoning scholarly literature.[1]

The core puzzle that this book seeks to explain is why these parties have established a clear presence in national parliaments in recent years in a diverse array of democracies – such as Canada, Norway, France, Israel, Russia, Romania, and Chile – and even entered coalition governments in Switzerland, Austria, the Netherlands, New Zealand, and Italy – while failing to advance in comparable nations such as Sweden, Britain, and the United States. Their rise has occurred in both predominantly Catholic and Protestant societies, in Nordic and Mediterranean regions, in liberal Norway and conservative Switzerland, as well as in the European Union and in Anglo-American democracies. The puzzle is deepened by the fact that they have surfaced in many established democracies, affluent post-industrial 'knowledge' societies, and cradle-to-grave welfare states with some of the best-educated and most secure populations in the world, all characteristics which should generate social tolerance and liberal attitudes antithetical to xenophobic appeals.[2] Moreover, radical right parties are not confined to these countries; they have also won support within certain post-Communist nations, as well as in some Latin American democracies. Their rise is all the more intriguing given the remarkable resilience of established party systems and the difficulties that left-libertarian insurgents, exemplified by Green parties, have commonly encountered when trying to break through into elected office.

Despite extensive interest, little consensus has emerged about the reasons for this phenomenon. This book reexamines classic questions about the underlying conditions facilitating the rise of the radical right, the nature of electoral change, and the drivers behind patterns of party competition. Building on ideas of rational voters and rational parties developed nearly half a century ago, this phenomenon is understood here through the concept of a regulated political marketplace which distinguishes between public 'demand' and party 'supply,' both operating within the context of the electoral rules. On the 'demand side,' the book suggests that certain conditions in the mass electorate, notably the growth of political disaffection and partisan dealignment in contemporary democracies, make it easier for supporters to defect, at least temporarily, from mainstream parties. The rising salience of cultural protectionism, in a backlash against globalization and population migration, has altered the public agenda in each country, providing sporadic openings for new parties. But these developments are common across contemporary societies, so they are insufficient by themselves to account for the varying fortunes of the radical right. The theory developed here argues that the key to radical right success depends upon the complex interaction of public demand and party supply under conditions of imperfect competition in a regulated electoral marketplace. Each section of the book is organized to explore a different dimension of this account.

- Part I provides an overview and introduction.
- Part II examines the broader institutional context of the type of

regulated marketplace, comparing the formal *rules* determining the nomination, campaigning, and election process.

- Part III considers the role of public *demand*, notably conditions of widespread political disaffection and attitudes sympathetic toward cultural protectionism.
- Part IV analyzes how far party *supply* matches electoral demands, in particular whether radical right parties emphasize either ideological or populist appeals within this environment, contributing toward sporadic electoral gains, and – the condition necessary for persistent success – whether the radical right manages to build and consolidate effective party organizations.

This theory is tested against survey evidence derived from almost forty societies. The conclusions drawn from the study are designed to contribute toward informing the debate about the role of the radical right in contemporary democracies, by dismissing certain common fallacies while highlighting other underemphasized causes. By contrast, the study establishes that remarkably little evidence supports many other popular myths about the reasons for their success, for example the claim that the radical right have advanced most strongly in societies with rampant unemployment or strong waves of immigration, or that they appeal most strongly to socially disadvantaged sectors of the electorate. Nor does this account emphasize, as others commonly suggest, that radical right fortunes depend primarily upon where other mainstream center-right and center-left parties locate themselves across the ideological spectrum, or that charismatic leaders are vital to their success. Taken by themselves, none of the core propositions advanced in this book can claim to provide particularly striking or original insights; indeed, they can be regarded as fairly conventional assumptions pervasive in many standard rational choice accounts of electoral systems, voting behavior, and party competition. The book borrows from, and thereby builds upon, the substantial literature in these subfields, rather than seeking to reinvent the intellectual wheel. Nevertheless, the combination and dynamic interaction of these factors have been insufficiently understood theoretically, still less demonstrated empirically, to explain this particular phenomenon.

THE RISE OF RADICAL RIGHT PARTIES

Before setting out the key components of the argument developed at the heart of this study, and discussing how this argument relates to the previous literature, for those unfamiliar with this phenomenon, the study first briefly sets the stage by describing the basic facts concerning where and when the radical right have advanced most successfully during the postwar era – and where they have failed. The precise definition and categorization of parties within the radical right family are discussed in detail in subsequent chapters, but here, for an overview of this phenomenon, some of the best-known contemporary cases are highlighted.

In the postwar decade, the remnants of the radical right existed at the shadowy fringe of party politics in established democracies. The most significant parliamentary party which could trace its origins to Europe's fascist past was the Movimento Sociale Italiano (MSI), although in postwar German politics the Nationaldemokratische Partei Deutschlands (NPD) remained active at the margins. In the United States, powerful forces of racist right-wing reaction included the Ku Klux Klan and George Wallace's American Independent Party. The most dramatic new insurgent, which shocked established party systems, arose in France, where the Poujadists registered sudden albeit short-lived gains during the 1956 general election. By the early 1970s, however, initial signs suggested that the deep tectonic plates of European party politics were starting to shift elsewhere. In 1972, Mogens Glistrup established the Danish Fremskridtspartiet (FP). Tremors reverberated throughout Western Europe when, just a year later, they became the second largest party in the Danish Folketing, gaining 16% of the vote on a radical antitax program. Other leaders sought to emulate their success in Britain (with the National Front, founded in 1967), France (Le Pen's Front National, FN, founded in 1972), and Norway (the sister Fremskrittspartiet, or FrP, created in 1973). The initial electoral record of these parties remained erratic and uncertain during this decade: by the early 1980s, national parliaments in Western democracies contained only a half-dozen parties which could be classified as constituting part of the radical right family, even by the most generous definition.

Today, by contrast, multiple contenders jostle for power. To give just a few illustrations of their contemporary success, as well as the recent contests in France and the Netherlands mentioned earlier, in Italy, the government was returned to power in May 2001, resting on the support of the xenophobic Lega Nord (LN), led by Umberto Bossi, and the Alleanza Nazionale (AN), led by Gianfranco Fini (with roots in the fascist MSI). In Austria, in 1999 Jörg Haider's Freiheitliche Partei Österreichs (FPÖ) won 26.9% of the vote and the FPÖ (although not Haider) became part of the new coalition government led by the conservative Österreichische Volkspartei (ÖVP). In the 2001 Danish general election, the Dansk Folkeparti (DF), headed by Pia Kjaersgaarg, got 12% of the vote. In Norway that year, Carl Ivar Hagen's Fremskrittspartiet won 14.7% of the vote, becoming the third largest party in the Storting. In Belgium, in October 2000, the Vlaams Blok, or VB (led by Frank Vanhecke), became the biggest party on Antwerp City Council, winning twenty out of fifty seats. During the June 2004 European elections, Vlaams Blok won the second largest share of the Belgian vote. In Switzerland, the Schweizerische Volkspartei (SVP) consolidated gains in the October 2003 elections with 26.6% of the vote, becoming the largest party in the Swiss Parliament, with 55 out of the 200 seats in the Nationalrat, gaining an additional seat in the executive Federal Council. By no means all these peaks were sustained in subsequent elections. Nevertheless each temporary surge administered a sharp shock to mainstream parties and generated considerable alarm in popular media commentary.

So far we have only mentioned some recent electoral gains for the more successful contemporary radical right parties in Western Europe. The list remains far from complete. As will be discussed in Chapter 3, in Anglo-American democracies similar parties include New Zealand First, the Canadian Reform Party (subsequently known as the Alliance and then the Conservative party),[3] the British National Party (BNP) and the UK Independence Party (UKIP), Ross Perot's Reform Party in the United States, and One Nation in Australia. In post-Communist Europe, ultranationalist right-wing forces emerging since the fall of the Berlin Wall in Central and Eastern Europe are exemplified by the Hungarian Justice and Life Party, the Slovene National Party, the Greater Romania Party, the Romanian National Unity Party, and the Liberal Democratic parties in Russia and the Ukraine.[4] In regional elections, the National Democratic Party (NDP) and the German People's Union have also registered some modest gains in the former Communist eastern Germany. Comparisons elsewhere include the Independent Democratic Union and National Renewal parties in Chile, and the National Religious Party and National Union (IL) in Israel.

Figure 1.1 summarizes some of the basic trends in party support. The graph illustrates the proportion of votes cast for seven relevant radical right parties in Western Europe which contested a continuous series of national elections since the early 1980s. This includes votes cast for the Italian MSI/AN, Austrian FPÖ, Swiss SVP, Danish FP/DF, Norwegian FrP, Belgian VB, and French FN. All these parties are defined as 'relevant' as they have achieved over 3% of the vote in one or more national parliamentary elections during this period, and they represent some of the more consistently successful radical right contenders in Western Europe. The figure

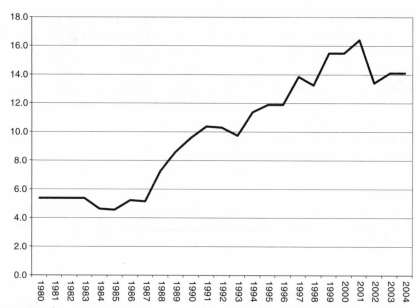

FIGURE 1.1. Mean Vote for Seven Radical Right Parties in Western Europe, 1980–2004. This figure summarizes the average share of the vote in the lower house from 1980 to 2004 for the following parties in Western Europe, all of which have contested a continuous series of national parliamentary elections since 1980: Italian MSI/AN, Austrian FPÖ, Swiss SVP, Danish FP/DF, Norwegian FrP, Belgian VB, French FN. All these parties can be defined as 'relevant'; i.e., they have achieved over 3% of the vote in one or more national parliamentary elections during this period. In the Italian and Danish cases, splits occurred within parties, but there are still recognizable continuities in renamed successor parties. *Sources:* Thomas T. Mackie and Richard Rose. 1991. *The International Almanac of Electoral History.* London: Macmillan; Thomas T. Mackie and Richard Rose. 1997. *A Decade of Election Results: Updating the International Almanac.* Studies in Public Policy. 295. Glasgow: University of Strathclyde; recent elections from *Elections around the World.* www.electionsworld.org.

demonstrates the dramatic advance of these parties: in the early 1980s, support remained flat and the radical right was often excluded from parliament through failing to meet the necessary vote thresholds over successive elections. The surge gathered momentum from the mid-1980s onwards until these parties eventually reached a slight plateau in 2001, with the support of around one in six European voters. To summarize, during the last two decades, popular support for these parties almost tripled.

By now, too many gains have occurred in too many countries to accept the idea that the radical right is simply a passing fad or fashion, a temporary phenomena which will eventually fade away on the contemporary political scene. Still, the success of the radical right should not be exaggerated: for example, the British National Party, the German NDP, and Australian One Nation currently remain stranded at the peripheries of power, attracting disproportionate media angst and headline news coverage despite, so far, only sporadic and limited electoral success. 'Flash' parties, exemplified by Lijst Pym Fortuyn, enjoy a meteoric rise but an equally precipitate fall. Elsewhere, however, as will be discussed in Chapter 10, some other contenders such as Lega Nord, the Norwegian FrP, and the Belgian Vlaams Blok have managed the successful transition from fringe into minor party status. After their initial entry into local government or national parliaments, parties which have consolidated support over successive elections have gradually gained status, resources, and legitimacy, which they can use to build grassroots party organizations, select more experienced candidates, and expand access to the news media and to public campaign funding, all of which can provide a springboard for further advances. Access to legislative office often provides important opportunities to accumulate valuable political resources such as access to public funding, political patronage, and media coverage between elections, which are denied to fringe parties persistently excluded from power.

ALTERNATIVE EXPLANATIONS IN THE LITERATURE

Of course, no shortage of alternative explanations for the rise of the radical right is available, as will be discussed further in subsequent chapters. The reasons for this phenomenon have attracted widespread speculation in popular commentary and in the academic literature.[5] Research on the extreme right is hardly new; indeed classics in political sociology published during the late 1950s and early 1960s focused on understanding grassroots support for fascism and Nazism (Adorno et al., Lipset), the French origins of Poujadism (Hoffman), and the American phenomenon of McCarthyism (Bell).[6] One summary of the literature by Rydgren developed the following 'shopping list' of reasons which had been proposed in research to explain the emergence of contemporary radical right parties:

1. A postindustrial economy.
2. Dissolution of established identities, fragmentation of the culture, multiculturalization.
3. The emergence or growing salience of the sociocultural cleavage dimension.

4. Widespread political discontent and disenchantment.
5. Convergence between the established parties in political space.
6. Popular xenophobia and racism.
7. Economic crisis and unemployment.
8. Reaction against the emergence of New Left and/or Green parties and movements.
9. A proportional voting system.
10. Experience of a referendum that cuts across the old party cleavages.[7]

Other commentators have identified ten distinct 'theories' of the radical right.[8] Yet it remains unclear how these various ad hoc causes relate to each other theoretically. Nor is it evident how structural developments which are thought to be common in most postindustrial nations, such as political disaffection, can account satisfactorily for contrasts in the electoral fortunes of the radical right within or among similar societies, such as Wallonian and Francophone Belgium, or western and eastern Canadian states. Many common propositions, such as the assumed role of economic conditions or patterns of immigration, have found only limited or mixed support in the literature. The research also remains divided in part because, rather than offering systematic comparative analysis with testable generalizations, the subfield remains heavily dependent upon descriptive narratives about specific national case studies. As a result, contingent factors emphasized as critical for the rise of specific radical right parties in some particular countries (or elections) are reported as unimportant in others. Many of these explanations are discussed and considered further throughout this book but found to be less closely and consistently linked to the rise of the radical right in many countries than the account developed here.

To make sense of the contemporary literature, and as a brush-clearing exercise, the predominant perspectives can be categorized analytically into three main schools. The most common sociological approach has long emphasized structural trends altering popular demands in mass society, notably developments in the socioeconomic background and political attitudes of the electorate, which are thought to have generated opportunities for new parties. Alternatively, more recent institutional accounts have often focused more heavily upon supply-side factors, including the strategic activities of parties as rational agents and where they choose to locate themselves across the ideological spectrum when seeking to compete for votes and seats. Finally, the traditional approach found in the literature on electoral systems has long stressed the importance of the institutional context, emphasizing the formal electoral rules constraining both supply and demand in the regulated marketplace.

Social Structure and Public Demand

Essentially, one-level models based on how changes in the social structure have fueled public demand for the radical right are by far the most pervasive approach in the previous literature, drawing upon sociology, social psychology, and political economy. These accounts emphasize long-term 'bottom up' generic conditions and secular trends in mass society – notably the growth of a marginalized underclass in postindustrial economies, patterns of migration flows, and/or the expansion of long-term unemployment – which are thought to have facilitated public demand for these parties as an outlet for political frustrations among the losers in affluent societies.[9] Specific arguments within this perspective claim, alternatively, that the radical right is strongest under conditions where: (i) new waves of immigration, asylum seekers, and refugees have raised public concern about this issue; (ii) the electorate has become widely discontented with the mainstream parties and mistrustful of the political system; (iii) a breakdown has occurred in the traditional class and religious cleavages structuring mainstream political affiliations and party loyalties; (iv) a cultural backlash is evident against the rise of postmaterial values; and/or (v) cuts in the welfare state, growing levels of job insecurity, and rising patterns of unemployment have generated new forms of social risk and disadvantage. These conditions are regarded as largely 'structural' in the sense that they are understood as persistent and enduring developments in mass society which constrain the behavior of all actors in the political system. This relationship between society and parties involves some endogeneity; in the long term, public policies can gradually transform society, for example through cuts in the welfare state expanding the number of households living in poverty, or through legal restriction on the influx of immigrants, asylum seekers, and refugees.[10] Politicians seek to shape and alter public opinion, for example by populist rhetoric heightening fears of 'outsiders,' or by proposing new legislation restricting immigration, thereby raising the salience of the issue on the policy agenda. Nevertheless, demand-side approaches treat mass society as the 'given' context within which political parties have to fight any particular election.

Although frequently assumed, for example by commentators in the news media, in fact some of the most popular explanations fail with just a cursory glance at the comparative evidence. Many accounts blame job insecurity and unemployment rates in each society, assuming that radical right support is strongest among poorer and less-educated groups, who feel threatened by rapid socioeconomic change. Contemporary accounts commonly echo postwar theories in social psychology offered by Adorno et al., suggesting that low-status individuals are more prone to suffer from 'authoritarian personalities,' where frustration born of experience of urban overcrowding, poverty, and joblessness in industrial societies is translated into hostility and prejudice against 'outsiders.'[11] Studies emphasize the rise of 'new social cleavages' which are believed to facilitate these parties, for example if the politics of resentment is concentrated among an 'underclass' of low-skilled and low-qualified workers in inner-city areas, experiencing growing levels of job insecurity and underemployment, who have fallen through the welfare safety net in affluent societies.[12] Yet, contrary to these predictions, the survey evidence presented in Chapter 6 in fact establishes little support for this popular view. Some radical right parties do draw heavily upon the socially disadvantaged populations among the poorest and least-educated social sectors; others attract a mix of social sectors. Class-based explanations fail to account for radical right support found among the comfortably self-employed bourgeoisie, as well as among the lower working class.[13] Moreover, if we compare the aggregate evidence, the contemporary radical right has surged ahead in European nations where unemployment rates are relatively low (Switzerland and Austria) as well as fairly high (France).[14] Simple accounts of structural change have limited capacity to explain this phenomenon.

Nor can this rise be attributed in any straightforward, mechanical, and mono-causal fashion simply to a backlash against the growth of the 'borderless' European Union, and waves of population migration, 'guest workers,' political refugees, and asylum seekers.[15] As will be discussed later in Chapter 8, contemporary radical right-wing parties have failed to enter the German Bundestag, the Swedish Riksdag, and the British House of Commons, for example, despite the fact that these countries have absorbed some of the highest proportions of asylum seekers in Western Europe. United Nations' estimates suggest that during the 1990s there were almost 1 million refugees and asylum seekers in Germany, 200,000 in the UK, and 175,000 in Sweden.[16] By contrast, Italy hosted about 7,000 refugees and asylum seekers during this decade, yet during the 2001 general elections the Alleanza Nationale elected two dozen deputies with the support of more than one in ten voters. Other variants within this perspective include those who claim that a backlash has occurred in Western Europe against powerful cultural tides and the

rise of post-materialist values.[17] But the classic 'value change' thesis of
Ronald Inglehart predicted the gradual emergence of left-libertarian and
Green parties in postindustrial societies, due to long-term cultural shifts
in values among the secure younger generation, and the gradual process
of population replacement, but not a return to the authoritarian past.[18]
Simple path-dependent historical explanations also fail: the radical right
has advanced in Austria and Italy, scarred by memories of fascism, but
also in Norway, at the forefront of Allied resistance.

What of protest politics? The 'politics of resentment' is often brought
into explanations where the populist rhetoric of the radical right is believed to tap into deep-seated public disaffection with the political system,
an erosion of trust in the institutions of representative government, and
the expression of disgust against 'all of the above.'[19] There is also considerable survey evidence that the rise of the radical right in recent decades
has been accompanied in many established democracies by growing popular disaffection with political institutions and with mainstream parties.[20]
But despite the apparent links between these trends, if the rise of political
disaffection is fairly universal, why should this estrangement generate the
rise of the radical right in Austria and not Germany, why Norway and not
Finland, why New Zealand and not Britain? As will be discussed further
in Chapter 7, the assumed direction of causality in this relationship can
also be questioned: on the one hand, voters may indeed seek an outlet
for expressing disaffection with 'all of the above' by casting ballots for
the radical right. Alternatively, on the other hand, 'losers' who support
fringe and minor parties on the radical right which consistently fail to
win legislative and government office may rationally come to feel greater
disaffection with the political system and mistrust of the institutions of
representative democracy.[21]

Another prime candidate concerns theories of partisan dealignment. In
political science, a wealth of survey evidence indicates a loosening of the
lifelong bonds tying loyalists to mainstream parties in many established
democracies.[22] This process is also believed to have occurred throughout
postindustrial societies, due to common structural developments (rising
educational levels, generating greater cognitive skills, and the ubiquity of
nonpartisan sources of information through the spread of the electronic
media). Where more voters are 'up for grabs' this should facilitate electoral volatility and sudden surges in popular support, including for newer
challengers. Although closer to the mark, again these accounts only take
us so far. In particular, they remain silent about the reasons why the beneficiaries of this process should necessarily be Le Pen, Haider, and Hagen,

[handwritten marginal note: how can path dependency fail? why in some countries + not others?]

for example, rather than multiple other challengers and insurgent minor parties in the crowded electoral marketplace, whether Green, regional-nationalist, ethno-religious, left-wing populist, or reformed Communist. Moreover, since the causes of partisan dealignment are thought to lie in social processes and structural trends common in most affluent postindustrial societies, by itself this explanation fails to account for marked cross-national *variations* in popular support for the radical right. As will be discussed in Chapter 10, some of the clearest evidence for partisan dealignment can be found in Ireland, West Germany, and Britain, all nations where the radical right has failed to establish a serious challenge. By contrast, the proportion of partisan identifiers has not fallen so dramatically in Denmark and Belgium, both countries where radical right parties have made considerable advances into legislative office.

In short, separate demand-side accounts frequently expressed in popular and academic commentaries often contribute an important part of the puzzle, and they can provide building blocks useful for developing more comprehensive theories. But their failure to provide an overall explanation is clear from even a simple glance at the clear contrasts in radical right fortunes found between neighboring states which appear to share similar cultural values, postindustrial service-sector economies, and comparable institutions of representative democracy, such as the differences in these parties between the Netherlands and Germany, France and Britain, or Canada and the United States.

Party Agency: The Role of Supply-Side Factors

By contrast, two-level models emphasizing supply-side factors have recently become more common in the literature, for example in historical-institutional accounts, descriptive case studies, and rational choice theories of political economy, as well as in theories linking challenger and insurgent parties with the rise of new social movements. This approach suggests that demand-side analysis is too simple and instead we need to give far greater emphasis to what parties can do through their own actions as strategic agents. Supply-side approaches focus upon patterns of party competition, including where mainstream parties decide to place themselves – to the left, center, or right across the ideological spectrum – as well as the actions taken by the radical right themselves, and the dynamic interaction of both these factors. In particular, research working within this perspective has emphasized factors such as the anti-immigrant and economic policies carried in radical right manifestos; the communication channels, populist styles, and rhetorical strategies these parties use when targeting voters; the characteristics and popularity of their leadership; and the financial resources and organization of each party.[23]

One of the most influential theories along these lines, developed by Herbert Kitschelt, suggests that the spatial location of mainstream parties across the ideological spectrum constrains the opportunities for the radical right to expand. In particular, in countries where the major parties of the left and right converge in the moderate center of the political spectrum, and where the mainstream parties fail to address issues of race relations, immigration, and free market economics that concern the electorate, Kitschelt suggests this allows the most space for the radical right to maximize their support.[24] Following a similar logic, van der Brug et al. also suggest that radical right parties are more successful when the largest mainstream right-wing competitor, in particular, occupies a centrist position.[25] Carter argues that the electoral fortunes of the radical right may also depend upon the ideological position that these parties choose to adopt within the available political space, along with cross-national variations in their party leadership and organization.[26] Alternatively, others such as Martin Schain theorize that when mainstream parties seek to articulate and coopt the radical right signature issues of political disaffection and anti-immigration, or where they accept them as coalition partners, this may serve to legitimize radical right parties in the eyes of the electorate.[27] This general approach assumes that the electorate's 'demand' for public policies can be regarded as constant across affluent nations, on the basis that broadly similar processes of globalization, population migration, structural unemployment, and multiculturalism have transformed most postindustrial societies. Variations in the success of the radical right across similar nations are therefore attributed to how far parties respond effectively to public demands through their own actions and strategies. Radical right parties are believed to react as rational actors to the opportunities arising from the ideological position of other mainstream parties, as well as, in turn, influencing the position of their rivals.

Electoral Rules: The Role of the Institutional Context

By themselves, however, supply-side explanations suffer from some important limitations; for example, during the postwar decade many established democracies experienced a broad social and economic consensus, with most mainstream parties clustered within the moderate center of the political spectrum, agreeing about the importance of maintaining the welfare state and Keynesian planned economies, yet in most places, although there was much ideological space to develop, radical right parties remained marginalized throughout this era. Chapter 9 will compare expert perceptions of party locations and establish the relatively poor fit between the type of radical right party found in a range of European democracies and either the size of the ideological gap between the mainstream center-left and center-right parties (the Kitschelt thesis), or the size of the 'right-wing' space (the van der Brug thesis). What is needed is a more comprehensive understanding of this phenomenon which provides insights into the interaction of the distribution of public opinion ('electoral demand') with how parties respond in their ideological locations ('party supply'). Recognizing party 'supply' as well as electoral 'demand,' while representing an important step forward, is also limited in the sense that in practice party competition is imperfect; instead supply and demand operate within a regulated electoral marketplace. Three-level nested models emphasize the institutional context of the political system, notably the formal and informal rules determining the nomination, campaign, and election process, which, in turn, influence both party supply and public demand.

Ever since the seminal work of Maurice Duverger, the 'mechanical' effects of the electoral rules are well known, with majoritarian systems depressing the seat share of minor parties, and this process is often assumed to affect smaller radical right parties.[28] The rules can also set a legal threshold of exclusion, or the minimum share of the vote stipulated in the constitution to secure a seat. Whether parties and candidates can get ballot access or equal campaign funding is also shaped by the formal rules. What is less well established, by contrast, are the psychological ('informal' or 'indirect') effects concerning how the legal rules shape the informal norms, attitudes, and behavior of parties and citizens, including their strategic calculations made in anticipating how the formal mechanisms work.[29] Such psychological effects include strategic contests (whether and where parties contest seats), strategic campaign communications (which electors parties target and why), and strategic voting (whether citizens vote for their second-choice party, if they regard ballots cast for smaller radical right parties as 'wasted votes'). The institutional context of the electoral system is also partly dependent upon party activity, for example where the governing parties pass legislation controlling the nomination process, campaign funding, and ballot access which restricts or even excludes minor parties. But during any contest, the electoral rules can be regarded as largely stable constraints operating upon all parties and candidates, and thereby shaping patterns of ideological competition.

Building upon this literature, theories of new social movements developed by Gamson and Tarrow popularized the idea of a 'political opportunity structure.'[30] Several accounts have utilized this concept when emphasizing the opportunities which new radical right insurgents face within the external constraints set by existing electoral rules and the established patterns of party competition.[31] Yet rather than using this framework, it seems preferable to keep the electoral system and patterns of party competition as logically separate. In the long term, formal electoral rules operating at the level of the political system are usually the stable and fixed institutional context within which patterns of party competition evolve and develop in the medium to short term, for example as parties adjust their ideological position and programmatic policies between elections and even within campaigns. Governing parties can and do alter the formal rules at irregular intervals. Occasional radical reforms transform the basic electoral system, as exemplified by major changes in the early 1990s in New Zealand, Italy, and Japan. More commonly, modest incremental adjustments amend the legal and administrative rules governing the nomination, campaign, and election process, for example the regulations used in U.S. presidential elections for campaign funding, constituency redistricting, and presidential debates. But the basic institutional context usually proves far more stable than the policy platforms and specific position of parties across the political spectrum, which are more commonly adjusted from one contest to another. Patterns of party competition are also best understood as an interactive and dynamic process, where radical right parties both respond to the position of other mainstream parties and in turn also influence them. Mixing both patterns of party competition and the electoral rules into a 'political opportunity structure' is conceptually confusing and adds little clarity to the analysis of the radical right. As Koopmans argues, some versions of the 'political opportunity' model overstretch the context to include aspects which are not political nor structural, or which just happen to fit the particular case study.[32] As such, this book avoids the term altogether and instead analyzes the impact of how party agencies position themselves ideologically and programmatically in any contest within the given context of formal electoral rules.

The institutional rules governing nomination, campaigning, and election are both formal and informal. *Formal* electoral rules are understood here as the legislative framework governing nomination, campaigning, and election, as embodied in official documents, constitutional conventions, legal statutes, codes of conduct, and administrative procedures, authorized by law and enforceable by courts. It is neither necessary nor sufficient for rules to be embodied in the legal system to be effective; social norms, informal patterns of behavior, and social sanctions also create shared mutual expectations among political actors.[33] Nevertheless the formal rules which will be compared in Chapters 4 and 5 are important as these are the core instruments of public policy, open to amendment whether by legislation, executive order, constitutional revision, judicial judgment, or bureaucratic decree. Although there is a gray overlapping area, by contrast most social norms are altered gradually by informal processes such as social pressures, media campaigns, and cultural value shifts located outside of the formal policy arena.

This study will examine evidence supporting both demand and supply perspectives with a critical eye, but it will also build upon previous studies to offer an alternative and more comprehensive middle way of understanding the dynamics of this phenomenon. Taken in isolation, each of these perspectives – emphasizing popular demands, party responses, and the context of electoral rules – provides limited insights. But in combination, if we understand their interaction, these factors go a long way toward explaining variations in the rise of the radical right. This book seeks to develop an integrated approach, where the varying fortunes of the radical right are understood to be the product of the way in which the formal institutional rules set the context of, and thereby interact with, both party supply and public demand in any election. It develops a theoretical framework for understanding the role of parties as strategic actors crafting their ideological appeals to match public demands, within the constraints set by electoral rules. This deceptively simple analytic step, developed in an earlier book, provides an extremely powerful and comprehensive lens through which to understand the dynamics of public opinion and party competition.[34] The challenge is to understand how shifts in attitudes toward cultural protectionism, coupled with partisan dealignment and growing political disaffection, have altered the distribution of public opinion in mass society (demand); how mainstream and radical right political parties have responded strategically to, and contributed toward, these changes in public opinion when emphasizing their party platforms and ideological values (supply); and how both demand and supply are constrained by the formal rules regulating the nomination, campaigning, and election processes, thereby determining which parties get into power.

Understanding the puzzle of the sporadic rise (and occasional fall) of these parties is important, even where the radical right remain marginalized on the fringes of public life, for a number of reasons. As will be explored in the final section of the book, there are plausible grounds to believe that successful radical right parties are exerting growing influence over public policy, especially on their 'signature' issues of race and immigration, by encouraging the center-right parties to adopt more restrictive policies toward refugees and asylum seekers. The dynamic theory of party competition presented here suggests that where radical right parties succeed, they expand the perceived 'zone of acquiescence,' so others will follow in subsequent contests. Their success could also signify a profound realignment of traditional party systems, as well as potentially legitimating greater social intolerance in contemporary democracies. Yet at the same time it is also true that some of the more alarmist concerns commonly expressed by popular commentators about the consequences of their rise for the overall health of democracy may well be exaggerated.

THE THEORETICAL FRAMEWORK: THE INTERACTION
OF STRUCTURE, AGENCY, AND RULES

If social structure, party agency, and electoral rules are the key analytic building blocks of this theory, how are they theorized to interact? Rather than a 'one size fits all' approach, the argument developed here seeks to explain significant variations in the strategic appeals and electoral success of parties within the radical right family, for example the sharp contrasts evident between the political fortunes of the U.S. and the Canadian Reform parties, or the French and British National Fronts, or the radical right in Norway and Sweden. The focus is primarily upon explaining the outcome of contemporary elections, and the consequences of this for party competition and for political systems, rather than upon individual-level voting behavior, although the latter helps to underpin the former. The core argument is evaluated against alternative explanations and competing counter-hypotheses offered in the literature, using national-level and survey data drawn from almost forty countries. This account unfolds in far greater depth throughout the book, along with the supporting evidence, but here the logic of the main argument is sketched out as a series of theoretical propositions.

(i) The Proximity Model of Voter Demand and Party Supply

The theory at the heart of this study starts from conditions of perfect electoral competition, and then modifies this position subsequently to account more realistically for behavior under a regulated marketplace. The traditional Downsian rational choice axiom assumes that both voters and

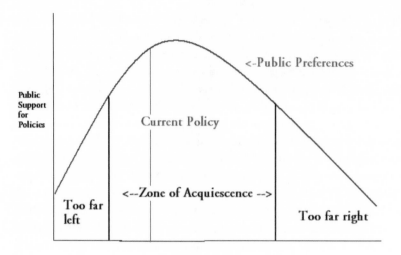

Policy Options: Left to right

FIGURE I.2. The Theoretical Model of Party Competition

parties are located at ideal points across an ideological spectrum ranging from left to right.[35] The proximity model of voting behavior assumes that each voter can locate him- or herself at a point in this space reflecting the voter's ideal preference. The position of each party can also be represented by a point in the same space. The theory assumes that under conditions of perfect competition, rational voters will choose the party whose position is closest to their own ideological preference and will shun the parties furthest away.[36] This process generates voter demand for parties. At the same time, rational parties seek to maximize their share of votes and seats by adopting the ideological position closest to the median voter, thereby generating party supply.

Further, the distribution of public opinion across the ideological spectrum is assumed to follow a normal curve (Figure I.2). Some issues do not fall into this pattern, for example if opinion is heavily skewed toward one side of the distribution, but as we shall demonstrate in subsequent chapters, public opinion reflects a normal distribution on most major issues, such as preferences for tax cuts versus public spending, or attitudes toward tolerance of ethnic minorities. In the ideological space, the theory assumes that some policy options are located too far left for the public's acceptance, some are located too far right, and there is an asymmetrical zone of acquiescence between them with a range of choices that are acceptable to the public.[37] A broad public consensus exists about issues and values within this zone. Typically, these are exemplified by the desirability of bread-and-butter 'valance' public policies, such as broad agreement about the importance of maintaining economic growth, basic standards of health care, educational services, law and order, and national security, as well as a consensus about shared social and political values such as the desirability of social tolerance, protection of human rights, and support for democratic processes and principles. Mainstream center-left and center-right parties typically compete primarily over which team is more competent to manage these valance issues. The public acquiesces to policies within this central zone because the differences among the alternative policy proposals are relatively minor, involving incremental more-or-less shifts rather than absolute black-and-white options. In democratic societies with competitive party systems, elected representatives are assumed to respond fairly sensitively to the distribution of public preferences. Rational politicians wish to maintain popular support (and hence office) by remaining safely within the zone of acquiescence, where the public is in accord with policy proposals and social values, rather than moving too far across the ideological spectrum to either the extreme left or right, where they risk gaining some votes but also losing others. Most politicians therefore implement policy changes step by step, broadly in terms of their perceptions of what the public wants. It follows that successful parties shape their policy platforms, rhetorical appeals, and values to maximize their popularity within the public's zone of acquiescence. Citizens converge in this zone and hence a center position generates the greatest electoral rewards and the least risks for parties.

(ii) The Dynamics of Public Demand

Yet the zone is not static. At a certain stage, the theory suggests, public preferences on the demand side may shift toward either the right or left. These movements are assumed to occur in response to 'shocks' to the status quo, which may include: (i) the impact of external events (exemplified by the sudden and dramatic impact of 9/11 on American perceptions of threats to national security); (ii) public reactions to major changes in government policies (such as the implementation of drastic reductions in public spending or taxation); (iii) the gradual and cumulative influence of long-term cultural trends (typified by growing public concern about the environment, rising support for gender and racial equality, or greater tolerance of homosexuality); or the persuasive arguments and rhetoric of politicians.[38] This specific account assumes that external events are important to the dynamics of public opinion, notably the impact of globalization in all its manifestations. But from the point of view of the general argument, the theory is broadly agnostic about the impact of different exogenous factors in causing shifts in public opinion. The essential assumption made here is that public opinion is not static, irrespective of the exact cause of such change. An expanding literature based on the analysis of long-term trends in opinion polls, for example by Page and Shapiro, suggests that mass public opinion shifts fairly rationally and predictably in response to these sorts of social and political developments.[39] The theory suggests that government policies, however, often continue to overshoot the new public consensus, until policymakers become aware of the shift and move back into line with the zone of acquiescence. If politicians fail to perceive a significant change in public sentiment, or else fail to respond to the shift, they face the threat of electoral defeat. In the short term, the link between public preferences and electoral outcomes remains crude and imperfect, since parties and candidates may be returned to power on successive occasions for many reasons, such as distortions of the electoral system, the personal popularity of charismatic leaders, or the impact of media campaign coverage, even when the policy mood is slowly moving against them. In the longer term, however, the theory assumes that in democracies, politicians remaining outside the zone of acquiescence and unable to turn the tide of public sentiments will eventually suffer electoral defeat.

The challenge facing rational office-seeking politicians is therefore to maintain their position close to the zone of acquiescence in public opinion where they can maximize their support among electors. The art of politics is like a circus dog balancing on a rolling balloon. Politicians may lag behind public opinion if they believe that certain policy options remain popular, such as programs promising tax cuts, even though the public has now shifted preferences toward public spending. Alternatively, policymakers may also run ahead of public opinion, for example if they are more liberal than the electorate in their own attitudes toward political refugees. Perceptual and information barriers often hinder how far political leaders can identify public preferences with any degree of accuracy.[40] But when lagging or leading, politicians face an electoral penalty. Assuming the proximity model of voting behavior, where rational voters seek to maximize their utility by opting for the party closest to their ideological preferences, and against parties furthest away, in the longer term any growing disjunction between public preferences and the actions of policymakers can be expected to produce an electoral response that 'throws the rascals out' in favor of others more in tune with the national mood.

(iii) The Impact of Globalization Has Functioned as an External 'Shock' to Public Opinion, Driving the Rising Demand for Cultural Protectionism

If we accept that the zone of acquiescence is not static, the study theorizes that one such major external shock, which has altered demand-side public opinion during recent decades, can be identified as growing emphasis on the values of cultural protectionism. The key catalyst for the value change, we theorize, is not just patterns of immigration flows per se, but rather the broader impact of globalization in all its multiple manifestations. Globalization is a complex phenomenon which is understood here to refer to the expansion in the scale and speed of flows of capital, goods, people, and ideas across borders with the effect of decreasing the effects of distance. Multiple studies have documented patterns of globalization using indicators such as levels of international trade, communications, and migration.[41] We assume that public opinion has reacted most strongly to some of the most visible manifestations of this phenomenon, especially to perceived threats arising from growing rates of immigration, ethnic diversity, and job losses arising from the greater permeability of national borders during recent decades. As we shall demonstrate later, attitudes toward cultural protectionism represent a powerful force, tapping into older nationalist sentiments. The radical right are far from the exclusive beneficiaries of the public reaction against globalization; certain core protectionist beliefs, such as suspicion and mistrust about the consequences of untrammeled free trade and the hegemony of multinational corporations, are also advocated by diverse parties and social movements on the libertarian left. Nevertheless, the more xenophobic and least tolerant dimensions of cultural protectionism have become, in many ways, the signature issue of the radical right. The rising salience of this issue in recent decades, as a parochial backlash against globalization and cosmopolitanism, has created openings for these parties and problems for all governments in established democracies.

(iv) Radical Right Parties Have Responded Most Effectively to This Shift in Public Opinion by Articulating Concerns and Supplying Policies about Cultural Protectionism, Thereby Meeting Popular Demand

Within this context, on the supply side, the strategic challenge facing radical right parties is how to mobilize sufficient support to carve out a niche section of the electoral market which is not already occupied by

Is it the parties that change stances + morph or does the surrounding culture cause it' (17)

the established parties on the center and center-right. The study theorizes that they can do this in at least three distinct ways.

One supply-side strategy open to the radical right is an attempt to compete with the established center-left or center-right parties on consensual left-right values, by stressing their ability and competence to manage the economy, public services, or national security. Yet party competition remains fiercest on these valance issues. Without the experience, legitimacy, and authority that come from an established record in government, or the resources derived from elected office, new radical right parties face serious problems in establishing their credibility and authority on these issues.

Rather than emphasizing their positive competence, the radical right may instead seek to undermine support for the political system by negative attacks, especially those directed against the performance and record of the main party or party coalition in government, or by sowing general mistrust of political institutions and politicians as a class. Populist rhetoric directed against 'all of the above,' fueling popular resentment about the political system, is commonly used by outsiders. Parties can thereby hope to gain support during any period of government unpopularity, although, of course, this is a risky strategy since they cannot be certain whether any voter dissatisfaction will benefit them, whether it will boost support for other alternative opposition parties, or whether citizens will simply stay home and fail to participate at the ballot box.

Alternatively, radical right parties may seek to appeal positively to the electorate by supplying specific values and supplying policy proposals perceived to lie outside of the zone of acquiescence, and therefore neglected by the mainstream parties in the center. Minor parties can seek to gain 'ownership' of these values. Given the normal distribution of public opinion on issues to the extreme left or right, new parties may thereby maximize support among the smaller sectors of the electorate located at these poles. Radical right parties therefore emphasize the values associated with cultural protectionism in a strategic attempt to build support, emphasizing signature issues such as the repatriation of immigrants, the closure of borders to 'foreigners,' and economic protectionism. They may also advocate more diverse economic and social policies only loosely related to cultural protectionism, such as proposing harsh anticrime laws or stringent requirements to qualify for public services and welfare benefits, although they can be framed and understood implicitly as coded attacks upon 'foreigners' and 'outsiders.' These issues and values are usually regarded as too far outside the public's zone of acquiescence to be adopted by the mainstream center-right parties: by emphasizing these values, any marginal gains major parties might make from the small proportion of extreme right voters carry serious risks of counterbalancing losses from the larger number of moderate center-left voters. But new radical right parties are assumed to be less risk averse, since they also contain fewer incumbents facing potential electoral losses. If radical right parties succeed in gaining popular support by advocating these values, then the theory predicts that mainstream parties will probably move toward the right flank in subsequent elections, adjusting their perceptions of the state of public opinion, as a rational strategy to keep within the shifting zone of acquiescence.

(v) Facilitating Demand-Side Conditions: Partisan Dealignment and Political Disaffection

Within this context, support for the radical right is further assisted by demand-side processes of partisan dealignment which loosen voter loyalties and by growing disaffection with government, both of which weaken habitual support (brand loyalty) for mainstream center-left and center-right parties, and thereby encourage electoral volatility. This should provide opportunities for newer competitors to attract supporters, especially short-term voter defections in second-order elections, exemplified by midterm contests for regional bodies and for the European Parliament. In occasional 'deviating' and 'critical' elections these contests can provide important breakthroughs for the radical right, whether on a short-term or longer-term basis. But, as will be discussed in depth in subsequent chapters, it would be a mistake to regard partisan dealignment and political disaffection as sufficient in themselves for explaining the rise of radical right parties; any weakening of traditional party-voter loyalties and any upsurge of protest voting could be channeled equally into support for a range of other minor parties and candidates seeking to provide 'a choice not an echo,' whether Green, regional, ethno-nationalist, ethno-religious, 'personalist,' or 'independent,' as well as encouraging nonvoting or 'exit.' Not surprisingly, as a result indicators of political disaffection and partisan dealignment are expected to prove significant but relatively weak predictors of electoral support for the radical right.

(vi) Yet under Conditions of Imperfect Competition, in a Regulated Marketplace, Radical Right Parties Face Institutional Barriers to Nomination, Campaigning, and Election

So far, we have sought to explain the dynamic interaction between the demands of rational voters and the supply of public policies and ideological values by rational parties under conditions of perfect competition.

The theory is simple and parsimonious. Far from being novel, the main assumptions are those conventionally accepted within the rational choice literature on proximity models of voting behavior and party competition. The account generates certain potentially testable propositions open to examination against the empirical evidence. The theory is powerful because it seeks to provide a general explanation applying to the strategic behavior of political parties in electoral democracies, not limited to the fortunes of specific radical right parties and their leaders in particular countries, whether the charismatic charm of Haider, the financial resources of Perot, or the legacy of Italian fascism.

Yet the theory developed in this book modifies traditional Downsian models by recognizing and emphasizing that the pursuit of office is also constrained in important ways by electoral institutions. In practice, it is more realistic to assume a regulated electoral marketplace, rather than conditions of perfect competition. In particular, this account assumes that the electoral system determines how the share of the popular vote translates into seats, patterns of voter and party behavior, and whether just a few major parties are represented in national parliaments or whether multiple parties are included. If electoral systems were perfectly proportional then there would be no need to bring in this intervening condition: any party's share of seats would automatically reflect its share of the vote. But in practice, no electoral system is perfectly proportional. The most important features of electoral systems that affect party competition include the effective electoral threshold (the average percentage of votes needed to gain a seat) and also, to a lesser extent, the structure of opportunities regulating ballot access and party finance. These regulate competition and constrain both demand- and supply-side factors.

The assumption that the electoral system matters for the distribution of seats is also hardly contentious, let alone original; ever since the classic work of Maurice Duverger and Douglas W. Rae, an extensive literature has established that basic electoral rules shape the degree of party fragmentation, and thus influence the electoral fortunes of minor parties of any political stripe and ideological persuasion.[42] As discussed earlier, the direct or 'mechanical' impact of rules is widely acknowledged, for example, how the legal threshold prevented the NDP from entering the Bundestag in 1969, or how the temporary shift to proportional representation (PR) in the 1986 French parliamentary elections helped Le Pen's Front National. But the *indirect* impact of these rules on party ideological strategies is often overlooked, especially in studies limited to comparing radical right parties in Western European parliamentary elections, which include few majoritarian electoral systems. Chapters 4 and 5 discuss the reasons for this relationship and confirm the proposition that the electoral system represents an important part of the explanation for cross-national variations in the emergence and consolidation of radical right parties, although these rules function as necessary, but not sufficient, conditions for their rise.[43]

(vii) The Electoral System Also Shapes the Success of Emphasizing Core Ideological Values or Vaguer Populist Appeals

Building upon these insights, the seventh proposition of this theory is that within the established system of electoral rules constraining actors, *the effectiveness of adopting either ideological or populist strategies to maximize potential seat gains depends in part upon the type of electoral system.* In this regard, parties are not just prisoners of their environment, but rather can become masters of their electoral fate. All radical right parties are located, by definition, toward the far right section of the ideological spectrum (for example, ranged from seven to ten on the conventional left-right ten-point scale), but nevertheless they are expected to differ systematically in the ideological appeals they adopt to maximize their support under different types of electoral systems.

Strategies emphasizing core ideological values work best in proportional representation electoral systems with low effective thresholds. The theory predicts that in this context, radical right parties can gain seats by adopting 'bonding' strategies emphasizing the 'signature' ideological appeals which distinguish them most clearly from mainstream competitors on the center-right and center-left. Under these rules, minor radical right parties can gain seats by focusing their appeals almost exclusively upon the values of cultural protectionism, emphasizing hard-line xenophobic rhetoric, proposing racist anti-immigration and anti-refugee policies, and advocating radical economic and social policies, such as a 'flat tax' or the abolition of welfare eligibility for noncitizens. The extreme nature of these proposals means that they are rejected by the majority of the electorate in most democracies, but there remains some support for these values among the public located to the extreme right. Low effective vote thresholds, common in PR elections, allow radical right parties to gain elected office through this strategy based on a relatively modest share of the popular vote. The theory predicts that party systems under proportional rules will therefore be centrifugal, with competition dispersed throughout the ideological spectrum and issue space.[44]

By contrast, vaguer populist strategies work best in contests with higher effective electoral thresholds to gain seats, common in majoritarian systems. In this context, radical right parties will fail to gain office unless they also expand their policy platform and ideological appeals beyond cultural protectionism to encompass a broader range of values and if they dilute their ideology with populist appeals. An effective electoral strategy requires radical right parties to advocate more diverse social and economic values, and to emphasize vague rhetoric and simple slogans, largely devoid of any substantive policy content. Majoritarian electoral systems have higher electoral hurdles, since parties need a simple plurality or a majority of votes in each district to win. Under these rules, successful parties commonly adopt populist strategies designed to gather votes among diverse sectors of the electorate.[45] This proposition suggests many important consequences, not least that under majoritarian electoral rules electorally successful radical right parties such as the Canadian Reform Party (subsequently the Alliance and the Conservative Party) have to appeal beyond narrow single-issue anti-immigration or antitax policies to expand their electoral support. Of course, radical right parties, such as the UK National Front and Australia's One Nation, may decide to focus only on their core values, emphasizing single-issue xenophobic antiforeigner cultural protectionism, prioritizing ideological purity over electoral popularity. But under majoritarian electoral rules, given the distribution of public opinion on these issues, the theory suggests that such parties will repeatedly fail to surmount the hurdles to become elected on a sustained basis and they will remain marginalized at the periphery of power. The theory therefore predicts that party systems under majoritarian rules will prove more centripetal, clustered closely around the center point of the ideological spectrum. Other accounts, notably work by Kitschelt and by van der Brug et al., have also emphasized patterns of party competition, but they have usually treated these patterns as static, and have often regarded radical right parties as passive actors in the process, rather than developing theories of the dynamics of party competition within institutional constraints.[46]

(viii) For Sustained Success, New Radical Right Challengers Also Need to Develop and Consolidate Party Organizations

The theory assumes that parties need effective ideological strategies to gain support. But for persistent success over a series of elections they also need to build and consolidate their organizational structure. Here the evidence remains more fragmentary, but nevertheless case studies suggest that new radical right fringe parties can occasionally enjoy sudden electoral success, but whether they manage to sustain their position over successive elections depends upon what ideological or populist strategies they adopt *and also* whether they manage to develop effective organizational structures. This includes agreeing on the formal procedures facilitating leadership succession and internal decision-making processes, as well as maintaining party discipline in parliament, and fostering a grassroots base among party activists, members, and voting loyalists in local communities. If parties remain poorly institutionalized, then they are more likely to capsize following developments such as internal factional splits, legal difficulties, or the loss of their founder-leader. The process of institutionalization also means that parties qualify for public funds allocated for election campaigning and full-time party staff; gain access to the powers of patronage to favor supporters; develop links with the news media, access to election broadcasting, and networks of volunteers to manage political communications; and build the modern infrastructure which maintains contemporary party organizations through good times and bad.

(ix) Where Radical Right Parties Have Surged in Popularity in One Election, by Meeting Popular Demand for Cultural Protectionism, Other Mainstream Competitors Will Respond by Attempting to Appeal to the Electorate on Their Issues in Subsequent Elections

If radical right parties are perceived as expanding their electoral popularity due to public demand for cultural protectionism, then the theory predicts that other parties within the same country will not simply stay static; instead they will seek to emulate their success by adopting their rhetoric and taking a more right-wing position on their signature issues of immigration, anticrime, and cultural protectionism in subsequent elections. The zone of acquiescence thereby expands further towards the right. Again this poses challenges for the sustained electoral success of newer parties, if established competitors can 'steal their clothes' and also appeal more effectively on mainstream issues, such as economic performance and public service delivery. Any 'contagion of the right' over issues of cultural protectionism is likely to have significant consequences for the public policy process and for government, for example by encouraging more restrictive immigration laws, as well as for patterns of party competition.

What about the vertical axis?

EVIDENCE FOR THESE PROPOSITIONS?

Are the core propositions arising from these assumptions supported by good evidence? Ever since seminal work by Douglas Rae and Arend Lijphart, there is certainly an established literature in comparative politics demonstrating that the parliamentary fortunes of minor parties are directly determined by the type of electoral system.[47] What is less well understood is how the structural context interacts with party strategies and the distribution of public opinion to explain the fortunes of the radical right. The analysis of party strategies is a complex and difficult area of study. This book does not seek to analyze *direct* evidence for campaign and electoral appeals, since it is difficult to gauge these reliably and consistently, especially across the wide range of countries contained in this study. Data from the Manifesto Research Group/Comparative Manifestos Project, coding party platforms published from 1945 to 1998 in twenty-five nations, allows comparison of left-right party policy programs within a common content analysis framework across many Western democracies.[48] This material is invaluable for tracking the ideological position and electoral fortunes of parties in countries such as France, Austria, and Norway, as will be seen later in Chapter 11. Unfortunately it has certain limitations as a guide that could be used to classify the range of parties contained in this study. In particular, the dataset excludes some important contenders, such as the British National Party, Perot's Reform Party in the United States, and Lijst Pym Fortuyn in the Netherlands, as well as radical right parties in the newer democracies in post-Communist Europe and Latin America. The coding scheme, developed in 1979, also focuses primarily upon the economic and social policy concerns most commonly dividing the major parties in Western democracies during the postwar era, exemplified by issues of nationalization, economic planning, and the welfare state. It was not designed to track detailed information about many signature radical right issues which have become increasingly salient during the last decade, including policies hostile toward asylum seekers, refugees, and immigrants. In recognition of the need for updating, the coding scheme and methodology are in the process of being revised.[49]

Alternative qualitative attempts to determine party electoral strategies directly, for example by asking campaign managers which voters and regions they targeted, or by interviewing party leaders about their priorities, encounter serious problems of accessibility to pre-hoc 'war room' campaign plan secrecy, and the dangers of post-hoc self-serving 'spin' rationalizations after the event. Indeed rational parties, like rational voters, may even be following certain strategies unconsciously, adapting to their institutional constraints without ever realizing the reasons behind their actions. Another alternative approach is to estimate party positions using proxy measures, such as indicators of party election spending on certain target voters, or content analysis of media coverage, campaign speeches, party websites, and election literature.[50] But again this evidence is simply not available on a functionally equivalent reliable basis for a wide range of parties and countries, and it is also often contextually driven; for example spending limits and control of TV advertising are often determined by campaign finance laws and broadcasting regulations.

The most reliable alternative research strategy for a consistent cross-national comparison is to define party families from 'expert surveys' which ask a sample of political scientists in each country to locate each party on a left-right ten-point ideological scale, or an equivalent scale on specific issues. This technique has been widely used in the literature and, building on previous studies, this book draws upon expert (and public) judgments for the location of parties contained within the CSES survey, and also the most recent expert survey, conducted in 2000 by Marcel Lubbers.[51] Chapter 2 uses these measures to define and classify which parties can be regarded as falling within the radical right family. Subsequent chapters then analyze and compare the attitudes, values, and social characteristics of supporters of these parties with other voters in the mass electorate. Under PR systems, where radical right parties are predicted to focus on mobilizing core voters on their core 'signature' issues, including appeals to xenophobia, nationalism, and cultural protectionism, their supporters are expected to be fairly homogeneous in their values, and ideological cues are predicted to be stronger guides to voting choices. Under majoritarian systems, by contrast, where radical right parties need to broaden their appeal to succeed in gaining office, their supporters are expected to prove more heterogeneous in their attitudes and values, and populist appeals are expected to be more important than ideological cues in determining voter choice. The theory predicts that the type of electoral rules will have important results for the campaign strategies adopted by successful radical right parties. These appeals can be tested empirically by examining survey evidence about the characteristics of party supporters in many nations, as well as by comparing selected detailed case studies illustrating historical processes in specific countries.

Most analysis of voting behavior is conventionally conducted at the individual level with comparisons made among groups of party supporters within each country. Cross-national comparisons then add a second level, for example by comparing the class basis of voting for the Austrian FPÖ and the Italian Lega Nord,[52] examining contrasts between supporters of the Flemish Vlaams Blok and the Wallonian Front National in Belgium,[53] or analyzing trends over time in political attitudes among supporters for radical right parties in one or two countries.[54] But with comparative studies limited to just a few countries it is difficult, or even impossible, to isolate institutional effects, such as the role of electoral and party systems on voting support for different parties. As a result, explanations which appear to be based on the social or ideological profile of voters for particular parties may, in fact, be due to the electoral and party systems in operation in each country.

Given this understanding, this study compares individual voters clustered in their support for relevant radical right parliamentary parties (defined as those with over 3% of seats in the lower house) within national elections. In turn, national elections are clustered into different types of electoral systems. The type of electoral institutions, and the socioeconomic conditions in each country, are classified and gauged at macrolevel. This data is combined with survey evidence monitoring voting behavior, political attitudes, and social characteristics, all measured at individual level. This evidence is compared across a wide range of nations, thirty-nine in total, including established and newer democracies from many regions in the world, using the thirty-two-nation Comparative Study of Electoral Systems 1996–2001 (CSES) and the twenty-two-nation European Social Survey 2002 (ESS) as the primary survey datasets. In combination, as will be discussed in detail in the next chapter, these recent large-scale cross-national surveys allow us to compare electoral support for radical right parties at individual level within varying institutional contexts. The comparative framework contains established and newer democracies, as well as industrial and postindustrial societies, including countries in Western, Central, and Eastern Europe, North and South America, and Asia-Pacific.

Plan of the Book

The challenge for this book is to explore the evidence supporting the strategic agency theory compared with alternative accounts. The theory does not claim to be particularly novel in its components. Many have regarded either the direct impact of electoral systems, or the breadth of the policy appeal of the radical right, or the rise of cultural protectionism, as important parts of the explanation for their success. The combination of these factors, however, has been insufficiently emphasized to explain exactly how successful party strategies respond to different electoral contexts. Chapter 2 explains the comparative framework and sources of survey and 'expert' data used in this study. Chapter 3 clarifies the party classification, an important preliminary step in order to examine whether parties identified as located within the radical right family share common social and ideological characteristics, as commonly assumed, as well as describing patterns of support for the most important parties on the radical right in each country.

Building on this foundation, Part II then starts to test the empirical evidence for the importance of formal rules in explaining the rise of the radical right in some affluent societies and established democracies, but not in others. Chapter 4 focuses upon the impact of ballot access and campaign finance rules, while Chapter 5 considers how far electoral systems generate patterns of party competition and opportunities for minor parties.

On this basis, Part III examines three dimensions of electoral demand. Chapter 6 considers survey evidence to see whether contemporary radical right support is drawn disproportionately from the petit bourgeoisie, as with classic fascist movements during the interwar era, or whether today these parties mobilize an 'underclass' of the less affluent and less educated strata who feel resentment against ethnic minorities, so that radical right support is concentrated within disadvantaged sectors, or instead whether processes of partisan dealignment mean that these parties gain votes from different social sectors and classes. Chapter 7 focuses upon the 'protest politics' thesis, which suggests that support for the radical right is essentially motivated by negative evaluations of the performance of the party in government, the lack of electoral choices due to closure of the gap between the center-left and center-right, or a more diffuse rejection of democratic institutions. Chapter 8 looks in more depth at attitudes toward immigration, multiculturalism, xenophobia, and cultural protectionism, and, in particular, how far electoral support for the radical right is linked to lack of tolerance toward ethnic minorities, asylum seekers, and refugees.

Part IV turns to the role of agency, representing the strategic appeals, ideological values and policy proposals that parties present to the electorate. Chapter 9 compares the impact of the perceived ideological location of radical right parties, leadership popularity, and partisanship. The study also uses case studies to see whether their ideological location is more strongly associated with votes for radical right parties in countries with PR rather than majoritarian electoral systems, as predicted by the strategic agency theory. Yet the analysis of cross-national survey evidence remains limited in its capacity to document processes of party change over time, and how some radical right parties move from the periphery to becoming minor partners in coalition governments, while others fail. Chapter 10 outlines the importance of organizational development and consolidation for sustained success and then illustrates this by selected case studies in nations where the radical right has, and has not, advanced into power.

Lastly, Part IV considers the wider consequences of this phenomenon for party competition, public policy, and the political system. Chapter 11 recaps the theoretical framework, summarizes the major findings established throughout the book, and also seeks to understand the broader implications of this development for representative democracy. Many liberals are alarmed by the contemporary resurgence of the radical right, but are these concerns actually justified? The conclusion reflects on whether these parties represent a healthy outlet for the expression of genuine public concern about issues of multiculturalism, thereby contributing toward public debate and diffusing tensions, or whether the growing legitimacy and power of the radical right poses substantial threats to social tolerance, political stability, and therefore the fundamental health of democracy.

2

Classifying the Radical Right

This chapter starts by clarifying the comparative framework and the primary sources of survey data employed in this study. The book is based upon the 'most different' research design, including thirty-nine countries with contrasting democratic histories, patterns of industrial development, and political institutions, as well as divergent electoral fortunes for the radical right. Countries are compared if included in either of the primary survey data sources: the European Social Survey 2002 and the Comparative Study of Electoral Systems 1996–2001. The national variations are important since they provide insights into the underlying conditions facilitating electoral support for these parties. The chapter then discusses the best way to conceptualize and define parties such as the French Front National, the Austrian FPÖ, and the Belgian Vlaams Blok, and explains the party typology used in this study. For a consistent classification, this book uses both 'expert' and 'voter' judgments to identify the location of parties across the ideological spectrum. This chapter draws upon the most recent expert survey, conducted in 2000 by Marcel Lubbers, supplemented by those contained in the Comparative Study of Electoral Systems and by similar sources.[1] Careful classification is an important preliminary step before examining whether parties within the radical right family share certain similar social and ideological characteristics, as so often assumed. On this basis, Chapter 3 then goes on to briefly summarize the electoral fortunes of the most significant contemporary radical right parties studied in depth throughout the rest of the book.

THE COMPARATIVE FRAMEWORK AND DATA SOURCES

The most common approach adopted by comparative studies of the radical right is to adopt the 'most similar' framework.[2] Edited volumes have often focused upon right-wing party fortunes within Western Europe, post-Communist Europe, or Latin America. Or they have sought to compare advanced industrial societies or established democracies. The virtue of the 'most similar' design is that these countries are believed to share certain similar historical traditions, levels of development, and cultural characteristics; this design can also draw upon the national expertise of area and regional specialists. By 'controlling' for certain common features, such as the length of experience of democracy, or the strength of Catholic or Protestant religious traditions, the analyst can thereby exclude these factors from the analysis and focus upon those conditions that *do* vary systematically within the selected universe, such as levels of unemployment or patterns of immigration. Given the common problem of too many variables and insufficient cases, this research design is attractive yet it is also limited. In particular, the 'most similar' framework can overlook certain structural and institutional arrangements which may be critical in explaining the success of the radical right, simply because they do not vary within a specific region or type of democracy under comparison. For example, studies confined to Western Europe cannot easily compare the role of electoral systems because nearly all established democracies in the region use proportional representation. Older postwar dichotomies between Western and post-Communist Europe, based on the Cold War era, may overlook growing convergence and the emergence of striking similarities, such as those shared today by member states within the expanded twenty-five-nation European Union, drawing upon centuries of shared cultures. Moreover it may be dangerous to expand generalizations beyond each region, for example to assume that the results of research analyzing the fifteen existing members of the European Union, or the nineteen nations contained in Western Europe, can be applied to the broader range of contemporary democracies found today in Central and Eastern Europe, Latin America, and Asia.

By contrast, the diverse range of thirty-nine nations included in this study requires the adoption of the 'most different' comparative framework. The advantage is that this approach allows us to examine systematic variations in patterns of voting support for radical right parties under many conditions, whether in terms of types of electoral systems (including majoritarian, combined, or proportional systems), rates of economic development, levels of dissatisfaction with government performance, or ethnic heterogeneity or homogeneity. A comparison covering many (although not all) Western European nations and Anglo-American democracies, as well as some Latin American and post-Communist states, expands the scope of the empirical generalizations that can be explored under a wide variety of contexts.

Yet this approach also carries certain well-known limitations. In particular, due to the multiplicity of variables under comparison it remains difficult to establish whether the factors thought to explain the rise of the radical right in this study are indeed the key drivers. Taken in isolation, no single indicator, set of data, national case study, or analytical technique can provide a comprehensive picture or definitive evidence. As with other controversies in the social sciences, the core concepts, definitions, and measures concerning electoral support for radical right parties can be understood and operationalized in many alternative ways. Any one piece of the puzzle can be reasonably challenged by skeptics and the results should be taken with a strong pinch of salt. But where alternative approaches using multiple indicators, social surveys, and methods of analysis produce patterns found consistently across a wide range of nations, and where a logical and parsimonious theory can account for the relationships, then their cumulative effect increases confidence in the reliability and robustness of the results and the conclusions become more compelling.

In particular, rather than making up ad hoc theories to account for the popularity of the radical right, it is far more satisfactory to relate explanations to what is already known more broadly from the established literature on patterns of voting behavior, party competition, and elections. This book provides a general theory, based on standard rational choice explanations of voting and parties, that remains open to further development. Area studies specialists can explore the theory further to see whether it fits by using more detailed qualitative case studies of the rise of the radical right within specific nations, while regional experts can expand the scope of the inquiry to consider how far the explanation works in other societies. This research is limited to examining the evidence from three main sources: (i) trends in national election results in many countries, including the percentage votes and seats won by the radical right during the postwar era; (ii) analysis of survey data in the thirty-nine countries included in the European Social Survey 2002 and the Comparative Study of Electoral Systems 1996–2001; and lastly (iii) case studies of party competition in selected elections and content analysis of party platforms collected by the Manifesto Research Group/Comparative Manifestos Project. The cases

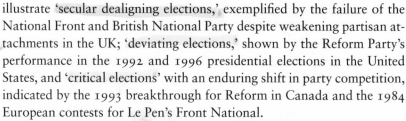

illustrate 'secular dealigning elections,' exemplified by the failure of the National Front and British National Party despite weakening partisan attachments in the UK; 'deviating elections,' shown by the Reform Party's performance in the 1992 and 1996 presidential elections in the United States, and 'critical elections' with an enduring shift in party competition, indicated by the 1993 breakthrough for Reform in Canada and the 1984 European contests for Le Pen's Front National.

A major source of survey data for this book is the twenty-two-nation European Social Survey 2002.[3] This study is designed to chart and explain the interaction between Europe's changing institutions and the attitudes, beliefs, and behavior patterns of its diverse populations. The survey includes a wide range of items designed to monitor voting behavior, partisanship, and an extensive range of social and political attitudes, including multiple items which can be used to develop scales of attitudes toward immigration and refugees, as well as indicators of political interest, efficacy, trust, subjective well-being, family and friendship bonds, and a rich array of detailed sociodemographic data including household composition, work status, dependence on state benefits, ethnicity, type of area, and occupational class. The size of the total pooled sample (with over forty thousand cases) allows us to monitor voting behavior among smaller population subgroups, such as ethnic minorities. The survey includes four nations in Scandinavia (Norway, Sweden, Finland, Denmark), eight nations in Northern Europe (Austria, Britain, France, Germany, Luxembourg, Ireland, the Netherlands, and Switzerland), six from Mediterranean Europe (Greece, Spain, Italy, Portugal, Turkey, and Israel), and four post-Communist societies in Central Europe (the Czech Republic, Hungary, Poland, and Slovenia). As shown in Table 2.1, all these countries fall within the category of electoral democracies, classified by Freedom House in 2001–2002 as fully 'free' in their political rights and civil liberties, using the Gastil index. Most can also be categorized as affluent postindustrial economies, with an average per capita GDP in 2002 ranging from sixteen thousand dollars (in Greece) to thirty thousand dollars (in Norway), although all of the post-Communist states except Slovenia fall below this level. The ESS facilitates comparison across a range of advanced industrialized societies in Western Europe sharing a broadly similar cultural heritage and level of development.

This survey is supplemented by the Comparative Study of Electoral Systems 1996–2001. This project is based on work by an international team of collaborators who have incorporated a special battery of survey questions into the national election studies, using a representative sample of the electorate in each country. Data from each of the separate election studies was coordinated, integrated, and cleaned by the Center for Political Studies, Institute for Social Research, at the University of Michigan.[4] The dataset is designed to facilitate the comparison of macro- and micro-level electoral data. Module 1 of the CSES (released in July 2002) used in this study allows us to compare surveys of a representative cross-section of the electorate in thirty-seven legislative and presidential national elections in thirty-two countries. The geographic coverage includes countries containing in total over 1.2 million inhabitants, or one-fifth of the world's population. The focus on voters' choices, the cross-national integration, and above all the timing of the data collection (within a year following each of the elections) provide a unique opportunity to compare voting behavior in a way that is not possible through other common sources of comparative data. Throughout the book, the national elections under comparison in the CSES are those held from 1996 to 2002 for the lower house of the national parliament and for presidential contests.

The 'most different' research design is particularly well suited to the societies included in these surveys as they range from low- or middle-income developing nations, such as Thailand, Mexico, Ukraine, Belarus, and Romania (all with a per capita purchasing power parity (PPP) GDP of less than five thousand dollars in 1998), to some of the most affluent societies in the world, including Switzerland, the United States, and Japan (with an equivalent per capita GDP of more than $30,000). Table 2.1 illustrates some of the basic charactistics of these nations. The countries under comparison in the CSES have varied political institutions, rates of population migration, levels of democratization, and cultural historical traditions, all of which can be incorporated into comprehensive explanations of patterns of right-wing support. Ethnically homogeneous societies such as Poland, Norway, and Britain are included, as well as plural societies with multiple social cleavages, exemplified by Israel and Belgium. The length of time that each country has experienced democratic institutions also varies considerably, as measured by the mean score 1972–2003 on the Gastil index measured by Freedom House, which can be expected to have an important impact upon electoral behavior and patterns of party competition. While Australia and Sweden are long-established democracies, countries such as Spain and Portugal experienced their democratic revolutions in the early 1970s, while still others like the Ukraine, Russia, and Belarus are characterized by unstable and fragmented opposition parties, ineffective legislatures, and limited checks on the executive, with a patchy record of civil liberties and political rights.[5]

TABLE 2.1. *The Comparative Framework*

Nation	Abrv.	HDI rank 2001 (UNDP 2003)[a]	GDP per capita PPP 2000 (World Bank 2002)[b]	Total pop. 2002 (World Bank 2002)	Freedom House Mean Political Rights & Civil Liberties[c] 1972–2003	Freedom House Rating Political Rights & Civil Liberties[c] 2002	Region	Type of electoral system (IDEA 1997)[d]	% Vote radical right 2000–2004
1 Australia	AUS	4	25,693	18,880,000	1.0	1.0	Asia-Pacific	AV	4.3
2 Austria	AUT	16	26,765	7,705,000	1.0	1.0	W. Europe	List PR	10.0
3 Belarus	BLR	53	7,544	10,236,000	5.9	6.0	C. & E. Europe	Two round	.
4 Belgium	BEL	6	27,178	10,161,000	1.1	1.0	W. Europe	List PR	13.6
5 Canada	CAN	8	27,840	31,147,000	1.0	1.0	N. America	FPTP	25.5
6 Chile	CHL	43	9,417	15,211,000	3.9	1.5	S. America	List PR	44.2
7 Czech Rep.	CZE	32	13,991	10,244,000	4.6	1.5	C. & E. Europe	List PR	1.0
8 Denmark	DNK	11	27,627	5,293,000	1.0	1.0	Scandinavia	List PR	12.6
9 Finland	FIN	14	24,996	5,176,000	1.5	1.0	Scandinavia	List PR	0.0
10 France	FRA	17	24,223	59,080,000	1.5	1.0	W. Europe	Two round	13.2
11 Germany	DEU	18	25,103	82,220,000	1.4	1.0	W. Europe	CD	0.3
12 Greece	GRC	24	16,501	10,645,000	2.1	1.5	W. Europe	List PR	2.2
13 Hungary	HUN	38	12,416	10,036,000	3.8	1.5	C. & E. Europe	CD	4.4
14 Iceland	ISL	2	29,581	281,000	1.0	1.0	Scandinavia	List PR	0.0
15 Ireland	IRL	12	29,866	3,730,000	1.1	1.0	W. Europe	STV	0.0
16 Israel	ISR	22	20,131	5,122,000	2.1	2.0	Middle East	List PR	9.7
17 Italy	ITA	21	23,626	57,298,000	1.4	1.0	W. Europe	CD	16.3
18 Japan	JPN	9	26,755	126,714,000	1.4	1.5	Asia-Pacific	CI	0.0

19	Korea, Rep.	KOR	30	15,054	46,844,000	3.7	2.0	Asia-Pacific	CI	0.0
20	Lithuania	LTU	45	7,106	3,670,000	4.5	1.5	C. & E. Europe	CI	1.3
21	Luxembourg	LUX	15	46,833	431,000	1.1	1.0	W. Europe	List PR	0.0
22	Mexico	MEX	55	9,023	98,881,000	3.6	2.0	N. America	CD	0.0
23	Netherlands	NLD	5	25,657	15,786,000	1.0	1.0	W. Europe	List PR	5.7
24	New Zealand	NZL	20	20,070	3,862,000	1.0	1.0	Asia-Pacific	CD	10.4
25	Norway	NOR	1	29,918	4,461,000	1.0	1.0	Scandinavia	List PR	14.5
26	Peru	PER	82	4,799	25,662,000	3.8	2.5	S. America	List PR	0.0
27	Poland	POL	35	9,051	38,765,000	3.8	1.5	C. & E. Europe	List PR	0.0
28	Portugal	PRT	23	17,290	9,875,000	1.8	1.0	W. Europe	List PR	0.0
29	Romania	ROM	72	6,423	22,327,000	5.2	2.0	C. & E. Europe	List PR	21.0
30	Russia	RUS	63	8,377	146,934,000	5.4	5.0	C. & E. Europe	CI	11.5
31	Slovenia	SVN	29	17,367	1,986,000	4.5	1.0	C. & E. Europe	List PR	4.4
32	Spain	ESP	19	19,472	39,630,000	2.1	1.0	W. Europe	List PR	0.1
33	Sweden	SWE	3	24,277	8,910,000	1.0	1.0	Scandinavia	List PR	1.4
34	Switzerland	CHE	10	28,769	7,386,000	1.0	1.0	W. Europe	List PR	29.5
35	Taiwan	TWN	.	.	22,401,000	4.0	2.0	Asia-Pacific	CI	0.0
36	Thailand	THA	74	6,402	61,399,000	3.6	2.5	Asia-Pacific	CD	0.0
37	Ukraine	UKR	75	3,816	50,456,000	5.2	4.0	C. & E. Europe	CI	0.1
38	UK	GBR	13	24,455	58,830,000	1.2	1.0	W. Europe	FPTP	0.2
39	U.S.	USA	7	34,142	278,357,000	1.0	1.0	N. America	FPTP	0.0
TOTAL			38	38	39	39	39	39	39	38

[a] The United Nations Development Program (UNDP) ranking of all nations worldwide according to the Human Development Index in 2001. The HDI is based on longevity, as measured by life expectancy at birth; educational achievement; and standard of living, as measured by per capita GDP (PPP $U.S.). A high rank represents greater development. Human Development Report, 2003.

[b] Gross Domestic Product (2000) measured in $U.S. in Purchasing Power Parity. World Bank Development Indicators, 2002.

[c] Freedom House Gastil index: A 7-point scale used by Freedom House, measuring political rights and civil liberties every year, where high equals most democratic. www.Freedomhouse.com.

[d] International IDEA.

41

This study therefore compares a wide range of older democracies, newer democracies, and a few nondemocratic states. To classify levels of democratization on a systematic and consistent basis, the book uses indices developed by Freedom House, monitoring political rights and civil liberties since 1972. Recent years have seen increasingly sophisticated attempts to develop effective measures of democracy. These include minimalist definitions, such as the dichotomous classification of all political systems into democracies and autocracies developed by Przeworski et al., multidimensional scales used by the World Bank to rank national levels of corruption, stability, and rule of law, and immensely rich and detailed qualitative 'democratic audits' conducted in just a few countries.[6] Alternative summary indices emphasize different components. All suffer from certain conceptual or methodological limitations in their reliability, consistency, and validity. Nevertheless, a comparison of nine major indices of democracy by Munck and Verkuilen concluded that, despite these methodological differences, in practice simple correlation tests showed considerable similarity in how nations were ranked across different measures: "For all the differences in conceptualization, measurement and aggregation, they seem to show that the reviewed indices are tapping into the same underlying realities."[7] Systematic biases may be generated from reliance by all the indices on similar sources of evidence, or from common data limitations, but the correlation of outcomes suggests that the adoption of one or another measure is unlikely to generate widely varying classifications of countries. The Gastil index, used by Freedom House, is adopted here from the range of alternatives, as in previous work by the author, because it provides comprehensive coverage worldwide, including all nation-states and independent territories around the globe.[8] The index also facilitates time-series analysis of trends in democratization, since an annual measurement for each country has been produced every year since the early 1970s. The index has become widely accepted as one of the standard measures providing a multidimensional classification of political rights and civil liberties. Table 2.1 shows the mean annual Freedom House ratings calculated from 1972 to 2003, as an indicator of democratic histories, and it also provides the most recent rating available (2003) for comparison.[9]

Based on this measure, *older democracies* are defined as the thirty-nine states around the world with at least twenty years continuous experience of democracy from 1983 to 2003 and a Freedom House score of 1.0 to 1.5 in the 2002 rating. *Newer democracies* are classified as the forty-seven states with less than twenty years experience with democracy and a 2002 Freedom House rating of 1.0 to 1.5. Another forty-seven states were classified as *semi-democracies* (Freedom House describes them as 'partly-free'; others use the terms *transitional* or *consolidating* democracies); these states have been democratic for less than twenty years and have Freedom House ratings in 2002 of 2.0 to 3.5. *Nondemocracies* are the remaining sixty-two states, with a Freedom House score in 2002 from 4.0 to 7.0; they include military-backed dictatorships, authoritarian states, elitist oligarchies, and absolute monarchies. Russia, Ukraine, and Belarus are rated as more authoritarian today than the other countries under comparison; nevertheless they are included since they provide an opportunity to examine support for the radical right in a few of the societies with more restricted political rights and civil liberties.

CLASSIFYING PARTY FAMILIES

Within this comparative framework, how can parties on the radical right be defined and classified? Political scientists have developed numerous typologies based on perceived similarities in certain party characteristics, whether in terms of shared programmatic policies and doctrinal appeals, common formal organizational structures, similar social characteristics of their supporters, networks through transnational organizational links, or even party names.[10] Certain categories of party families are now well established and clearly recognized in the literature, such as the 'Greens,' 'Socialists,' or 'Communists.' Yet it remains unclear whether a single phenomenon labeled 'the radical right' exists, even as a loose category. Parties commonly seen as exemplifying the radical right, such as Lega Nord, the Freiheitliche Partei Österreichs, and the Dansk Folkeparti, can also be regarded as highly diverse in their ideological appeals, organizational structures, and leadership rhetoric.[11] The classification process is relatively straightforward through membership of international party organizations. Most Social Democratic, Socialist, and Labour parties, for example, recognize common affiliations through membership of the Socialist International, even when parties within this family diverge in their ideological positions and programmatic stances, such as contrasts over economic and foreign policy between Blair's Labour Party and Schroeder's Social Democrats. Radical right parties represented within the European Parliament have developed some common transnational party networks, notably affiliation with the Group of Independents for a Europe of the

Nations, which includes the Austrian FPÖ, the Belgian VB and FN, the French FN, and the Italian AN, among others.[12] But not all parties within this family share this affiliation, even within the EU.[13]

Consistency in the literature is not helped by the transience of many fringe radical right parties, where these organizations collapse, splinter, merge, or reinvent themselves under new leadership and labels when fighting successive elections. In the Netherlands, for example, the extreme nationalist Nederlanden Volksunie fragmented and was succeeded by both the Centrum Partij (Center Party – CP) and a splinter group, Centrum Partij' 86, eventually becoming the Centrumdemocraten (Center Democrats – CD). Under the leadership of Hans Janmaat, the CD campaigned on anti-immigrant sentiments, law-and-order issues, and populist antipolitics rhetoric, winning only 1% or 2% of the vote over successive elections, peaking with three seats in 1994 before suffering a dramatic decline in more recent elections. The rise of the more successful Lijst Pym Fortuyn tapped electoral support based on a similar appeal, becoming the major opposition party with 17% of the vote on their first attempt in 2002, before they subsequently fell by two-thirds in parliamentary elections the following year; then they crashed and burned in the 2004 elections to the European Parliament. Another illustration comes from Canada, where the radical right fought successive elections as the Reform Party (in 1988, 1993, and 1997), the Canada Reform Conservative Alliance (or Alliance for short) in the 2000 Canadian election, and then, after merging with the Progressive Conservatives, the Conservative Party of Canada (in 2004).

Nor are a common nomenclature and terminology shared among parties on the radical right, in part because deep-rooted social sanctions against the fascism indelibly associated with Hitler and Mussolini makes modern parties disown this historical tradition. Orwellian doublespeak is also common, notably the adoption of 'democratic' and 'progressive' labels by parties which stand for neither of these things. Standard reference works use alternative typologies and diverse labels categorizing parties as 'far' or 'extreme' right, 'new right,' 'anti-immigrant,' 'neo-Nazi' or neofascist,' 'antiestablishment,' 'national populist,' 'protest,' 'ethnic,' 'authoritarian,' 'antigovernment,' 'antiparty,' 'ultranationalist,' or 'neoliberal,' 'libertarian,' and so on. Some commentators suggest that it may prove misleading to categorize parties together conceptually, as is common, into a single family. Instead it might be more precise to discern two or three distinct 'subfamilies,' for example 'neoliberal,' 'anti-immigrant,' or 'populist' strands. In Central and Eastern Europe, for example, Ramet classifies radical right parties (seen as sharing organized intolerance) into five discrete strands: ultranationalists, fascist and crypto-fascist, clerical, ultraconservative, and radical-populist.[14] Each category carries certain distinct historical associations, ideological identities, and philosophical ideas.

The label *new right* is perhaps the most inappropriate since it has become closely associated with the promarket economic ideas of privatization and rolling back the frontiers of the state, as propagated by Thatcherism and Reaganism.[15] *Neoconservatism* falls into the same category; for example many of those at the heart of the Bush administration's interventionist foreign policy and tax-cutting economic agenda are popularly known as the 'neocons,' including Richard Perle, Paul Wolfowitz, James Woolsey, Donald Rumsfeld, and Dick Cheney. Kitschelt has argued persuasively that *neofascist* would be an inaccurate label, since parties such as the Austrian FPÖ, the French FN, and the Swiss Democrats deny any links with historic fascism, they derive support from a different class base, and they do not espouse many of the characteristic ideas traditionally associated with this ideology, such as the strong anticapitalist populist appeal to the 'common man' against the forces of big business and corporatist economic policies: "The fascist rhetoric was authoritarian, communitarian, and anti-capitalist, a rather different blend of appeals than that of the NRR."[16]

The nomenclature *extreme right* is another common alternative, but this can imply groups well beyond the legal boundaries of democratic politics that are willing to use violent direct actions, or even terrorist tactics. In Europe, incidents of racist violence by right-wing social movements and youth groups are monitored by organizations such as Human Rights Watch and Amnesty International. Reports document direct acts of anti-Semitism (such as hate mail and vandalizing synagogues), terrorist intimidation of immigrant communities, and neo-Nazi bombings against foreigners. In America, violent pro-life groups employ acts of bombing and arson against abortion clinics and physicians in the United States, while paramilitary groups in the Patriot or Militia movement also fall into the extreme right category.[17] Examples of genuinely extreme right ultra-fringe parties include the Norwegian Fedrelandpartiet (the Fatherland Party) and Hvit Valgallianse (the White Electoral Alliance), the National Democratic Party of Austria, and the Partei Rechtstaatlicher Offensive (Law and Order Party) in Hamburg, Germany. By contrast, the parties studied within this book compete using conventional electoral channels and disown the explicit adoption or use of violent tactics and terrorist practices.

Whereas many of these terms have various weaknesses, the term *rad-ical right* presents certain advantages. The concept is well established; it was first popularized by Daniel Bell in *The Radical Right*, published in 1963, and it became widely adopted by other American social scientists during this era.[18] The German literature also commonly used this term following the lead of the Office for the Protection of the Constitution, which prohibited certain parties from standing for election. The value of this terminology is that it avoids prejudging the programmatic content or rhetorical appeal of these parties, for example by labeling these par-ties 'anti-immigrant,' 'nationalist,' 'antisystem,' or 'populist,' which can generate a circular logic in any empirical analysis. It remains to be seen whether or not parties actively espouse these policies and stances. The ex-ercise of analytical classification and typologies for its own sake may be a somewhat arid pursuit, unless it tells us something more theoretically or empirically, for example in identifying the drivers of electoral support or in understanding the impact of these parties on public policy. At the same time, the label adopted in this study denotes that these parties are located toward one pole on the standard ideological left-right scale where par-ties are conventionally arrayed, and it remains to be determined if these parties do or do not share other important characteristics.

Classifying Party Ideology

The question arises whether diverse parties, conventionally classified as belonging to the radical right party family can, indeed, be regarded as hav-ing shared ideological goals, core identities, or social characteristics.[19] The study uses systematic evidence to classify contemporary parties based on expert judgment surveys. This approach has been widely used in the liter-ature on party politics, including a pioneering study in 1984 by Castle and Mair, replicated in 1992 by Laver and Hunt, and again in 1995 by Huber and Inglehart's study covering a broader range of nations.[20] Coppedge conducted a similar exercise covering Latin American parties.[21] The most recent expert survey in Western Europe, conducted by Marcel Lubbers in January 2000, sent a questionnaire to a random sample of 290 po-litical scientists in all fifteen member states of the European Union as well as in Norway and Switzerland. The survey achieved a satisfactory response rate (150 or 52% of the questionnaires were successfully com-pleted and returned). The questionnaire asked respondents to place polit-ical parties in their country on scales ranging from 0 to 10. These scales represented (i) the current position of each party on an ideological scale ranging from 'left' (0) to 'right' (10); (ii) the current position of each party on an immigration scale ranging from 'not very restrictive' (0) to 'very restrictive' (10); the past position of each party in 1990 on a similar immigration scale. Information was also gathered about party organizations and leadership. There was a high degree of inter-coder reliability, and the results of the left-right Lubbers scale were compared with the 1995 Huber and Inglehart survey as an additional cross-check on external validity. The scores on the two independent expert scales were highly correlated (R = .99).

Figure 2.1 shows the pattern of party competition in each country according to the ideological placement of each party, with the left-right scale plotted on the vertical axis and the restriction of immigration scale shown on the horizontal axis. The size of each party is also illustrated in terms of its share of the vote in the most recent national legislative elections. The results show that parties scored by experts as most right-wing on the left-right Lubbers scale were also usually scored as most restrictive on the immigration Lubbers scale. For example, according to these scales, the Austrian FPÖ, Belgian VB, French FN, and UK BNP are all consistently located in the top right corner of the scatter-gram for each country. By contrast, European Green and Communist parties are usually located in the bottom left position. Only one case (Norway) shows a more divergent pattern among parties on the right. Accordingly these two scores were combined for analysis. Parties were classified in this book as part of the radical right if their mean scores on the combined left-right and immigration 10-point scales in the Lubbers survey were greater than 8.0. This list was cross-checked against the literature and found to be consistent with most previous classifications, although there is dispute about borderline cases and the appropriate cut-off point on any measures.[22]

Yet unfortunately the Lubbers expert survey covers only seventeen European nations. To supplement this resource with comparisons from a wider range of countries, where appropriate this study also draws upon expert judgments made in the 1995 study by Huber and Inglehart, by Coppedge for parties in Latin America, as well as studies by Ramet and by Lewis of party systems in Central and Eastern Europe, and by the principal investigators in the thirty-two-nation Comparative Study of Electoral Systems 1996–2001, who were asked to classify the parties included in this study along a ten-point left-right scale.[23] These judgments were

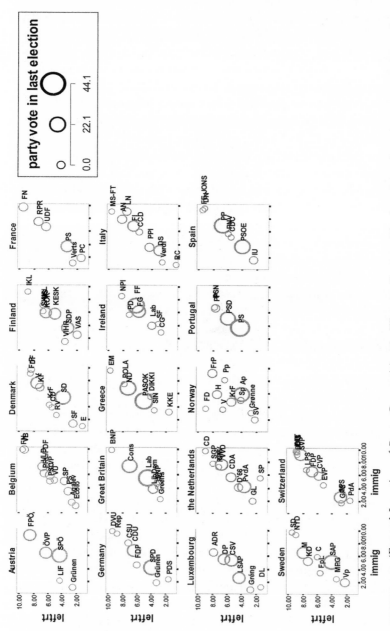

FIGURE 2.1. 'Expert' Location of Party Competition in Western Europe. The location of parties on ten-point scales measuring left-right economic positions (vertical axis) and tolerance of immigration (horizontal axis). *Source:* Marcel Lubbers [principal investigator]. 2000. *Expert Judgment Survey of Western-European Political Parties 2000.* Nijmegen, the Netherlands: NWO, Department of Sociology, University of Nijmegen.

supplemented in a few cases where such evaluations are not available by careful judgments based on a review of the existing research and standard reference sources.[24]

Classifying Party Strength

As well as their ideological position, the electoral strength of radical right parties also needs to be classified systematically based on their share of votes or seats. Some fringe parties in this family struggle to contest local, regional, or national parliamentary elections, but gain no more than a handful of seats, if that, in one or two contests before simply fading away. Indeed some extraparliamentary parties, which function more like interest groups or social movements, never contend national elections. Other parties on the radical right gradually develop a substantial base of supporters in the electorate, allowing members of parliament to be returned to office consistently over a series of elections, with all the legitimacy and credibility that this process entails. Within each election, parties can have a sudden breakthrough in support, or they may experience an equally rapid decline in their fortunes. By definition, 'flash' parties are particularly prone to this volatility, for example the sudden wave of sympathy for Lijst Pym Fortuyn triggered by the assassination of their leader and their subsequent fall from popularity. Party fragmentation also complicates estimates of party strength, where parties split into contending factions, or where they relaunch themselves under new labels, because it makes it difficult to establish whether there is genuine continuity in any one party organization. In Italy, for example, there was an identifiable continuity when the MSI, which had operated throughout the postwar era, dissolved and relaunched their party in January 1995 as the Alleanza Nazionale. In Denmark, however, the older Fremskridtspartiet (FP), founded by Mogens Glistrup in 1972, suffered a leadership split in 1995 and were gradually displaced in subsequent elections by the more radical Dansk Folkeparti, founded by Pia Kjaersgaard.

To exclude some of these volatile fluctuations, and to develop a more reliable and consistent classification, contemporary party strength is measured here as the mean share of votes or seats won over the series of national legislative elections held since 1990. This historical watershed is selected because of the major discontinuities in party systems brought about by the collapse of the Soviet Union and the end of Communist party hegemony in Central and Eastern Europe. Party systems in some established democracies (notably Italy and New Zealand) were also transformed in the early 1990s, following major reforms to the electoral system producing the disintegration of older patterns of party competition. *Electoral parties* are defined in this study as those parties contesting seats in the lower house of the national legislature (excluding purely regional parties fighting only local contests).

Electoral parties can be further subdivided based on their share of the vote in elections to the national legislature since 1990. *Relevant* electoral parties are defined as those achieving at least 3.0% of the mean share of the vote. By contrast, *fringe* electoral parties achieve 2.9% or less of the vote.[25] The relevant parties are also the most politically influential, through winning the greatest share of parliamentary seats and exercising the strongest impact upon public policy and the political system, although their legislative representation depends on the electoral system. Elections results are derived from Mackie and Rose, *The International Almanac of Electoral History*, and subsequent publications in this series, supplemented in the most recent contests by results from *Elections around the World*.[26] The study compares more than forty parties, of which about half can be classified as 'relevant' with the remainder 'fringe.'

It should be recognized that these distinctions remain imprecise. There is room for debate about borderline cases, such as the Belgian Front National (falling just below the threshold) or the Danish Fremskridtspartiet (just above). Nevertheless, the criterion adopted here is the conventional cut-off point for monitoring party strength and counting the effective number of parties adopted by many other studies.[27] The results are also sensitive to marginal differences in periodization, for example if the mean share of the vote is estimated from a slightly earlier or later year. Moreover these measures do not take account of other indicators of party popularity, such as vote or seat gains in local councils, regional assemblies, or the European Parliament, support for parties monitored in regular opinion polls, or other indicators of party membership, finances, or organizational strength. Often minor parties can be excluded from national parliaments while demonstrating pockets of strong support in local areas or municipalities, especially in federal systems; for example the share of the vote for the Belgian Front National is far greater if measured in the Francophone region of Wallonia rather than across the whole of Belgium. Despite these limitations, the selected indicators do provide a consistent and reliable nationwide yardstick that can be used to compare party strength across different countries and political systems. Alternative measures were tested and it is doubtful if the inclusion or exclusion of any particular borderline case would cause fundamental revisions to the main conclusions drawn from the study. The distinction is an important one; in contrast to fringe parties, relevant parties are more likely to be in a position to consolidate support over a series of elections, for example building up a grassroots network of local volunteers and activists, institutionalizing internal party bodies, creating official rules of candidate nomination and leadership succession, formalizing decision-making processes in the party organization, establishing party discipline and coordination within parliament, developing a body of experienced and well-known legislators at local, regional, and national levels, and accumulating organizational and financial resources which can lead to further electoral success. In short, there are no guarantees that minor parties will succeed in institutionalizing their organization, but they are closer to power and, even with sporadic successes, fringe parties are more likely to prove transient. Indeed the occasional election which symbolizes the shift from fringe to minor party status, which we will discuss in Chapter 10, is a critical one for new challengers to party systems.

Given this approach, how far are the electoral fortunes of radical right parties determined by their broader institutional context? Where have they succeeded in establishing a beachhead in elected office and where have they failed to gather any substantial popular support? Before analyzing the causes of this phenomenon, the next chapter first describes the main parties that are then analyzed throughout the rest of the book.

3

Comparing Parties

During the postwar era, party systems in established democracies enjoyed considerable stability. The standard explanation for this phenomenon was provided by Lipset and Rokkan's seminal work, which suggested that patterns of party competition in Western Europe were 'frozen' from the 1920s until the mid-1960s between the block of Social Democratic, Labour, and Communist parties on the left and the block of Christian Democratic, Liberal, and Conservative parties on the right, in a mold established with the expansion of the working-class franchise decades earlier.[1] Yet from the late 1960s or early 1970s onwards, challenges to established party systems emerged sporadically at intervals in some Western democracies, with occasional electoral successes catalyzed by diverse issues, movements, and parties. One of the first indicators occurred with the sudden success of the radical right Fremskridtspartiet (FP, or Danish Progress Party), which became Denmark's second largest party in 1973. This led observers such as Mogens Pedersen to detect evidence of greater electoral volatility in some European democracies, notably in France, Germany, Denmark, and Norway. Yet stability continued elsewhere, such as in Austria, Switzerland, and Sweden, where the relative strength of parties hardly changed from one election to the next.[2] Since the mid-1980s, many indicators have confirmed observations of growing party fragmentation and electoral volatility following the rise of new challenger parties, including those on the radical right.

This chapter compares legislative election results for radical right parties in established democracies in Western Europe and Anglo-American societies since 1945 with similar patterns in selected newer democracies in post-Communist Europe and in Latin America since 1990. Leaving

aside the ultramarginal extraparliamentary parties and social movements as well beyond the scope of this study, Table 3.1 summarizes the
contemporary electoral parties of the radical right in the nations under
comparison. Parties are identified as falling within this family if located at
or above 8.0 on the expert 10-point combined ideological scales described
in the previous chapter, or (if not included in the Lubbers comparison)
from other standard expert judgments and reference sources.[3] In total,
forty-three parties meet this criterion. These are then further subdivided
according to their contemporary electoral strength into the categories of
'relevant' and 'fringe' parties (relevant parties are defined as those with
an average of 3.0% or more of the vote in national legislative elections
held during the 1990s).

In older democracies, the relevant parties on the radical right that are
the focus of this study include the Italian MSI/AN, the Italian LN, the
Austrian FPÖ, the Dutch LPF, the Swiss SVP, the Danish FP, the Danish
DF, the Norwegian FrP, the Belgian VB, the French FN, Pauline Hanson's
One Nation, New Zealand First, and the Canadian Reform/Alliance/
Conservative Party. Similar parties in selected post-Communist European
nations under comparison include the Hungarian Justice and Life Party,
the Slovene National Party, the Greater Romania Party, the Romanian
National Unity Party, and the Liberal Democratic Party in Russia and the
Ukraine. Comparisons also include the Independent Democratic Union
and National Renewal in Chile, and the National Religious Party and
National Union in Israel. The heart of this book focuses upon explaining
the popular success of these parties – and yet the failure of any equivalent breakthroughs in other established democracies where any similar
sister parties remain marginalized in terms of winning popular support,
exemplified by the German NDP, the BNP in Britain, and the Belgian
Front National. It should be acknowledged that the distinction between
relevant and fringe becomes less clear-cut where smaller parties display
strength within particular local communities or regional assemblies, or
where their candidates are elected to the European Parliament, even if
failing to break through successfully as effective players over a sustained
series of national contests. Yet the basic contrast remains between relevant
parties playing an important role in national legislatures and the public
policy process, with all the legitimacy, status, resources, and media publicity which flow from elected office, and fringe parties which fail to break
through this critical barrier even if fighting national or European elections.
Another category includes the ultrafringe radical right parties, factions,
and organizations which prioritize direct action and extraparliamentary

TABLE 3.1. *Classification of Contemporary Radical Right Electoral Parties, Thirty-Nine Nations*

Nation	Party	Party trans.	Year founded	Abrv.	Lubbers expert scale	Type of party	Mean % vote in elections since 1990[a]	Latest year[b]	% Votes	% Seats
Australia	Pauline Hanson's One Nation	One Nation	1997	ON		Relevant[c]	6.4	2001	4.3	0.0
Austria	Freiheitliche Partei Österreichs	Freedom Party	1956	FPÖ	8.8	Relevant	19.6	2002	10.0	9.8
Belarus	Liberalna-Demokratyčnaja Partja	Liberal Democrat	1994	BPP		Fringe		2001	0.9	0.9
Belgium	Vlaams Blok	Flemish Block	1978	VB	9.6	Relevant	9.0	2003	11.6	12.0
Belgium	Front National	National Front	1983	FN	9.7	Fringe	1.7	2003	2.0	0.7
Canada	Reform	Reform	1988	RP		Relevant	21.2	2000	25.5	21.9
Chile	Unión Demócrata Independiente	Independent Democratic Union	1988	UDI		Relevant	18.2	2001	22.0	29.1
Chile	Renovación Nacional	National Renewal	1987	RN		Relevant	14.4	2001	12.0	18.3
Czech Rep.	Republikanska Strana Ceská	Republican Party	1990	RSC		Relevant	4.0	2002	1.0	0.0
Denmark	Dansk Folkeparti	Danish People's Party	1995	DF	9.2	Relevant	9.7	2001	12.0	12.3
Denmark	Fremskridtspartiet	Progress Party	1973	FP	8.9	Relevant	4.0	2001	0.6	0.0
Finland	Isanmaallinen Kansallis-Liitto	Patriotic National Alliance	1993	IKL	9.1	Fringe	0.0	2003	0.0	0.0
France	Front National	National Front	1972	FN	9.6	Relevant	13.0	2002	11.3	0.0
France	Mouvement pour la France	Movement for France		MPF	8.5	Fringe	0.8	2002	0.8	0.2

Country	Party	Party (English)	Year	Abbr.		Classification		Year		
France	Mouvement National Republicain	National Republican Movement	1999	MNR		Fringe	1.1	2002	1.1	0.0
Germany	Die Republikaner	Republican Party	1983	Rep	9.1	Fringe	1.5	2002	0.3	0.0
Germany	Deutsche Volksunion	German People's Union	1987	DVU	9.6	Fringe	0.9	2002	0.0	0.0
Germany	Nationaldemokratische Partei Deutschlands	National Democratic Party	1964	NPD		Fringe	0.2	2002	0.0	0.0
Greece	Laikos Orthodoxos Synagermos	Populist Orthodox Rally	2003	LAOS		Fringe	2.2	2003	2.2	0.0
Greece	Eliniko Metopon	Greek Front	1994	EM	9.7	Fringe	0.1	2003	0.0	0.0
Hungary	Magyar Igazsag es Elet Partja	Hungarian Justice & Life Party	1993	MIEP		**Relevant**	3.8	2002	4.4	0.0
Iceland	None	None				None	0.0		0.0	0.0
Ireland	None	None				None	0.0		0.0	0.0
Israel	Mifleget Datit Leumit	National Religious Party	1956	Mafdal		**Relevant**	5.7	2003	4.2	5.0
Israel	Ha-Lkhud Ha-Leumi	National Union	1999	IL		**Relevant**	3.3	2003	5.5	5.8
Italy	Alleanza Nazionale	National Alliance	1995	AN	8.0	**Relevant**	12.0	2001	12.0	3.8
Italy	Lega Nord	Northern League	1989	LN	8.3	**Relevant**	7.5	2001	3.9	4.9
Italy	Movimento Sociale-Fiamma Tricolore	Social Movement 3 Color Flames	1995	MsFt	9.4	Fringe	0.7	2001	0.4	0.0
Japan	None	None				None	0.0		0.0	0.0
Korea, Rep.	None	None				None	0.0		0.0	0.0
Lithuania	Lietuvos Laisves Sajunga	Lithuanian Freedom Union	1992	LLaS		Fringe	1.1	2000	1.3	0.7
Luxembourg	None	None				None	0.0		0.0	0.0
Mexico	None	None				None	0.0		0.0	0.0

(continued)

TABLE 3.1 (*continued*)

Nation	Party	Party trans	Year founded	Abrv.	Lubbers expert scale	Type of party	Mean % vote in elections since 1990	Latest year	% Votes	% Seats
Netherlands	Lijst Pym Fortuyn	List Pym Fortuyn	2002	LPF		Relevant	11.4	2003	5.7	5.3
Netherlands	Centrumdemocraten	Center Democrats	1986	CD	9.3	Fringe	0.8	2003	0.0	0.0
New Zealand	New Zealand First	New Zealand First	1993	NZFP		Relevant	9.1	2002	10.4	10.8
Norway	Fremskrittspartiet	Progress Party	1973	FrP	8.7	Relevant	12.1	2001	14.7	15.8
Norway	Fedrelandspartiet	Fatherland Party	1991	FLP		Fringe	0.3	2001	0.1	0.0
Peru	None	None				None	0.0		0.0	0.0
Poland	None	None				None	0.0		0.0	0.0
Portugal	None	None				None	0.0		0.0	0.0
Romania	Partidul România Mâre	Greater Romania Party	1992	PRM		Relevant	9.9	2000	19.5	24.2
Romania	Partidul Unității Nationale Române	Romanian National Unity Party	1992	PUNR		Relevant	5.2	2000	1.5	0.0
Russia	Liberal'no-Demokratischeskaja Partija	Liberal Democrat Party	1988	LDPR		Relevant	15.5	2003	11.5	8.0
Slovenia	Sovenska Nacional Stranka	Slovene National Party	1991	SNS		Relevant	5.9	2000	4.4	5.7
Spain	Falangistas	Falange		Fal		Fringe	0.1	2000	0.1	0.0
Sweden	Sverigedemokraterna	Swedish Democrats	1988	SD	9.6	Fringe	0.5	2002	1.4	0.0
Sweden	Ny Demokrati	New Democracy	1990	NyD	9.1	Fringe	2.0	2002	0.0	0.0
Switzerland	Schweizerische Volkspartei	Swiss People's Party	1971	SVP	8.7	Relevant	19.2	2003	26.6	55.0

Country	Party (native)	Party (English)	Abbrev.	Founded	Score	Status	Mean % [a]	Election year [b]	Vote % [b]	Seats % [b]
Switzerland	Eidgenossische Demokratische Union	Union of Federal Democrats	EDU		9.0	Fringe	1.2	2003	1.3	2.0
Switzerland	Schweizer Demokraten	Swiss Democrats	SD	1991	9.4	Fringe	2.3	2003	1.0	1.0
Switzerland	Lega dei Ticinesi	Ticino League	LdT		9.3	Fringe	1.3	2003	0.4	1.0
Switzerland	Freiheits Partei der Schweiz	Freedom Party	FPS	1985	9.2	Fringe	2.6	2003	0.2	0.0
Taiwan	None	None	None			None	0.0		0.0	0.0
Thailand	None	None	None			None	0.0		0.0	0.0
Ukraine	Ukrainska Natsionalna Asambleya	Ukrainian National Assembly	UNA	1990		Fringe		2002	0.1	0.0
UK	British National Party	British National Party	BNP	1983	9.7	Fringe	0.2	2001	0.2	0.0
UK	National Front	National Front	NF	1967		Fringe	0.1	2001	0.0	0.0
UK	Independence Party	Independence Party	UKIP	1993		Fringe	0.2	2001	1.5	0.0
US	None	None	None			None	0.0	2004	0.0	0.0

Note: 'Radical right parties' are defined as those scoring 8.0 or more on the combined 10-point Lubbers expert judgment scale or, where not included, from other reference sources. Only *contemporary parties* are listed, defined as those contesting the most recent national legislative elections, excluding historical parties which have subsequently declined in national elections.

[a] Mean share of the vote in national parliamentary elections held from 1990 onwards.

[b] The share of the vote and seats for each party in the latest parliamentary elections (date specified), held from 2000 to 2004.

[c] *Relevant electoral parties* are defined as those winning at least 3 % of the mean vote in national parliamentary elections held since 1990.

Sources: Marcel Lubbers [principal investigator]. 2000. *Expert Judgment Survey of Western-European Political Parties 2000* [machine readable dataset]. Nijmegen, the Netherlands: NWO, Department of Sociology, University of Nijmegen. Thomas T. Mackie and Richard Rose. 1991. *The International Almanac of Electoral History.* Washington DC: CQ Press; Tom Mackie and Richard Rose. 1997. *A Decade of Election Results: Updating the International Almanac.* Studies in Public Policy 295. Glasgow: University of Strathclyde; *Elections around the World.* www.electionworld.org; Richard Rose, Neil Munro, and Tom Mackie. 1998. *Elections in Central and Eastern Europe since 1990.* Studies in Public Policy. Glasgow: University of Strathclyde; Sabrina P. Ramet. Ed. 1999. *The Radical Right in Central and Eastern Europe since 1989.* University Park: Pennsylvania State University Press.

organization over contesting national elections, as well as the extreme right social movements, but these groups fall well beyond the scope of this study.

To provide a brief overview of support for these parties, Figure 3.1 illustrates trends in the share of the radical right vote in national parliamentary elections in older democracies during the postwar era. The graphs show how these parties have moved from margin to mainstream in recent decades, although marked contrasts are apparent in the patterns of electoral support among these nations. The illustrations highlight the erratic fluctuations in their electoral fortunes in Denmark and Norway, for example, by contrast to their strong surge in popularity experienced in Canada, Switzerland, and Austria. Figure 3.2 maps voting support for radical right parties in Europe in the most recent national legislative election, showing the patchwork quilt of popularity rather than any simple geographic concentration in any one region. A brief summary description of the main players and their electoral fortunes during the postwar era in each major region (including (i) continental Western Europe, (ii) Anglo-American democracies, (iii) post-Communist Europe, and (iv) Latin America) familiarizes us with their basic features before we go on to analyze the main factors driving their support in subsequent chapters.

(i) The Radical Right in Continental Western Europe

France

In France, a dramatic seismic political tremor occurred in January 1956 when the established parties were rocked by the success of Poujade's party, the Union for the Defense of Merchants and Artisans (UDCA), which gained fifty-eight deputies and 12.3% of the vote at their first national election. Under Pierre Poujade, a grocer, the party represented a coalition of petty bourgeoisie, independent artisans, shopkeepers, entrepreneurs, and peasant farmers attracted by populist rhetoric directed against taxes, big business, and big government.[4] Their aim was to preserve the economic viability of the independent self-employed petite bourgeoisie, threatened by large corporations and government regulations, but under assault from the government and established parties, their rebellion proved short lived. Perhaps the best known of the contemporary radical right parties in Western Europe is the Front National (FN), a persistent presence in French politics since it was founded in 1972 by Jean-Marie Le Pen.[5] For years, the party could not make a decisive breakthrough at national level; in 1981, for example, Le Pen failed to scrape together the

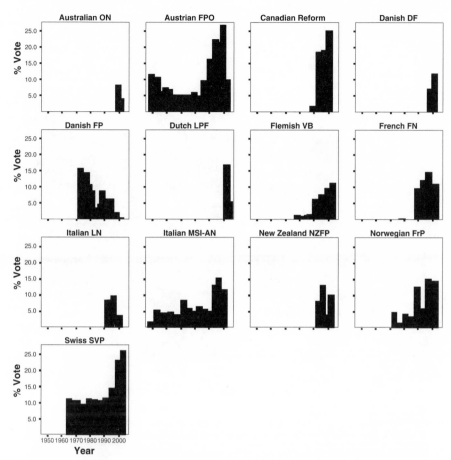

FIGURE 3.1 Percentage Vote for Relevant Radical Right Parties in Established Democracies, 1950–2004. This summarizes the percentage share of the vote in nation elections to the lower house of parliament from 1950 to 2004 for the following parties in established democracies: Australian One Nation, Austrian Freedom Party, Canadian Reform Party, Danish Progress Party, Danish People's Party, Dutch Lijst Pym Fortuyn, Flemish Vlaams Blok, French Front National, Italian Lega Nord, Italian MSI/AN, New Zealand First, Norwegian Progress Party, and the Swiss People's Party. *Sources:* Thomas T. Mackie and Richard Rose. 1991. *The International Almanac of Electoral History.* Washington, DC: CQ Press; Thomas T. Mackie and Richard Rose. 1997. *A Decade of Election Results: Updating the International Almanac.* Studies in Public Policy 295. Glasgow: University of Strathclyde; recent elections from *Elections around the World.* www.electionsworld.org.

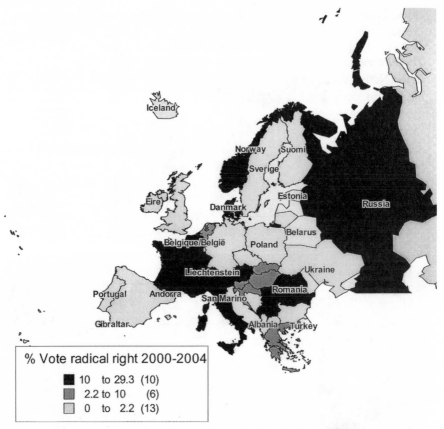

FIGURE 3.2 Percentage of Votes Cast for Radical Right Parties in Europe, Latest National Legislative Elections. For the classification of parties see Table 3.1. The percentage share of the vote is for the most recent national legislative elections for the lower house (held between 2000 and 2004). *Sources:* Thomas T. Mackie and Richard Rose. 1991. *The International Almanac of Electoral History.* Washington, DC: CQ Press; Thomas T. Mackie and Richard Rose. 1997. *A Decade of Election Results: Updating the International Almanac.* Studies in Public Policy 295. Glasgow: University of Strathclyde; recent elections from *Elections around the World.* www.electionsworld.org.

minimum 500 signatures needed to contest the presidential election. Yet in April 2002, Le Pen shocked commentators by coming second with 17% of the vote, gaining over six million ballots, in the first round of the French presidential elections. The Parti Socialiste Prime Minister, Lionel Jospin, was knocked out of the race. Millions of French citizens were jolted out of electoral apathy, and massive protests erupted spontaneously in many cities, before the final round ballot two weeks later eventually assured President Chirac's Gaullist defeat of Le Pen.[6]

The Netherlands

In the Netherlands, Koekoek's Farmers' Party (BP) came closest to French Poujadism, opposing European integration and development aid. The BP peaked in the 1960s, winning seven seats in the Tweede Kaamer in 1967. In 1971, they lost much of that support, and never really regained it, losing their last remaining seat in 1981. The main Dutch radical right party was the Nederlanden Volksunie (Netherland People's Union), which was succeeded by the Centrum Partij (Center Party, or CP) and the splinter Centrum Partij '86 (Center Party '86). The Centrumdemocraten (Center Democrats, or CD) was formed in 1986, gaining marginal support throughout the 1990s (peaking with 2.5% of the vote in 1994). In May 2002, the assassination of Pym Fortuyn just before the Dutch general election led to a sudden surge of support for his party, the anti-immigrant Lijst Pym Fortuyn (LPF). Founded just three months earlier, the LPF entered parliament as the second largest party in their first attempt, becoming part of a coalition government led by the Christian Democrats. Their initial success caused shock waves in the Dutch political system although, lacking experienced leaders or clear policies, and with scandal and divisions destabilizing the coalition, the government did not last for long. In the subsequent January 2003 general election, the LPF vote faded from 17% to 5.7%, causing the loss of two-thirds of their elected members. The party achieved a marginal share of the vote and had no members elected in the 2004 elections to the European Parliament.[7] The May 2002 election exemplified a 'deviating' election, providing a radical jolt to the party system, but one that ultimately proved short lived.

Belgium

Next door, in the Flanders region of Belgium, the xenophobic Vlaams Blok (Flemish Block, or VB) began in 1978 as a split from the more moderate Volksunie (People's Union). VB support has been concentrated in the city of Antwerp, where they gradually expanded their vote, rising from the smallest party in 1982 to the largest in 1994. In October 2000 the party won a third of the vote, and almost half of the seats, in Antwerp City Council elections, where support crumbled for the traditional Christian Democrats and Social Democrats who traditionally divided up power.[8] Building on this base, in parliamentary elections on May 2003, the party surged to 11.6% of the national vote, including 17.9% in their home

region of Flanders. Vlaams Blok had campaigned under the slogan 'Our
people first!', demanding that Belgium close its borders to immigrants
and prohibit multicultural education, as well as under a radical platform
advocating regional independence.[9] Although these are their defining issues, the party also stand for a broader range of right-wing positions,
by defending traditional moral values, evoking hard-line anticrime measures, and fostering free market economic policies.[10] By contrast, in the
Francophone Wallonian region the Front National, born in 1985, remain
far weaker, based largely on groups of radical activists but suffering from
ineffective leadership. Their peak of support was 7.9% of the Wallonian
vote (2.9% Belgium-wide) achieved in the 1994 elections to the European
Parliament. The Belgian FN follow the model of Le Pen's Front National,
with similar slogans and policy platforms, but with less success.

Austria
In Austria the Freiheitliche Partei Österreichs (FPÖ, or Freedom Party)
was founded in 1956 by former Nazi Anton Feithaller, with support from
Nazi sympathizers. During the 1970s the party adopted more moderate
policies, ejecting extremist elements, and in 1983 they joined a governing
coalition with the Socialists. This collapsed in 1986 with the election as
the new party chairman of Jörg Haider, who shifted the party toward
the right. Jörg Haider was notorious for alleged Nazi sympathies and his
plans to halt immigration, a particularly sensitive issue given Austria's past
history. The party gained support from the early 1990s onward, until by
the time of the 1999 election the FPÖ had become the second largest party
in Austria with 26.9% of the vote and fifty-five seats in the Nationalrat.[11]
The entry of the FPÖ into government, in coalition with the conservative
Österreichische Volkspartei (ÖVP, or Austrian People's Party), triggered
an international outcry and diplomatic sanctions mounted against Austria
by the European Union and the United States. Haider was forced to resign
as leader and the FPÖ subsequently lost ground in national elections in
November 2002, although they remain in coalition government with the
ÖVP, as well as holding pockets of electoral strength in local and regional
politics.[12]

Switzerland
In Switzerland, the most notable challenge to the mainstream right is the
Schweizerische Volkspartei (SVP, or Swiss People's Party). Support for the
SVP, which had averaged about one in ten Swiss voters since the party was
founded in 1965, suddenly jumped to 14.9% in 1995 and then to 23.3%

in 1999. As in the Austrian case, the most plausible explanation for this rise is the outspoken views of their charismatic leader, Christoph Blocher, shifting the SVP sharply rightward in the mid-1990s by emphasizing a populist, anti-immigrant, and anti-EU platform. Nor was this election a deviating case; the gains registered by Schweizerische Volkspartei were consolidated in the October 2003 elections, when they became the largest party in the Swiss parliament with 26.6% of the vote and 55 out of the 200 seats in the Nationalrat. Victory led to the inclusion of two SVP members in the Federal Council, not one, the first change to the 'magic formula' traditional division of cabinet spoils in Switzerland for over forty years.[13] The result stunned commentators, not least because it had occurred in one of the most affluent and stable democracies in Europe. The SVP are not alone; other smaller radical right parties on the fringe of Swiss politics include the National Aktion Party, which became the Schweizer Demokraten (SD - Swiss Democrats) in 1991, and the regional Lega dei Ticinesi (Ticino League).[14]

Germany

In Germany, extreme right parties have been subject to strong social sanction as well as legal regulation by the Office for the Protection of the Constitution, due to the historical legacy of the breakdown of the Weimar Republic and the scar of National Socialism. The 1949 constitution banned parties and organizations that reject basic liberal-democratic principles, such as political pluralism, respect for human rights, and free elections. Nevertheless, various radical right parties have enjoyed sporadic electoral success, although they are generally marginalized in national elections well below the 5% voting hurdle required for representation in the Bundestag. In West Germany about two dozen right-wing extremist parties, such as the Sozialistische Reichspartie (SRP) and Deutsche Reichspartei, fought elections after 1949, achieving limited support in the early years of the Federal Republic, but this waned with the stabilization of the party system and growing economic prosperity after 1952. The Nationaldemokratische Partie Deutschlands (NDP), founded in 1964, represent the start of a second wave of the radical right, along with the Deutsche Volksunion (German People's Union or DVU, established in 1971). After several years of intermittent success in Länder elections, in 1969 the NDP peaked with 4.3% of the second (party list) votes in Bundestag elections, narrowly missing the 5% threshold for entry.[15] Since then the NDP appear to have declined in terms of popular support, down to an estimated five thousand members, although in September 2004 the NDP achieved 9% of the vote in regional elections in Saxony, above the 5% exclusion threshold, gaining seats in the Länder assembly for the first time since 1968. In neighboring Brandenburg, the Deutsche Volksunion polled above 6% in simultaneous contests. Their success has been attributed to welfare cuts by the Schroeder government coupled with high levels of long-term unemployment, with almost one in five out of work in eastern Germany. Some observers have also identified a 'third wave' of the radical right with support for the hard-core Republikaner, founded in 1983, with their strongest organizational base in Bavaria and Baden-Württemberg. The Republikaner achieved only modest and sporadic bursts of support in second-order elections, achieving their best nationwide result (7.1% of the vote) in the 1989 European Parliamentary elections, and subsequently gradually fading during the 1990s. Nevertheless, estimates suggest that recruitment to militant neo-Nazi extreme right groups has expanded, particularly in the new Länder of unified Germany, and there are indications that racially motivated violent offenses have also increased.[16]

Italy

German radical right parties have enjoyed limited success. Until the 1990s, a similar pattern was evident across the border in Italy where the neofascist Movimento Italiano Sociale (MSI, or Italian Social Movement, founded in 1946), achieving very modest electoral support, had long been isolated from other parties. For this reason, however, they were less afflicted by the charges of sleaze which engulfed many of their rivals in the early 1990s. The breakdown of the postwar party system, with the Christian Democrats and the Socialist Party in disarray, expanded the opportunities for radical electoral change.[17] As a result, in the March 1994 election the MSI share of the vote more than doubled from 5.4% to 13.5%, producing 109 deputies in the lower chamber.[18] A month later, the MSI entered coalition government with Silvio Berlusconi's Forza Italia – the first time a radical right party had served in government in Europe since the Second World War. The MSI reinvented themselves officially in January 1995 as the Alleanza Nazionale (AN), based on a nationalist platform against immigration and multiculturalism, and they strengthened their vote to 15.7% in the 1996 elections. In 2001 they maintained their role in supporting the government coalition with Berlusconi, holding several cabinet posts, and their leader, Gianfranco Fini, served as Italy's deputy prime minister.

The populist Lega Nord (LN) was founded by Umberto Bossi in 1991 based on a merger between the Liga Veneta and Lega Lombarda. The early campaigns of Lega Nord stressed an ethno-regional appeal in demanding a federal state and the creation of a new independent region in the north, Padania, breaking away from the poorer south. In the early years, the party also emphasized the appeal of 'clean government' in standing against Tangentopoli in Rome and the widespread problems of corruption, clientelism, the mismanagement of public finances, and vote rigging. The party subsequently focused upon attacking multiculturalism and presenting a populist antiestablishment message against immigrants, refugees, homosexuals, Communists, Roma, and poorer southern Italians, tapping into political disaffection. In recent years, the party have fueled popular fear of immigration, globalization, crime, and social change. The Lega Nord won 8.4% of the vote and 117 seats in the 1994 Italian general election, benefiting from their concentration of support in the new system of single-member districts, becoming the largest single party in parliament following the dramatic breakdown of Christian Democratic hegemony. Lega Nord were included in Berlusconi's coalition cabinet with Forza Italia. Within a decade, the Lega had risen to become the largest electoral force across much of northern Italy.[19] But LN broke suddenly with the coalition by withdrawing over the planned pension reforms, and they brought down the government. In the 1996 general election, the LN share of the vote improved to 10.1% but they did less well by holding only fifty-nine seats. Following the 2001 general election, support fell further to only 3.9% of the vote and thirty seats, although members were still appointed to three ministries in the new Berlusconi cabinet, with Umberto Bossi becoming the new Minister for Devolution. It can be argued that the Lega Nord are more populist in their antisystem appeal, and so they may not be strictly part of the radical right, based on the perceived ideological self-location of their voting supporters.[20] The Lubbers expert survey confirms that the LN are located at 7.55 on the 10-point left-right ideological scale, less extreme in this regard than the Alleanza Nazionale and the fringe Movimento Sociale-Fiamma Tricolore (MsFt). This does make their classification more ambiguous than other parties in this comparison. Nevertheless, the Lubbers estimate of Lega's position on the anti-immigration scale placed them at 9.0 on the 10-point scale, making the party clearly within our scope.

Spain and Portugal

By contrast to the situation in Italy, during the last decade the radical right have attracted minimal popular support in Spain, where the Falange parties have divided into rival splinter factions which have been unable to

shake off their association with their ultra-authoritarian and antidemocratic history, and the fascism of the Franco regime.[21] In Portugal, as well,
the radical right remain marginalized, attracting negligible support in the
electorate.[22] It seems likely that the authoritarian history of these countries produced a public reaction against radical right-wing parties in the
new democracies.

Denmark

In Scandinavia, the strong liberal and egalitarian culture permeating the
smaller welfare states of northern Europe, along with the fact that these
are some of the most prosperous countries in the world, might be expected
to have immunized these countries against this phenomenon. Not so.[23]
Indeed the rise of the radical right in Europe was sparked in the early
1970s when Denmark witnessed the success of the Fremskridtspartiet
(FP, or Danish Progress Party), which became Denmark's second largest
party in 1973 under Mogens Glistrup's leadership on a neoliberal, antitax, and antistate platform.[24] The Fremskridtspartiet generated a minor
earthquake in this election, gaining 15.9% of the vote, and encouraging
the development of a similar party in Norway. The party subsequently
split into contending factions, due to leadership problems. The successor
Dansk Folkeparti (DF, or Danish People's Party), founded in 1995, rose
to became the third most popular party in the November 2001 general
elections. Under the leadership of Pai Kjaersgaard DF adopted a more
extreme platform than FP, advocating radical tax cuts, law-and-order reforms, and the exclusion of immigrants. Favoring the preservation of a
traditional Danish culture, including strong internal and external security,
the party oppose the European Union. As the statement of principles on
their website states: "Denmark is not an immigrant-country and has never
been so. Therefore, we will not accept a transformation to a multiethnic
society. Denmark belongs to the Danes and its citizens must be able to
live in a secure community founded on the rule of law, developing only
along the lines of Danish culture."[25]

Norway

In Norway, following the wave of success for the Danish party, in 1973
Anders Lange founded the Party for the Substantial Reduction in Taxes,
Duties, and Governmental Interference. The party achieved 5% of the
vote and four seats in their first contest but the leadership was racked by
dissent and for the next three elections they struggled to stay above the
4% legal threshold required for seats in the Storting, despite relaunching

the party in 1977 as the Fremskrittspartiet (FrP). Under the leadership of Carl Hagen, the anti-immigrant wing of the party became more prominent and the fiscal conservatives deserted the party. In 1989 the party experienced a major breakthrough on this platform, when their share of the vote surged from 3.7% to 13.0%.[26] The Fremskrittspartiet then stayed around this level (with a temporary dip in 1993) in the subsequent parliamentary elections in September 2001, making them the third largest parliamentary party in Norway, with about one-sixth of all seats. Although excluded from ministerial office, due to an informal cordon sanitaire among the major players, the party have lent support to the center-right Høyre minority coalition consisting of the Christian People's Party and Liberals, and the Fremskrittspartiet may have sometimes exerted 'blackmail' influence over their immigration policies.[27]

Sweden

In Sweden, Ny Demokrati (New Democracy, or NyD) emerged in 1990 on a platform of cutbacks in state services and taxes, anti-EU membership, and anti-immigration, and they won 6.7% of the national vote and twenty-four seats in their first parliamentary election the following year. Yet contrary to developments in Norway and Denmark, NyD failed to consolidate their support and they lost all their seats in the 1994 election, in part due to internal leadership squabbles, before practically disappearing in the 1998 contest. Another contender, the Sverigedemokraterna (SD, or Sweden Democrats), have failed to achieve any significant success to date at national level, where they remain marginalized, although they are represented at local level in thirty municipalities. Moreover a growing range of anti-EU, anti-asylum, and anti-immigrant movements are active in Sweden, as well as neo-Nazi and skinhead groups, and it has been argued that the conditions are ripe in Sweden for the emergence of a radical right party.[28]

Elsewhere in the Nordic region, although the usual scattering of ultrafringe radical right groups and organizations exists in Finland and Iceland, no contemporary party has managed to gain any substantial support in either country.[29]

(ii) The Radical Right in Anglo-American Democracies

One possible explanation for the rise of the radical right could lie in the expansion and deepening of the European Union as an agency of multinational governance, which could have triggered a public backlash against the loss of national autonomy compared with the fiat of Brussels bureaucrats. This might sound plausible if this phenomenon was confined to European Union member states. But it is not. Anglo-American democracies have also seen growing radical right challenges to the mainstream pattern of party competition in Canada, New Zealand, and Australia (see Table 3.1). These parties have proved most successful where their votes are geographically concentrated; they have faced stronger hurdles in gaining parliamentary seats under majoritarian electoral systems where their support is dispersed geographically.

Australia

In Australia the most notable breakthrough was achieved by Pauline Hanson's One Nation party. In 1996 Pauline Hanson first stood for the Federal Parliament as a Liberal candidate in Queensland. She was officially disowned by the party two weeks before polling day for racist comments although she won as an independent. Her maiden speech to the Federal Parliament later that year caused a sensation when she claimed that Australia was in danger of being swamped by Asians. She denounced the inequality of giving welfare money to Aborigines that was not available to other Australians. Many other groups came in for criticism during the speech, including government bureaucrats, fat cats, do-gooders, big business, foreign investors, and the United Nations. The outrage following this speech made her a national figure and she founded the One Nation party with a few close associates in 1997. The party's positions on Aboriginal issues, multiculturalism, and Asian immigration gained extensive media coverage, playing the 'race card,' heightening the issue of immigration on the policy agenda. Hanson attempted to link Australian economic insecurities to the issues of globalization, proposing protectionist tariffs, economic nationalism, and other policies to reduce unemployment. The party gained support from other far-right groups, such as Australians against Further Immigration, the League of Rights, and National Action.

In their first contest in the Queensland state election in 1998, the party won almost one-quarter of the vote (23%), gaining eleven out of seventy-eight seats, on a platform combining opposition to Asian migrants and Aboriginal rights with support for gun ownership. After this result, Prime Minister John Howard moved his party sharply to the right by introducing a controversial but popular policy of turning away boatloads of asylum seekers before they could reach Australia's shores. In the November 1998 federal elections, One Nation won 8.4% of the first preference vote and no seats, and this share of the vote fell to just 4.3% in the 2001 election. This

pattern was consistent with the high vote hurdles facing minor party challengers in the Australian preferential voting system used for the House of
Representatives, where the major Labour-Liberal/Nationalist parties remain predominant.[30] In January 2002 Hanson announced her retirement
from politics as she was deeply damaged by legal charges of electoral
irregularities in party registration and campaign finance. She was found
guilty of illegally using the names of five hundred members of a support
group to register One Nation as a political party, as well as fraudulently
obtaining almost A$500,000 (US$325,000) in electoral funds. She was
discredited by a three-year jail term awarded in August 2003, although
it was suspended on appeal three months later. Given the publicity, and
lacking effective leadership, doubts surround whether One Nation represent a continuing serious presence in Australian party politics, given that
they only achieved just over 1% of the vote in the October 2004 federal
elections. In retrospect, their success in the 1998 Queensland contest can
probably be best understood as a classic example of a 'deviating' election, or a 'flash' party phenomenon, rather than signaling any significant
challenge to the status quo in Australian party politics.[31]

New Zealand

New Zealand had an entrenched two-party 'Westminster' system during
most of the twentieth century. Government office rotated between the
conservative National Party and the center-left Labour Party, excluding
minor party contenders from legislative and government office. Dealigning trends weakened party identification during the 1980s, and electoral
volatility rose, but with little effect on parliamentary politics due to the
use of the first-past-the-post single-member electoral system.[32] The major
shock to the system came from the introduction of the mixed-member proportional (MMP) electoral system in 1993, which fragmented the party
system. This produced opportunities for the rise of the anti-immigrant
populist New Zealand First party, founded by Winston Peters in 1993.
The party won 8.3% of the vote and two seats in their first general election, rising to 13.4% of the vote and seventeen seats in 1996. Following
this result, in conjunction with the National Party, New Zealand First
unexpectedly formed the first coalition government in the country since
the 1930s. The coalition fell apart in August 1988, producing some internal party divisions. Their support subsequently slumped to just five seats
in the 1999 general election but it rebounded again in the 2002 election,
where New Zealand First were the third most popular party, with 10%
of the parliamentary vote and thirteen MPs.[33]

New Zealand First can be seen as more moderate than some of the other parties under comparison, for example in their policies on health care, unemployment, and the environment, and yet they can also be regarded as part of the radical right family through their strong emphasis on economic and cultural nationalism. The party currently remain protectionist in their economic policy, calling for New Zealand ownership of key assets and infrastructure, arguing against economic globalization, and favoring limits on the extent of foreign ownership in the country. In this regard, they are similar to One Nation. At the same time, the statement of party principles on their official website, and contained in leadership speeches, presents a strong defense of cultural nationalism, including criticism of the legal rights enjoyed by the Maori aboriginal population under the Treaty of Waitangi. Winston Peters, for example, argued that

The public has legitimate concerns over the influx of immigrants – the dramatic changes in the ethnic mix – culture – and the other aspects of national identity – and the mindless, unthinking way change is inflicted on our society. In their contempt for the past, Labour and National have swept away many of the old landmarks – often selling them off to overseas investors – and have dismantled much that was valued and cherished by New Zealanders.... There are many apparent threats to our way of life from open door immigration policies, through to a growing obsession with the fundamentalism which has sprung up around the Treaty of Waitangi and to the disturbing increase in lawlessness in our society.

Their party website opens with a poster image of Winston Peters and the classic slogan that could be adopted by many of the parties under comparison: "Immigration's up. Treaty costs up. Crime's up. Had enough?"

Canada

In 1987 Canada experienced the rise of the Reform Party, formed with a base in Ontario by Preston Manning as a populist neoconservative party reflecting alienation with the established party system.[34] The Reform Party can be regarded as sharing concerns about the issues of multiculturalism and out-group threats to 'nativism' with many of the other parties under comparison, although they blended these issues with an antiwelfare, antitax, small-government, free market philosophy where they were close to the 'old-right' Progressive Conservatives. While initially regarded as a temporary protest in 1993, where Reform benefited from the meltdown of the Progressive Conservatives, the party subsequently consolidated their position by becoming the largest opposition party in subsequent elections. They repackaged under the label of the 'Canada Reform Conservative

Alliance' to expand their regional western base, winning 25.5% of the
vote in the November 2000 general election. They subsequently merged
on 15 October 2003 to become the new Conservative Party of Canada,
and today it remains unclear to most observers whether this party can be
regarded as legitimately constituting part of the radical right.[35] The declaration of principles issued on merger was fairly moderate, emphasizing
the older conservative tradition in Canada, characterized by tolerance of
multiculturalism combined with free market economics. Yet at the same
time, tensions within their leadership, and certain remarks by parliamentary candidates on issues such as abortion rights and gay marriage during
the June 2004 campaign, indicated a strong strain of social conservatism
within the new party. Some Progressive Conservatives campaigned for
Liberal candidates, although others remained within the new party. The
2004 federal election produced a Liberal minority government. The Conservatives, under Stephen Harper's leadership, became the main opposition, with ninety-nine MPs and 29.6% of the vote, although not doing as
well on polling day as opinion polls had predicted. A series of campaign
gaffes, and the perception that the party's position remained ambiguous
and uncertain on many policies, appear to have caused some support to
drain away during the final stages of the general election.

Britain

In Britain, the mid-1970s saw growing concern about the virulently anti-
immigration National Front, which achieved a very modest share of the
vote where they contested local and general elections.[36] Their greatest support was located in urban working-class areas with high immigrant populations, notably the East End of London, cities such as Wolverhampton
and West Bromwich in the West Midlands, Leicester in the East Midlands,
and Bradford in West Yorkshire. The National Front were replaced in the
early 1980s by the British National Party (BNP), which broke away in
1983. The BNP have subsequently been marginalized in general elections;
for example in 2001 the BNP contested only thirty-four parliamentary
seats, achieving 3.7% of the vote in these constituencies.[37] Their best
result was 16% of the votes cast in both Oldham constituencies, after
race-related riots in the area. The BNP have registered more gains at local
level but these still remain strictly limited; for example, the party fielded
more than two hundred candidates on an anti-asylum-seeker platform
in the May 2003 English local council elections, becoming the official
opposition party briefly on Burnley District Council, and making seat
gains in Oldham Council, a traditional working-class area in Northwest

England with a high Asian population. Despite these gains, the BNP have regularly attracted national attention in the news media out of all proportion to their level of electoral popularity and their threat to the major parties.

The most recent right-wing challenge to mainstream politics has arisen with the UK Independence Party (UKIP), founded in 1993 to seek Britain's withdrawal from the European Union. The official manifesto of the party claims that they are nonracist and moderate in orientation, thereby distancing themselves from the National Front and the BNP, and their primary focus is to detach Britain from Brussels. The party also argue that they favor maintaining asylum for genuine refugees fleeing political persecution. Nevertheless the official party policy is against unlimited European immigration, or 'overcrowding' in their own words: "With the fourth largest economy in world, the UK is the very attractive destination for people seeking a better life. The trouble is the UK is already full up."[38] Moreover survey analysis of the 2004 European elections found that many UKIP voting supporters shared many political attitudes with, and also sympathized with, the BNP.[39] The party won only 1.4% of the vote in the 1994 European elections, rising to 7% and three seats in 1999. The party failed to make much of a mark in the 2001 UK general election, however, with 428 candidates gaining only 1.5% of the UK vote, despite the fact that, with the demise of the Referendum Party, UKIP were the sole vehicle for the anti-European cause.[40] In the June 2004 elections, however, the party won twelve seats to the European Parliament with 16% of the vote, more than doubling their share and thereby beating the Liberal Democrats into third place. In simultaneous elections, they also came fourth and won 10% of the second-preference votes in the London mayoral contests. It remains to be seen how UKIP develop in their Euroskeptic ideological location and the level of popular support for the party in subsequent elections.

The United States

In the United States, multiple extreme right groups, social movements, and radical organizations have flourished on the fringes of American politics, from the Klu Klux Klan and neo-Nazi skinheads to the militia movement.[41] Yet contemporary third parties of any ideological persuasion have had an exceptionally difficult time in gaining traction against the Democrats and Republicans, due, in part, to the structural barriers of single-member plurality districts used for elections to Congress, the majoritarian Electoral College employed for presidential contests, and the implementation of restrictive state registration procedures determining ballot access in primary and general elections, which will be described in the next chapter.[42] The distinctive history and traditional culture of the United States, founded upon successive waves of immigrants which continue today, but also marked by the scar of African slavery, have left a deep and enduring imprint upon racial politics and discourse, which contrasts sharply with the colonial history and more recent experience of immigration in many European democracies.

Despite the steep institutional hurdles, during the postwar era, occasional right-wing challenges to the two-party system in America have proved effective. In 1948, the splinter-group States Rights or Dixiecrat Party broke away from the Democrats over the civil rights platform of President Harry Truman. The party, led by South Carolina governor Strom Thurmond, won thirty-nine Electoral College votes from four southern states, gaining over one million ballots nationwide (representing 2.4% of the popular vote). Although defined in terms of states rights, the party's main goal was continued racial segregation and maintaining the Jim Crow laws which sustained it. In the 1968 election, a deep split over the 1964 Civil Rights Act, polarizing liberal and conservative wings within the Democratic Party, led to the formation of Governor George Wallace's prosegregationist American Independent Party, which gained 12.9% of the popular vote and forty-six Electoral College votes. America was rocked by turbulent race riots and anti–Vietnam war protests during this era. Wallace went on to contest the 1972 and 1976 presidential elections on a states' rights platform, but he never recovered fully from an attempted assassination in 1972 which left him permanently paralyzed.

In recent elections, the Libertarian Party, although extremely marginalized, persist in fielding presidential candidates on an individualistic antistate, antitax platform, yet one also tolerant of the rights of immigrants. Although it clearly differed ideologically from contemporary radical right parties in Europe, arguably the strongest challenge from a populist party in recent years came from the billionaire Ross Perot's Reform Party, gaining almost one-fifth of the popular vote (18.3%) in the 1992 presidential election and 9% in 1996. As will be discussed further in Chapter 10, the party subsequently fragmented into contending leadership factions, and Pat Buchanan, who tacked further to the right, failed to sustain the momentum as their figurehead in the 2000 presidential elections. In 2004, the party officially endorsed consumer advocate Ralph Nader as their candidate, gaining him ballot access in Florida, thereby leading Reform in a very different direction.

(iii) The Radical Right in Post-Communist Europe

In post-Communist Europe, complex and fluid patterns of party competition are evident during the transition and consolidation stages experienced by newer democracies. In most of the newer democracies in
Central and Eastern Europe, for example, the process of party formation
is by no means complete, although parties have increasingly developed
characteristics which allow them to be compared with West European
counterparts. In these nations, the basic concept of ranging parties across
the left-right ideological scale is widely familiar, although there are commonly greater difficulties in classifying parties consistently into a single
category called the 'radical right,' or even identifying parties using the left-
right ideological continuum that is conventional in Western Europe.[43] For
example, the traditional conservative appeal of maintaining familiar social
values and a nostalgic return to the past has often been most strongly associated with orthodox Communist parties or their successor movements
on the left which have not reconstructed themselves into social democratic organizations.[44] The most suitable equivalent to the radical right
in Western Europe is probably the more extreme ultranationalist parties,
which have established a presence, although often achieving marginal electoral success, in most countries in the region. These parties have played a
critical role in the politics of the Balkans, however; well after conflict sub-
sided, the Serbia Radical Party (SRS) became the largest party with over
one-quarter of the vote (28%) in the December 2003 legislative elections.

A comprehensive comparative overview provided by Paul Lewis identified a range of radical right nationalist parliamentary parties in Central and Eastern Europe.[45] Subsequent detailed case studies, by Ramet
and by others, serve to confirm this basic classification.[46] Based on these
sources, the most important parties in this category in the countries under comparison include the Hungarian Justice and Life Party, the Slovene
National Party, the Greater Romania Party, and the Romanian National
Unity Party. To this list should be added, in Russia, the xenophobic and
ultra-nationalist Liberal Democratic Party of Vladimir Zhirinovsky and
the sister party in Belarus. Table 3.1 provides a summary of voting support
for these parties, both during the 1990s and in the latest national legislative election.[47]

The Hungarian Justice and Life Party (MIEP) was launched in 1993 on
an explicitly anti-Semitic platform. Their growing influence was apparent
through organizing antigovernment rallies before they secured fourteen

seats in the 1998 legislative elections. In the subsequent 2002 Hungarian general election, however, the MIEP won only 4.4% of the vote, dropping below the minimum legal threshold. The Slovene National Party (SNS) stand for a militarily strong and sovereign Slovenia, and the preservation of the country's cultural heritage. The SNS won 9.9% of the vote and twelve seats in December 1992, before slipping in support after experiencing leadership divisions. In the last two general elections, four members were elected to parliament, qualifying as a relevant party with about 3% to 4% of the vote. In Romania, the extreme nationalist Partidul Românía Măre (Greater Romania Party, or PRM) achieved a modest share of the vote during the 1990s until the November 2000 elections, when their legislative representation jumped to eighty-four seats in the lower house and thirty-seven in the upper, with a fifth of the vote, second only to the Social Democrats. The Romanian National Unity Party (Partidul Unitătii Naţionale Românĕ – PUNR) adopted a hard right platform. After some initial success in the 1992 election, internal tensions developed during the mid-1990s, and the party subsequently achieved poor showings at the polls. In Russia, the Liberal Democratic Party (Liberal'no-Demokratischeskaja Partija Rossii – LDPR) was founded in March 1990. Their controversial leader, Vladimir Zhirinovsky, won over six million votes (7.8%) in the 1991 presidential poll on a series of extravagant promises. The party ran even more strongly in the 1993 legislative contest, coming second with more than a fifth of the national vote. In subsequent contests, however, support slipped so that the party came third in the 1995 legislative ballot, and only fifth in the 1996 and 2000 presidential contests. The Liberal-Democratic Party of Belarus (Liberalna-Demokraticheskaya Partiya Belarusi, LDPB) is an extremist party, dedicated to restoring the USSR. It opposes NATO and what it calls 'international monopolies.' The party has no democratic structure, but is run by its leader, Sergey Haidukevich. The party gathers its main support from ex-servicemen and those bent on restoring the Soviet Union, and it is especially strong in Minsk, Vitchsk, and some regional cities. The LDPB's main domestic ally is the Patriotic Party, and it has links to vague business circles.

This classification of contemporary radical right parties in the selected post-Communist nations under comparison is far from comprehensive. The definition remains less clear-cut than the situation in established democracies, given only partial democratization in Eastern Europe, and the fluidity of many party systems in this region. But this identification can be used to explore whether supporters of these parties can indeed be consistently related to their radical right counterparts in Western Europe and elsewhere, whether in terms of their social characteristics or their ideological orientations.

(iv) Radical Right Parties in Latin America

The diverse range of consolidating democracies in Latin America also displays complex patterns of party competition and there have been a number of attempts to develop typologies categorizing these patterns.[48] It is particularly difficult to array contemporary parties across the familiar left-right socioeconomic spectrum in Latin American nations, where party leaders usually gather temporary factions around personalistic and clientalistic electoral appeals, especially in presidential contests, rather than developing cohesive party organizations and policy platforms with distinctive ideological positions, ideas, or interests. In Brazilian politics, for example, modern presidential campaigns often revolve primarily around the personalities of alternative leaders, rather than involving serious and sustained debate about substantive policy issues and each party's collective programmatic platform.[49] Catchall, fluid, and personalistic congressional parties in Brazil support popular presidents in temporary alliances, but these coalitions often disintegrate when leaders fall from public esteem in difficult times.[50] Weak party discipline in the Brazilian Congress, and minimal accountability of elected members to grassroots party members or local constituents, generate few effective sanctions if politicians cast legislative votes contrary to the party line, or if they switch party affiliations and cross the floor.[51] Moreover, throughout Latin America, a retreat from radical ideological politics occurred during the 1990s, as countries consolidated political rights and civil liberties, and moved toward neoliberal markets with economic restructuring. The history of military-backed juntas and right-wing dictators abusing human rights in the region had discredited support for older parties expressing a fascist or neofascist discourse, such as the Chilean Parti Nacista. The revolutionary left was also in retreat following the downfall of the Soviet Union and the growth of democracy.

Despite these difficulties, some populist relevant right-wing parties can be identified in Chile, which includes parties from the extreme right to the revolutionary left, although not in Peru and Mexico, the other Latin American nations under comparison.[52] Coppedge also used the methodology of an expert survey to distinguish ideological competition among Latin American parties existing in the region until the mid-1990s, comparable to the approach already discussed. The study identified a range of Latin American parties that could be regarded as either on the 'secular' or 'Christian' right, distinguished from the center-right.[53] In Chile this procedure identified the Unión Demócrata Independiente (Independent Democratic Union, or UDI) and Renovación Nacional (National Renewal, or RN) as relevant opposition parties, fighting in coalition after 1997 as the Union for Chile, located on the radical right of the political spectrum. In the 2001 elections, the Union for Chile held 57 out of 120 seats in the Chamber of Deputies of the National Congress, and a slim majority in the Senate. Other far right ultramarginal Chilean parties include the National Advance Guard (AN), with links to the state intelligence operation under Pinochet. Again, it remains to be determined whether the background and ideas of voters for these parties are similar or different to supporters of radical right parties in Western Europe.

(v) Middle East and East Asia

Lastly, the comparative framework in this book includes a few other party systems from other world regions. In East Asia, the study includes Japan, Thailand, Taiwan, and the Republic of Korea. Although these countries contain a variety of small right-extremist groups, most intensely nationalist, and also moderate conservative and neoliberal parties, no relevant radical right parties were identified from standard reference sources.[54] As in Latin America, political parties in the newer democracies of East Asian often tended to consist of elected legislators grouped around leadership factions and splinter groups, usually poorly institutionalized, with centrist competition, rather than presenting a clearly defined ideological profile, stable organization, and party program. In the contemporary Korean Republic, for example, political parties are described as fluid, dominated by personalities, and all centrist or conservative in parliament.[55] In Taiwan, the primary cleavage revolves around issues of national identity and divergent views toward relationship with mainland China, rather than socioeconomic left-right issues such as social welfare.[56]

In the Middle East, Israel represents a special and particularly complex case. In most European countries, contemporary radical right parties have been largely secular in orientation, reflecting the predominant social values in this region. In Israel, however, the extreme right has been sharply defined by the role of ultra-orthodox religious factions within the Knesset and by attitudes toward the primary cleavage revolving around Zionism and the Palestinian question.[57] The extreme fragmentation of the party system, the existence of multiple splinter ultranationalist organizations, the depth of violent conflict in Middle East politics, and the existence of many shifting electoral alliances, also complicate the analysis.[58] The main contemporary contenders which can be identified as relevant parties on the radical right today include the National Religious Party (Mafdal), dedicated to the principles of religious Zionism and evolving into a militantly nationalist group calling for the outright annexation of the West Bank, and the National Union, formed as an electoral alliance, including the Homeland Party (Moledet), an ultra-Zionist secular party also calling for the annexation of the occupied territories. Both parties formed part of the coalition government headed by Prime Minister Ariel Sharon.

EXAGGERATING THEIR RISE?

This brief review can only sketch out thumbnail portraits giving the basic characteristics of the most important parties in the countries under comparison. Yet in summarizing their electoral fortunes, critical skeptics could point out that the contemporary success of the radical right may have been exaggerated, in this account, for a series of reasons.

First, some electoral breakthroughs have proved extremely short lived. This pattern might be expected to prove common if antiestablishment parties encounter problems in maintaining their image as outsiders when they enter governing coalitions.[59] Temporary extremist 'flash' parties, notably the Poujadists in France, have suddenly surged and then faded away in the past, leaving only a faint enduring imprint upon the body politic.[60] Other radical right parties, however, have now maintained a significant presence in a succession of national parliamentary elections for more than two decades, notably the Freiheitliche Partei Österreichs in Austria (which shifted rightwards during the mid-1980s), the Front National in France, and the Schweizerische Volkspartei (which became more radical in 1999). Measuring support for radical right parties according to their average share of the vote in successive elections held for the lower house of parliament during the 1990s should avoid some of the problems of electoral volatility encountered in studies of smaller parties, by evening out peaks and troughs.

It can also be argued that, rather than representing a consistent shift in patterns of party competition across postindustrial societies, the specific factors leading toward the breakthrough of radical right parties in each country can be regarded as almost accidental, or at least highly contingent upon particular historical factors, events, or circumstances, which differ from place to place. It remains extremely difficult to generalize systematically about the role of party leadership, for example Ross Perot's millions bankrolling his idiosyncratic and quixotic 1992 presidential campaign for the Reform Party, Pauline Hanson's populist rhetoric in Queensland, Australia, or Jörg Haider's charismatic appeal in Austria. For this reason, detailed case studies of the development of specific parties, and the processes of building electoral support over many years, need to be used to supplement cross-national comparisons across a wide range of countries.

Another difficulty is that scholars often unintentionally overemphasize the strength of the radical right by 'selecting cases on the dependent variable,' that is, by focusing attention exclusively upon the 'success' stories, and thereby neglecting countries and regions where the radical right remains peripheral.[61] Yet the characteristic features which generate cross-national variations can only be distinguished by comparing levels of party support consistently and systematically across the universe of postindustrial societies, or among a wide range of electoral democracies. This error is common in the literature; for example van der Brug and Fennema caution against this tendency, yet their own study focuses upon the seven West European nations with the largest parties of the radical right, rather than comparing all fifteen countries contained in their dataset, the 1999 European Election Study.[62] The macro conditions underlying cross-national variations in party support, for example the role of electoral systems or political culture, can only be fully grasped if studies systematically compare countries where the radical right have, and have not, advanced. Focusing attention exclusively upon the most successful parties, such as the French Front National or the Italian Alleanza Nazionale, neglects the way that elsewhere equivalent parties failed to achieve equivalent breakthroughs, for example in Britain, Finland, Greece, Spain, Sweden, and Ireland. Another tendency common in the literature is to exaggerate support by citing the peak vote achieved by radical right parties at any level, whether in subnational, national, presidential, or European elections.[63] It makes more sense to compare their average share of votes or seats won consistently over a series of equivalent contests.

Any exaggeration is not simply a matter for scholars; the popular press often overplays the success of the radical right in banner headlines, even when parties win only modest support or a handful of seats in local elections. Journalists, commentators, and politicians commonly express alarm about any gains by the radical right and the implications of such gains, whether for political and social instability, for race relations, for asylum and immigration policy, or for what this signifies about the rejection of mainstream parties, the legitimacy of the radical right, and public attitudes toward democracy. Support for these parties is often associated in popular accounts with public sympathy for more extreme right groups, organizations, and social movements who use violence, such as skinheads, neo-Nazi sympathizers, and terrorist organizations, including racist attacks, anti-Semitic and anti-Muslim incidents, and aggressive acts of brutality directed against asylum seekers, guest workers, and immigrant populations. Post 9/11, this issue has become of growing concern.[64] Yet although they are commonly assumed to be related, with the radical right legitimizing racist and antiminority rhetoric, in fact there may also be little association between voting for radical right parties and active support for violent manifestations of racism or ethnic hatred. Indeed some commentators have suggested that a trade-off exists between these phenomena, if radical right parties provide an outlet for social pressures that might otherwise be channeled into antiminority violence.[65]

All of these reasons can often lead toward overstating the level of support for radical right parties; nevertheless, even acknowledging these tendencies, this does not mean that nothing important is going on here. During the last decade there have been just too many electoral gains for parties which can be loosely regarded as coexisting within the extended family of the radical right, occurring in too many different countries, to dismiss this development as simply a passing short-lived phase, or the coincidental conflux of specific causes within each specific nation.

Based on these definitions and sources of evidence we can now proceed to examine some of the structural explanations for the rise of the radical right, in particular how far the electoral fortunes of these parties are shaped by the institutional context set by nomination and campaign regulations (Chapter 4), the electoral system and vote thresholds (in Chapter 5), and by 'new' social cleavages (in Chapter 6). All these factors are regarded as part of the puzzle, representing necessary but not sufficient structural conditions helping to explain their success.

PART II

THE REGULATED MARKETPLACE

4

Ballot Access and Campaign Finance

Electoral laws and regulations structure opportunities for party competition within each country. Far from being neutral, these can provide formidable constitutional, legal, and administrative barriers for smaller parties. This chapter sets out a conceptual framework to understand these issues. The study then analyzes evidence for the impact of the formal rules and legal regulations governing all steps in the process of winning elected office, namely: (i) the *nomination* stage (including ballot access and party registration); (ii) the *campaign* stage (including the distribution of party funds, state subsidies, and access to party political broadcasts); and (in Chapter 5) (iii) the *election* stage (including the major type of electoral system, the effective threshold, and the use of compulsory voting).[1] The study examines how formal rules governing this process influence the electoral fortunes of radical right parties, measured by their national share of votes and seats in legislative elections in the nations under comparison. The logic is straightforward: minor parties seeking to break into office (and thus many radical right parties) are generally expected to perform well in political systems which facilitate more egalitarian conditions of party competition, for example where all parties are equally entitled to ballot access, free campaign media, direct public funds, and indirect state subsidies. By contrast, minor parties face a harsher environment where such public resources are allocated in a 'cartel' arrangement biased toward established parties already in the legislature, thereby protecting incumbent politicians.[2] Minor challengers face even more serious limitations in regimes holding manipulated elections, where the rules for the allocation of public resources, such as media airtime, are grossly biased toward the ruling party.

The main conclusion, from the case-study evidence considered in this chapter, is that nomination rules are probably important for the electoral success of minor parties on the radical right in some countries, exemplified by the difficulties that American third parties experience in gaining ballot access, the constitutional restrictions on extremist parties in Germany, and limits on hate speech generating legal charges against the radical right in Belgium. Although minor parties should also benefit from rules giving them equitable access to public funds, state subsidies, and free media party campaign broadcasts, in fact no consistent link could be established in the available evidence between the existence of these formal rules and the electoral fortunes of the radical right. Subsequent chapters develop the arguments further by considering the impact of electoral systems, on the grounds that proportional representation elections with low thresholds are commonly regarded as a necessary, although not sufficient, condition facilitating opportunities for extremist parties.

THE CONCEPTUAL FRAMEWORK

Most attention in the literature has focused on how electoral systems shape party competition. Yet this represents only the final hurdle faced by minor parties, which may be excluded from the contest well before reaching this stage, either by legal restrictions on ballot access or by lack of financial resources and media access. In the United States, for example, the use of single-member plurality districts in winner-take-all elections makes it difficult for minor parties to mobilize votes, but their task is even harder where they are unable to secure enough signatures to even appear on the ballot or, once on the ballot, if they cannot afford TV ads to mobilize support.

The process of winning elected office can be understood as a sequential process, illustrated in Figure 4.1, including three stages. *Nomination* includes the legal regulations governing party registration and the process whereby parties nominate candidates on the official ballot paper. The *campaign* stage includes the legal regulations governing access to electoral resources, including the allocation of any free advertising time on broadcast media and the distribution of public funds or state subsidies for parties. The *election* stage revolves primarily around the minimum share of the vote required for a party to win a seat. Each stage can be seen as progressively narrowing the opportunities to gain office, where some potential contenders fall by the wayside, while others remain in the contest, rather like a complex game of musical chairs. Moreover the process is not

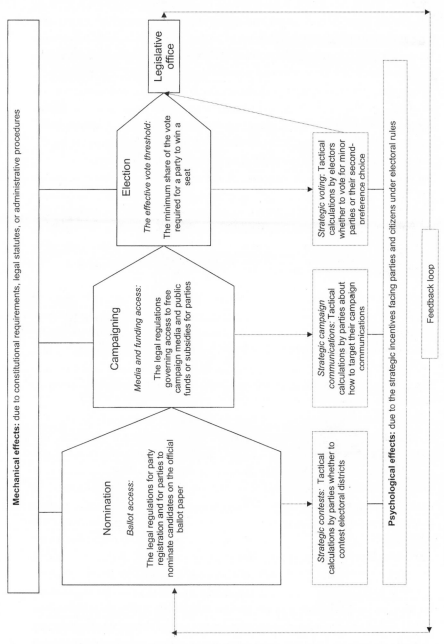

Mechanical effects: due to constitutional requirements, legal statutes, or administrative procedures

Nomination

Ballot access:

The legal regulations for party registration and for parties to nominate candidates on the official ballot paper

Campaigning

Media and funding access:

The legal regulations governing access to free campaign media and public funds or subsidies for parties

Election

The effective vote threshold:

The minimum share of the vote required for a party to win a seat

Legislative office

Strategic contests: Tactical calculations by parties whether to contest electoral districts

Strategic campaign communications: Tactical calculations by parties about how to target their campaign communications

Strategic voting: Tactical calculations by electors whether to vote for minor parties or their second-preference choice

Psychological effects: due to the strategic incentives facing parties and citizens under electoral rules

Feedback loop

FIGURE 4.1. The Sequential Model of the Main Stages to Elected Office

neutral or free from partisan bias, since incumbents holding elected office have the power to shape the legal and constitutional rules of the game (illustrated via the feedback loop), along with the courts and judiciary.

Rules governing the process can be categorized into three broad ideal types. *Egalitarian* regulations are designed to be fairly permeable and open, facilitating plural party competition among multiple contenders at all stages, with equal access to public resources and minimal legal restrictions on which parties and candidates appear on the ballot. *Cartel* regulations, by contrast, limit party competition through a variety of restrictive practices designed to benefit established parties in parliament or in government, including the requirements for ballot access, the regulations governing the allocation of public funding, and the rights to free campaign broadcasts and state subsidies for related services such as postage and staff. Cartels are designed to skew resources toward insiders, with a high effective vote threshold protecting against outside challengers. *Autocratic* regulations are explicitly skewed toward the ruling party, restricting all opposition parties and dissident movements, to prop up repressive regimes and one-party states. Most liberal democracies attempt to strike a balance between totally open competition, which could result in hundreds of parties and candidates on the ballot, extreme party fragmentation in parliament, and political instability in government, and unduly restricted competition, thereby limiting basic political rights and civil liberties.

Following Duverger, the model recognizes that the effects of electoral laws and regulations can be regarded as both mechanical and psychological.[3] *Mechanical (formal* or *direct)* effects can be conceptualized as those which depend upon the implementation of the formal rules governing the requirements of nomination, campaigns, and election, for example the legal threshold of exclusion, or the minimum share of the vote stipulated in the constitution to secure a seat. Formal rules are understood here as the legislative framework governing elections, as embodied in official documents, constitutional conventions, legal statutes, codes of conduct, and administrative procedures, authorized by law and enforceable by courts. It is neither necessary nor sufficient for rules to be embodied in the legal system to be effective; social norms, informal patterns of behavior, and social sanctions also create shared mutual expectations among political actors. Formal rules are important as core instruments of public policy which are open to amendment by the political process, whether by legislation, executive order, constitutional revision, judicial judgment, or bureaucratic decree.[4]

By contrast, *psychological (informal* or *indirect)* effects concern the way that the legal rules shape the informal norms, attitudes, and behavior of parties and citizens, including their strategic calculations made in anticipating how the formal mechanisms work. Such psychological effects include most importantly strategic contests (whether and where parties contest seats), strategic campaign communications (which electors parties target and why), and strategic voting (whether citizens vote for their second-choice party, if they regard ballots cast for smaller radical right parties as wasted votes). Although there is a gray overlapping area, most social norms are altered gradually by informal processes, located outside of the formal policy arena. While in practice it remains difficult to disentangle mechanical and psychological effects from the analysis of national election results (which combine both), the distinction is an important one which is frequently overlooked in the literature. This chapter focuses upon the 'mechanical' or 'direct' impact of formal rules on the nomination and campaign stages. How parties react to the context of opportunities set by the formal electoral rules through strategic campaigns, and how the public responds to electoral choices through strategic voting, will be examined in subsequent chapters, using individual-level survey data.

I THE NOMINATION STAGE: PARTY REGISTRATION
AND BALLOT ACCESS

The primary mechanical obstacle to the first hurdle – getting nominated – includes any legal regulations or constitutional requirements designed to limit or prevent minor parties from either registering, nominating candidates for office, or otherwise gaining official ballot access. Under the most egalitarian regulations, parties are only loosely governed by law. Party organizations are regarded as private associations which should freely determine their own internal rules, procedures, and structures, much like other voluntary sector interest groups in civil society. Any intervention or regulation by the state, beyond the normal legal framework governing all voluntary organizations, can conflict directly with the basic principles of civil liberties, free speech, freedom of association, and freedom of assembly, which are central to liberal conceptions of human rights and representative democracy. Given these assumptions, most established democracies have been reluctant to impose any strong regulations limiting party competition. Yet minor parties commonly encounter some cartelized barriers, with varying degrees of severity, including routine administrative requirements for ballot access (exemplified by the United States); civil law affecting all parties, where some radical right organizations have fallen foul of campaign funding and race relations legislation (exemplified by Australia, Belgium, and the Netherlands); outright legal bans on extreme parties advocating violence or terrorist tactics (exemplified by Germany and Spain); and, where autocratic regulations exist, repression and intimidation of opposition parties, manipulation of electoral law, and serious limits on free speech and association in the most authoritarian regimes (exemplified in this comparison by Belarus and Ukraine).

Registration Requirements

In a few countries, including France, Sweden, and Ireland, there are no requirements for parties to register with official authorities before appearing on the ballot. But in many countries requirements have generally increased in recent years, in part due to the provision of public campaign funds, and in some, parties face complex and lengthy bureaucratic requirements to register legally, the first step to gaining ballot access. Party registration processes vary cross-nationally (as well as among states in America) but common requirements are that these organizations have to deposit with the electoral authorities a written declaration of principles and the party constitution, statutes, statement about the organizational structure, and rulebook, as well as a list of party officers, and the names of a certain minimum number of party members or signatures.[5] There are sometimes regional distributional requirements and parties need to contest a minimum number of candidacies. Some illustrative examples of these practices, with brief extracts from the official regulations and laws governing parties, published by the national election commissions in each country, are as follows:

Mexico: "For an organization to be registered as a national political party, it must fulfill two fundamental requirements: Submit a declaration of principles, as well as a consistent program and bylaws to regulate its activities. Account for three thousand members in at least ten of the thirty-two federal entities, or 300 in at least 100 of the 300 single-member districts in which the country is divided for electoral purposes, although the law sets forth that the total number of its members may never amount to less than 0.13% of the registered voters in the national electoral roll used in the ordinary federal election that preceded the submission of the register application."

Canada: "To become eligible to be registered, a party must include in its application for registration the following information: A resolution of the party appointing the leader, certified by the leader and another officer of the party. The names, addresses and signed consent of at least three officers in addition to the leader. The names, addresses and signed declarations of at least 250 members. A signed declaration by the leader that one of the fundamental purposes of the party is to participate in public affairs by endorsing one or more of its members as candidates and supporting their election. Registered and/or eligible parties must provide an annual statement by the leader about the party's fundamental purpose, in addition to the already required annual update of its registration information."

Australia: "Essential features of federal registration are that a party: Must be established on the basis of a written constitution; must have at least 500 members who are entitled to be on the Commonwealth Electoral Roll, or at least one member who is a member of the Parliament of the Commonwealth; cannot rely on a member who has been used by another party for the purposes of registration (i.e. the list of members upon which a party bases its registration must be unique to that party); may have the registered party name or abbreviation printed beside the names of its endorsed candidates on ballot papers for House of Representatives and Senate elections; qualifies for election funding in respect of those of its endorsed candidates who obtain at least 4% of the formal first preference votes in the election contested; must lodge annual financial disclosure returns; must appoint an agent to be responsible for receipt of funding and its disclosure obligations; and is subject to compliance audits by the Australian Electoral Commission."

UK: To register with the Electoral Commission a party must: "complete an application form giving details of: the party name; at least two party officers; where in the UK the party is to be registered; and whether the party will have any accounting units; submit a copy of the party's constitution; submit a financial scheme showing how the party will comply with the financial controls; and include a fee of £150."

Radical right parties are not necessarily unduly disadvantaged by these types of regulations, but insofar as they represent a barrier for all new challengers and minor players then these could deter some contenders. Any specific requirements specifying that parties have to share certain democratic goals and principles, as will be discussed later in the case of Germany, can certainly affect some of the more extreme right organizations.

Ballot Access

Once parties are officially registered, regulations intended to limit the nomination of frivolous candidacies include required payment of an official deposit prior to election (common in majoritarian systems), or the collection of a certain number of valid signatures per candidate or party list. In most democracies, the deposit required for a candidate to stand for election is relatively modest, for example (in U.S. dollars per candidate)

$125 in New Zealand, $140 in France, $180 in Australia, and $350 in Ireland.[6] The deposit rises to $640 in Canada, $735 in Britain, and a hefty $22,400 in Japan. Deposits are often returnable if candidates or parties achieve a minimal share of the valid votes, for example over 5% in New Zealand and the UK. But when high deposits are combined across multiple candidacies, the requirements can deter serious contenders with limited financial resources; for example, if they lost every deposit by falling below the minimum 5% threshold, it would cost the Greens almost half a million dollars to contest every seat in a UK general election.

The requirements for signature petitions collected prior to nomination are often fairly modest, and parties already represented in parliament are exempt from some of these requirements. Austria and Belgium, for example, specify collecting 200–500 signatures per district, while Italy requires 500 signatures for candidates in single member districts and 1,500–4,000 for party lists. But some petitions are more demanding; Norway, for instance, requires 5,000 signatures to register a party. Perhaps the clearest case of overt partisan manipulation of the rules is the United States, where Democrats and Republicans appear automatically on the ballot, but third parties and independents have to overcome a maze of cumbersome legal requirements for ballot access which vary from state to state, posing serious barriers, especially in presidential contests.[7] Formal requirements are fairly easy to achieve in some states, yet others such as New York, Georgia, and Oklahoma implement stringent limits on which third parties are entitled to ballot access, for example requiring the collection of a certain percentage of valid electors' signatures on petitions within a specified period prior to each contest before a candidate's party affiliation is listed on the official ballot paper. In Georgia, for example, state law requires all third-party candidates to obtain signatures from 5% of the registered voters living in the district they wish to represent. Because of the rigorous validation process, candidates must get substantially more signatures than the state minimum in order to compensate for those that will be discarded because they cannot be verified. For candidates seeking statewide or congressional office, this means obtaining tens of thousands of signatures. To qualify for all state ballots, each third-party presidential candidate needs volunteers or pay staff to gather over a million signatures. Historically this process has strained the already limited resources of many third-party candidates over the years, including George Wallace, Eugene McCarthy, and John Anderson, as well as deterring Ross Perot's Reform Party, as will be discussed further in Chapter 10. In the November 2004 presidential elections, Ralph Nader secured a place on the ballot in thirty-seven states, including those with close races in Florida, New Mexico, and Pennsylvania. But in the process he faced bitter opposition from the Democrats, with court challenges to his ballot petitions across the nation.

Laws Governing Civil Society

Recent years have seen growing legal regulation of internal party organizations, including the process of nominating legislative candidates and campaign funding. Some radical right leaders have fallen foul of such laws and, because these parties remain poorly institutionalized, they are vulnerable to sudden collapse or setback. Examples include Pauline Hanson's One Nation party in Australia; when its leader was imprisoned in 1999 on charges of electoral misrepresentation and fraud, after One Nation was found guilty of solicited bribes from candidates in federal election, the party assets were frozen and the party was officially deregistered in New South Wales.[8] Previous instances of party leaders who have encountered serious legal problems, dragging down their party support, include Mogens Glistrup, founder of the Danish Progress Party, who was convicted in 1979 of tax fraud and sentenced to three years imprisonment, before being expelled from the Folketing a few years later.[9] Both party leaders and followers have also been associated with protest skirmishes, street fracases, and violent brawls. In France, for example, Jean-Marie Le Pen was convicted of assaulting a French Socialist candidate during the 1988 election campaign, and as a result he was temporarily banned by the European Court from taking his seat in the European Parliament, although the resulting media furor may not have damaged his popularity among his supporters.

Party organizations, along with other associations in the voluntary and public sector, have also found themselves subject to an increasing body of legal regulations governing race relations and hate crimes, and certain court cases implementing these laws have had an important impact upon the radical right.[10] In Belgium, the anti-immigrant Vlaams Blok was subject to tough financial and operating restrictions in April 2004, just before regional and European elections, when a Ghent court ruled that it had broken antiracism laws. The court noted that the Vlaams Blok regularly portrayed foreigners as "criminals who take bread from the mouths of Flemish workers" and found it guilty of "permanent incitement to segregation and racism." Associations which managed the party's finances were severely fined by the court. As a result, Vlaams Blok closed down and relaunched itself with a new label as Vlaams Belang (Flemish Interest) to avoid financial collapse. Moreover proposed legislation would strengthen Belgian antiracist legislation and allow authorities to ban financing of parties which violate human rights. Similar fines for inciting racial hatred were imposed in the mid-1990s on the Centrum Partij in the Netherlands, contributing toward its electoral decline. Britain has seen attempts to ban mass marches organized by the British National Party near ethnic minority communities, on the grounds that these actions could exacerbate racial tensions, provoke incidents of violent clashes with Anti-Nazi League opponents, and possibly generate outbreaks of mass rioting.

Legal Bans on Extremist Party Organizations

Certain important exceptions to liberal principles of party competition have always been made for undemocratic party organizations advocating violence or using terrorist tactics. Postwar Germany developed some of the strictest requirements with the Federal Constitutional Court responsible for banning extremist and undemocratic parties from organizing and contesting elections. These requirements are embodied in Article 21 of the Basic Law (or constitution), which specifies:

(1) The political parties shall participate in the forming of the political will of the people. They may be freely established. Their internal organization shall conform to democratic principles. They shall publicly account for the sources and use of their funds and for their assets. (2) Parties which, by reason of their aims or the behaviour of their adherents, seek to impair or abolish the free democratic basic order or to endanger the existence of the Federal Republic of Germany shall be unconstitutional. The Federal Constitutional Court shall decide on the question of unconstitutionality.

The court has outlawed two parties over the years, including the Sozialistische Reichspartei in 1952, which proclaimed itself neo-Nazi to the extent of acknowledging Admiral Donitz, Hitler's designated successor, as the only legitimate authority, as well as a far left Communist party. In 2001 the German Government also tried to disband the far right National Democratic Party. But the attempt suffered a serious setback after a number of NDP members brought forward to give evidence in the case were revealed to have been government informants. The court has also banned many xenophobic skinhead groups, ultranationalist organizations, and neo-Nazi movements which were actively engaged in violent acts of intimidation and hate crimes against asylum seekers, Turkish migrants, foreigners, and the Jewish community, for example the German branch of an international white supremacist group, Blood and Honor.[11]

Elsewhere, hard-line fringe parties associated with terrorist acts of violence have also been outlawed, such as the Chilean September 7 Command, which claimed responsibility for murdering several government opponents following the 1986 attempt on General Pinochet's life, and the neofascist National Alliance, banned by the Czech government in April 2000. In Russia, the deputy leader of the paramilitary and anti-Semitic Russian Revival (Russkoye Vozrozhdeniye) was arrested in 1995 on suspicion of inciting racial hatred and threatening murder, and its Moscow branch was banned for violating federal statutes. In Spain, legal actions have been directed against Batasuna, the political wing of ETA, which demands separatism in the Basque region; Batasuna was banned in March 2003 for being associated with a series of terrorist bombings and assassinations of local policemen and political leaders. France has used a 1936 law allowing the government to dissolve private militias to ban a number of far right groups – such as the neofascist New Order and the Defence Union Group (GUD) – as well as the 1970s left-wing urban guerrilla group Action Directe. In July 2002 the French authorities resorted to this law when they outlawed Radical Unity, a tiny neo-Nazi group, after one of its members tried to assassinate President Chirac during a Bastille Day Parade. Radical Muslim parties have also faced bans, such as the Welfare Party, the largest parliamentary party at the time in Turkey, which was shut down in 1998 by the Constitutional Court, despite mobilizing considerable reservoirs of popular support. In March 2003 the Constitutional Court also moved to ban Turkey's only legal Kurdish party, the People's Democracy Party (HADEP). The authorities claim that the party has links with the militant separatist Kurdistan Workers' Party (PKK), which announced in 2002 that it would disband and reform under a new name. In Britain, broadcasting bans were imposed on Sinn Fein by Mrs. Thatcher's government, although this policy was lifted in 1994, and the party has always been allowed to contest elections, mobilizing growing support in recent years.

Repression of Opposition Parties

Cases of autocratic regulations can be found among the most repressive regimes, which hold flawed plebiscitary elections and have employed a variety of draconian tactics to restrict opposition party activities and to limit challenges to their rule, including using rigged and manipulated polls, and employing intimidation and imprisonment of party leaders and dissidents who challenge the government. Amnesty International, Freedom House, and Human Rights Watch document multiple cases of such malpractices in one-party regimes around the globe which outlaw, persecute, intimidate, or repress opposition movements, including Syria, Eritrea, Laos, Saudi Arabia, and North Korea. One of the best-known cases concerns the Burmese military junta's refusal to hand over power, and the house arrest of Aung San Suu Kyi and party members, after the National League for Democracy won an overwhelming landslide in the 1990 election.

Among the countries included in this comparison, Belarus exemplifies the poorest human rights record.[12] The government staged deeply flawed parliamentary elections in 2001 and President Lukashenka maintained his grip on power by manipulation and repression. State agents were associated with the 'disappearance' of some well-known opposition figures, and the country witnessed a spate of political show trials staged against government critics by the Supreme Court. In the run-up to 2001 parliamentary elections the government intensified its crackdown on the opposition, which struggled to remain unified in calling for a boycott. Due to extensive election violations, no intergovernmental organization recognized the legitimacy of the election results.[13] Human rights observers also report that Ukraine and Russia have suffered from recent incidents of informal political censorship, progovernment bias in television election news, and even outright manipulation of election results, depressing support for opposition movements.[14] In the comparison, these states also registered the lowest Freedom House ratings in their record of civil liberties and political rights.

Therefore the case studies suggest that, even in liberal democracies, under certain conditions, cartelized rules can seriously limit the opportunities for party competition, including those regulations facing radical right parties. Restrictions range from cumbersome and onerous administrative requirements for third parties to register and obtain ballot access in the United States to constitutional bans on extremist parties and legal regulations covering hate crimes found in some Western European states, and even outright intimidation or repression of opposition parties found in a few of the undemocratic regimes under comparison. Court cases and judicial decisions, implementing the legal and constitutional hurdles, generate the 'mechanical' or direct effects of these rules on patterns of party competition.

But, as Duverger noted, as well as certain mechanical effects, we would also expect that certain 'psychological' or indirect effects would flow from these rules, concerning the strategic calculations that parties make about whether it is worth while to fight certain contests or districts.[15] If parties regard their chances of ballot access or their electoral prospects as poor, or even hopeless, then they may well be discouraged from running, preferring to conserve their limited organizational and financial resources for other campaigns. In majoritarian electoral systems, for example, minor parties such as the BNP are highly selective in targeting just a few chosen council seats and parliamentary constituencies in their heartland regions, such as Burnley, Bradford, and Oldham, after estimating that they cannot mobilize sufficient support to stand a realistic chance of winning many seats across the whole country. All other things being equal, the more stringent the formal requirements for party registration and ballot access, the stronger we expect the psychological effects of electoral rules to be on the strategic nomination decisions of smaller radical right parties. Like Sherlock Holmes' 'dog which didn't bark,' the strength of minor parties needs to be assessed where they did, and did not, stand. In this regard, it is misleading to compare the average party share of the vote achieved in selected districts or heartland regions which they contested, such as VB's vote in the Antwerp town hall or the FPÖ's success in the southern Austrian province of Carinthia, rather than their share of the national vote across all seats which they could legally contest.

II THE CAMPAIGN STAGE: FUNDING AND MEDIA ACCESS

Once parties are officially entitled to nominate candidates, then the next stage in the process concerns the official rules and statutory regulations governing direct public funding, indirect state subsidies, and access to campaign broadcasting. All of these requirements can limit opportunities for minor party challengers to campaign effectively or on an equal basis with the major players.[16] Access to money and television are two of the most important factors that help parties in conveying their message and mobilizing potential supporters. Studies suggest that many West European parties have experienced steady erosion in their mass membership since the 1960s, losing activists who used to function as an important source of revenue and volunteer labor during campaigns.[17] As a result, parties have become increasingly dependent upon other sources of funding to sustain the costs of routine interelectoral activities and election campaigns, particularly revenue streams from direct public funding provided for members of parliament, parliamentary party groups, or national and regional party organizations. Parties also receive many indirect state subsidies, such as the provision of matching funds, tax incentives, and services. Another important resource concerns the allocation of party political and election broadcasts, free of charge, provided in all established democracies except the United States. The growth of public resources has driven greater demands for transparency and accountability in how campaign funds are used, and more stringent regulatory policies, including bans and limits restricting either campaign fundraising or expenditures.[18] Katz and Mair argue that in countries where campaign finance regulations function to protect established political cartels, then parties that are already in office can use their control over the allocation of resources to promote their interests and thereby deter challengers: "Because these subventions are often tied to prior party performance or position, whether defined in terms of electoral success or parliamentary representation, they help to ensure the maintenance of existing parties while at the same time posing barriers to the emergence of new groups."[19] More egalitarian systems of public finance and state subsidies, however, such as those used by electoral commissions to allocate public funds and campaign broadcasts equally to all parties in Mexico and Russia, should generate a more level playing field for challengers and for smaller parties struggling to enter office.

Although the logic is clear, we are only starting to develop a systematic classification of the formal statutes and regulations governing state funding of political parties in many countries across the world. The most comprehensive guide currently available is the handbook published in 2003 by International IDEA: *Funding of Political Parties and Election Campaigns.*[20] This source includes a matrix classifying the major finance laws and regulations governing parties and elections at the national level in 111 countries around the world, including 33 nations under comparison in this book.[21] The study was developed from primary sources, including the original laws, administrative decrees, and official regulations. The twenty-eight categories in the IDEA matrix focused on the official regulation and enforcement of the financing of political parties, the disclosure of income, ceilings of expenditure, and both direct and indirect public funding provisions. Of these, ten criteria were chosen as most relevant to shaping the electoral opportunities for minor parties. The assumption behind the selected indicators is that smaller parties (and therefore radical right minor parties) should face a more equal election contest where states specify maximum ceilings on levels of campaign contributions and/or spending, and where parties have access to campaign resources derived from direct public funding, rules governing free media access, and/or state subsidies. By contrast, elections are expected to provide more unequal competition, with biases toward established parties, where there is minimal regulation over campaign spending and fund raising (thereby benefiting incumbents over challengers) and where there is no provision of state subsidies, free media, or public funding of parties.

Table 4.1 lists the indicators included in this study. Summary scales were constructed by adding items (all coded as binary variables where yes = 1) covering the regulation of party finances and access to public resources, as well as an overall score on all these items. In addition, the way that public funding and media access are allocated may also prove important. For example, if resources are distributed based on the percentage of seats in the current legislature, as in Switzerland or the Netherlands, such provisions can act as a cartel allocating public goods to incumbent politicians and established parliamentary parties. On the other hand, minor challengers have more opportunities to benefit if these resources are distributed on a more egalitarian basis, either via the percentage of votes cast in the previous or the current election (such as in Spain), via the number of candidates running in the present election (used to determine party broadcasts in the UK), or on a wholly equal basis across all registered parties (as in Russia). For comparison, to 'eyeball' the data, the last two columns in Table 4.1 summarize the share of the votes and seats won by radical right parties in the most recent national elections. The IDEA matrix classification indicates substantial contrasts in the regulations of campaign funding across the countries included in the study, with minimal provisions in Austria, Finland, Iceland, and Switzerland and, by contrast, the most equitable formal regulations of campaign funding and broadcasting access in countries such as Russia, Italy, Mexico, and Spain. The countries are ranked in the table according to the summary scale from the least regulated down to the most regulated, in the assumption that, all other things being equal, greater regulation of party finances and greater access to campaign resources should benefit minor parties (including those on the radical right).

Despite the plausible arguments that more egalitarian provision should logically benefit minor parties (and thereby many smaller parties of the radical right), in fact the results of correlation analysis provide *no* support for this hypothesis. Table 4.2 indicates no significant relationship could be established between the share of votes or seats won by the radical right and the indicators of party funding regulations and access to public resources. Moreover this pattern cannot simply be attributed to the small number of nations included in the comparison, as the direction of the relationship between electoral support for the radical right and each of the

TABLE 4.1. Regulations Governing Party Funding and Campaign Media Access

	Degree of party financial regulation				Access to public resources				ALL	Allocation criteria[a]		Most recent election	
Nation	Is there a system of regulation for financing parties? (i)	Is there provision for disclosure for contributions to parties? (ii)	Is there a ceiling on contributions to parties? (iii)	Is there a ceiling on party election spending? (iv)	Do parties receive direct public funds? (v)	Are parties entitled to free media access? (vi)	Are parties entitled to tax exempt status? (vii)	Do parties receive indirect public subsidies? (viii)	Summary scale (i–viii)	What is the basis for direct public funding?	What is the basis for allocating free broadcasting time?	% Vote radical right	% Seats radical right
1 Austria	Yes	No	No	No	Yes	No	No	No	2	% seats	None	10.0	9.8
2 Finland	Yes	No	No	No	Yes	No	No	No	2	% seats	None	0.0	0.0
3 Iceland	No	No	No	No	Yes	No	Yes	No	2	% votes	None	0.0	0.0
4 Switzerland	No	Yes	No	No	Yes	No	No	Yes	2	% seats	% seats	29.3	59.0
5 Australia	Yes	Yes	No	No	Yes	No	No	No	3	% votes	None	4.3	0.0
6 Denmark	No	Yes	No	No	Yes	Yes	No	No	3	% votes	Equal	12.6	12.3
7 Norway	No	Yes	No	No	Yes	Yes	No	No	3	Mixed	Mixed	14.8	15.8
8 Sweden	No	No	No	No	Yes	Yes	No	Yes	3	Mixed	Equal	1.4	0.0
9 United States	Yes	Yes	Yes	No	No	No	No	No	3	None	None	0.0	0.0
10 Chile	Yes	Yes	No	No	No	Yes	Yes	No	4	None	% votes	34.0	47.4
11 Ireland	Yes	Yes	Yes	No	Yes	No	No	No	4	% votes	None	0.0	0.0
12 Netherlands	Yes	Yes	No	No	Yes	Yes	No	No	4	% seats	% seats	5.7	5.3
13 New Zealand	Yes	Yes	No	Yes	No	Yes	No	No	4	None	Mixed	10.4	10.8
14 Peru	Yes	Yes	No	No	No	Yes	No	Yes	4	None	Equal	0.0	0.0
15 Czech Republic	Yes	Yes	No	No	Yes	Yes	Yes	No	5	Mixed	N. cand	1.0	0.0

	Col 1	Col 3	Col 6	Col 18	Col 19	Col 24	Col 26	Col 28		Col 20	Col 25		
16 Germany	Yes	Yes	No	No	Yes	Yes	Yes	No	5	% votes	Mixed	0.3	0.0
17 Ukraine	Yes	Yes	Yes	Yes	No	No	No	No	5	None	Equal	0.1	0.0
18 Belgium	Yes	Yes	Yes	Yes	Yes	No	No	No	6	Mixed	% seats	13.6	12.7
19 Canada	Yes	Yes	No	Yes	Yes	No	No	Yes	6	Mixed	Other	25.5	21.9
20 France	Yes	Yes	Yes	Yes	Yes	No	Yes	No	6	Mixed	% seats	13.2	0.2
21 Hungary	Yes	Yes	No	No	Yes	Yes	Yes	Yes	6	Mixed	Equal	4.4	0.0
22 Poland	Yes	Yes	Yes	Yes	Yes	No	No	No	6	% votes	Mixed	0.0	0.0
23 United Kingdom	Yes	Yes	No	Yes	Yes	No	Yes	Yes	6	% seats	N. cand	0.2	0.0
24 Israel	Yes	Yes	Yes	Yes	Yes	Yes	Yes	No	7	% seats	Mixed	9.7	10.8
25 Japan	Yes	Yes	Yes	No	Yes	Yes	Yes	Yes	7	Mixed	N. cand	0.0	0.0
26 Lithuania	Yes	Yes	Yes	Yes	Yes	Yes	Yes	No	7	% votes	Equal	1.3	0.7
27 Portugal	Yes	Yes	Yes	Yes	Yes	Yes	Yes	No	7	Mixed	Equal	0.0	0.0
28 Romania	Yes	Yes	Yes	No	Yes	Yes	Yes	Yes	7	Mixed	Mixed	21.0	24.2
29 Russian Federation	Yes	Yes	Yes	Yes	Yes	No	Yes	Yes	7	Equal	Equal	11.5	8.0
30 Thailand	Yes	Yes	No	Yes	Yes	Yes	Yes	Yes	7	Equal	% seats	0.0	0.0
31 Italy	Yes	Yes	Yes	Yes	Yes	Yes	Yes	Yes	8	% seats	Equal	16.3	8.7
32 Mexico	Yes	Yes	Yes	Yes	Yes	Yes	Yes	Yes	8	Equal	Mixed	0.0	0.0
33 Spain	Yes	Yes	Yes	Yes	Yes	No	Yes	Yes	8	% votes	Equal	0.1	0.0
TOTAL	28	28	15	15	28	26	14	13					
IDEA MATRIX[b]	Col 1	Col 3	Col 6	Col 18	Col 19	Col 24	Col 26	Col 28		Col 20	Col 25		

[a] Equal: all parties get an equal allocation; % votes: depends upon the proportion of votes won in the previous or current election; % seats: depends upon the proportion of seats won in the previous or current election; n. cand: depends upon the number of candidates fielded in the previous or current election; mixed: a mixture of these rules is used; none: no campaign funds or media access are allocated.

[b] For the relevant coding, see the IDEA matrix of each column labeled 'Col.'

Source: International IDEA. 2004. *Funding of Political Parties and Election Campaigns*. Stockholm: International IDEA.

TABLE 4.2. *Campaign Regulations and Support for Radical Right Parties*

Scales	Elections 1990–2004			Most recent election				Number of countries
	% Votes[a]	% Seats[a]	Ratio[a]	% Votes[a]	% Seats[a]	Ratio[a]	ENPP[b]	
Degree of party financial regulation[c]	−.18	−.27	−.24	−.14	−.29	−.21	.09	33
Access to public resources[d]	−.05	−.06	.00	.00	−.05	−.09	−.17	33
All campaign regulations[e]	−.15	−.22	−.16	−.09	−.23	−.20	−.04	33

Note: The figures represent the simple correlation coefficients between support for the radical right parties and indicators of campaign regulations, without any prior controls. None of the correlation coefficients proved significant at the conventional 0.05 level (two-tailed).

[a] *% Votes and seats won by radical right parties and the ratio:* See Table 3.1.

[b] Effective number of parliamentary parties, calculated following the method of Laakso and Taagepera (1979).

[c] A summary 4-point scale constructed from columns i–iv in Table 4.1.

[d] A summary 4-point scale constructed from columns v–viii in Table 4.1.

[e] A summary 8-point scale constructed from columns i–viii in Table 4.1.

regulatory indicators usually proved in the contrary direction (negative) to that predicted. This means that radical right parties did better where there was *less* regulation of party funding and access to public resources, not more. The cases of Austria and Switzerland illustrate the way that radical right parties have sometimes been extraordinarily successful in elections despite minimal regulation of campaign financing or access to public resources in these countries, while by contrast such parties are marginalized in Spain, Mexico, and Portugal, where these regulations are some of the most egalitarian for all parties. Examining the allocation criteria used to distribute direct public funding and free broadcasting time also failed to unravel this puzzle. Distribution of resources can be equal among all parties, or given out on the basis of current representation in the legislature, the vote performance at the previous or the current election, the number of candidates nominated in the present election, or some mixed criteria combining some of these requirements. Logically, systems where these resources were distributed on a more egalitarian basis (either equally among all parties contesting an election or as a proportion of votes won) should benefit minor parties more than cartel arrangements, where these resources served to reinforce incumbents (through being distributed on the basis of the proportion of seats held in parliament at a previous election). Yet in fact the share of votes and seats for radical right parties was higher under cartel allocation criteria, such as in Switzerland.

This is a puzzle which cannot be resolved by the available evidence but there are several reasons why the hypotheses may have failed to be supported by this evidence. First, it should be noted that although IDEA provides the most comprehensive available cross-national data, the handbook matrix reflects the *formal* requirements for campaign media and party funding. This provides only an imperfect guide to practice, as implementation depends upon whether courts and election officials enforce the regulations, as well as many detailed matters within specific statutes. For example, in Russia, by law all registered parties are entitled to equal access to the free party political advertising which is broadcast on television during campaigns. This should level the playing field but, with the multiplicity of parties and television ads, the impact of this access in mobilizing support for any one party is inevitably diluted. Every party, large or small, gets its thirty-second moment of fame. By contrast many reports by official observers have documented a heavy progovernment bias in the television campaign news shown on all main channels, which strongly benefited presidents Boris Yeltsin and Vladimir Putin in successive elections.[22]

Moreover, many other factors are generating support for the radical right, so their effects may outweigh specific provisions regulating party funding and campaign media. What might matter more, for example, is the organizational ability of parties to raise independent funds from private sources and voluntary contributions, and their ability to use multiple channels of communications to get their message out during elections through free media, exemplified by the extensive publicity (albeit much of it negative) which radical right parties often attract in the news headlines. The cumulative effects of newspaper and TV news throughout the campaign may easily outweigh the impact of one or two party election broadcasts. In addition, as with many attempts to measure institutional effects, the indicators of campaign regulation and funding remain extremely crude and imperfect. If the devil is in the details, patterns of party competition may be influenced by the specific *level* of any ceiling on campaign spending, whether the free access to party political broadcast is supplemented by the ability to purchase paid advertisements, or the extent to which parties depend upon direct public campaign funds versus independent sources of revenue. Any campaign finance regulation and public funding may effect all parties fighting an election fairly evenly, in which case those on the radical right would not be particularly advantaged compared with other minor challengers, such as the Greens or left-libertarians.

Or the hypotheses, no matter how intuitively plausible, may simply be wrong. Others have tested the impact of changes in ballot access, media access, and state subsidy rules from the 1960s to the 1990s, and also found no systematic link between these rules and the measures of party system change, such as in the proportion of independents, in the effective number of electoral parties (ENEP), or in the effective number of parliamentary parties (ENPP).[23] The soundest judgment we can probably make is that the available evidence considered here provides no support for the claim that minor parties on the radical right *necessarily* benefit from more egalitarian regulations governing financial and media access, but given limitations in the available cross-national evidence, this proposition cannot be conclusively ruled out. The detailed case studies later in the book provide another opportunity to consider these issues in greater depth.

CONCLUSIONS

This chapter outlined the main reasons why the laws and regulations governing ballot access for nominations and funding access for campaigning are expected to generate a permissive or inhospitable structure of opportunities for minor party challengers, and analyzed the cross-national evidence in the thirty-nine nations under comparison. The results suggest certain main findings relating to the processes outlined in the conceptual model.

Nomination: Case studies suggest that the legal requirements governing party registration and ballot access at nomination probably play an important role in limiting opportunities for radical right parties under four main conditions:

- Where the process of ballot access proves cumbersome and burdensome for minor parties (as in the United States);
- Where these parties fall foul of civil law, notably race relations legislation governing hate speech (as in Belgium and the Netherlands), or campaign finance regulations (as in Australia and Denmark);
- Where constitutional provisions and court decisions ban extremist or antidemocratic parties (exemplified by Germany, Chile, and Spain); and
- In repressive regimes holding manipulated and flawed elections where the ballot access and campaign rules are grossly biased toward the ruling party (illustrated by Belarus).

Few liberal democracies ban radical right parties outright, or even implement strict limits on party competition, on the grounds that this would interfere with basic human rights and civil liberties in free elections. But there are specific cases – in Germany, Spain, and Chile – where fringe extremist right party organizations associated with violence or terrorism have been forced to disband and sometimes reorganize under new labels. The fragile institutionalization of minor parties also means that the fortunes of radical right parties remain vulnerable to specific legal challenges, such as the prosecution of party leaders charged with electoral irregularities or the propagation of hate speech.

Campaigning: There are many reasons why the legal statutes and formal regulation governing access to campaign media and party funding either could also serve as a political cartel, reinforcing the power of incumbent parties already in elected office, or could generate a more level playing field which could boost opportunities for minor party challengers, including those on the radical right. Despite this logic, the evidence compared here could find no significant relationship between the formal legal requirements for financial and media access and national levels of support for the radical right (or more general patterns of party competition).

Several limitations mean that we should be cautious about drawing any strong inferences from the available evidence, but at best the claim must be regarded as essentially unproven. Subsequent case studies allow us to return to this issue later. The next step is to examine the role of the electoral system, the final stage in the pursuit of elected office, to which we now turn.

5

Electoral Systems

Electoral laws and regulations structure opportunities for party competition within each country. Building upon the framework developed in
the previous chapter, here we can focus upon the final stage in the pursuit of elected office, including the impact of the major type of electoral
system, the effective threshold, and the use of compulsory voting.[1] Using the same approach, this chapter analyzes the impact of these formal rules on the electoral fortunes of radical right parties, measured by
their national share of votes and seats in legislative elections in the nations under comparison. Much attention in the literature has focused
on how electoral systems shape party competition; in particular the use
of proportional representation (PR) is often regarded as a necessary,
although not sufficient, condition facilitating opportunities for extremist parties. Yet the evidence needs to be reexamined because, although
widely assumed, the validity of this claim has been challenged.[2] Moreover the contrast is not simply between all majoritarian and all proportional electoral systems, since important variations exist among nations using PR: for example, Israel's combination of a single nationwide
constituency with a low legal vote threshold (1.5%) allows the election
of far more minor and fringe parties than Poland, which has a 7% legal vote threshold and fifty-two small electoral districts for party lists.
As a result, we also need to examine the effects of specific components
of electoral systems, such as the impact of any national legal or effective threshold of exclusion, the mean district magnitude, and the level of
proportionality.

The main conclusion, from the evidence we shall consider in this chapter, is that electoral laws do have an important impact on the electoral

fortunes of the minor parties on the radical right. But this impact is generated primarily through their mechanical effects in translating votes into seats (especially the role of legal thresholds in PR systems), more than their psychological effects in deterring voting support. In this regard, the conventional wisdom about how far PR facilitates extremist parties is only partially correct. Subsequent chapters develop the arguments further by considering the main reasons underlying these patterns, using individual-level survey evidence to explore strategic campaigning by parties and strategic voting by citizens.

THEORETICAL FRAMEWORK

Where minor parties manage to overcome inequalities of ballot access and funding access, the main mechanical hurdle remaining at the election stage concerns the barriers created by the electoral system and, in particular, the effective threshold that all parties have to surmount before being eligible to gain any seats. The conventional wisdom suggests that PR systems are an important contextual constraint on the electoral fortunes of the radical right. Ignazi summarizes this view: "As with every new/minor party, extreme right parties need low institutional/electoral thresholds to enter the political arena. The thresholds are low when the electoral system is proportional, the requirements to participate (financial deposits, signatures, etc.) are minimal, and when the first electoral contest is run as a 'second-order' election."[3] Critics commonly charge that PR systems with low thresholds facilitate party fragmentation and extremism, which, in turn, is associated with hung parliaments, unstable and ineffective governments, and, in extreme cases, even state failure. An extensive literature providing systematic comparisons of the relationship between electoral systems and party systems has developed since the seminal work of Douglas Rae.[4] Much of this has focused upon the evidence surrounding Duverger's first 'law': (1) "The plurality single-ballot rule tends to party dualism." The second claim is that (2) "The double-ballot system and proportional representation tend to multipartyism."[5] While these claims were originally stated as universal lawlike regularities, without exception, Duverger subsequently suggested that they were only weaker probabilistic generalizations.[6] The conditions under which these relationships hold, and their status as laws, have attracted considerable debate in the literature marked by continued reformulations of the original statement and many efforts to define precisely what is to 'count' as a party in order to verify these claims.[7]

Much of the literature, notably Lijphart's classic study, supports Duverger's generalization that plurality electoral systems tend toward party dualism, while PR is associated with multipartyism.[8] My previous study compared the results of the most recent national election for the lower house of parliament in 170 contests held worldwide from 1995 to 2000.[9] The research found that the mean number of parliamentary parties (based on the simplest definition of parties holding at least one seat) was 5.22 in the countries using majoritarian systems, 8.85 in combined (or mixed) systems, and 9.52 in societies with proportional representation electoral systems. In other words, nations using any form of PR had almost twice as many parliamentary parties as countries using any form of majoritarian electoral system.[10] Confirming this broad pattern, although with less of a sharp contrast between the major types of electoral system, the comparison of the mean number of *relevant* parties in these elections (holding over 3% of parliamentary seats) was 3.33 in all majoritarian systems, 4.52 for combined systems, and 4.74 for all proportional systems. Party systems are usually more competitive and fragmented in PR elections, while majoritarian systems often restrict opportunities for minor parties.

The literature has also established evidence supporting the thesis that extremist parties flourish best under PR.[11] For example, Katz compared the ideological position of parties in established democracies, using expert scales by Castle and Mair, and also by Laver, as discussed earlier, under different electoral systems. The study concluded that a wider range of parties stood for election in PR than in single-member plurality systems: "Clearly, PR is associated with more small parties and with more extreme and ideological parties, while single-member plurality and other barriers to the representation of small parties are associated with fewer parties and a tendency towards an abbreviated political spectrum."[12]

Moreover, 'before-and-after' case studies, monitoring the impact of electoral reform over successive elections within particular countries, lend credence to the conventional assumption that these rules matter for radical right party fortunes. In France, for example, the Front National won no seats in the 1981 parliamentary elections (held under the second-ballot majoritarian electoral rules), suddenly gained thirty-five deputies (6.3%) under the proportional representation system tried in the 1986 parliamentary election, and then plummeted to only one deputy in 1988, despite an unchanged share of the vote, after PR was repealed.[13] Only a few FN candidates have ever been elected to the National Assembly under the second-ballot system, but by contrast they have been far more successful under PR rules in European and regional contests. The impact of electoral reform can also be demonstrated by the electoral opportunities of New Zealand First under the Mixed Member Proportional system adopted in 1993, when a two-party system became a multimember system overnight.[14] Although 'before' and 'after' natural experiments within each country are persuasive, they cannot furnish conclusive proof. Much else can change over successive elections – the issue agenda, the leaders, or the government's performance – which can also alter party fortunes. Moreover the exact conditions under which electoral systems constrain the success of radical right parties are only imperfectly understood.

Despite the body of evidence, the claim that PR necessarily depresses popular support for extremist parties, although common, has been questioned elsewhere in the literature. Kitschelt, for example, compared voting support for the radical right in different countries in Western Europe during the 1980s and found that this did not vary significantly and consistently under majoritarian, combined, or proportional electoral systems. On this basis, he dismisses the role of these institutional rules: "While electoral laws have a non-negligible impact on party formation and the fragmentation of party systems taken by themselves, they explain very little about the actual dynamics of competition."[15] Another recent study by Carter compared the electoral formulas used in sixteen West European countries and estimated the mean share of the vote won by extreme right-wing parties from 1979 to 2002 under each major type of system. The conclusion agreed with Kitschelt, suggesting that, contrary to popular assumptions, PR systems do not promote party extremism: "The share of the vote won by the West European parties of the extreme right in the period 1979–2002 appears unrelated to the type of electoral system in operation in the various countries."[16]

The idea that the type of electoral system should affect support for minor parties is based on the notion of strategic voting. In highly disproportional systems, in Duverger's words: "The electors soon realize that their votes are wasted if they continue to give them to the third party, whereas their natural tendency to transfer their vote to the less evil of its two adversaries."[17] The basic simple idea of *strategic* voting (also known as *tactical*, *insincere*, or *pragmatic* voting) is that these considerations come into play among voters whose favorite party has a poor chance of winning in their constituency, but who have a preference between the parties perceived to be in first and second place.[18] The necessary but not sufficient conditions for casting a tactical vote are threefold: voters need to have a clear *rank order* of preferences among parties; voters need to have certain *expectations* based on the available information about how well each party is likely to do in their constituency; and, lastly, voters need to *rationally calculate* that the benefit of casting a ballot for their second-preference party outweighs the costs of not supporting their favorite party. The 'wasted vote' thesis assumes that higher thresholds commonly found in majoritarian elections deter rational citizens from casting a ballot for minor parties on the radical right, if they believe that their chosen party stands little chance of entering parliament, let alone government office. Such rational supporters of the radical right, the wasted vote thesis assumes, should either stay home, thereby reducing levels of turnout, or they should switch support to another party on strategic or tactical grounds. Citizens are expected to cast a strategic vote for their second-preference choice, in the belief that casting a ballot for smaller radical right parties under these rules will generate no direct policy benefits. This thesis assumes that people are instrumentally rational; that is, they care about whom they vote for only insofar as this affects the outcome in seats, thereby maximizing their utility in terms of policy outcomes. They are not concerned to express their symbolic support for a party, nor do they wish to swell the national vote share for their favorite party, nor attempt to exercise indirect influence over the policy platforms of other parties.

EVIDENCE

The basic proposition to be explored is that the type of electoral system, and specific aspects of electoral law, will shape support for the radical right. In particular, compared with systems of proportional representation, majoritarian elections characterized by high electoral thresholds are expected to create greater mechanical and psychological hurdles for minor parties, and hence to prevent many radical right contenders from gaining office. To reexamine the basis for these claims with systematic evidence, electoral systems in the thirty-nine countries under comparison are classified in this study into three major families, as listed in Table 5.1, each including a number of subcategories: *majoritarian* formulas (including first-past-the-post, second ballot, the block vote, single nontransferable vote, and alternative voting systems);[19] *combined* systems (incorporating both majoritarian and proportional formulas); and *proportional* formulas (including party lists as well as the single transferable vote systems).

The Effect of the Electoral System on Radical Right Votes

Based on this classification, Table 5.2 compares the share of the votes and seats won by radical right parties in the nations under comparison.

TABLE 5.1. *The Thirty-Nine Electoral Systems under Comparison*

Type of district	Year of election	Electoral system	Party list	Formula	Total n. of MPs	MPs N. of SMD	MPs N. of list	Total number of district for lists	Average VAP per member	Mean district magnitude	% Nat vote Legal threshold	% Nat vote Effective threshold	% Nat vote Prop.	ENPP	Max. years between elections
Majoritarian															
Australia	1996	AV	None	Majority	148	148	0	0	91,500	1.0	None	50.0	84	2.61	3
Belarus		2nd ballot	None	Majority	260	260	0	0	29,432	1.0	None	50.0		2.98	5
Canada	1997	FPTP	None	Plurality	295	295	0	0	78,300	1.0	None	35.0	83	3.70	5
France		2nd ballot	None	Majority	577	577	0	0	77,161	1.0	None	50.0	75	2.11	5
UK	1997	FPTP	None	Plurality	659	659	0	0	68,400	1.0	None	35.0	80	1.99	5
USA	1996	FPTP	None	Plurality	435	435	0	0	436,700	1.0	None	35.0	94		2
Combined Independent															
Japan	1996	FPTP+PR	Closed	d'Hondt	500	300	200	11	193,400	18.0	None	4.0	86	2.93	4
Korea, Republic	2000	FPTP+PR	Closed	LR-Hare	299	253	46	1	114,900	46.0	5	5.0	84	2.36	4
Lithuania		2nd+PR	Open	Hare	141	71	70	1	21,653	70.0	5	5.0	76	4.20	4
Russia	1999	FPTP+PR	Closed	LR-Hare	450	225	225	1	242,700	225.0	5	5.0	89	5.40	4
Taiwan	1996	SNTV+PR	Closed	LR-Hare	334	234/27	100	2	42,900	50.0	5	5.0	95	2.46	4
Ukraine	1998	FPTP+PR	Closed	LR-Hare	450	225	225	1	86,500	225.0	4	4.0	86	5.98	5
Dependent															
Germany	1998	FPTP+PR	Closed	LR-Hare	656	328	328	1	100,000	328.0	5	5.0	94	3.30	4
Hungary	1998	FPTP+PR	Closed	d'Hondt	386	176	110	20	20,000	6.0	None	11.3	86	3.45	4
Italy		FPTP+PR	Open	Hare	630	475	155	1	75,131	155.0	4	4.0	90	6.69	5
New Zealand	1996	FPTP+PR	Closed	St-Laguë	120	65	55	1	21,400	55.0	5	5.0	96	3.78	3
Mexico	1997	FPTP+PR	Closed	LR-Hare	500	300	200	5	110,800	40.0	2	2.0	91	2.66	3
Thailand	2001	FPTP+PR	Closed	LR-Hare	500	400	100	1	85,000	100.0	5	5.0		3.05	4

Proportional

Austria		PR Lists	Open	Hare	183	0	183	9	35,319	20.3	4	4.0	99	3.41	4
Belgium	1999	PR Lists	Open	d'Hondt	150	0	150	20	53,300	7.5	None	9.2	96	9.05	4
Chile	1996	PR Lists	Open	Binomial	120	0	120	60	80,289	2.0	None	29.2	86	5.18	4
Czech Republic	1996	PR Lists	Closed	LR-Droop	200	0	200	8	39,300	25.0	5	5.0	89	4.15	4
Denmark	1998	PR Lists	Open	St-Laguë	179	0	179	17	23,000	7.9	2	2.0	98	4.92	4
Finland		PR Lists	Open	d'Hondt	200	0	200	14	20,779	14.3	None	5.0	92	5.15	4
Greece		PR Lists	Open	Hare	300		288	56	26,311	5.1	3	3.0	88	2.12	4
Iceland		PR Lists	Closed	Hare	63	0	63	9	3,121	6.3	None	10.8	97		
Ireland		STV	Open	Droop	166	0	166	41	16,156	4.0	None	16.3	89	2.99	5
Israel	1996	PR Lists	Closed	d'Hondt	120	0	120	1	30,700	120.0	1.5	1.5	96	5.63	5
Luxembourg		PR Lists	Open	Droop	60	0	60	4	5,600	15.0	None	4.8	92		
Netherlands	1998	PR Lists	Closed	d'Hondt	150	0	150	1	80,000	150.0	0.67	0.7	95	4.81	4
Norway	1997	PR Lists	Closed	St-Laguë	165	0	165	19	20,000	8.7	4	4.0	95	2.35	4
Peru	2000	PR Lists	Open	d'Hondt	120	0	120	1	127,000	120.0	None	0.6	98	3.81	4
Poland	1997	PR Lists	Open	d'Hondt	460	0	460	52	60,700	8.8	7	7.0	82	2.95	4
Portugal		PR Lists	Closed	d'Hondt	230	0	230	22	33,935	10.5	None	6.7	90	2.61	4
Romania	1996	PR Lists	Closed	d'Hondt	343	0	343	42	48,800	8.2	3	3.0	82	3.37	4
Slovenia	1996	PR Lists	Open	LR-Hare	90	0	90	8	17,000	11.0	3	3.0	84	5.52	4
Spain	1996	PR Lists	Closed	d'Hondt	350	0	350	52	88,600	7.0	3	3.0	93	2.73	4
Sweden	1998	PR Lists	Open	St-Laguë	349	0	349	29	19,800	10.7	4	4.0	97	4.29	4
Switzerland	1999	PR Lists	Panachage	d'Hondt	200	0	200	26	28,700	7.7	None	9.0	93	5.08	4
AVERAGE	1997				296	140	154	14	69,037	48.6	4	11.5	90	3.92	4

Source: Pippa Norris. 2004. *Electoral Engineering.* Cambridge: Cambridge University Press. For definitions, see the notes for *Electoral Engineering*, table 4.5.

TABLE 5.2. *Electoral Systems and Support for Radical Right Parties*

Major type of electoral system	Elections 1990–2004			Most recent election			Number of countries
	% Votes	% Seats	Ratio	% Votes	% Seats	Ratio	
Majoritarian system	8.6	3.5	0.40	7.2	3.8	0.52	6
Combined system	4.4	2.1	0.48	3.6	2.3	0.64	12
Proportional system	7.9	8.7	1.10	7.1	9.9	1.39	21
TOTAL	6.9	5.9	0.85	6.1	6.6	1.08	39
R (Sig.)	.059	.255	.375*	.065	.226	.319*	

Note: The results summarize the mean percentage of votes and seats won by radical right parties in elections for the lower house in the national legislature. For the classification of electoral systems by nation see Table 5.1 and also Pippa Norris. 2004. *Electoral Engineering.* Cambridge: Cambridge University Press, chapter 2.

Sources: Thomas T. Mackie and Richard Rose. 1991. *The International Almanac of Electoral History.* Washington, DC: CQ Press; Tom Mackie and Richard Rose. 1997. *A Decade of Election Results: Updating the International Almanac.* Studies in Public Policy. Glasgow: University of Strathclyde; *Elections around the World* www.electionworld.org; Richard Rose, Neil Munro, and Tom Mackie. 1998. *Elections in Central and Eastern Europe since 1990.* Studies in Public Policy 300. Glasgow: University of Strathclyde.

Two periods are selected for analysis, to check whether the results are robust and consistent across both periods: the mean vote and seat share won by radical right parties in national elections held in each country since 1990, and, for comparison, the votes and seats share in the most recent national elections (held from 2000 to 2004).

The results in Table 5.2 suggest two main conclusions. First, contrary to the conventional wisdom, *the share of the vote achieved by radical right parties in the most recent national legislative elections was similar under majoritarian (7.2%) and proportional (7.1%) electoral systems.* How do we explain this pattern, which is consistent with Kitschelt and Carter, given that it runs counter to the 'wasted vote' thesis? There are at least two possible reasons suggested by the proximity model of voting used in this book why the 'wasted vote' assumption could be misspecified. First, any instrumental calculation by voters depends, in part, upon the proximity or distance of parties across the ideological spectrum. Moderate parties are placed in an optimal position to be affected by strategic voting, since because they are the halfway house it is relatively easy for their supporters to switch either to or from other second-preference parties on either the center-left or center-right. In the 1997 British general election, for example, the closure of the ideological gap between the main opposition parties – with Tony Blair stealing Liberal Democrat clothes on constitutional issues and Paddy Ashdown campaigning on Labour's territory of education and health – may have significantly reduced the costs facing voters of transferring from one to the other. The main opposition parties offered more of an echo than a choice. If both parties were perceived to favor similar policies, then strategic considerations made it easier for voters to switch their vote more effectively in seats where this mattered. The 1997 election saw a considerable flow of the vote between Labour and Liberal Democrat supporters designed (successfully) to defeat the Conservative government.[20] Yet the ideological position of radical right-wing parties is usually located well away from mainstream contenders across the political spectrum, which makes it more costly for their supporters to cast a strategic or tactical vote for another candidate, even if their favorite party faces little hope of winning any seats. Other parties on the center-right, whether Christian Democrats, Conservatives or Liberals, are simply located too far away from their ideal policy position. For this reason, we might expect little strategic voting among supporters of the radical right, even if their preferred party cannot win office.

Moreover, if we relax the assumption of instrumental rationality, supporters of the radical right could be understood to be seeking political benefits beyond electing members to the legislature who can have a direct impact upon the public policy process. If people want to cast an 'expressive' or 'symbolic' ballot, such as registering disgust with the immigration policies adopted by both the mainstream governing and opposition parties, they might well remain willing to vote for a radical right party, even if their chosen candidate or party cannot hope to gain office.[21] By sending a message through the ballot box, radical right supporters may still hope to influence public policy indirectly, for example causing the governing party to adopt more restrictive policies toward refugees and asylum seekers, even if not gaining any elected parliamentary representatives. The rational choice facing supporters of smaller radical right parties in majoritarian elections is therefore exit (staying home) or else casting an expressive ballot for the radical right, with a potential indirect impact upon public policy, rather than switching to a party which is located far away from their ideal ideological location. The evidence supporting this proposition is explored more fully in Chapter 7, analyzing individual-level survey data to see whether voter defection is less common among radical right than moderate center parties.

The Effects of the Electoral System on Radical Right Seats

Despite these patterns, and confirming the conventional wisdom, the mechanical effects of the electoral formula on the ratio of votes-to-seats are also strikingly evident. The second major finding in Table 5.2 is that, despite having roughly the same share of the vote, *radical right parties were more than twice as successful in gaining seats under PR as under majoritarian elections.* In the most recent elections, radical right parties won 3.8% of seats under majoritarian rules and 9.9% under PR. Another way of summarizing this data is to calculate the votes:seats ratio.[22] Under majoritarian systems, with 7.2% of votes, radical right parties won 3.8% of seats, or a ratio of 0.52. Under combined or 'mixed' systems the ratio is 0.64. Under PR it becomes 1.39, meaning that radical right parties win a far higher share of seats than they get votes. Similar patterns were evident in the comparison of all national legislative elections held since 1990. The effect of majoritarian systems was therefore *not* to depress the popular vote for radical right parties, contrary to expectations of strategic voting, but rather to limit their access to legislative office and all the trappings of power and legitimacy that flow from this position. In this regard, majoritarian electoral systems work exactly as proponents claim by excluding extreme parties from parliament. Combined systems prove the intermediate position, as predicted, because they include elements from both the majoritarian and PR systems. In confirmation of the conventional wisdom, radical right parties reaped their greatest parliamentary rewards under PR elections. The outcome for their share of seats is politically important because, in turn, it determines the power, legitimacy, status, and resources that flow from elected office. The type of electoral system is therefore critical in constraining the legislative influence of extreme parties, even where they tap into reservoirs of popular support.

These patterns can be illustrated in more detail by classifying types of radical right parties by their electoral strength (measured by their average share of the national vote during the 1990s). Table 5.3 shows the relative success of these parties under different electoral systems. Three relevant radical right parties (gaining on average over 3% of the vote) compete in nations with majoritarian electoral systems (Pauline Hanson's One Nation in Australia, the Canadian Reform Party, and the French Front National),

TABLE 5.3. *Types of Electoral System and Radical Right Electoral Parties*

Majoritarian		Combined		PR	
Nation	Party	Nation	Party	Nation	Party
Relevant Parties					
Australia	One Nation	Hungary	Hungarian Justice & Life Party	Austria	Freedom Party
Canada	Reform	Italy	National Alliance	Belgium	Flemish Block
France	National Front	Italy	Northern League	Chile	Independent Democratic Union
		Russia	Liberal Democrat Party	Chile	National Renewal
				Czech Rep.	Republican Party
				Denmark	People's Party
				Denmark	Progress Party
				Israel	National Religious Party
				Israel	National Union
				Netherlands	List Pym Fortuyn
				New Zealand	New Zealand First
				Norway	Progress Party
				Romania	Greater Romania Party
				Romania	Romanian National Unity Party
				Slovenia	Slovene National Party
				Switzerland	Swiss People's Party
	(3)		(4)		(16)
Fringe Parties					
Belarus	Liberal Democrat	Germany	Republican Party	Belgium	National Front
UK	British National Party	Germany	German People's Union	Finland	Patriotic National Alliance

(continued)

TABLE 5.3 *(continued)*

Majoritarian		Combined		PR	
Nation	Party	Nation	Party	Nation	Party
UK	National Front	Germany	National Democratic Party	France	Movement for France
		Italy	Social Movement 3 Flames	France	National Republican Movement
		Ukraine	Ukrainian National Assembly	Greece	Populist Orthodox Rally
		Lithuania	Lithuanian Freedom Union	Greece	Greek Front
				Netherlands	Center Democrats
				Norway	Fatherland Party
				Spain	Falange
				Sweden	Swedish Democrats
				Sweden	New Democracy
				Switzerland	Union of Federal Democrats
				Switzerland	Swiss Democrats
				Switzerland	Ticino League
				Switzerland	Freedom Party
	(3)		(6)		(15)
None					
U.S.	None	Japan	None	Iceland	None
		Korea Rep.	None	Ireland	None
		Mexico	None	Luxembourg	None
		Taiwan	None	Peru	None
		Thailand	None	Poland	None
				Portugal	None
	(1)		(5)		(6)

Note: Radical right parties are classified on the basis of the Lubbers expert survey (where included) or by other reference sources, as discussed in Chapter 2. *Electoral parties* are defined as those radical right parties contesting seats in the lower house of the national legislature. *Relevant* electoral parties are defined as those with an average of 3.0% or more of the vote in national legislative elections held during the 1990s. *Fringe* electoral parties are defined as those with an average of 0.1 to 2.9% in national legislative elections held during the 1990s. *None* are where no parties meet these criteria.

Source: Classified from Tables 2.1 and 3.1.

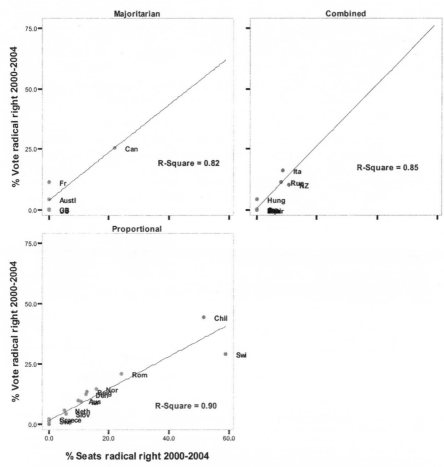

FIGURE 5.1. The Ratio of Votes-to-Seats Won by Radical Right Parties, 2000–2004. The proportion of votes and seats won by radical right parties in the most recent national legislative election for the lower house (held from 2000 to 2004). The regression line summarizes the relationship between votes and seats. *Source:* See Table 5.1.

along with a few fringe parties. Four relevant radical right electoral parties exist in countries using combined (or 'mixed') electoral systems. By contrast, there are sixteen relevant radical right parties under PR systems (including all those parties that have ever entered governing coalitions), along with fifteen fringe radical right parties.

The impact of the electoral rules is also illustrated by Figure 5.1, showing the proportion of votes to seats achieved by radical right parties under the three basic types of electoral system. The majoritarian systems provide the least proportional results for these parties, notably in France, where Le Pen's Front National gain minimal deputies in the French National Assembly, due to the second-ballot majoritarian system, despite having the support of more than one in ten voters. In Canada, by contrast, as mentioned earlier, the Reform Party do relatively well in Parliament, because of the regional nature of Canadian electoral politics. The combined systems, used for national legislative elections in countries such as Hungary, Russia, Italy, and New Zealand, prove moderately proportional. And the PR electoral systems, used in places such as Switzerland, Romania, and Norway, prove most proportional for radical right contenders.

Electoral Thresholds

The evidence considered so far confirms that, compared with PR, majoritarian electoral systems usually limit how far radical right candidates and parties succeed in entering legislative office, unless their vote is spatially concentrated within a specific region where they can overcome these hurdles – for example the Canadian Reform Party tapped into regional anti-Québécois sentiments in Western Canada. Yet there remain substantial variations in the success of radical right parties, even within PR systems: for example their considerable success in Switzerland and Israel, compared with their marginalization in Sweden and Spain. If all PR schemes were perfectly proportional then we would not have to investigate further conditions, but in fact these vary a great deal depending on specific arrangements such as the mean district magnitude and the use of legal thresholds. To explore variations between and within the main types of electoral systems, we need to compare specific components, including the legal and effective electoral thresholds that minor parties face. Under the second-ballot electoral system used in France, for example, Front National parliamentary candidates need to get an absolute majority (50%+) of the vote in their department to enter the National Assembly, and the same barrier faces One Nation under the Australian Alternative Vote system. British National Party candidates standing in single-member plurality districts, with at least three rivals, often need to get a third of the vote or more to win a Westminster seat, a barrier which they have consistently failed to overcome. These are all far more daunting obstacles than that faced by Mifleget Datit Leumit (Mafdal) when seeking office in the highly proportional Knesset elections, where parties have to win just 1.5% of the national vote to overcome the minimum legal threshold for representation.[23]

Two basic types of threshold determine the minimum vote that a party needs to obtain in order to be represented. Some proportional or combined electoral systems specify a *legal* (otherwise known as a *formal* or *artificial*) threshold, representing the minimal percentage share of the vote in the electoral district or the whole nation which all party lists must meet in order to be eligible for a seat. Parties falling below the specified legal threshold are automatically excluded from office. Examples include the German Nationaldemokratische Partei Deutschlands, which won 4.3% of the second (party list) votes in the 1969 federal elections, falling below the 5% threshold for entry into the Bundestag, before declining in popular support in subsequent contests.[24] The aim of formal thresholds is to reduce party fragmentation by excluding fringe and extreme parties from the legislature. Electoral laws differ according to their level of application (whether there needs to be a minimum share of the vote achieved at the district or the national level, or both); the percentage specified for any legal threshold (ranging from 0.67 in the Netherlands to 10% of the vote in Turkey); whether the threshold is applied to the first or any subsequent stage of any seat allocations; and whether the threshold varies for parties and for party alliances.[25] Moreover the effects of the legal threshold depend on the context; in Germany, for example, as already observed, the 5% threshold proved critical for the NDP, whereas the 3% legal threshold in Greece has little effect since many minor parties fail to get elected due to the use of fifty-six districts for party lists. A national legal threshold (as in Germany) applied across the whole country limits minor parties such as the Party of Democratic Socialism (PDS), who are strongest in the east but who fell below the 5% level nationally in the 2002 Bundestag election, whereas a district-level legal threshold (such as that used in Spain) will not affect small parties such as the Basque Nationalists, who are returned in their regional strongholds.

In other PR systems, if no legal threshold is specified by electoral law, then there is an *informal* (sometimes known as the *natural* or *mathematical*) threshold. This is strongly influenced by the mean district magnitude, meaning the average number of legislators returned per district, ranging from one member of Parliament per constituency elected to the British House of Commons, and two Congressional deputies per district in Chile, up to 150 members in the Netherlands. But the informal threshold can also be affected, to a lesser extent, by the working of the electoral formula translating seats into votes (for example differences in proportionality among the d'Hondt, Sainte-Laguë, LR-Droop, and Hare formulas), and by the number of political parties competing in a seat. It has two

boundaries: the threshold of *representation* is the minimum percentage
of the vote that can earn a party a seat under the most favorable circumstances. The threshold of *exclusion* is the maximum percentage of
the vote that, under the most favorable conditions, may be insufficient
for a party to win a seat. These can be understood as representing the
upper boundaries (where it is possible to win a seat) and lower boundaries (where it is guaranteed to win a seat). Following Lijphart, the informal threshold is calculated as the mean of the threshold of representation and exclusion, so that it is assumed to be half-way between the
upper and lower threshold.[26] Estimating the informal threshold at national level, however, is not a precise matter as this represents a range,
which can also vary from district to district.[27] Any national estimates
have to remain approximate because the precise conditions under which
electoral thresholds curtail opportunities for minor parties depend heavily upon the distribution of party support and the number of members
returned within each district. For example, even in first-past-the-post majoritarian elections, smaller parties can overcome vote thresholds and gain
districts if their support is spatially concentrated, such as the Reform
Party, which picked up substantial votes and seats in their heartland of
Western Canada. At the same time, even in proportional systems, minor parties with popularity dispersed across many regions can be heavily
penalized; Poland, for example, has open list PR but sets a 7% legal
national voting threshold which smaller parties must surmount to gain
a single parliamentary seat. Nevertheless, the basic proposition expected
here is that the higher thresholds commonly found in majoritarian systems
will restrict opportunities for minor parties, including smaller parties on
the radical right, compared with the lower thresholds usually evident in
PR systems.

The two types of threshold can be combined for analysis. The *effective*
national-level electoral threshold is defined as either the *legal* threshold
(in countries where this is specified at national level) or, where this is
not specified by electoral law, the *informal* threshold at national level. To
examine the effects of specific features of electoral systems on the vote
and seat shares for radical right parties, as well as on the effective number
of parliamentary parties (ENPP) in a country, we can compare a number
of indicators, including the legal and the effective electoral threshold at
national levels, as well as the mean district magnitude (the average number
of representatives elected per district), and the index of proportionality.
The specific measures used are listed under Table 5.4.

TABLE 5.4. *Electoral Rules and Support for Radical Right Parties*

| | Elections 1990–2004 | | | Most recent election | | | | |
	% Votes	% Seats	Ratio	% Votes	% Seats	Ratio	ENPP[a]	Number of countries
Legal electoral thresholds in PR systems[b]	−.358	−.481**	−.432**	−.302	−.366*	−.493**	−.314	21
Effective thresholds in all systems[c]	.171	.026	−.163	.192	.038	−.148	−.204	39
Index of proportionality[d]	.004	.098	.137	−.061	.048	.134	.218	38
Mean district magnitude[e]	−.002	−.096	−.067	−.101	−.121	−.017	.281	39

Note: The figures represent the simple correlation coefficients between support for the radical right parties and electoral rules.

[a] Effective number of parliamentary parties, calculated following the method of Laakso and Taagepera (1979).

[b] This is the minimum share of the vote (in the district or nation) required by law to qualify for a seat.

[c] Following Lijphart (1994), the legal threshold, where available, or else $\frac{50\%}{M+1} + \frac{50\%}{2M}$, where M is the district magnitude.

[d] Calculated as the difference between a party's share of the vote and its share of the total seats in parliament, summed, divided by two, and subtracted from 100. Theoretically it can range from 0 to 100. This is a standardized version of the Loosemore-Hanby index. For details see Rose, Munro, and Mackie (1998).

[e] The average number of seats (representatives returned to parliament) per electoral district.

Sig. .001 = ***; sig. .01 = **; sig. .05 = *.

Source: See Table 5.1.

The results in Table 5.4 demonstrate that PR systems with low legal thresholds, exemplified by Israel or the Netherlands, facilitate the share of seats won by radical right parties. This process is critical: through winning even a handful of parliamentary seats, radical right parties thereby gain legitimacy and a public platform which they can use to consolidate their power and gradually expand their influence. But the results also suggest that legal thresholds do not affect the share of the *vote* for the radical right. Other features of electoral systems which are under comparison, including the effective threshold, the index of proportionality, and the mean district magnitude, also fail to affect the vote or the seat share won by the radical right, and the ENPP measure of party competition.

One reason why the national level of effective thresholds may prove less important than expected is the role of electoral geography; in particular where support for the radical right is concentrated in particular regions and areas, what matters for their exclusion is the effective threshold at *district*, not national, level. If parties can mobilize votes in their heartland areas, they can overcome the effective threshold in these areas, whether in majoritarian or proportional electoral systems. The results provide further confirmation of Lijphart's findings that the electoral system is not a strong instrument in shaping the party system, especially the effective number of elective parties.[28] It appears that, although each of these specific aspects could affect the radical right, it is use of PR systems in general, and the use of restrictive legal thresholds in particular, which has a significant impact upon their share of seats.

Compulsory Voting

In addition to these features, other specific variations in the electoral rules could also shape the fortunes of minor parties. Electoral laws and administrative procedures cover numerous matters including the administration of voting facilities, the frequency of contests, the drawing of constituency boundaries, and citizenship qualifications for the franchise. Discussing how all these matters could affect the electoral fortunes of radical right parties would take us too far from the main subject of this book, but nevertheless we should consider the impact of compulsory voting, as a plausible explanation which has been discussed in the literature. These laws have been suggested as one factor influencing the success of the Vlaams Blok in Antwerp, for example, since under these rules citizens are required to cast a ballot, even where they are dissatisfied by the performance of the major parties, and so they may be tempted to cast a protest vote for the radical right as an expression of antiparty sentiment.[29] Similar patterns may be evident in some of the other nations using compulsory voting, such as Italy and Australia.

Worldwide, twenty-three countries currently use compulsory voting in national parliamentary elections, including Australia, Belgium, Greece, Luxembourg, and Italy. This practice is also used in a few provinces in Austria and in Switzerland, and (until 1970) in the Netherlands. Table 5.5 compares the share of the vote and seats won by radical right parties in the countries which did and did not use such regulations. The results show that the radical right did fare slightly better in the eight nations which use compulsory voting, with perhaps an extra two to three percentage points

TABLE 5.5. *Compulsory Voting and Support for Radical Right Parties*

	Elections 1990–2004			Most recent election			
	% Votes	% Seats	Ratio	% Votes	% Seats	Ratio	Number of countries
Compulsory voting is not used	6.3	5.1	.41	5.9	5.9	.41	31
Compulsory voting is used	9.0	7.5	.37	8.8	8.6	.37	8
Difference	+2.7	+2.4	.04	+2.9	+2.7	.0.4	39

Note: The results summarize the mean percentage of votes and seats won by radical right parties in elections for the lower house in the national legislature. For the classification of compulsory voting by nation see Pippa Norris. 2004. *Electoral Engineering*. Cambridge: Cambridge University Press. Chapter 7. The mean difference in the proportion of votes and seats won by radical right parties between countries which did and did not use compulsory voting were *not* significant at the conventional .95 confidence level when tested by ANOVA (Aanalysis of Variance).

Source: See Table 5.1.

in the vote. This evidence is suggestive but, given the limited number of cases, not surprisingly the modest difference was not statistically significant at the conventional level. This suggests that we need more conclusive proof from survey evidence at individual level before we can safely conclude that the radical right do indeed benefit from compulsory voting laws.

One reason why the results are ambiguous is that the strength of any effect may depend upon how strictly compulsory voting regulations and any associated sanctions are implemented and enforced.[30] In practice, legal rules for voting may be de jure or de facto. The most common legal basis is statutory law, although the obligation to vote may also be rooted in constitutional provisions. Implementation ranges from minimal de facto enforcement to the imposition of various sanctions. Fines are most common, as in Luxembourg, although other punishments include the denial of official documents like passports, identity cards, drivers' licenses, or government benefits, used in Italy and Greece, and even occasionally the threat of imprisonment as a criminal offence. The effectiveness of any legal penalties is dependent upon the efficiency of the prior registration process and, where the initiative falls upon the elector, whether there are fines or other penalties associated with failure to register.[31]

CONCLUSIONS

The study examined evidence for the impact of electoral systems and electoral thresholds, particularly the standard claim that PR facilitates support for smaller extremist parties. The results suggest three main findings:

  i. A revised version of the conventional wisdom is partially correct: *electoral systems do affect the seats gained by minor radical right parties*, with their rise facilitated by PR systems with low legal thresholds.
 ii. Nevertheless the evidence suggests an important and overlooked qualification to the conventional wisdom: the effect of electoral systems works through determining their share of seats *not* votes. The effects here are mechanical rather than psychological, for reasons discussed below.
iii. And lastly, within PR systems, legal thresholds also exert a critical mechanical impact on the radical right share of seats.

The clear role of electoral systems and thresholds on the distribution of seats can be illustrated by a few examples. Under majoritarian elections, for example, Le Pen's Front National have been stranded on the sidelines of French politics for decades. By contrast, after gaining a similar share of the vote (11–12%) in the most recent national general elections, under PR the Vlaams Blok constitute one-tenth of the members of the Belgian Parliament, while Alleanza Nazionale hold ministerial office in Berlusconi's cabinet. Politically this process is vital, since parliamentary representation provides the radical right with legitimacy, resources, and power. Through PR, parties gain access to a platform on the national stage, allowing them to propagate their views, influence debates, and mobilize popular support via the national news media, not just gain sporadic bursts of publicity during occasional election campaigns.

There is one important qualification to these conclusions, as it should be noted that the evidence about the impact of electoral systems in newer democracies remains limited, and the direction of causality in this relationship, in particular, cannot be determined from cross-sectional evidence alone. What this means is that we cannot say whether majoritarian electoral systems penalize and thereby discourage extremist parties from competing, or, alternatively, whether newer democracies containing multiple parties dispersed widely across the political spectrum are more likely to adopt PR rules in their electoral laws and constitutions. What we can conclude, however, is that in established democracies which have had relatively stable electoral systems over successive decades, or even for centuries, in the long term it seems plausible that the rules of the game (adopted for whatever reason) will constrain *subsequent* patterns of party competition. In Britain, for example, the system of plurality single-member districts has persisted in elections for the House of Commons since the Great Reform Act of 1832, with the exception of a few dual-member seats which were finally abolished in 1948. This system has greatly limited the opportunities for minor center parties to challenge the Labour and Conservative predominance at Westminster, despite growing patterns of partisan dealignment and surges of popular support for the Liberal Democrats in recent decades. In the 2001 general election, the 'manufactured majority' bias for the governing Labour Party was the largest since World War II.[32] Where electoral rules have persisted unchanged for many decades, we can conclude that they determine how parties respond strategically to the structure of opportunities they present.

The conventional wisdom remains partially *in*correct; although the institutional context of the electoral system might be expected to influence popular support for minor parties, with majoritarian systems having a psychological effect in depressing their vote share for the radical right, this turns out not to be the case. The 'wasted vote' thesis does not hold for these parties; given the proximity theory of voting, their supporters are located too far away from other contenders across the ideological spectrum for them to switch to their second-preference choice for tactical or strategic considerations. Fuller support for this argument is presented in Chapter 7, examining survey evidence of protest and strategic voting.

In subsequent chapters in this book we also need to consider other psychological effects of electoral rules, in particular whether the basic type of electoral system exerts an important indirect impact upon the campaign strategies and ideological positions adopted by minor parties on the radical right. As will be explored in detail later, majoritarian rules with higher thresholds are expected to generate incentives for rational vote-seeking parties to adopt bridging strategies, appealing to citizens across different ideological persuasions and social backgrounds. By contrast, under proportional systems with lower thresholds, rational parties have greater incentive to adopt bonding strategies, appealing more exclusively to their home base.[33] Far from being irrelevant, therefore, the strategic agency theory presented in this book regards the electoral system as central to understanding variations in the electoral success of the radical right, as well as how these parties respond to the institutional constraints on their behavior. The next step is to examine the social background and ideological profile of radical right supporters.

PART III

ELECTORAL DEMAND

6

The 'New Cleavage' Thesis

The Social Basis of Right-Wing Support

Demand-side accounts focus upon developments in the mass electorate which are believed to have fueled the popularity of radical right appeals, whether structural changes in the socioeconomic basis of postindustrial society, the rise of political disenchantment, or shifts in public opinion toward immigrants and ethnic minorities. Ever since early work on the origins of fascism and authoritarianism, a series of studies in political sociology have explored these issues. Three distinct strands emerged in the literature.[1] Classic accounts published during the 1950s and 1960s sought to explain the phenomenon of the rise of fascism in Weimar Germany, as well as Poujadism in France, and McCarthyism in the United States, as a *revolt against modernity* led primarily by the petite bourgeoisie – small entrepreneurs, shopkeepers, merchants, self-employed artisans, and independent farmers – squeezed between the growing power of big business and the collective clout of organized labor.[2] Echoing and updating these concerns, contemporary theorists argue that a *new social cleavage* has emerged in affluent societies. In this view, some residual elements of the appeal of the radical right among the petite bourgeoisie can still be detected, but during the last decade their populist rhetoric has fallen upon its most fertile ground among a low-skilled blue-collar underclass, with minimal job security, and among those populations most vulnerable to new social risks who have tumbled through the cracks within affluent societies.[3] Alternatively, theories of *partisan dealignment* suggest that today the appeal of the radical right is not based upon a single identifiable social cleavage common in all countries, whether the unskilled working class or the petite bourgeoisie. Rather, the theory predicts significant variations in the social basis of support for parties within the radical right

129

family, and an erosion in how far social structure and partisan loyalties are related to voting behavior.

Section I discusses the reasons underlying the alternative theoretical frameworks and considers the rival hypotheses in more detail. The chapter then compares evidence to analyze the social basis of the radical right vote across fifteen nations, using data from the European Social Survey 2002 and the Comparative Study of Electoral Systems 1996–2001. Previous case studies analyzing voting support for specific parties, such as Vlaams Blok or Lega Nord, have often reported inconsistent results. These variations may be attributed to genuine contrasts found in the national electorates, or they may be due to the use of inconsistent classifications of social stratification and occupational class employed in alternative studies, as well as the common problems of limited sample size and measurement error.[4] The number of respondents included in the pooled cross-national samples in the surveys used in this book, combined with the consistency of the measures and the range of indicators they tap across different countries, allows us to surmount some of these problems. Section II focuses upon the role of social stratification while Section III considers the enduring gender gap and patterns of generational support. The conclusion considers the implications of these results for understanding the basis of radical right popularity, and for the stability and longevity of these parties.

I THEORETICAL FRAMEWORK AND RIVAL HYPOTHESES

Classic Sociological Accounts: A Crisis of Modernity?

The classic account of voting behavior by Lipset and Rokkan emphasized that social cleavages shaped patterns of party competition in Western Europe.[5] They argued that the enduring foundations for political parties were formed from historical divisions in the electorate, existing at the time of the expansion of the mass franchise, between Catholics and Protestants, core and peripheral regions, and owners and workers. Parties were thought to reflect and channel these interests into the public sphere. These structural theories in political sociology are rooted in broader processes of societal modernization, identifying multiple long-term secular trends associated with the rise of industrial and postindustrial societies.[6] The most fundamental economic developments shaping European societies during the early twentieth century include the consolidation of large-scale manufacturing industry through the economies of scale generated by assembly-line production, the unionization of the labor force, and the growth of professional and managerial white-collar employees in the service sector. These developments were closely associated with the expansion of secondary and higher education, rising middle-class affluence, and growing standards of living.

The early seminal accounts in political sociology linked these economic and social developments to the roots of support for fascism in Italy and Germany, and for McCarthyism in America. These ideas were contained in a series of essays in *The New American Right*, edited by Daniel Bell, first published in 1955, and in *Political Man*, published by Seymour Martin Lipset in 1959. Fearing downward mobility and loss of social status, Lipset and Bell argued, radical right-wing movements tapped fears and insecurities among those who lost out to industrialization: "Extremist movements have much in common. They appeal to the disgruntled and psychologically homeless, to the personal failures, the socially isolated, the economically insecure, the uneducated, unsophisticated, and the authoritarian persons."[7]

In particular, Lipset argued, it was the small individual entrepreneurs, especially those lacking education and those socially isolated in rural areas and small towns, who formed the traditional bedrock support for fascism, trapped between the threat of big business and manufacturing industry on the one hand, and the collective strength of organized labor on the other. The petite bourgeoisie consisted of small entrepreneurs, shopkeepers, urban merchants, self-employed craftsmen, and independent family farmers. These groups differ in many regards. What they share in common is that they risk their own modest reserves of capital, and they lack the security that comes from managerial and professional careers employed in large organizations or from the collective bonds of trade union membership. The self-employed, working in family businesses, are exposed to market forces and they remain vulnerable to sudden economic downturns, hyperinflation, or rising interest rates. Bell and Lipset emphasized, however, that it was the threat of loss of *status* by the petite bourgeoisie in industrial societies, more than purely economic threats, which triggered their resentment against big business and organized labor, boosting the appeal of American movements offering simple populist solutions, exemplified by Coughlinism in the 1930s, McCarthyism in the 1950s, and the John Birch Society in the 1960s, as well as mass support for fascist movements in Germany and Italy. Subsequent historical research on the origins of European fascist movements during the interwar period lends further support to these conclusions.[8] If there is some historical continuity in the social basis of contemporary politics, then the theory predicts that electoral support for radical right parties will be concentrated most strongly among the petite bourgeoisie.

Modern Sociological Accounts: A 'New Social Cleavage'?

Modern sociological explanations echo, but also update, some of these concerns. The core ideas and ideological appeals that characterized populism and fascism in earlier decades differ sharply from modern right-wing movements today, and these shifts may attract a different social base. The traditional platform of interwar fascism advocated corporatist and state-controlled economies, with strong government authority built around a hierarchical political leadership, in sharp contrast to the free market, small government, and antistate appeal of the contemporary right.[9] The signature issue mobilizing support for the radical right today, however, is not primarily fear of big business and organized labor per se, but rather the threat of 'the other,' driven by patterns of immigration, asylum seekers, and multiculturalism. The radical right have responded to the way that modern postindustrial societies have been transformed during the late twentieth century by multiple social developments which have transformed living conditions, life chances, and patterns of socio-economic inequality in advanced industrial societies. These include processes of globalization, reducing national barriers for labor, trade, and capital mobility; the liberal restructuring of economic markets and the shrinkage of the welfare state, reducing social protection; and the decline of local communities and traditional working-class formal organizations, exemplified by trade unions and labor cooperatives. Contemporary sociological accounts emphasize that these processes have largely benefited those social groups with the educational and cognitive skills, geographic mobility, and professional career flexibility to take advantage of the new economic and social opportunities in affluent societies.[10]

At the same time, commentators argue that these developments have left behind a residual 'underclass' of low-skill workers, who face shrinking life chances, poorer opportunities for full-time employment and well-paid secure careers in the job market, reduced state benefits, and growing conditions of social inequality.[11] The less-educated poor face being stuck in low-skill, low-wage casual work, usually with minimal job security. It might be thought that these groups would naturally gravitate toward mainstream socialist, social democratic, labor, and Communist parties of the center-left and extreme left, the traditional advocates for the socially disadvantaged; or mainstream conservative parties that stand for security, law and order, and national identity. But instead, theorists argue, mainstream parties have been unable or unwilling to respond to a displaced constituency generated by increased economic inequality and social insecurity among the losers of modernity, combined with growing multiculturalism. These conditions have encouraged the politics of resentment against immigrants, kindling the conflagration sparked by populist rhetoric and fanned by extremist party leaders.

The old left may have proved unresponsive to these concerns, and social inequality may have worsened, where these parties have become increasingly catchall in pursuit of support among the rapidly expanding middle classes, and where the forces of globalization and international market pressures have constrained the autonomy of center-left governments to pass protectionist measures.[12] Traditionally the left has been concerned with protection against the type of social disadvantage that seriously limits the capacity of wage earners to extract an income from the labor market, such as industrial accidents, unemployment, disease, invalidity, or old age. Protection against these social risks became the key objective of the welfare states throughout postwar Western Europe and elsewhere, with social policies developed primarily by Social Democratic parties in alliance with the labor movement, as well as by Christian Democratic parties. Where mainstream center-left parties have failed to recognize or respond to the emergence of populations experiencing new social risks, and where patterns of economic retrenchment mean that spending on the welfare state has been sharply reduced, this may create new social cleavages in the electorate which can be exploited by entrepreneurial new parties. At the same time, Betz suggests that social individualization and fragmentation have eroded the mass membership of traditional collective organizations, social networks, and mass movements that used to mobilize working-class communities, exemplified by workers' cooperatives and the trade union movement. Socialist and Social Democratic parties functioned in the past as a channel for the collective organization and expression of working-class grievances.

It is these new socially disadvantaged groups, Betz suggests, who are most prone to blame ethnic minorities for deteriorating conditions, to support cultural protectionism, and to criticize government for failing to provide the growing prosperity and social security that was characteristic of postwar Europe. The failure of center-left political elites to restore a sense of security and prosperity to the unemployed and underprivileged in Western Europe, this account argues, fuels support for populist leaders who do make such promises.[13] In short, the politics of resentment are believed to generate conditions favorable to populist leaders offering simplistic solutions. Some empirical evidence sustains this argument; for example, Lubbers, Gijsberts, and Scheepers report that in Western Europe radical right support at individual level is significantly stronger among the unemployed, blue-collar workers, the retired, and less-educated sectors, as well as among younger voters, the nonreligious, and men.[14] Yet these were specific, not diffuse effects: they did not find stronger right-wing voting in nations with higher levels of unemployment.[15] The gender gap in support for extreme right parties has been a well-established and persistent pattern, although the reasons for this are not clearly understood.[16] In a five-nation comparison, Niedermayer also found that white-collar employees and professionals are consistently underrepresented in the electorates of radical right parties, although he also demonstrated that the proportion of blue-collar workers and those with low educational achievement varied substantially among different parties such as the Austrian FPÖ, the German Republicans, and the Danish Progress Party.[17]

Some aggregate-level studies have also found a relationship between national unemployment rates and the share of the vote cast for far right parties in each country, for example work by Jackman and Volpert.[18] The authors emphasized that the effects of macroeconomic conditions were expected to operate at sociotropic level, affecting all groups within a society, but not necessarily at egotropic level, so that support for the radical right was not anticipated to be stronger among those individuals with direct personal experience of long-term unemployment, among unskilled workers, or among poorer social sectors. A similar link has been found between unemployment and radical right voting patterns when analyzing regional variations in France and Austria.[19] Golder, however, argues that there is an interaction effect, reporting that unemployment only matters where immigration is high.[20] The new cleavage thesis therefore emphasizes that 'bottom up' secular trends common in affluent postindustrial societies, particularly the growth of disadvantaged populations subject to contemporary social risks, have created a disgruntled pool of citizens open to the appeals of the radical right. If this account is supported by the survey evidence, then we would expect to find that contemporary voting support for the parties under comparison should be disproportionately drawn from unskilled manual workers, the less educated, and those people with personal experience of unemployment or job insecurity.

Partisan Dealignment and Weakening Social Cues

Yet not all the evidence is consistent with this thesis; for instance van der Brug, Fennema, and Tillie compared support for seven radical right parties, reporting that they attracted support equally across all social strata. After controlling for ideological proximity and political attitudes, the study found that the indicators of social stratification were rarely significant associated with party support (including the role of social class, income, religion, and education), and no significant patterns were found consistently across all parties.[21] Studies of French voting behavior also suggest that the class and the religious profiles of electors fail to prove a particularly powerful predictor when explaining support for the Front National.[22] General processes of social and partisan dealignment may have eroded any distinctive social profile of the radical right voter, along with the role of class and religious cleavages in predicting support for many mainstream parties on the center-left and center-right. A large body of research suggests that the class cleavage in party politics has gradually faded over the last three decades in many postindustrial societies, with more cross-cutting cleavages arising in multicultural societies, and growing partisan dealignment weakening traditional voter-party loyalties.[23] The most recent review of the evidence by Dalton and Wattenberg compared indicators of party attachments across a wide variety of advanced industrialized democracies, based on time-series survey analysis of Eurobarometer and national election studies. They concluded that over time the total number of the electorate expressing a party identification had eroded significantly (at the .10 level) in thirteen out of nineteen nations under comparison, and nonpartisanship had spread most widely among more politically sophisticated and better-educated citizens, as well as among the younger generation.[24]

If the rocklike ballast of class and partisan identities no longer anchors voters to mainstream parties over successive elections, this may have significant consequences for patterns of growing volatility in electoral behavior and in party competition, opening the door for more split-ticket voting across different levels and the occasional sudden surge of support for the parties based on protest politics, as well as more vote switching within and across the left-right blocks of party families.[25] The dealignment thesis suggests that the radical right may be able to capitalize on protest politics, particularly benefiting from any temporary widespread disaffection with governing parties, in second-order elections held during periods of mid-term blues, or from sudden events (exemplified by the wave of support for Lijst Pym Fortuyn following the assassination of their leader), to pick up votes generally across the board, rather than presenting a distinctive social profile. At the same time, this thesis also suggests that any short-term gains for the radical right may be dissipated in subsequent elections, as they will not be based on stable social and partisan cleavages which make supporters stick with parties through good times and bad.

II COMPARING THE SOCIAL BASIS OF SUPPORT

To recap the core alternative hypotheses, the roots of the contemporary radical right will continue to reflect patterns of electoral support for interwar fascism in the crisis of modernity thesis if the evidence demonstrates that their vote is disproportionately concentrated among the petite bourgeoisie, whether in self-employed professional and managerial workers, such as family farmers, freelance architects, and restaurant proprietors, or in own-account manual occupations, such as self-employed builders, taxi drivers, and casual plumbers. On the other hand, modern sociological accounts of the emergence of a new social cleavage will be confirmed if radical right support in many countries draws disproportionately upon the most socially disadvantaged and poorer sectors of the electorate. And the partisan dealignment thesis will be demonstrated if social cleavages are only weakly related to voting behavior today.

What evidence could be used to test these propositions? Previous survey analyses of the social basis of the radical right vote have often been hampered by poor measurement of vulnerability to new social risks, experience of job insecurity, and socioeconomic inequality (including fairly crude measures of social class categories). This problem is compounded by the limited sample size of most standard social surveys, restricting analysis of the small number of radical right voters contained within each sector. Moreover, due to the limitations of survey data and the available measures, previous analysis has often failed to distinguish in sufficient detail among distinct segments of the 'new' working class, such as examining any similarities in voting behavior among self-employed professionals and own-account skilled manual workers, as well as party support among those with direct experience of job and financial insecurity.

To examine the systematic cross-national evidence, this study draws upon the European Social Survey 2002 and the Comparative Study of Electoral Systems 1996–2001. These surveys facilitate consistent comparisons across fifteen industrial and postindustrial nations containing relevant right parties, including diverse Anglo-American, West European, and post-Communist states, to see whether there are similarities in the electorate across and within societies. These sources also allow analysis of more finely grained measures of the social and attitudinal structure of support for radical right parties at individual, party, and country levels. The ESS 2002 survey includes several indicators of social deprivation and experience of long-term unemployment. Ratio measures are used to present the results, as the clearest and most straightforward way to compare how far support within each group is greater or less than the average party vote among all the electorate in each country. Ratios are measured as the proportion of each group who voted for the radical right divided into the proportion of the national electorate who voted for the radical right in each country. A ratio of 1.0 suggests that the proportion of a group voting for the radical right reflects the share of the vote that the party received from across the whole electorate (e.g., if the Lega Nord received 10% of the national vote and the support of 10% of the unskilled working class). A ratio less than 1.0 indicates that, compared with the national average, the group is underrepresented in voting for the radical right. And a ratio greater than 1.0 (flagged in tables in **bold**) suggests that, compared with the national average, the group is overrepresented in voting for these parties.

To test the impact of social stratification with systematic evidence, we follow the fivefold Goldthorpe-Heath classification of occupational class, used by Heath, Jowell, and Curtice for understanding the British electorate, on the basis of a schema originally developed by the sociologist John Goldthorpe.[26] This distinguishes among five groups: (i) the *salariat* (employees who are managers and administrators, supervisors, and professionals, with relatively high career security, salaries, and status); (ii) *routine non-manuals* (employees such as accounts clerks, sales workers, and personal assistants, with lower work security, income, and prestige); (iii) the *petite bourgeoisie* (self-employed farmers, small proprietors, and own-account manual workers, exposed to market risks through reliance upon their own capital); (iv) the *skilled working class* (manual employees including electricians, machinists, and crafts persons); and (v) the *unskilled working class* (more casual employees, such as plant operatives, laborers, and domestic helpers, with the lowest job security, pay, and status). Respondents were classified by their own work, based on the ISCO88 occupational code, if employed in the paid workforce, rather than by head of household. We focus in this chapter upon simple descriptive models measuring the direct effects of social cleavages upon voting support, leaving aside for the moment any indirect effect that may run from social cleavages through political attitudes to party support.

The first model in Table 6.1 presents the results of a binary logistic (logit) regression model, including the unstandardized beta coefficients (B), the standard errors, and their significance, in the pooled eight-nation

TABLE 6.1. *The Social Structure of Radical Right-Wing Votes, ESS 2002*

	Predictors of voting for the radical right, pooled eight-nation European sample		
	B	Std. error	Sig.
(Constant)	−3.08		
Demographic background			
Age (in years)	.005	.002	**
Sex (male = 1, female = 0)	.307	.074	***
Ethnic minority (ethnic minority = 1, else = 0)	−1.04	.249	***
Socioeconomic status			
Education (highest level attained on a 6-point scale from low to high)	−.051	.030	N/s
Salariat (professional and managerial employees)	−.267	.120	*
Petite bourgeoisie (self-employed)	.297	.105	**
Skilled manual working class	.372	.119	**
Unskilled manual working class	.390	.102	***
Ever been unemployed (for more than 3 months)	.198	.085	**
Religiosity (self-identified as religious on a 7-pt scale)	−.033	.012	**
Nagelkerke R^2	.025		
Percentage correctly predicted	93.1		

Note: The model presents the results of a binary logistic (logit) regression model including the unstandardized beta coefficients (B), the standard errors, and their significance, in the pooled eight-nation European sample weighted by design and population size. The nations were selected from all those in the ESS 2002 based on whether they contained a relevant party on the radical right (including Austria, Belgium, Switzerland, Denmark, Israel, Italy, the Netherlands, and Norway). France was excluded from the pooled sample because the standard occupational classification was not measured in the survey. The dependent variable is whether the respondent voted for a radical right party. All coefficients were confirmed to be free of multicollinearity errors. The pooled sample contained 13,768 respondents in total, including 932 voters for the radical right (6.8%). The routine non-manual category of social class was dropped as the default (comparison) case in this model.
Sig. .001 = ***; sig. .01 = **; sig. .05 = *.
Source: Pooled sample eight nations, European Social Survey 2002 (ESS).

European sample. Countries were selected from all those in the ESS 2002 based on whether they contained a relevant radical right electoral party, defined as those with over 3% of the vote, including Austria, Belgium, Switzerland, Denmark, Israel, Italy, the Netherlands, and Norway. The dependent variable is whether the respondent voted for a radical right party. The results of the pooled model confirm that nearly all the basic social indicators were significant at the conventional .95 probability level and coefficients pointed in the predicted direction; the one exception was education, which was negatively related to support for the radical right, as predicted, but which was only significant at the .90 probability level. The results confirm what many others have found in previous studies; namely in these nations support for the radical right was significantly stronger among the older generation and men, and ethnic minority voters were underrepresented. The analysis by social class indicates that support for the radical right was underrepresented among the salariat, and overrepresented among the petite bourgeoisie, as well as skilled manual and unskilled manual workers. Moreover support for these parties was greater among those who had experienced unemployment, as well as among the less religious. This social profile of radical right voters broadly reflects that found earlier by Lubbers et al. based on analysis of other cross-national surveys conducted in Western Europe in the mid-1990s, strengthening confidence in the stability of these findings.[27]

Overall these patterns suggest that structural characteristics continue to differentiate radical right voters; lacking consistent time-series data, we cannot establish whether the impact of these variables has weakened over the years, as theories of partisan dealignment suggest. What we can conclude with more confidence, however, is that radical right parties are not simply appealing across all social sectors equally, for example based on temporary protest politics and a period of widespread public disenchantment with mainstream politics, as some previous studies suggest.[28] The continued attraction of the petite bourgeoisie to the contemporary radical right, for example, indicates that there are deeper roots which also characterized interwar fascism. To go further, the pooled results need to be broken down by nation and by type of social cleavage, as well as being compared with the social profile of the radical right electorate in other Anglo-American and post-Communist countries, to see whether there are consistent patterns across postindustrial societies.

Table 6.2 summarizes the ratio measures of class voting for the radical right in thirteen countries containing relevant radical right parties, without any prior controls. The evidence confirms that support for these parties remains disproportionately overrepresented among the petite bourgeoisie, as well as the skilled manual and the unskilled manual working class, in most of the countries under comparison. In particular, compared with the general electorate, support for the radical right is at least twice as strong among the petite bourgeoisie in Hungary, Italy, and Romania, showing the greatest resemblance to the classic roots of European

TABLE 6.2. *The Class Basis of Radical Right Voters*

Nation	Party(s)	% Who voted for the radical right, all voters	The ratio of voting support for the radical right in each class compared with the national average share of the vote				
			Salariat	Routine non-manual	Petite bourgeoisie	Skilled manual	Unskilled manual
Austria	FPÖ	3.2	1.0	0.8	0.8	1.9	1.8
Belgium	VB, FN	4.4	0.5	0.9	1.3	2.3	1.4
Czech Rep.	RSC	5.6	0.9	0.7	0.7	2.0	1.5
Denmark	DF, FP	6.8	0.3	0.9	0.9	1.4	1.6
France	FN	3.2			0.8		
Hungary	MIEP	2.2	**1.4**	0.5	2.0	0.7	1.0
Israel	Mafdal, IL	4.6	**1.7**	0.9	1.1	1.3	0.5
Italy	AN, LN, MsFt	6.1	1.2	0.7	2.0	0.3	0.7
Netherlands	PF, CD	11.5	0.6	1.2	1.1	1.1	1.1
New Zealand	NZFP	10.9	0.8	0.9	1.0	1.3	1.1
Norway	FrP, FLP	11.9	0.5	0.8	1.1	1.3	**2.0**
Romania	PRM, PUNR	3.2	0.3	1.3	2.4	1.3	0.9
Switzerland	SVP, EDU, SD, LdT, FPS	8.8	0.9	0.9	1.7	0.8	1.0
MEAN		6.2	0.8	0.9	1.3	1.3	1.2

Note: The figures represent the ratio of each group's support for the radical right compared with the national average (measured as the proportion of each group who voted for the radical right divided into the proportion of the national electorate who voted for the radical right in each country). A coefficient of 1.0 suggests that the group was perfectly proportional to the national average. A coefficient of less than 1.0 suggests that group was underrepresented among radical right voters. A coefficient greater than 1.0 (in **bold**) suggests that the group was overrepresented among radical right voters. For the list of parties included, see Table 3.1.

Sources: Austria, Belgium, Switzerland, Denmark, France, Israel, Italy, the Netherlands, and Norway analyzed from data in the ESS 2002. The Czech Republic, New Zealand, Romania, and Hungary analyzed from data in the CSES 1996–2001. Note that 'self-employment' was not classified in Canada, Russia, and Slovenia, necessitating dropping these nations from the comparison in this table, while standard occupational category was not classified in France.

fascism. By contrast, the salariat are underrepresented within the radical right electorate in every country except for Hungary, Italy, and Israel. This remains the radical right's greatest area of electoral weakness, given the substantial expansion in professional and managerial employees in service sector economies, and the limited size of the petite bourgeoisie. Some important cross-national differences are also apparent, exemplified by the more blue-collar base of the Austrian FPÖ (confirming the substantial growth of their support among the working class in elections during the 1990s, documented elsewhere),[29] in contrast to the greater attraction of the Romanian PRM and PUNR among lower-middle-class voters and the Lega Nord's strongest base among the petite bourgeoisie. Later chapters examine whether these social differences relate to systematic patterns of ideological support, as case-study comparisons suggest that the different class base found in the FPÖ and the Lega Nord can be explained by their divergent programmatic appeals, with Lega Nord maintaining their advocacy of radical free market neoliberal policies while the FPÖ altered their platform under Haider to favor more protectionist measures.[30]

The educational profile of voters is broken down in more detail in Table 6.3, showing a not dissimilar pattern across nations, which is not surprising given the close link between prior educational achievement and subsequent social status. Again the radical right in Hungary (MIEP), Israel (Mafdal and IL), and Italy (AN, LN and MsFt) draw disproportionately upon those with better education, just as they have a stronger imprint among the salariat. In nearly all other countries, support for the radical right tends to be stronger among those with low or moderate education. Nevertheless there are variations in these patterns, and it would be an exaggeration to claim that party support is confined to early schoolleavers with the lowest level of educational attainment and cognitive sophistication.

We can go beyond these basic indicators to also see whether those with experience of being unemployed and the poorest groups living in low-income households are more prone to support the radical right, as many suggest. This is important given that many aggregate-level studies in political economy argue that rising levels of unemployment, coupled with the perceived threat of migrant foreign workers to job security, play a major role in explaining the rise of the radical right in the European Union.[31] We can also examine the location of respondents, to see whether votes for these parties are concentrated either within poorer inner-city urban neighborhoods, or else, as classic accounts of fascism suggested,

So it varies by country

Electoral Demand

TABLE 6.3. *The Educational Background of Radical Right Voters*

Nation	Party(s)	% Who voted for the radical right, all voters	The ratio of voting support for the radical right in each group compared with the national average share of the vote		
			Low education	Moderate education	High education
Austria	FPÖ	3.2	1.1	1.0	0.8
Belgium	VB, FN	4.4	1.3	1.0	0.3
Canada	RP	18.9	0.9	1.1	0.9
Czech Rep.	RSC	5.6	1.4	1.1	0.6
Denmark	DF, FP	6.8	1.4	1.1	0.1
France	FN	3.2	1.5	0.5	0.5
Hungary	MIEP	2.2	0.8	1.0	1.7
Israel	Mafdal, IL	4.6	0.2	0.8	1.8
Italy	AN, LN, MsFt	6.1	0.7	1.3	1.4
Netherlands	PF, CD	11.5	1.1	1.0	0.7
New Zealand	NZFP	10.9	1.5	1.1	0.8
Norway	FrP, FLP	11.9	1.3	1.2	0.4
Romania	PRM, PUNR	3.2	0.6	1.2	1.3
Russia	LDPR	1.5	1.3	1.5	0.7
Slovenia	SNS	2.2	0.5	1.3	1.1
Switzerland	SVP, EDU, SD, LdT, FPS	8.8	0.7	1.2	0.5
MEAN		6.2	1.0	1.1	0.9

Note: The figures represent the ratio of each group's support for the radical right compared with the national average (measured as the proportion of each group who voted for the radical right divided into the proportion of the national electorate who voted for the radical right in each country). A coefficient of 1.0 suggests that the group was perfectly proportional to the national average. A coefficient of less than 1.0 suggests that group was underrepresented among radical right voters. A coefficient greater than 1.0 (in **bold**) suggests that the group was overrepresented among radical right voters. For the list of parties included, see Table 3.1.

Sources: Austria, Belgium, Switzerland, Denmark, France, Israel, Italy, the Netherlands, and Norway analyzed from data in the ESS 2002. Canada, the Czech Republic, New Zealand, Romania, Russia, Slovenia, and Hungary analyzed from data in the CSES 1996–2001.

within rural areas and small villages. Table 6.4 demonstrates that those with experience of unemployment were overrepresented among supporters of the radical right in about half the nations under comparison, with particularly strong effects in the Czech Republic and the Russian Federation. Yet the results can hardly be seen as providing strong confirmation for claims that individual experience of job insecurity and unemployment is a major factor behind the success of these parties. The comparisons

TABLE 6.4. *Social Indicators, Type of Area, and Radical Right Voters*

Nation	Party(s)	% Who voted for the radical right, all voters	The ratio of voting support for the radical right in each group compared with the national average share of the vote			
			Unemployed during the last 5 years	Low income	Live in rural area or village	Live in a large city
Austria	FPÖ	3.2	0.8	0.8	**1.2**	0.6
Belgium	VB, FN	4.4	**1.6**	**1.1**	**1.2**	0.9
Canada	RP	18.9	0.9	0.9	1.0	1.0
Czech Rep.	RSC	5.6	**2.3**	**1.1**	**1.2**	0.1
Denmark	DF, FP	6.8	**1.1**	**1.2**	0.9	0.8
France	FN	3.2	0.8	0.9	0.8	0.6
Hungary	MIEP	2.2	**1.5**	1.0	1.0	**2.2**
Israel	Mafdal, IL	4.6	0.8	0.6	**1.6**	0.9
Italy	AN, LN, MsFt	6.1	0.8	0.6	0.8	**1.7**
Netherlands	PF, CD	11.5	**1.4**	0.9	1.0	0.9
New Zealand	NZFP	10.9	**1.1**	**1.5**	**1.3**	0.9
Norway	FrP, FLP	11.9	**1.1**	0.7	1.0	0.9
Romania	PRM, PUNR	3.2	0.3	0.8	1.0	1.0
Russia	LDPR	1.5	**2.0**	**1.5**	0.8	**1.1**
Slovenia	SNS	2.2	0.8	0.7	1.0	1.0
Switzerland	SVP, EDU, SD, LdT, FPS	8.8	0.6	0.9	**1.1**	0.2
MEAN		6.2	**1.1**	0.9	**1.1**	0.9

Note: The figures represent the ratio of each group's support for the radical right compared with the national average (measured as the proportion of each group who voted for the radical right divided into the proportion of the national electorate who voted for the radical right in each country). A coefficient of 1.0 suggests that the group was perfectly proportional to the national average. A coefficient of less than 1.0 suggests that group was underrepresented among radical right voters. A coefficient greater than 1.0 (in **bold**) suggests that the group was overrepresented among radical right voters. For the list of parties included, see Table 3.1.

Sources: Austria, Belgium, Switzerland, Denmark, France, Israel, Italy, the Netherlands, and Norway analyzed from data in the ESS 2002. Canada, the Czech Republic, New Zealand, Romania, Russia, Slovenia, and Hungary analyzed from data in the CSES 1996–2001.

among low-income households were even more equivocal: support for the radical right was only overrepresented in this group among one-third of the nations under comparison. The analysis by area also demonstrates that there were mixed patterns, with six countries where the radical right was stronger in rural areas and only three cases where they gained more votes among urban residents. On balance, the interpretation of the contemporary right as simply being the product of disaffection among the poorest and least-educated social sectors appears to be an exaggerated stereotype; while it is true that radical right parties in Austria, Denmark, and the Czech Republic do derive considerable reservoirs of support from these social sectors, at the same time these parties attract considerable votes across the spectrum in Hungary and the Netherlands, and they gain slightly greater than average support among the petite bourgeoisie and the highly educated in Italy and Israel.

III DEMOGRAPHIC FACTORS: GENDER AND GENERATION

Research on gender differences in the electorate has been a recurrent theme in political science ever since the earliest systematic surveys of voting behavior.[32] Many hoped, and others feared, that once women were enfranchised there would be a distinctive women's vote. Gender was not regarded as a primary electoral cleavage, equivalent to class, region, and religion, because women and men experienced many cross-cutting forces, but the seminal account of European voting behavior by Lipset and Rokkan viewed gender as one of the secondary cleavages shaping the electoral base of party politics.[33] The early classics in the 1950s and 1960s established the orthodoxy in political science: gender differences in voting were generally fairly modest, but women were likelier than men to support center-right parties in Western Europe and in the United States, a pattern that has been termed the traditional gender gap.[34] Most explanations of this phenomenon emphasized structural differences between men and women in religiosity, longevity, and labor force participation; for example, women in Italy and France were more likely to attend churches associated with Christian Democratic parties.[35] During this era, women were also commonly assumed to be more conservative in their political attitudes and values, producing an ideological gap underpinning their party preferences.[36] Yet at the same time many studies suggested that men were far more likely to belong to extreme right parties, such as the fascist movement.[37] The traditional gender gap on the center-right gradually faded and the literature suggested that the old thesis of female conservatism was apparently no longer evident; instead, the situation in the 1980s seemed contingent upon political circumstances: in some established democracies women seemed to lean toward the right, in others to the left, and in still others no significant differences could be detected.[38] By the end of the 1990s, however, women had shifted toward the center-left of men in many established democracies.[39] What is the pattern on the extreme right, and have there been parallel shifts?

The results of the comparison by gender in Table 6.5 confirm a consistent pattern; men continue to be overrepresented among the radical

TABLE 6.5. *The Gender Gap among Radical Right Voters*

Nation	Party(s)	% Who voted for the radical right, all voters	The ratio of voting support for the radical right in each group compared with the national average share of the vote	
			Men	Women
Austria	FPÖ	3.2	1.3	0.7
Belgium	VB, FN	4.4	1.2	0.8
Canada	RP	18.9	1.2	0.8
Czech Republic	RSC	5.6	1.4	0.6
Denmark	DF, FP	6.8	1.3	0.7
France	FN	3.2	1.3	0.8
Hungary	MIEP	2.2	1.2	0.9
Israel	Mafdal, IL	4.6	1.0	1.0
Italy	AN, LN, MsFt	6.1	1.4	0.7
Netherlands	PF, CD	11.5	1.0	1.0
New Zealand	NZFP	10.9	1.0	1.0
Norway	FrP, FLP	11.9	1.2	0.7
Romania	PRM, PUNR	3.2	1.2	0.8
Russia	LDPR	1.5	1.6	0.7
Slovenia	SNS	2.2	1.0	1.0
Switzerland	SVP, EDU, SD, LdT, FPS	8.8	1.2	0.9
MEAN		6.2	1.2	0.8

Note: The figures represent the ratio of each group's support for the radical right compared with the national average (measured as the proportion of each group who voted for the radical right divided into the proportion of the national electorate who voted for the radical right in each country). A coefficient of 1.0 suggests that the group was perfectly proportional to the national average. A coefficient of less than 1.0 suggests that the group was underrepresented among radical right voters. A coefficient greater than 1.0 (in **bold**) suggests that the group was overrepresented among radical right voters

Sources: Austria, Belgium, Switzerland, Denmark, France, Israel, Italy, the Netherlands, and Norway analyzed from data in the ESS 2002. Canada, the Czech Republic, New Zealand, Romania, Russia, Slovenia, and Hungary analyzed from data in the CSES 1996–2001.

right electorate in a dozen of the countries under comparison, and in the remainder there is no gender difference. The gender gap in support is greatest in support for the Liberal Democrats in Russia, the Republikanska Stiana Česká (RSC) in the Czech Republic, and the AN, LN, and MsFt in Italy. Although some parties such as Le Pen's Front National have made a particular effort to change their traditional male-dominated image by picking more women candidates for elected office, nevertheless the leadership and the grassroots base of these parties remain predominately male. It remains to be seen in subsequent chapters whether this pattern is

TABLE 6.6. *The Age Profile of Radical Right Voters*

Nation	Party(s)	% Who voted for the radical right, all voters	The ratio of voting support for the radical right in each group compared with the national average share of the vote		
			Younger	Middle	Older
Austria	FPÖ	3.2	0.9	0.8	1.8
Belgium	VB, FN	4.4	1.0	1.2	0.8
Canada	RP	18.9	0.8	1.1	1.1
Czech Rep.	RSC	5.6	1.3	1.2	0.2
Denmark	DF, FP	6.8	1.2	0.8	1.4
France	FN	3.2	0.3	1.4	1.3
Hungary	MIEP	2.2	0.7	1.1	1.1
Israel	Mafdal, IL	4.6	0.9	1.2	0.9
Italy	AN, LN, MsFt	6.1	0.7	1.1	1.0
Netherlands	PF,CD	11.5	0.7	1.1	0.9
New Zealand	NZFP	10.9	0.7	1.0	1.6
Norway	FrP, FLP	11.9	0.9	1.0	1.1
Romania	PRM, PUNR	3.2	1.0	1.1	0.9
Russia	LDPR	1.5	1.2	1.1	0.7
Slovenia	SNS	2.2	1.7	0.6	0.3
Switzerland	SVP, EDU, SD, LdT, FPS	8.8	0.7	1.2	1.3
MEAN		6.2	1.0	1.0	1.0

Note: The figures represent the ratio of each group's support for the radical right compared with the national average (measured as the proportion of each group who voted for the radical right divided into the proportion of the national electorate who voted for the radical right in each country). A coefficient of 1.0 suggests that the group was perfectly proportional to the national average. A coefficient of less than 1.0 suggests that group was underrepresented among radical right voters. A coefficient greater than 1.0 (in **bold**) suggests that the group was overrepresented among radical right voters. For the list of parties included, see Table 3.1.

Sources: Austria, Belgium, Switzerland, Denmark, France, Israel, Italy, the Netherlands, and Norway analyzed from data in the ESS 2002. Canada, the Czech Republic, New Zealand, Romania, Russia, Slovenia, and Hungary analyzed from data in the CSES 1996–2001.

due to the issues and policies advocated by the radical right, such as their xenophobic and antistate appeals, or whether it can be attributed more generally to long-standing gender differences toward the use of violence, and the association of extreme right movements with acts of aggression and direct-action radical tactics.

The generational profile is important as this can tell us much about the future of these parties. If their support is overrepresented among the older generation, reflecting a nostalgic appeal to the past, then in the long term these parties may gradually fade in popularity through the usual process of population replacement and the shrinkage of their mass base. If, however, they manage to attract and retain a younger generation, for example appealing strongly to unemployed male youth, then this could contribute toward their future expansion. Table 6.6 demonstrates the age profile of radical right voters; the results show that there is little consistency across countries; in some (notably post-Communist Russia, Slovenia, and the Czech Republic) the younger generation are disproportionately attracted to these parties, but in others (New Zealand, Switzerland, and Austria, in particular) their appeal is stronger among the older generation. This suggests that the specific age-related profile of these parties varies cross-nationally, which may be due to their historical roots in each society and their leadership images, campaign strategies, and ideological appeals among different groups of voters.

CONCLUSIONS

One of the classic ways of explaining patterns of party support relates to the distribution of social cleavages in the electorate. Where parties are based upon distinct social sectors, then they can forge enduring ties with these groups, representing their interests and concerns in the political system. Where such ties have weakened, through social and partisan dealignment, then we would expect greater electoral volatility and more potential for protest voting. What do the results suggest about enduring patterns of support for the radical right?

The comparison of the social class profile of radical right voters, including indicators of social inequality, suggests that they are disproportionately overrepresented both among the petite bourgeoisie – self-employed professionals, own-account technicians, and small merchants – *and* among the skilled and unskilled working class. In many countries patterns of individual-level voting support among the unemployed and among low-income households are not as strong as suggested by many aggregate-level accounts in political economy. This cross-class coalition means that we should look skeptically upon the idea that radical right parties are purely a phenomenon of the politics of resentment among the new social cleavage of low-skilled and low-qualified workers in inner-city areas, or that their rise can be attributed in any mechanical fashion to growing levels of unemployment and job insecurity in Europe. The social profile is more complex than popular stereotypes suggest. It remains to be seen in subsequent chapters whether, as some claim, it is the particular combination of experience of unemployment and anti-immigrant attitudes which matters, rather than job insecurity alone.[40] At the same time the traditional gender gap persists, with men fueling support for these parties. Moreover, although the pooled analysis suggests that there are some common factors, the results disaggregated by nation show considerable variations in who voted for the radical right. Chapter 10 considers in more detail the systemic impact of 'dealigning elections' and the consequences of weakening voter-party loyalties for patterns of party competition and the opportunities facing new radical right challengers. In some countries, we demonstrate that dealignment has facilitated the rise of these parties, with either 'deviating' or 'critical' elections, whereas in others cases, such as Britain and the United States, despite widespread evidence of a long-term erosion of partisan identities, radical right parties have failed to surmount the electoral barriers to make a sustained series of gains.

Therefore, based on this evidence we can conclude that classic sociological theories of a crisis of modernity, or modern accounts emphasizing the emergence of a new social cleavage, only take us so far in explaining variations in the success and failure of radical right parties. What we need to understand is not just how social conditions might facilitate their rise, but, even more importantly, how parties respond to these factors in crafting their strategic and programmatic appeals, in building their organizations, and in consolidating their support. To consider these issues further, we need to look more closely in the next chapter at the politics of resentment thesis, and how far there is any direct evidence that widespread political disaffection drives party popularity.

7

'None of the Above'

The Politics of Resentment

The demand-side politics of resentment thesis regards rising support for the radical right as essentially expressing a negative protest against the status quo, and hence an indicator of rising political disaffection with democratic politics. This perspective is commonly used in the academic literature on new parties, for example to explain support for Ross Perot's Reform Party in the United States, One Nation in Queensland, Canadian Reform, and New Zealand First.[1] This argument is not necessarily antithetical to the new cleavage thesis, as these explanations can be combined where it can be suggested that political disaffection is concentrated among disadvantaged social sectors. Nevertheless these explanations remain logically distinct. Betz articulates one of the strongest versions of this argument, suggesting that the rise of populist politics in Europe has been fueled by resentment and alienation from the political institutions of representative government:

> A majority of citizens in most Western democracies no longer trust political institutions that they consider to be largely self-centered and self-serving, unresponsive to the ideas and wishes of the average person, and incapable of adopting viable solutions for society's most pressing problems. . . . It is within this context of growing public pessimism, anxiety and disaffection that the rise and success of radical right-wing populism in Western Europe finds at least a partial explanation.[2]

This claim is also commonly heard in popular commentary where the growth of widespread political cynicism, civic malaise, and social alienation, particularly disaffection with mainstream parties (*parteienverdrossenheit*), is believed to have provided a springboard for radical right antiestablishment appeals.[3] The language of party leaders from Glistrup and Haider to Le Pen and Bossi is richly flecked with vivid antiparty and antiestablishment sentiments and it is believed that this constitutes an essential part of their appeal.[4]

Despite the popularity of the politics of resentment thesis, and its intuitive plausibility, systematic empirical studies that demonstrate the negative motivations of radical right voters remain scarce, and some research throws serious doubt on this thesis.[5] Evidence favoring the protest vote hypotheses has come from open-ended survey questions, where voters for anti-immigrant parties often mention that they were motivated by discontent with mainstream or governing parties. Nevertheless, as with other direct motivational questions, it remains difficult to know how much weight to put on these responses, whether regarded as reasons or rationalizations for support.[6] One of the most sophisticated comparative analyses of this question has been conducted by Wouter van der Brug and colleagues, who classified voting motivations into four categories: idealistic, pragmatic, clientalistic, and protest.[7] Idealistic voters are seen as those who rationally cast a vote on the basis of ideological proximity. Pragmatic voters (who can also be regarded as 'strategic' or 'tactical') take account of ideological proximity plus the size of the party, on the grounds that it is perfectly rational to vote for a second-choice party which is close to one's policy positions if this party stands a better chance of getting into power. Clientalistic voters rationally cast a ballot for concrete material benefits, such as the delivery of individual or public goods ('pork'). Protest voters are regarded as the default category in the analysis, understood as those whose objectives are to demonstrate a rejection of all other parties. Based on this classification, van der Brug and colleagues used party preferences, measured by probability to vote for a party (not votes cast), as their dependent variable in the 1994 and 1999 European Election Studies. They concluded that in the 1994 elections, party preferences for seven radical right parties in the EU could be largely explained by the same mix of idealistic and pragmatic motivations that accounted for support for other parties. The propensity to vote for radical right parties in European Parliamentary elections could be accurately predicted by voters' ideological (left-right) proximity and their anti-immigrant attitudes, coupled with pragmatic considerations of party size. The only exception to this rule was found for one party (the Dutch Centrumdemocraten). Their replicated study in the 1999 European elections again confirmed a similar pattern concerning support for the FPÖ, Alleanza Nazionale, Dansk Folkeparti, and Vlaams Blok. Yet they also concluded that these factors could not satisfactorily explain party preferences for the Danish

Fremskridtspartiet, the French Front National, the Lega Nord, the Germany Republikaner, the Wallonian Front National, and the Dutch Centrumdemocraten, who could therefore have attracted support based on protest votes.

This provides one of the most thorough cross-national comparisons of radical right party preferences in second-order European elections, but the analysis suffers from the critical weakness that protest voting is regarded as the default category, so that their conclusions rely upon circumstantial evidence. The study fails to consider any direct evidence for or against protest voting, such as indicators of political disaffection, trust, and alienation among radical right supporters. As a result, as the authors acknowledge, the study cannot prove that the default category is actually motivated by a protest rejection of 'all of the above,' as they have no direct evidence of public attitudes toward the political system.[8] Their models might be misspecified by failing to consider other plausible explanations for supporting radical right parties, such as the attraction of charismatic leaders, the strength of party identification, the impact of other important demographic factors including gender or race (both commonly and consistently linked to radical right voting), and indeed any of the multiple salient policy issues in the European elections (such as attitudes toward the government's performance on education, health care, and crime) not included in their study. One of the well-known characteristics of elections to the European Parliament is that these are widely regarded by the public as a mid-term referendum upon the performance of national governments in each country, rather than determined by European-wide issues such as the adoption of the euro or the role of the Commission. As such, their claims about protest voting should be regarded as an interesting thesis but essentially unproven.

THEORIES OF PROTEST POLITICS

Moreover, much previous analysis of this issue remains underconceptualized as there are several distinct ways to interpret support for the radical right as an outlet for protest politics, each of which needs careful disentangling both analytically and empirically. Rather than seeing support for the political system as all of one piece, ever since the classic work of David Easton it is widely recognized that different *levels* or *objects* of support can be distinguished.[9] These can be understood to range from the most specific level, including support for individual politicians and party leaders, through support for the performance and institutions of the regime, to the most abstract level, representing support for the nation-state as a whole.[10] In the United States, for example, it is commonly found that people often trust particular politicians, such as the member of the House of Representatives elected from their district, and yet express cynicism about Congress as an institution.[11] Or they might express confidence in the U.S. Congress and yet still have little faith in the party controlling the White House. Or they might feel intensely patriotic about America and yet still mistrust most politicians in Washington, DC. There is no logical inconsistency in distinguishing among these different components of the political system. People may also trust each other (social or interpersonal trust) and yet have little or no confidence in political institutions.[12]

Any interpretation of how far support for the radical right reflects protest politics depends upon how deeply any disaffection is thought to extend. The protest politics thesis implies that negative reasons are the primary drivers of support for the radical right, and these factors are expected to outweigh any positive motivations in electoral decisions, for example if supporters are attracted by the radical right because they see themselves as ideologically close to their positions on salient issues such as immigration or taxes, or because they admire the charisma, rhetoric, and leadership of figures such as Jean-Marie Le Pen, Umberto Bossi, or Jörg Haider. Theories of protest politics assume that voters support the radical right primarily for negative reasons, but they differ in how they conceptualize the objects of such negativity. This could be because:

i. Radical right voters may be deeply dissatisfied with the performance of the government over specific issues, such unemployment rates, European integration, or immigration policies; or,

ii. They may be alienated and socially intolerant citizens lacking interpersonal trust (the social capital argument associated with Putnam); or alternatively

iii. They could be deeply unhappy with the general workings of the political system and lack confidence in representative democratic institutions in their country (the Betz view).

In other words, any disaffection tapped by the radical right could be directed mainly against the government's record, against society in general, or against the major institutions of representative government. Negative protest voting could be expressed at each level, but we need to distinguish among these in order to determine the significance and consequences of the rise of the radical right.

(i) Dissatisfaction with the Government's Record

The weakest version of this claim suggests that radical right support is generated primarily by retrospective evaluations of the record of the governing party or parties, most commonly triggered by general dissatisfaction with liberal policies about immigration following an influx of migrants and asylum seekers, perceived high rates of crime, or worsening levels of unemployment, or by dramatic government failures, such as headlines about sexual or financial scandals involving high-ranking officials. In this view, support for the radical right surges, especially in 'second-order' mid-term elections such as local, regional, or European contests, to send a message of public protest directed against those in power. Support is expected to subside again once government popularity recovers, for example if economic growth resurges, if rates of immigration subside, or if there are distinct improvements in the delivery of public services.

We can examine whether electors who vote for radical right parties express exceptionally high levels of dissatisfaction with the state of the health service and education and the state of the economy, as well as with the performance of the national government and the way democracy works in each country, after controlling for the social structural factors such as age, gender, and class that we have already demonstrated help predict radical right support. If we establish a consistent relationship, however, it remains difficult to regard this as a matter of great public concern, since negative voting to express dissatisfaction with government policies and performance essentially represents the essence of normal democratic politics.

(ii) Social Capital and Interpersonal Trust

In recent years theories of social capital have come into vogue, emphasizing that the United States has experienced a steep erosion of social capital during the postwar era, with a fall in *generalized reciprocity* (including social trust and social tolerance) and in *social connectedness* (including formal associational participation and informal socializing). Work by Robert Putnam suggests that the hemorrhaging of social capital has had important consequences for civic participation, and thus for the health and vitality of American democracy.[13] Putnam warns that multiple indicators display a consistent secular fall in America since the 1960s and 1970s, including membership of voluntary associations, indicators of traditional political participation, civic attitudes, the strength of informal social ties, and levels of social trust. The core claim of Toquevillian theories of social capital is that typical face-to-face deliberative activities and horizontal collaboration within voluntary organizations far removed from the political sphere – exemplified by sports clubs, social clubs, and philanthropic groups – promote interpersonal trust, social tolerance, and cooperative behavior.[14]

In turn, these norms are regarded as cementing the bonds of social life, creating the foundation for building local communities, civil society, and democratic governance. In a 'win-win' situation, participation in associational life is thought to generate individual rewards, such as career opportunities and personal support networks, as well as facilitating community goods, by fostering the capacity of people to work together on local problems. The causes of this phenomenon are complex but are argued by Putnam to include the modern pressures of time and money, the movement of women into the paid workforce and stresses in the two-career family, geographic mobility and suburban sprawl, and the role of technology and the mass media. The ubiquity of television entertainment, in particular, is thought to play a critical role in privatizing leisure hours for 'couch potatoes.'[15] If any erosion of social trust has occurred more generally across postindustrial societies, due to common social trends, then this could have reduced social tolerance, generated social alienation, and indirectly encouraged support for extreme political movements, groups, and parties.[16] Accordingly in this chapter we can explore whether there is a significant link at individual level between lack of social or interpersonal trust and voting support for radical right parties.

(iii) Or Deep-Rooted Alienation from Political Democratic Institutions?

The strongest version of the protest politics argument, expressed by Betz, interprets support for radical right parties as a deep-seated rejection of the core institutions of democracy, particular an erosion of confidence in political parties and parliaments, representing a crisis in the political system as a whole. "It is within this context of growing public pessimism, anxiety, and disaffection that the rise and success of radical rightwing populism in Western Europe finds at least a partial explanation."[17] Betz supports this claim by the response of Lega Nord, French Front National, and FPÖ voters in open-ended questions when they reported casting their vote as a protest act, as well as by the cross-class composition of these parties' support, suggesting that they gained protest votes by appealing to different social groups. Some limited survey evidence has been found for this view;

for example Lubbers et al. observed that, even with a battery of prior social controls, people dissatisfied with the workings of democracy were significantly more likely to vote for extreme right parties.[18] Yet, despite the popularity of the politics of resentment claim, and its important implications, the thesis needs further exploration as the available systematic evidence remains limited. We can examine whether radical right voters express less confidence and trust in a range of political institutions such as parliaments and the courts. In this argument, the rise of the radical right reflects a profound lack of confidence in core institutions of representative democracy, not just a rejection of the electoral choices offered by mainstream parties at the ballot box. If the ascendance of the radical right does represent a rejection of these institutions, as well as a lack of social tolerance for minority groups, then this could lead to serious consequences, especially in more fragile transitional and consolidating democracies, such as Russia and the Ukraine.

EVIDENCE

Before accepting or rejecting the protest thesis, it is important to examine direct evidence. We need to establish whether support for radical right parties can be accurately predicted by attitudes such as satisfaction with government performance, confidence in political institutions, and social or interpersonal trust. The European Social Survey 2002 contains a battery of items monitoring political and social attitudes. Factor analysis (shown in Table ??) confirmed that a series of selected items fell into three dimensions: social trust, satisfaction with government, and trust in political institutions. Scales were constructed based on these items. *Trust in institutions* (with each item measured on ten-point scales) included both international organizations such as the European Parliament and United Nations and national parliaments, politicians, the legal system, and the police, all of which formed one dimension. *Satisfaction with government* included evaluations of the state of education and the performance of the health service, the national government, the present state of the national economy, the way democracy works in each country, and satisfaction with life as a whole. There is some controversy about the most appropriate way to conceptualize the question about 'how democracy works,' in terms of whether it relates primarily to assessments of democracy as an abstract ideal or whether it taps a sense of how well the government is performing in each country.[19] On this scale, evaluations were clearly related to the latter interpretation. Lastly, *social or interpersonal*

TABLE 7.1. *Dimensions of Trust and Satisfaction*

	Component		
	Institutional trust	Satisfaction with government	Social trust
Trust in the European Parliament	.794		
Trust in the United Nations	.740		
Trust in country's parliament	.732		
Trust in politicians	.715		
Trust in the legal system	.677		
Trust in the police	.582		
State of education in country nowadays		.687	
State of health services in country nowadays		.663	
How satisfied with the national government		.648	
How satisfied with present state of economy in country		.647	
How satisfied with the way democracy works in country		.627	
How satisfied with life as a whole		.474	
Most people try to take advantage of you, or try to be fair			.819
Most people can be trusted or you can't be too careful			.797
Most of the time people helpful or mostly looking out for themselves			.726
Percentage of variance	22.9	17.8	15.05

Note: The coefficient represent the results of principal component factor analysis rotated by varimax with Kaiser normalization, in the pooled eight-nation European sample weighted by design and population size. The nations were selected from all those in the ESS 2002 based on whether they contained a relevant party on the radical right (including Austria, Belgium, Switzerland, Denmark, Israel, Italy, the Netherlands, and Norway). The pooled sample contained 13,768 respondents in total, including 932 voters for the radical right (6.8%).
Source: Pooled sample nine nations, European Social Survey 2002 (ESS-2002).

trust was gauged by three measures, again using ten-point scales, about how far people take advantage of you, how far most people can be trusted most of the time, and how helpful people are.

These scales were entered into the pooled eight-nation weighted sample with the logit regression model developed in the previous chapter, to

TABLE 7.2. *Trust, Satisfaction, and Radical Right Vote*

	Predictors of voting for the radical right, pooled eight-nation European sample		
	B	Std. Error	Sig.
(Constant)	−3.48		
Demographic background			
Age (In years)	.008	.003	***
Sex (male = 1, female = 0)	.322	.097	***
Ethnic minority (ethnic minority = 1, else = 0)	−.376	.336	N/s
Socioeconomic status			
Education (highest level attained on a 6-point scale from low to high)	.059	.040	N/s
Salariat (professional and managerial employees)	−.231	.165	N/s
Petite bourgeoisie (self-employed)	.597	.114	***
Skilled manual working class	.038	.186	N/s
Unskilled manual working class	.072	.148	N/s
Ever been unemployed (for more than 3 months)	.387	.115	**
Religiosity (self-identified as religious on a 7-pt scale)	−.042	.017	**
Indicators of trust and satisfaction			
Institutional trust (60-pt scale)	−.035	.005	***
Satisfaction with government (60-pt scale)	.035	.006	***
Social trust (30-pt scale)	−.025	.008	**
Nagelkerke R^2	.056		
Percentage correctly predicted	92.4		

Note: The model presents the results of a binary logistic (logit) regression model including the unstandardized beta coefficients (B), the standard errors, and their significance, in the pooled eight-nation European sample weighted by design and population size. For the construction of the scales for trust and satisfaction see Table 7.1. Note that France is not included in this model because it lacked the classification of occupational class.

Sig. .001 = ***; Sig. .01 = **; Sig. .05 = *.

Source: Pooled sample eight nations, European Social Survey 2002 (ESS-2002).

see whether these attitudes contributed toward explaining voting support for the radical right after controlling for the other demographic and social characteristics that we have already found to be important. The results in Table ?? show that in the pooled sample, after introducing all the prior

TABLE 7.3. *Trust, Satisfaction, and Radical Right Vote by Nation*

Nation	Party	Institutional trust (60-point scale)		Satisfaction with government (60-point scale)		Social trust (30-point scale)	
Austria	FPÖ	−2.8	*	+0.7	N/s	−1.3	N/s
Belgium	VB, FN	−8.7	***	−3.6	***	−2.8	***
Denmark	DF, FP	−6.2	***	−0.7	N/s	−2.1	***
France	FN	−6.4	***	−6.8	***	−1.9	***
Israel	Mafdal, IL	−2.9	N/s	+4.8	***	+2.6	***
Italy	AN, LN, MsFt	−0.5	N/s	+3.6	***	−0.5	N/s
Netherlands	PF, CD	−5.4	***	−2.5	***	−1.8	***
Norway	FrP, FLP	−4.4	***	−3.3	***	−2.4	***
Switzerland	SVP, EDU, SD, LdT, FPS	−2.4	***	−1.3	*	0.0	N/s
TOTAL		−3.4	***	−0.5	N/s	−0.5	***

Note: For the construction of the scales see Table 7.1. The coefficients represent the mean difference between the position of voters for radical right parties and all other citizens on these scales. The significance of the mean difference between groups is measured by ANOVA (Analysis of Variance). The sample was weighted by design and population size.
Sig. .001 = ***; Sig. .01 = **; Sig. .05 = *.
Source: European Social Survey 2002 (ESS 2002).

controls, the indicators of institutional trust and social trust proved significantly related to radical right support, in the expected negative direction. This suggests that people who voted for the radical right usually expressed lower confidence in institutions such as national and the European parliaments, politicians, and the legal system, and they also had less trust in people around them. By contrast, contrary to expectations, the measure of government satisfaction proved significant and positive, indicating that radical right voters had higher than average evaluations of government performance, not lower.

Alienation from Political Institutions?

In order to make more sense of these findings we need to see how far these attitudes vary across the nine countries in the survey which contain relevant radical right parties. The results in Table ?? describe the mean difference between the position of radical right voters on these scales and the average position of all other citizens in these nations, without any controls. Institutional confidence provides the clearest picture: overall, radical right voters were consistently more negative across all societies, displaying lower than average trust in a range of political institutions.

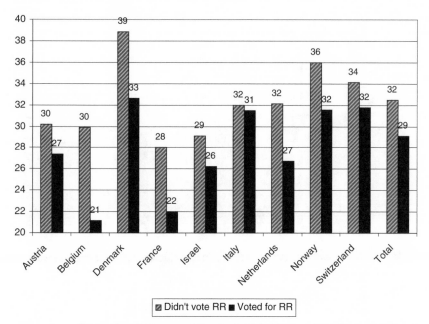

FIGURE 7.1. Institutional Trust and Radical Right Voters. For the institutional trust sixty-point scale, see Table 7.1. For the significance of the difference between groups, see Table 7.3. *Source:* European Social Survey 2002 (ESS 2002) weighted by design and population size.

The size of this trust gap on the sixty-point scale was not large overall and it varied among nations (see Figure ??), displaying the greatest gap in Belgium (8.7 points), France (6.4), Denmark (6.2 points), and the Netherlands (5.4 points), but it proved significant in every country except two (Israel and Italy), despite the limited number of radical right voters included in the national samples. This finding provides the most convincing evidence for the protest vote thesis: people supporting parties such as the Vlaams Blok, Danish Fremskridtspartiet, and Lijst Pym Fortuyn were consistently more cynical about some of the core institution of representative democracy, such as parliament and the legal system. As many suggest, there is a significant link between disenchantment with politics and radical right support. But does this prove causality? Not necessarily. What this evidence cannot resolve is (i) whether citizens were attracted toward these parties because these voters already held more cynical attitudes toward the workings of representative institutions, as many assume, or (ii) whether the populist rhetoric and antiestablishment language of these parties encourages greater suspicion of the state among their supporters, or alternatively (iii) whether supporters of radical right minor parties

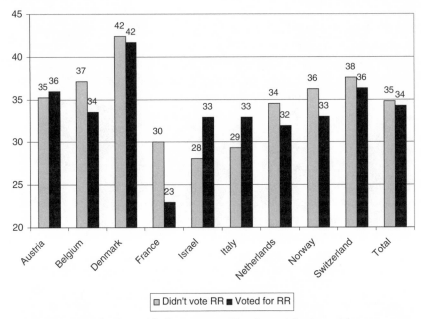

FIGURE 7.2. Satisfaction with Government. For the satisfaction with government sixty-point scale, see Table 7.1. For the significance of the difference between groups, see Table 7.3. *Source:* European Social Survey 2002 (ESS 2002) weighted by design and population size.

became more cynical because these parties sometimes fail to be elected or, if entering parliament, rarely tread the corridors of ministerial office.

Dissatisfaction with the Government's Record

Disentangling the direction of causality in this relationship is a complex matter, but the results of the comparison of satisfaction with government in each country throw some additional light on it (see Figure ??). In Italy and Israel, supporters of radical right parties were strongly and significantly more positive in their evaluations of government, and a fainter positive pattern was also detected in Austria (although this did not prove significant). By contrast, in the other six countries radical right voters were more negative in their assessment of the government, such as the performance of the education system, the health service, the state of the economy, and the performance of democracy.

Further exploration suggests that this pattern was not simply the result of the particular survey questions asked in the ESS 2002 and/or the limited number of cases of radical right voters in each country. The results could not be replicated exactly in the CSES, as in the previous chapter, as this dataset contained alternative questions monitoring satisfaction with government as well as a different range of countries. Nevertheless, the specific items and nations contained in the CSES facilitate some comparison of the general principle that supporters of minor parties included in governing coalitions expressed more positive orientations toward the political system than those excluded from power. The CSES monitored satisfaction with democracy, how far people felt that the last election was fairly conducted, and whether people felt that political parties care what ordinary people think. The dataset covered seven democracies containing relevant radical right parties in legislative elections (Canada, the Czech Republic, Denmark, New Zealand, Norway, Israel, and Switzerland), and in the last two nations these parties are in government. Again in most countries, compared with the general public, supporters of the radical right were consistently more negative in their evaluations across all three items. But in Israel and Switzerland, by contrast, radical right voters were more positive than average in their satisfaction with the performance of democracy, the fairness of the electoral process, and their sense of party responsiveness.

The results of both surveys therefore indicate that mistrust of government is not necessarily an inevitable feature of radical right support in every nation. Instead this evidence strongly suggests a more instrumental interpretation; either where radical right leaders hold ministerial office (as in Israel and Italy), or where right-wing governments in power are broadly sympathetic to their aims and values, then radical right followers hold more positive attitudes toward government and display related indicators of satisfaction with the political system. Where these parties are systematically persistently excluded from power, then, not surprisingly, radical right voters hold more critical attitudes toward the performance of the government. The exclusion or inclusion of minor parties in legislative and governmental office seems to influence approval of the government's record. In Italy, for example, where Lega Nord share ministerial office with Forza Italia, their supporters display far greater satisfaction with government than radical right supporters in France, where the Front National are persistently excluded from office due to the majoritarian second-ballot electoral system, despite gaining about one-fifth of the vote in recent legislative contests.

We can theorize that patterns of winners and losers from the political system are structured by the constitutional arrangements and, over a long period of time, this accumulated experience can be expected to shape general orientations toward the political regime.[20] At the simplest level, if people feel that the rules of the game allow the party leaders that they endorse to be elected to power, they are more likely to feel that policymaking processes are responsive to their needs and to approve of the government's performance. If they feel that the party they prefer persistently loses, over successive elections, they are more likely to feel that their voice is excluded from the decision-making process, producing dissatisfaction with government. Over time, where constitutional arrangements succeed in channeling popular demands into government outcomes, then we would expect this to be reflected, not just in specific support for particular government coalitions, but also in more diffuse support for the public policy process in general. In a series of studies, Christopher Anderson has demonstrated that system support is consistently influenced by whether people are among the winners or losers in electoral contests, defined by whether the party they endorsed was returned to government.[21] Following the same logic, the cross-national evidence suggests that dissatisfaction with government among radical right supporters does not seem to be an inherent characteristic of these supporters; instead attitudes depend upon the rational calculation of the exclusion of their party from power.

Social Trust

Explanations based on theories of social capital suggest that extremist parties may flourish under conditions of social intolerance and alienation; societies lacking interpersonal trust may provide suitable conditions nurturing the radical right. This taps into traditional images of radical right supporters as alienated individuals, isolated from the broader integrative bonds of family, community, and workplace. We tested the available survey evidence at individual level where social trust proved to be significantly more negative among radical right voters in five out of nine nations (Belgium, France, the Netherlands, Norway, and Denmark). In the remainder, either radical right voters did not differ significantly from the general population (in three nations), or else (as in Israel) they proved more trusting. The mixed pattern found in different societies suggests that although social mistrust is associated with radical right support in many countries, this fails to provide a consistent explanation for this phenomenon. The fact that attitudes are significantly more negative than average across the available indicators of institutional trust, satisfaction with government, and social trust in Belgium, France, the Netherlands, and Norway suggests that the radical right tap into the reservoir of disaffected citizens most strongly in these nations. But this pattern fails to hold consistently in the other five countries containing relevant radical right parties. As predicted earlier, theoretically demand-side factors do help provide part of the explanation of why the radical right succeed more in some countries rather than others, but the key concerns are how far parties manage to tap into reservoirs of popular disaffection, and hence the role of protest politics alone is not sufficient to account for variations in their share of votes and seats.

CONCLUSIONS

On the basis of this evidence, three main conclusions can be drawn. First, the overall results suggest that there is some systematic support for the protest politics thesis, but commentators should be careful not to exaggerate either the strength or the consistency of the indicators. Popular explanations common in journalism often claim that the ascendancy of the radical right in Europe since the mid-1980s has been fueled by various modern developments, including popular disillusionment with government due to their perceived failure to deliver public services; the growth of public cynicism with politics or deep disaffection with public affairs; and/or a widespread and pervasive erosion of social trust and social capital. The evidence suggests that the more lurid claims about the role of protest politics fueling radical right votes appear to be greatly overstated and oversimplified, and a more cautious judgment would be more appropriate.

Even where radical right voters express above-average political disaffection, there remain reasons to hesitate before concluding that growing cynicism automatically spurs their support. The results presented in this chapter throw doubt on the argument that radical right voters are exceptionally critical of government; instead the cross-national evidence suggests that evaluations of government performance, on matters such as the delivery of public services or the performance of the economy, are strongly shaped by whether parties are included or excluded from power. Where radical right parties become part of governing coalitions, or where conservative governments which are closely sympathetic to the aims of the radical right rise to power, then radical right supporters are more positive in their orientations toward government. Where parties are consistently excluded from power, then, not surprisingly, this may well encourage their supporters to mistrust the responsiveness and performance of government. Far from a deeply irrational rejection of democratic politics, as 'the authoritarian personality' thesis implied, instead less positive orientations toward the political system may be the rational product of the persistent exclusion of their preferred party from power, or the more general lack of responsiveness of the political system to the particular concerns and policy priorities of radical right supporters.

The most accurate interpretation of the evidence presented here confirms that those who cast their ballots for the radical right are indeed less trusting of a range of political and legal institutions. This does indeed provide partial support for one aspect of the protest politics thesis. Research also suggests that a gradual erosion of institutional trust and confidence has occurred among the public during recent decades in many established democracies, especially concerning trust in the core institutions of political parties and parliaments.[22] This process is likely to have swelled the potential constituency among the electorate who would be generally sympathetic toward radical parties emphasizing antiestablishment sentiments. But certain important points need to be borne in mind before jumping to the conclusion that the erosion of institutional trust has necessarily *caused* the rise of the radical right, or even contributed substantially to their success. Firstly, evidence suggests that mistrust of representative institutions has grown in many advanced industrialized democracies, so it becomes difficult to use this explanation to account for the substantial *variations* in the electoral fortunes of the radical right found in these countries, such as the dissimilarity noted earlier in the Nordic region between Norway and Sweden, or in the Mediterranean area between Italy and Spain, or even within countries, such as between Francophone or Wallonian Belgian regions, or Francophone and Anglophone Canada. Moreover, even though Belgian, Norwegian, and Dutch supporters of radical right parties were found to consistently express more negative attitudes across all the indicators, it remains difficult to disentangle the direction of causality here. It might be that those who are more disenchanted with mainstream parties, and more alienated from the political system, tend to gravitate toward the radical right, who articulate these concerns. Alternatively, the exclusion of these parties from power, coupled with the populist antiestablishment rhetoric of radical right leaders, could plausibly encourage greater mistrust of political institutions amongst their followers.[23]

To go further, we need to turn toward the specific issues which are thought to be most conducive to generating mass demand among the electorate, including the distribution of public opinion on matters such as immigration and cultural protectionism. We shall see in the next chapter whether these attitudes and values more strongly determine variations in the electoral success of radical right parties, and hence the major contrasts evident between the fortunes of these parties in Austria and Germany, Belgium and Portugal, Norway and Sweden, and Canada and the United States.

8

'Us and Them'

Immigration, Multiculturalism, and Xenophobia

Alternative variants of the demand-side thesis suggest that the rise of the radical right is fueled by shifts in public opinion generated by the growth of multiculturalism and more ethnically diverse societies found today in postindustrial nations. Social change is thought to be driven by many factors associated with processes of globalization, notably by patterns of long-term population migration, growing numbers of refugees and asylum seekers fleeing armed conflict, civil wars, and failed states, and more permeable national borders and more open labor markets.[1] Many accounts assume that a public backlash against these trends has triggered the success of outspoken leaders such as Le Pen and Haider, especially where mainstream parties and liberal elites in the European Union and Anglo-American democracies have failed to respond to any public resentment and growing hostility directed against 'foreigners' by setting stricter limits on immigration and asylum seekers.[2] Election results are often regarded as a direct indicator of the state of public opinion in a society; given their heated rhetoric about the need for cultural protectionism, the electoral popularity of the radical right in Austria, Switzerland, and Belgium is understood to reflect growing racial intolerance and widespread xenophobia throughout these societies.[3]

Although a popular argument, this account demonstrates that in fact no automatic and direct relationship exists between aggregate indicators of the growth of multiculturalism in society (including the inflow of immigrants, refugees, and asylum seekers into any country), the balance of public opinion on these issues, and the share of the vote won by radical right parties. Instead this study theorizes that a contingent relationship exists, mediated by the role of party strategists who decide how to craft and pitch their campaign appeals about the values of cultural protectionism to gain maximum advantage, within the context of the electoral rules. This chapter first sets out the theoretical framework and discusses the sources of aggregate and individual-level evidence. We demonstrate that the share of the vote won by the radical right at *national* level cannot be explained satisfactorily by a wide range of aggregate indicators of ethnic diversity, including both objective measures, exemplified by the official rate of immigration and asylum seekers entering each nation, and subjective measures, notably anti-immigrant attitudes found in public opinion within each country. Radical right parties can gain ground in societies where attitudes toward ethnic minorities remain relatively liberal and tolerant, such as Norway, as well as faring poorly elsewhere in countries where the public proves more hostile toward outsiders, such as Greece.

But at the same time, at individual level, attitudes toward cultural protection *do* help to explain why some people vote for these parties; the study demonstrates how negative feelings toward immigration, refugees, and multiculturalism predict whether somebody casts a ballot for a radical right party, even after including a range of prior controls for social background and political trust. Attitudes toward cultural protectionism prove far more significant predictors of radical right voting than economic attitudes. This pattern is found in nearly every country containing a relevant radical right party where we have data from the European Social Survey 2002, although there are two important exceptions to this pattern (Italy and Israel). The chapter's conclusion reflects on why different patterns emerge at individual and aggregate levels, and then considers the implications of these findings for the interpretation of election results and for understanding public opinion.

I THEORETICAL FRAMEWORK

In one of the most influential studies, as discussed in Chapter 1, Kitschelt argues that radical right party fortunes are not determined mechanically by structural trends in society; instead what matters is how parties respond (as agents) to social developments, within the context set by overall patterns of party competition.[4] In particular, he argues that where the ideological gap between moderate left and right parties closes – for example if a broad middle-of-the-road consensus develops around issues such as the need for social tolerance of ethnic diversity, the protection of displaced populations, and respect for the human rights of political refugees – this is believed to provide the ideal opportunity for radical right elites to harvest popular support among the public located on the far right of the ideological spectrum. In this context, the optimal platform for radical right parties, Kitschelt suggests, will combine anti-immigrant, xenophobic rhetoric with free market economic policies. The ideological appeals and policy positions which party agents adopt are assumed by Downsian theories to be largely autonomous free choices, under conditions of perfect competition. Like chess players, political strategists are thought to decide whether their party should tack toward the center ground, or to shift further right or left, in rational pursuit of maximum electoral advantage.

There are grounds for skepticism about Kitschelt's specific claim that the closure of patterns of mainstream party competition opened the right flank to advance by the more radical challengers, as will be demonstrated in the next chapter. Despite this important qualification, we can still build upon and further develop the general insights about parties as agents suggested by Kitschelt's theory. In particular, we agree that parties are not simply political epiphenomena bobbing willy-nilly on the tides of deep-rooted sociological trends; instead they can become masters of their fate through astute judgments and effective strategies tailored to respond to popular demands, within certain institutional constraints. Essentially Kitschelt's two-level model (consisting of the democratic market where party 'supply' of public policy issues needs to match public 'demands') should be recognized instead as a three-level nested model (combining the electoral regulations setting the context for both party supply and voter demand). The strategic agency theory developed in this book argues that parties should not be understood as purely autonomous rational actors competing against rivals for votes and seats. Instead, there is a regulated marketplace, and the most effective campaign appeals that parties adopt to mobilize popular support, and to maximize their potential seat gains, are constrained by the basic type of electoral system.

There are several building blocks in this theory. We have already demonstrated how the mechanical effects of electoral rules function as an important determinant for the entry of radical right parties into elected office and thus into government. The function of the rules controlling ballot access, campaign access, and election is analogous to protectionist regulations in the economic market, designed primarily by incumbent political parties and providing barriers, with different levels of severity, to reduce the seats awarded to minor challengers. What remains to be established in this chapter is whether the distribution of public opinion toward cultural protectionism is an important factor contributing toward the success of the radical right. On this basis, the next chapter can examine whether electoral rules also generate certain psychological effects upon strategic campaigning, by shaping the tactical calculations made by parties when crafting and targeting their broader ideological messages.

II EXPLAINING THE NATIONAL SHARE OF THE VOTE FOR THE RADICAL RIGHT

Electoral support for the radical right is commonly interpreted in demand-side accounts as representing a grassroots reaction by European publics directed against growing ethnic heterogeneity and multiculturalism in society. Structural theories in political economy and sociology suggest that the ascendancy of these parties is generated primarily by a public backlash directed against rising numbers of immigrants and asylum seekers, and the failure of mainstream governing parties to curb these numbers and protect national identities through effective public policy regulations.[5] As Betz claims:

> It should come as no surprise that the emergence and rise of radical right-wing populist parties in Western Europe coincided with the growing tide of immigrants and particularly the dramatic increase in the number of refugees seeking peace, security, and a better life in the affluent societies of Western Europe. The reaction to the new arrivals was an outburst of xenophobia and open racism in a majority of West European countries. . . . This has made it relatively easy for the radical populist Right to evoke, focus, and reinforce preexisting xenophobic sentiments for political gain.[6]

In effect, the distribution of public opinion in any country is read directly from election results.

Although this is a popular view, empirical studies investigating this relationship have generated somewhat mixed results; some have indeed confirmed that aggregate rates of immigration, and levels of refugees and asylum seekers in each country or subnational region, are linked to national levels of voting support for radical right parties, although others have reported finding little support for this relationship.[7] Kitschelt examined three measures – the proportion of the foreign-born population in a country, the change in rates of immigration during the 1980s, and the share of political refugees in a population – and concluded that there was no significant correlation between these measures and the voting strength of right-wing parties during the 1980s in Western Europe.[8] For example, Sweden (with a negligible far right presence) absorbed far more immigrants than Norway (where the FrP performed relatively strongly). By contrast, Lubbers et al. compared the proportion of non-EU citizens in a country, using multilevel models, and reported that this factor contributed toward cross-national variations in extreme right-wing voting support.[9] Further confirmation of this relationship was provided by Golder, who also examined this thesis by analyzing the proportion of the resident population living in each country who were 'foreign citizens.'[10]

Possible reasons for the inconsistent results in the literature is that national-level evidence remains extremely limited, characterized by an immense amount of 'noise' and measurement error.[11] Alternative indicators of levels of immigration, citizenship, asylum seekers, and ethnic heterogeneity are employed by different studies. Comparisons of the proportion of 'foreign citizens' in a country, for example, may generate some 'muddy' results, depending upon the relative ease or difficulty of obtaining legal citizenship in each nation, as well as the accuracy of any census data and the official government records used to monitor the proportion of illegal aliens resident within each country. Moreover the primary debate about cultural protectionism in the European Union today does not revolve around the presence of 'foreign citizens' per se; for example relatively little concern is heard about the proportion of Belgians living in Luxembourg, British citizens buying second homes in northern France, or German citizens working in Switzerland. By contrast, heated popular debate surrounds rates of refugees, asylum seekers, and guest workers drawn from outside of either Western Europe or the European Union, such as the arrival of displaced Somalians, Turkish Kurds, and Balkan exiles in Paris, Berlin, and Vienna. Countries differ in they way that they collect migration statistics and who they consider to be a migrant. Some statistics are based on administrative data, for example who applies for residency permits or citizenship, or border records, while others use survey data such as the official census. The time period for any data collection is also critical; for example whether measures capture past waves of immigration to Europe following earlier periods of decolonization, such as Algerians who moved to France or Ugandan Asians who entered Britain, or whether they focus upon more recent migration flows. And of course there may also be a substantial perceptual gap between official rates of population flows and public perceptions of these trends.

To reexamine the available evidence, we can first look at whether voting support for the radical right is related directly to a range of aggregate-level indicators of ethnic heterogeneity in each nation under comparison, utilizing a series of objective measures of the number of immigrants and asylum seekers entering each country (both the current number in 2002 and the total number of asylum seekers during the previous decade), as well as subjective indicators of ethnic heterogeneity from survey data.

At national level, the United Nations High Commissioner for Refugees (UNHCR) collects the most comprehensive series of international statistics monitoring the contemporary national inflow of refugees, asylum seekers, and other populations of related concern. There are reasons to be cautious about the reliability and consistency of these official statistics, for all the reasons already discussed, but nevertheless they remain perhaps the best that are currently available. These indicators suggest that the number of such displaced populations grew rapidly during the early 1990s, following the collapse of the Soviet Union, protracted armed conflict, and cases of human rights abuses or political repression. Some of the largest population inflows into advanced industrialized societies came from displaced refugees and asylum seekers from the Balkans, Afghanistan, Iraq, Sri Lanka, Sudan, Somalia, China, and Iran.[12]

Yet the number of refugees and asylum seekers does not take into account the impact of previous patterns of immigration on multiculturalism, exemplified by the 1950s influx of West Caribbeans and Asians into Britain following decolonization, North Africans moving into France, or patterns of labor mobility during the 1980s among Turkish 'guest workers' in Germany and Sweden. Unfortunately official census data provides unreliable cross-national estimates of the degree of ethnic heterogeneity within each country, in part because of varying national definitions of what constitutes an ethnic minority, as well as different measures of race, religion, and citizenship which have not been adequately standardized by international bodies. In this study, to gauge the degree of ethnic heterogeneity, we can also draw upon estimates derived from the European Social Survey 2002 to compare the proportion of residents of a country in the sample who report that they were not born in that country and also the proportion who say that they are not citizens. These reported figures may generate a systematic slight underestimate of ethnic heterogeneity, if any illegal immigrants are reluctant to admit to noncitizenship, but any such bias should be of roughly similar levels across countries. In addition, we also need to test for the effects of standardized aggregate rates of unemployment and also per capita GDP in each society. Studies of political economy report that the impact of immigration matters most under conditions of high unemployment, with an interaction effect where people blame 'foreigners' for job insecurity, low wages, or loss of employment.[13] Levels of average income may be important in countries where support for the radical right is drawn disproportionately from among poorer social sectors.

Two dependent variables are used to assess mass support for the radical right at national level in the countries under comparison: namely, the percentage share of the radical right vote won in the most recent (2000–2004) legislative elections and also the type of contemporary radical right party existing in each county (divided into 'none,' 'fringe,' or 'relevant' categories). The results of the comparison, presented in Table 8.1, show that, contrary to theories of political economy, *support for the radical right at national level is unrelated to any of the available aggregate indicators of ethnic diversity in the societies under comparison.* This pattern holds irrespective of the specific measure of ethnic heterogeneity which is considered, including the official number of refugees, asylum seekers, and the total population of concern to the UNHCR in the most recent year available, or the survey estimates of the proportion of noncitizens and residents born overseas. Figure 8.1 illustrates the pattern more clearly by showing how the total size of the population of concern to the UNHCR (including asylum seekers and refugees in each country) ranges substantially among the nations under comparison, with Germany, the United States, Britain, and Sweden containing some of the largest numbers, although none of these nations contain a relevant radical right party. None of the correlations in Table 8.1 prove significant, and some even point in the contrary direction to that predicted; for example the most recently available UNHCR figures suggest that an estimated fifteen thousand asylum seekers live in each of the seventeen nations containing a relevant radical right party, compared with more than twice this number of asylum seekers (thirty-seven thousand) living in the eleven nations without such a party. Similarly, the ESS estimates of the proportion of resident noncitizens suggest that this group constituted about 9.9% of the population sample in the countries without a radical right party, compared with 3.2% of the population in countries with a fringe radical right, and 2.8% of the population in countries with a relevant radical right party. This is the opposite of what is predicted by oversimple claims that the radical right are most successful in ethnically heterogeneous societies. Of course considerable care is needed in interpreting this relationship as this may involve a case of reverse causality; the presence of a successful radical right party gaining popular votes or seats in the legislature may well pressure the governing party or parties to further restrict the number of immigrants or asylum seekers who are allowed to enter the country legally, as commentators suggest has occurred in the Netherlands and France.[14] But under these circumstances it becomes even more difficult to argue that the success of the radical right in certain countries and their failure elsewhere are driven by structural population trends.

TABLE 8.1. *National-Level Indicators and Radical Right Support*

Indicators	Data source	Means by type of contemporary radical right party			Correlation with % radical right vote	
		None	Fringe party	Relevant party	R.	Sig.
Objective indicators						
Number of refugees, 2002	(i)	57,755	152,328	40,737	.015	N/s
Number of asylum seekers, 2002	(i)	37,429	17,517	15,290	−.059	N/s
Number of asylum seekers, 1992–2001	(iv)	158,530	426,310	147,760	−.128	N/s
Total population of concern, 2002	(i)	95,185	171,637	112,358	.117	N/s
Total pop. of concern standardized per 1,000 residents	(i)	.16	.46	.51	.194	N/s
Proportion of residents born overseas	(ii)	10.5	7.7	9.9	.109	N/s
Proportion of resident noncitizens	(ii)	9.9	3.2	2.8	−.018	N/s
Economic indicators						
Standardized rates of unemployment, 2002	(iii)	7.7	7.9	5.7	−.204	N/s
Per capita GDP 2000 (US$)	(v)	20,849	16,840	20,064	.060	N/s
Subjective indicators						
Anti-immigrant attitude 100-pt scale	(ii)	51.8	56.0	53.6	−.142	N/s
Number of countries		11	8	17	36	

Note: The coefficients represent the national-level means by the type of radical right party and the correlation with the proportion of radical right vote 2000–2004 in each country. None of the correlations or difference between means proved significant (at the 95% confidence level).

Sources: (i) UNHCR. July 2003. *Asylum Applications Lodged in Industrialized Countries: Levels and Trends, 2000–2002.* Geneva: UNHCR. http://www.unhcr.ch. The total population of concern to the UNHCR in each country includes all refugees, asylum seekers, refugees returning home, and people uprooted within their own countries (internally displaced persons).

(ii) Estimate from the European Social Survey 2002, weighted by design and population. For the 100-point standardized anti-immigrant attitude scale, see Table 8.2.

(iii) OECD *Main Economic Indicators* 2004. www.oecd.org.

(iv) OECD inflows of asylum seekers into selected OECD countries, 1991–2001. www.oecd.org.

(v) World Bank *World Development Indicators, 2002.* The per capita GDP is standardized by Purchasing Power Parity. www.worldbank.org.

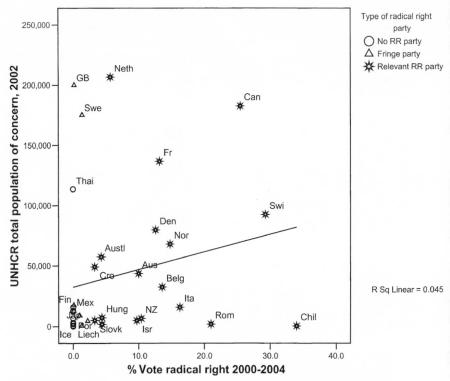

FIGURE 8.1. Number of Refugees and Radical Right Votes. The total number of refugees, asylum seekers, and others of concern to the United Nations High Commissioner for Refugees, 2002, by country of residence. Three countries (the United States, Russia, and Germany) each containing about 900,000 refugees, asylum seekers, and other populations of concern to the UNHCR are excluded as outliers in the data. The inclusion or exclusion of these countries does not change the substantive interpretation of the results. *Source:* UNHCR 2002 Statistics. http://www.unhcr.ch/cgi-bin/texis/vtx/statistics.

The results also suggest that similar national-level comparisons made with the standardized rate of unemployment and per capita income in each country are also insignificantly related to support for the radical right; for example 7.7% of the working population were unemployed in the societies under comparison where there was no relevant radical right party, whereas the rate was slightly lower (5.7%) where there was such a party. Figure 8.2 illustrates the lack of any consistent pattern even more clearly. Further attempts to uncover any interaction effects, for example by combining alternative indicators of ethnic heterogeneity with rates of unemployment, also failed to prove significant.

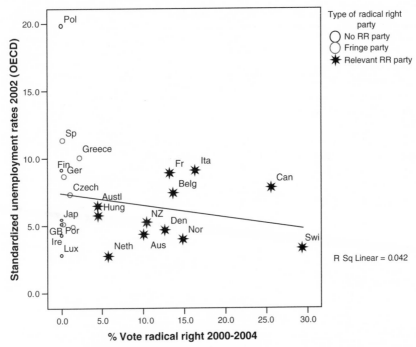

FIGURE 8.2. Unemployment Rates and Radical Right Votes. Standardized unemployment rates 2002 from OECD *Main Economic Indicators* 2004. www.oecd.org.

Subjective Attitudes toward Cultural Protectionism

An alternative plausible explanation of this phenomenon is that support of radical right parties may be generated less by the objective number of refugees and asylum seekers entering a country, or by the actual proportion of ethnic minorities living in any society, than by the subjective feelings toward the perceived threats from multiculturalism.[15] After all, few people may be aware of the exact number of immigrants, or their proportion of the population, but what may matter is whether many people believe that there are too many 'outsiders' and 'foreigners' who endanger traditional social values and norms in each national culture. This claim is, after all, the core focus of much contemporary radical right rhetoric. To explore this issue, the European Social Survey 2002 contains a wide range of suitable items carried in a special battery designed to tap attitudes toward immigrants, multiculturalism, and race relations. Exploratory factors analysis was used to reduce these items to four primary dimensions, listed in Table 8.2, concerning perceptions of the instrumental threat of

TABLE 8.2. *Dimensions of Cultural Attitudes, ESS 2002*

	Negative attitudes toward			
	Immigrants	Refugees	Multiculturalism	Economic equality
Immigrants take jobs away in country or create new jobs (1–10)	.716			
Immigrants harm economic prospects of the poor more than the rich (1–5)	.713			
Average wages/salaries generally brought down by immigrants (1–5)	.702			
Immigration bad or good for country's economy (1–10)	.680			
Immigrants make country worse or better place to live (1–10)	.649			
Country's cultural life undermined or enriched by immigrants (1–10)	.614		.408	
Immigrants make country's crime problems worse or better (1–10)	.478			
Government should be generous judging applications for refugee status (1–5)		.712		
Granted refugees should be entitled to bring close family members (1–5)		.684		
Financial support should be offered to refugee applicants while cases considered (1–5)		.663		
People applying refugee status should be allowed to work while cases considered (1–5)		.609		
Immigrants should be given same rights as everyone else (1–5)		.507		
Better for a country if a variety of different religions (reversed) (1–5)			.797	

	Negative attitudes toward			
	Immigrants	Refugees	Multiculturalism	Economic equality
Better for a country if almost everyone shares customs and traditions (1–5)			.672	
Government should reduce differences in income levels				.782
Employees need strong trade unions to protect work conditions/wages				.779
Percentage of variance explained by each factor	20.3	14.4	10.1	8.7

Note: Exploratory principal component factor analysis of cultural attitudes using varimax rotation with Kaiser normalization. The analysis is based upon the pooled twenty-two-nation European Social Survey weighted by design and population. Each scale was summed from these items and standardized into a 100-point scale.
Source: European Social Survey 2002.

immigration, attitudes toward refugee policy, the perceived threat of multiculturalism, and lastly, for comparison, economic attitudes.

Attitudes toward Immigration

Race relations and the integration of ethnic minorities from former colonies has long been a concern in European societies, such as the integration of Algerians in France, Indonesians in the Netherlands, and Asians in Britain, along with the role of 'guest workers' (*Gastarbeiter*), notably Turks recruited into the German labor force and North Africans who moved to France. The instrumental argument suggests that what matters are not levels of immigration per se, but rather the belief that any influx of new minorities could take away public benefits such as housing, depress wages in low-skilled jobs, or exacerbate unemployment rates. The rhetoric of the radical right is littered with such claims; for example Jean-Marie Le Pen propagated the slogan "Two million immigrants are the cause of two million French people out of work."[16] Haider's slogan, "Stop the *Uberfremdung*," or "over-foreignization," could have been well received where Austrians were already afraid of losing their jobs to Central and East European migrants, or of seeing their children attending schools with many Muslim immigrants.

To see whether this rhetoric fell upon sympathetic ears among radical right voters, the first scale measured 'instrumental' attitudes toward immigration, combining seven selected survey items monitoring how far these groups were regarded as an economic or cultural threat to the country, for example by depressing wages and taking away jobs, or by undermining cultural life. These items can be seen as tapping instrumental, pragmatic, or resource-based evaluations of the expected consequences of population migration, resting upon perceptions of threats to the material interests of white Europeans. The survey does not seek to define or measure the type of immigrant group, for example by distinguishing among Muslim or Catholic émigrés; instead the conception of what constitutes an immigrant is left to survey respondents in each society.

Attitudes toward Refugee Policy

Negative attitudes toward immigrants represent only one potential form of opposition to ethnic diversity in modern societies. The most recent wave of population migration during the last decade concerns the wave of asylum seekers and refugees, often from the Balkans, Central Europe, and Africa, seeking to live and work in the European Union, as well as seeking settlement in Australia and Canada. The second scale included five items which were designed to measure tolerant or restrictive attitudes toward government policy concerning asylum seekers and refugees, for example how far people felt that refugees should be given financial aid while their cases were being considered, how far they should be provided with work permits, or how far they should be entitled to bring close family members with them.

Attitudes toward Multiculturalism

The third attitudinal dimension examined attitudes toward multiculturalism, to see if broader aspects of cultural globalization have generated a backlash benefiting strongly nationalist parties. Public support for the radical right could also be triggered by a broader sense of the threat posed to national values by growing multiculturalism, or a more symbolic 'identity-based' opposition to ethnic diversity, based on perceptions of the threat of foreigners to national cultures (expressed through fears about the loss of the predominant language, religion, food, and so on). Processes of globalization have weakened the protection of national borders, symbolized by the worldwide proliferation of internationally traded consumer brands, the ascendancy of popular cultural icons and celebrities, and instantaneous communication through telecommunications, broadcasting, and the Internet around the globe.[17] Patterns of population migration have certainly accelerated these trends, but they are only part of a broader phenomenon driven by factors such as the burgeoning of new information and communication technologies, the expansion of free markets and trade, and greater political integration within the ever-widening EU. Multiculturalism is measured in the ESS by items monitoring attitudes toward the value of religious diversity and the importance of sharing cultural traditions, both of which can be regarded as representing a threat to cultural identities.[18]

Economic Attitudes

Lastly, attitudes toward traditional left-right economic policies could also help to explain the attraction of the radical right; Kitschelt argues that it is the combination of free market liberalism with traditional authoritarian policies toward minorities which has created the winning conditions for these parties.[19] To capture this dimension, the fourth economic scale monitored attitudes toward economic inequality and the need for strong trade unions. The available items were far from ideal, as they only cover a limited range of economic values, but they probably tapped two important attitudes that are strongly related to broader positions toward free market versus planned economies. Claims about income equality lie at the heart of traditional socialism, as do attitudes toward the role of trade unions. While not sufficient for any detailed analysis, these items allow us to test the Kitschelt thesis.

Each of these scales was constructed by recoding the direction of the items, combining them, and standardizing the final scales to 100 points, all in a negative direction (representing hostility to immigration, refugees, multiculturalism, and economic equality), for ease of interpretation. These measures can be used to examine the common claim that countries where radical right parties have succeeded in mobilizing electoral support most successfully are those where the general public is most hostile toward immigrants and least tolerant of refugees and asylum seekers. This proposition is widely assumed in popular commentary, where the popularity of parties promulgating racist antiforeigner policies, such as in Austria and Switzerland, is often taken as indicative of exceptionally strong racist sentiments in the general population as a whole.

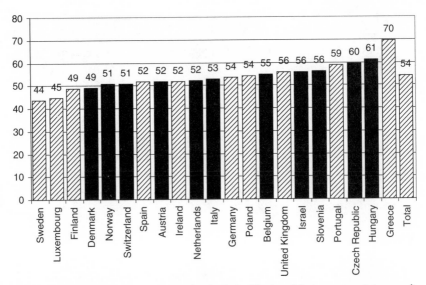

FIGURE 8.3. Anti-immigrant Attitudes Scale by Nation. Nations containing a relevant radical right party are highlighted in solid columns. For the construction of the 100-point attitudinal scale, see Table 8.2. *Source:* European Social Survey 2002 (ESS 2002).

Figure 8.3 demonstrates that anti-immigrant feelings do indeed vary across European countries, from the most tolerant (Sweden and Luxembourg) to the least (Hungary and Greece). Yet at aggregate level, the distribution of public opinion in each country fails to predict either the share of the vote won by the radical right or the existence of relevant radical right parties. The smaller liberal Scandinavian welfare states prove some of the most tolerant toward outsiders, whether Norway (with the FrP) and Denmark (with the DF and FP), or Sweden and Finland (without a relevant radical right party). By contrast, the least tolerant European nations include Greece and Portugal (without such a party), but also Hungary (with the MIEP) and the Czech Republic (with the RSC).

To compare this further, Figure 8.4 displays the average level of support for anti-immigrant attitudes in each country compared with the mean share of the vote won by radical right parties. Again no relationship is apparent at national level, and this remains true even if we exclude Switzerland as an outlier. Although we shall demonstrate that *individual* attitudes hostile toward cultural protectionism (toward foreigners, refugees, and ethnic diversity) do indeed predict whether a particular person will cast a ballot for a radical right party, this does not mean that the

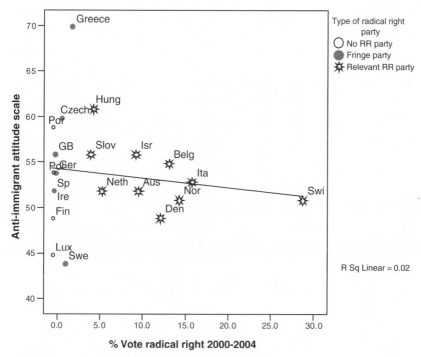

FIGURE 8.4. Anti-immigrant Attitudes and Support for the Radical Right. For the construction of the attitudinal scale, see Table 8.2. *Source:* European Social Survey 2002 (ESS 2002).

electoral success of these parties can be predicted at *national level* by public opinion in any country.

III EXPLAINING INDIVIDUAL SUPPORT FOR THE RADICAL RIGHT

So far this chapter has failed to detect any significant link between electoral support for the radical right, aggregate-level indicators of ethnic heterogeneity, and public opinion. Yet despite this pattern, attitudes on these issues do help to predict whether individuals vote for the radical right. The study ran a binary logistic (logit) regression model to analyze patterns of individual-level radical right voting within the pooled European sample, including the nine countries with a relevant right party that were contained in the ESS 2002. The results can be compared with the similar models used in previous chapters. The demographic and socioeconomic characteristics were first entered in the model, then the indicators of institutional trust, satisfaction with government, and social trust which we have already employed as significant predictors of radical right support. These factors act as prior controls in the multivariate model, assuming that background characteristics such as age, gender, and class will influence general orientations toward the political system, including patterns of institutional trust, social trust, and satisfaction with government. In turn, these factors are expected to shape more specific instrumental and identity-based attitudes toward immigration and political refugees, perspectives on cultural protectionism, and preferences for egalitarian economic policies.

The results of the pooled model in Table 8.3 confirm the significance of all the cultural attitudes: as expected, *negative attitudes toward immigration, refugees, multiculturalism, and economic equality all predicted individual radical right-wing votes, remaining significant even after including the full battery of prior controls*. The overall fit of the model still remained modest but it also strengthened (evaluated by the Nagelkerke R^2), compared with previous estimates. To go further, we again need to explore these patterns when broken down by nation, without any controls.

As Table 8.4 illustrates, the cultural indicators measuring negative attitudes toward immigration, refugees, and multiculturalism proved significant predictors of individual radical right voting in seven of the nine nations containing a relevant radical right party (in Austria, Belgium, Denmark, France, the Netherlands, Norway, and Switzerland). Compared with the attitudes of the general public, these indicators proved quite strong in these societies, such as strong anti-immigrant and anti-refugee sentiments expressed by supporters of the FPÖ in Austria and Lijst Pym Fortuyn in the Netherlands. Moreover, in these seven countries the indicators measuring negative attitudes toward economic equality failed to predict voting patterns. Admittedly the economic measures contained in the ESS 2002 remain limited; nevertheless, contrary to Kitschelt's thesis of a 'winning formula,' it appears that antiforeigner feelings and cultural protectionism provide far better explanations of the success of the radical right in Austria and Switzerland than any appeal to free market liberalism. In Italy there was a slightly different pattern, however, as support for the radical right in this country was more strongly related to economic attitudes than anti-immigrant feelings. The major exception to the general pattern concerns Israel, where none of these attitudinal scales proved to be significantly related to voting support for Mafdal and IL. It appears as though the deep religious cleavage in Israel, dividing secular and more orthodox Jews, as well as Jews and Muslims, and related attitudes toward issues of national security, the Palestinian question, and the role of the

TABLE 8.3. *Cultural Attitudes and the Radical Right Vote, Pooled Sample*

	Predictors of voting for the radical right, pooled eight-nation European sample		
	B	Std. error	Sig.
(Constant)	−5.887		
Demographic background			
Age (in years)	.010	.003	***
Sex (male = 1, female = 0)	.209	.109	*
Ethnic minority (ethnic minority = 1, else = 0)	−.007	.376	N/s
Socioeconomic status			
Education (highest level attained on a 6-point scale from low to high)	.016	.046	N/s
Salariat (professional and managerial employees)	−.201	.178	N/s
Petite bourgeoisie (self-employed)	.573	.129	***
Skilled manual working class	.118	.207	N/s
Unskilled manual working class	.156	.164	N/s
Ever been unemployed (for more than 3 months)	.364	.128	***
Religiosity (self-identified as religious on a 7-pt scale)	−.072	.019	***
Indicators of trust and satisfaction			
Institutional trust (60-pt scale)	−.017	.006	***
Satisfaction with government (60-pt scale)	−.004	.007	N/s
Social trust (30-pt scale)	−.016	.010	N/s
Cultural attitudes			
Negative attitudes toward immigration	−.013	.004	***
Negative attitudes toward refugees	.010	.004	**
Negative attitudes toward multiculturalism	.009	.003	***
Negative attitudes toward economic equality	.006	.003	*
Nagelkerke R^2	.218		
Percentage correctly predicted	91.2		

Note: The model presents the results of a binary logistic (logit) regression model including the unstandardized beta coefficients (B), the standard errors, and their significance, in the pooled eight-nation European sample weighted by design and population size. The dependent variable was whether the respondent had voted for a radical right party. For the construction of the cultural scales, all standardized to 100 points, see Table 8.1.
Sig. .001 = ***; Sig. .01 = **; Sig. .05 = *.
Source: Pooled sample eight nations, European Social Survey 2002 (ESS 2002).

TABLE 8.4. *Cultural Attitudes and the Radical Right Vote by Nation*

Nation	Party	Negative attitudes toward			
		Immigration	Refugees	Multiculturalism	Economic equality
Austria	FPÖ	11.3 **	10.3 **	10.8 *	7.0 N/s
Belgium	VB, FN	13.9 ***	12.9 ***	14.7 ***	−2.3 N/s
Denmark	DF, FP	14.7 ***	11.6 ***	13.7 ***	0.9 N/s
France	FN	18.5 ***	18.6 ***	9.0 ***	0.1 N/s
Israel	Mafdal, IL	−7.3 N/s	2.8 N/s	6.3 N/s	2.3 N/s
Italy	AN, LN, MsFt	0.6 N/s	2.6 ***	2.0 *	6.9 ***
Netherlands	PF, CD	9.3 ***	7.5 ***	10.0 ***	2.7 *
Norway	FrP, FLP	7.7 ***	7.5 ***	10.1 ***	3.5 N/s
Switzerland	SVP, EDU, SD, LdT, FPS	6.8 ***	9.6 ***	7.8 ***	9.0 ***
TOTAL		4.5 ***	10.3 ***	5.9 ***	5.6 ***

Note: For the construction of the 100-point standardized scales see Table 8.1. The coefficients represent the mean difference between the position of voters for radical right parties and all other citizens on these scales. The significance of the mean difference between groups is measured by ANOVA. The sample was weighted by design and population size.

Sig. .001 = ***; Sig. .01 = **; Sig. .05 = *.

Source: European Social Survey 2002 (ESS 2002).

West Bank, coupled with the unique history and origins of the Israeli state as a nation of immigrants and refugees, means that these attitudes fail to resonate in generating support for these particular parties.

CONCLUSIONS

It is widely assumed in popular commentary that secular trends in modern multicultural societies are critical for rising levels of support for radical right parties. In particular, patterns of population migration, the influx of immigrants and refugees, and the perceived cultural threat from globalization are generally believed to have encouraged more racist attitudes in the public, which leaders such as Le Pen and Haider have been keen to foster and exploit. Support for extremist political groups may also have been encouraged more recently by xenophobia directed against Muslim populations, indicated by reports of rising levels of hate crimes in the United States and within Europe in the aftermath of 9/11 and subsequent terrorist incidents.[20] Yet the previous literature examining the empirical link between aggregate indicators of ethnic heterogeneity and the proportion of votes cast for radical right parties has reported inconclusive results.

Two major conclusions can be drawn from the evidence analyzed here. First, this chapter has demonstrated that no significant relationship exists at national (aggregate) level between the national share of the vote cast for radical right parties and a wide range of indicators of ethnic diversity, whether measured objectively by estimated official rates of refugees and asylum seekers, the proportion of nonnationals and noncitizens living in a country, or subjectively by public opinion toward immigration. Parties such as the Vlaams Blok, the FPÖ, and One Nation have certainly emphasized racist rhetoric, antiforeigner diatribes, and the theme of cultural protectionism as the leitmotif recurring throughout their leadership speeches and at the heart of their manifesto policies. Other issues, such as criticism of the European Union powers and policies, or attacks on the welfare state, are also often implicitly framed in ways tapping into culturally protectionist sentiments. Although the electoral success of these parties is often interpreted by media commentators, news journalists, and some scholars as a public backlash directed against ethnic minorities in the countries where they do well, in fact the relationship proves far more complicated and nuanced.

At individual level, however, support for cultural protectionism does indeed predict who will vote for the radical right, as expected, with

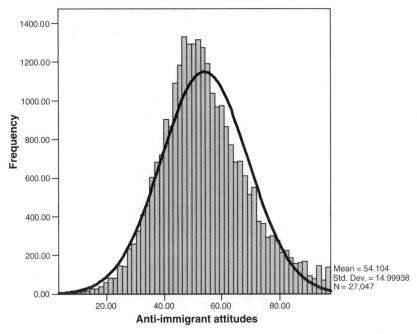

Cases weighted by All weight (dweight*pweight)

FIGURE 8.5. The Distribution of Anti-immigrant Attitudes in Public Opinion. For the construction of the attitudinal scale, see Table 8.2. *Source:* Pooled eight-nation European Social Survey 2002 (ESS 2002).

anti-immigrant and anti-refugee attitudes remaining significant variables even after applying a battery of prior social and attitudinal controls. This pattern is found consistently in many, although not all, of the nine countries in the ESS survey that contained a relevant right party. By contrast, the limited measures of attitudes toward free market or egalitarian economic policies failed to prove consistently significant predictors of radical right support in most nations.

Why do these results appear inconsistent at different levels? Quite simply, the well-known ecological fallacy suggests that we should not assume that patterns found at national level will also be found at individual level. And the individual fallacy means that we should not assume that patterns found at individual level will also exist among public opinion at national level.[21] The main reason for the disparity is the skewed nature of radical right votes; these parties usually gain the support of only a small sector of the electorate, even in countries where they qualify as relevant. Hence it is highly misleading to generalize on the basis of the attitudes held by their supporters to the general distribution of public opinion existing in the countries where they perform relatively well. Figure 8.5 illustrates the distribution of anti-immigrant attitudes more clearly, in the pooled European sample. There is a normal curve in this distribution, but in the polar extremes it is skewed toward the right. The group most hostile toward ethnic diversity forms the pool of potential electoral support most likely to vote for the radical right. But this does not mean that the outcome for the radical right in votes, still less in seats, can be read as an accurate indicator of the state of public opinion in each country.

The demand-side interpretation therefore does contribute part of the explanation for radical right success, and yet because both political disaffection and cultural protectionism are characteristic of many postindustrial societies, it is difficult to use these factors to explain where these parties have, and have not, advanced. Even at individual level, in the pooled model the combination of the social background of voters, their level of political trust, and their attitudes toward cultural protectionism only explained, at most, roughly one-fifth of the variation in voting for the radical right. On this basis, we need to also consider the supply side of the equation, and how parties respond to the public when crafting their ideological values and developing their organizational base, within the constraints set by the broader type of institutional context and electoral system.

PART IV

PARTY SUPPLY

Location, Location, Location

Party Competition

Previous chapters have established that the share of the national vote gained by radical right parties is not directly linked with structural trends in aggregate levels of immigration, multiculturalism, and ethnic diversity. Instead, supply-side theories suggest that parties play a critical role as active agents connecting social developments and political attitudes with voting behavior. What we have not yet had the opportunity to analyze is direct evidence for the role of party strategy. This includes (i) the ideological space created on the far right of the political spectrum by the location of the mainstream parties, (ii) where the radical right parties choose to place themselves in the same space, and also, the subject of Chapter 10, (iii) how effectively these parties build and consolidate their organizational base. Observers have commonly noted that some radical right parties emphasize core hard-right ideological values, while by contrast others characteristically prioritize vaguer populist appeals. We can see whether these strategies are an important predictor of their success. Moreover, so far we have been unable to compare whether the broader institutional context, particularly the electoral rules, affects party strategies in their choice of ideological locations. The analysis of relevant radical right parties contained in the European Social Survey 2002 has also limited the comparative analysis in another important regard, because nearly all are based in nations using proportional representation electoral systems in national contests.

To consider these issues, after setting out the theoretical framework and evidence, Section I of this chapter analyzes the relationship between radical right support and mainstream patterns of party competition, utilizing the Lubbers expert estimates for the location of parties. Section II then examines patterns of voting behavior in the broader range of parties and electoral systems contained in the Comparative Study of Electoral Systems. To consider the impact of majoritarian and proportional rules, Section III focuses upon analyzing voting support for the radical right in four selected case studies: Canada and France, selected as nations exemplifying majoritarian electoral systems, compared with Norway and Switzerland, illustrating elections under proportional representation. The conclusion considers the implications for how parties behave strategically as agents, and how voters react, under different rule-based constraints.

I THE IDEOLOGICAL SPACE GENERATED BY MAINSTREAM PARTY COMPETITION

Parties can be seen as competing by arraying themselves across an ideological space, conventionally from left to right on a ten-point scale. The supply-side thesis developed by Herbert Kitschelt suggests that support for radical right parties is fueled by a broader unhappiness with the electoral choices offered by the established mainstream parties, especially where there has been closure of the gap between the center-left and center-right on many major social and economic policy issues.[1] In postindustrial societies, any convergence of Social Democrat and moderate Conservative major parties, he argues, coupled in particular with an extended period of government by the center-right, creates the most opportune electoral opening for the radical right. In Britain, for example, the new Labour Party under Blair's leadership have adopted liberal free market economic policies on trade, taxation, welfare reform, and labor mobility. In periods when the Conservatives have hedged back toward the center ground on Europe and the welfare state, to try to recapture middle-of-the-road support, then this leaves parties such as the BNP and the UK Independence Party maximum room to expand their support on the far right by banging the nationalist antiforeigner, anti-Brussels drum. A middle-of-the-road consensus at elite level, for example a tacit agreement by major parties to avoid playing 'the race card,' may lead voters, unhappy with the mainstream electoral choices, to opt increasingly for alternative extremist parties that provide 'a choice not an echo.' Radical right parties do particularly well under these conditions, Kitschelt argues, as exemplified by Denmark, France, and Norway, if they offer a 'winning formula' combining neoliberal promarket policies on economic issues with an authoritarian stance on social issues concerning citizenship, lifestyle, or cultural politics.

As well as evidence presented by Kitschelt, support for this thesis has been found in some other studies. Abedi, for example, classifies party positions based on expert judgments and compares the proportion of votes cast for antiestablishment parties since 1945 in sixteen postindustrial societies. He concludes that the closure of the mainstream parties on the left-right dimension generated greater opportunities for the electoral success of antiestablishment parties (including, although not confined to, those of the radical right).[2] Following a similar line of reasoning, van der Brug et al. also suggest that radical right parties are more successful when the largest mainstream right-wing competitor, in particular, occupies a centrist moderate position. This is thought to facilitate an opening for radical right contenders, who can thereby pick up far right voters who would otherwise lack a home.[3] The study reported that the left-right position of the main right-wing competitor party was a significant predictor of the share of the vote won by more than two dozen radical right parties in EU nations; indeed this was the strongest factor in their models.

Nevertheless, this interpretation needs to be reexamined, since the evidence has been disputed. For example, Lubbers et al. reported that, contrary to Kitschelt and Abedi, support for radical right parties was not larger where there was greater space in party competition on the issue of immigration.[4] Another question concerns periodicity: Ignazi has argued that the specific timing of ideological shifts in party competition fails to support Kitschelt's claims. He points out that historically the mainstream center-right moved in a neoconservative direction following the rise of Reaganism and Thatcherism during the late 1970s and early 1980s, well before the ascendancy of the radical right occurred in the early 1990s.[5] We can reexamine the evidence for the Kitschelt thesis using the Lubbers expert scales monitoring the ideological position of parties, as discussed earlier. The normative implications of this theory are also important to consider. If support for radical right parties does indeed represent an alternative outlet of expression for those unhappy with the choices offered by the existing party system, for example frustration with the overwhelming predominance of the Republicans and Democrats in the United States, then the radical right could still function as a healthy part of political competition, by widening democratic choices at the ballot box, the scope of deliberative debate in public affairs, and the political agenda in legislatures. Classical liberal thinkers such as John Stuart Mill would disagree deeply with the xenophobic attitudes, intolerant sentiments, and the politics of hatred expressed by the radical right, but so long as parties acted nonviolently within the confines of the law, classical

TABLE 9.1. *Party Competition and Radical Right Parties*

	Major rightist party		Major leftist party		Left-right gap[a]	Right-wing gap[b]	Type of radical right party
France	7.50	RPR	3.36	PS	4.14	2.50	Relevant
Sweden	7.96	M	4.00	SAP	3.96	2.04	Fringe
Portugal	5.96	PSD	2.16	PCP	3.80	4.04	None
Italy	6.65	FI	3.00	PCI	3.65	3.35	Relevant
Norway	7.41	H	4.00	DNA	3.41	2.59	Relevant
Belgium – Francophone	6.61	PRL	3.26	PS	3.35	3.39	Relevant
Denmark	7.20	KF	3.97	SD	3.23	2.80	Relevant
Finland	6.43	KOK	3.21	FPDL	3.22	3.57	None
Belgium – Flemish	6.76	PVV	3.58	SP	3.18	3.24	Relevant
Netherlands	6.71	VVD	3.69	PvDA	3.02	3.29	Relevant
Spain	6.85	PP	3.96	PSOE	2.89	3.15	Fringe
Britain	7.07	Con	4.43	Lab	2.64	2.93	Fringe
Germany	6.36	CDU	3.96	SPD	2.40	3.64	Fringe
Greece	7.38	ND	5.08	Pasok	2.30	2.62	Fringe
Austria	6.25	OVP	4.31	SPO	1.94	3.75	Relevant
Ireland	5.93	FG	4.06	Lab	1.87	4.07	None
Mean relevant	6.89		3.65		3.24	2.88	
Mean fringe	7.12		4.29		2.84	3.89	
Mean none	6.11		3.14		2.96	3.11	

[a] The 'left-right' gap is calculated as the difference between the major rightist and major leftist party in each nation, to examine Kitschelt's claim that it is the closure of this gap which creates the greatest opportunities for radical right success.

[b] The 'right-wing' gap is calculated by subtracting the position of the major rightist party from ten, the maximum point on the left-right scale, to examine van der Brug et al.'s thesis that the radical right get most votes in countries where the major rightist party is most centrist.

Source: The position of each party is calculated from Marcel Lubbers [principal investigator]. 2000. *Expert Judgment Survey of Western European Political Parties 2000* [machine readable dataset]. Nijmegen, the Netherlands: NWO, Department of Sociology, University of Nijmegen.

liberals would defend their rights to articulate these views and stand for elected office.[6]

There are two hypotheses to examine. The Kitschelt thesis suggests that the closure of the ideological space between the major parties on the center-left and center-right provides opportunities for electoral advance by radical right parties. If correct, then we should expect to find that the smaller the ideological gap between the center parties, then the greater the popularity of the radical right. The alternative van der Brug version of

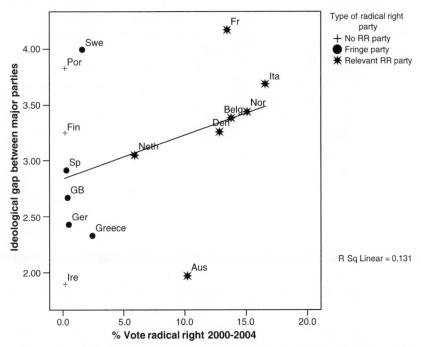

FIGURE 9.1. Party Competition and Radical Right Parties. For the estimates of the size of the ideological gap between major parties, see Table 9.1. For the classification of parties, and the percentage share of the vote for the radical right, see Table 3.1. *Source:* The size of the ideological gap between major parties is calculated from Marcel Lubbers [principal investigator]. 2000. *Expert Judgment Survey of Western European Political Parties 2000* [machine readable dataset]. Nijmegen, the Netherlands: NWO, Department of Sociology, University of Nijmegen.

this thesis claims that it is the location of the mainstream right-wing party in each nation, in particular, which is vital: the more centrist the right-wing party, the larger the spatial opportunity for radical right challengers. Evidence to test these two claims can be derived from the Lubbers expert ideological ten-point scales, used and discussed earlier, monitoring the position of all electoral parties located from extreme left (o) to extreme right (10).[7]

Table 9.1 and Figure 9.1 present the results in sixteen European societies without any prior controls for the type of electoral system, which might also be expected to influence patterns of party and ideological competition. All these nations are established democracies and postindustrial economies, to facilitate comparison of similar societies. The table identifies the ideological location of the major rightist and major leftist party in

each nation, and then calculates the size of the left-right gap (the difference between the two locations). To consider first the evidence concerning
the Kitschelt claim, the comparison of the mean ideological gap between
center-left and center-right was 3.24 in countries which contained a relevant radical right electoral party, compared with 2.84 in countries with
a fringe radical right electoral party, and 2.96 where there were no successful electoral radical right contenders. This evidence therefore fails to
support the Kitschelt prediction that the radical right will flourish most
successfully where the ideological gap between the main parties is smallest.
Figure 9.1 illustrates the correlations graphically; a cluster of countries,
notably Italy, Belgium, Norway, and Denmark, exhibit high ideological
polarization among the mainstream parties and also a flourishing share
of the vote for the radical right, the antithesis of the Kitschelt claim. At
the same time, there are many countries ranging across levels of party ideological competition, from low (Ireland) to high (Sweden), with minimal
voting support for contemporary radical right parties. In these sixteen
societies, no significant correlation existed between the size of the major party left-right gap and the mean share of the radical right vote or
seats (whether calculated by the average vote or seats for these parties in
elections held from 1990 to 2004, or during the most recent period, from
2000 to 2004).

The van der Brug variant of this thesis claims that it is the ideological
location of the mainstream *right*-wing party which is critical for maximizing or minimizing opportunities for the radical right. The size of the
right-wing gap is calculated in each society by simply subtracting the position of the major right-wing party from the maximum score (10) on the
ideological scale. Table 9.1 shows that the right-wing gap on the right was
slightly greater in nations where there was a relevant radical right party
(3.24) than in those countries where there were fringe parties (2.84), or
no radical right party (2.96), as expected, but this was only a very modest
difference. Of course there are a limited number of cases under comparison, and this restricts the analysis; nevertheless, again there was also an
insignificant correlation between the size of the right-wing gap and the
vote or seat share of the radical right (using the same periods as described
above). It appears that there are grounds for skepticism surrounding the
claim that the ideological positions of the mainstream parties provide
automatic opportunities for radical right parties. What might matter, instead, might be the ideological strategies radical right parties adopt to
maximize their support, within the constraints of the electoral rules and
the distribution of public opinion.

II THE CONSTRAINTS ON PARTY COMPETITION

Most supply-side rational choice theories treat parties as largely autonomous agents, deciding where to locate themselves across the ideological spectrum in pursuit of popular support, assuming conditions of perfect competition. By contrast, the account offered here suggests that the electoral rules serve to regulate both demand and supply factors, especially the electoral strategies that parties follow. As discussed in the Introduction, 'proximity' or 'spatial' theories of voting behavior start from the traditional Downsian rational choice axiom that both voters and parties are located at ideal points on the classic left-right ideological dimension.[8] The proximity model used here follows this tradition by assuming that voters can position themselves at a point in this continuum reflecting their ideal preference. The ideological position of each party can also be represented by a point in the same continuum. Building upon this foundation, the strategic agency theory developed in this book makes certain important claims about how:

(i) The electoral system generates incentives for either centripetal or centrifugal patterns of party competition, and, as a result;

(ii) The rules influence where rational parties decide to locate themselves on the left-right ideological spectrum; and, in turn,

(iii) Patterns of party competition shape how citizens respond to the available electoral choices, and the importance of ideological or populist appeals in voting behavior.

Proximity models of voting behavior assume that the distribution of public opinion on the left-right ideological spectrum usually follows a unimodal normal curve with a single peak in the center of the distribution. Public opinion commonly reflects this pattern on most major values, such as preferences for tax cuts over public spending, for free market liberalism over state-planned economies, or for stricter or liberal regulation of refugee entry. In this ideological space, as discussed in the Introduction, the theory assumes that some policy options are located too far left for the public's acceptance (such as allowing all refugees who apply into a country), some are located too far right (such as denying asylum even to refugees from bloody civil wars or victims of human rights abuses), and there is an asymmetrical zone of acquiescence between these poles with a range of intermediate policy choices (allowing some, but not all) that are broadly acceptable to the general public.[9] A broad consensus exists about valance issues found within this zone. Given the normal distribution of public opinion around most values, support for extremist values on the far right or far left usually remains confined to a minority of the electorate.

In this context, standard Downsian rational choice models assume that most parties have a strategic incentive to compete by emphasizing similar values in the middle ground of the ideological spectrum, since that is where most voters cluster.[10] If public opinion is normally distributed, rational vote-maximizing parties will try to position themselves within the left-right ideological space to maximize their appeal among as many citizens as possible. Under most circumstances, parties are therefore subject to strong centripetal pressures to emphasize values where there is widespread agreement, for example to suggest that they offer an experienced leadership team capable of managing economic growth, providing effective security, and maintaining a basic welfare safety net offering social protection against the problems of old age, unemployment, and ill health. Party policies and platforms are expected to converge with the position of the median voter on these issues. This account provides a logic consistent with predictions made in the mid-1960s about 'the end of ideology' (Bell) and the growth of 'catch-all' parties (Kirchheimer).[11] Simple proximity models provide a potential explanation for why major parties usually cluster in the center ground of politics, given the normal distribution of public opinion.

Yet standard proximity theories are less good at explaining why rational vote-maximizing and seat-maximizing radical right parties do not simply moderate their policy positions and tone down their heated rhetoric in the pursuit of popular support clustered in the center-right ground of the political spectrum. To go further, building upon arguments developed by Cox, we assume that the strategic incentives facing rational parties vary systematically according to the institutional context of the electoral system.[12] In particular, as already observed, the electoral threshold determines the number of parties elected to the legislature, and thus, as Cox suggests, it may shape the incentives for either centripetal patterns of party competition (where most parties and candidates advocate moderate policies clustered in the middle of the zone of acquiescence) and centrifugal patterns (where parties adopt more extreme positions ranged across the full ideological spectrum).

Earlier chapters have demonstrated how PR electoral systems with low thresholds allow minor parties to gain office even if they receive only a modest share of the popular vote. Under these rules, we theorize that radical right minor parties have a strategic incentive to win seats by adopting 'bonding' strategies which they can use to mobilize and activate niche cleavages within the electorate. Such appeals stress signature issues and hardline values characteristic of the far right of the ideological spectrum, notably xenophobic, anti-immigrant, and antiestablishment rhetoric. Such values distinguish radical right parties most clearly from their mainstream competitors, thereby generating support among their hard-core base. The theory assumes that it is easier for minor parties to mobilize certain distinct segments of the electorate, for example, for Green parties in Western Europe to attract the younger generation on environmental issues, or for reformed Communist parties to mobilize older voters in Central Europe by emphasizing the importance of maintaining welfare services and social security. By contrast, it is more difficult for minor parties to compete in the center ground of party politics, such as on consensual or valance issues of national security and competent management of the economy, since party competition is most crowded here, and many minor radical right parties lack the credibility derived from the experience of government office. By helping to mobilize supporters, raise funds, attract volunteers, and therefore contribute ultimately towards their electoral success, minor radical right parties can gain many benefits from prioritizing clear ideological principles, distinctive programmatic party platforms reflecting these goals, and a sense of one-of-us belonging to a clan with boundaries demarcating 'them' and 'us.'

By contrast, in contests under majoritarian rules, and/or with higher effective electoral thresholds, radical right parties will fail to surmount the barriers to elected office (and thus the rewards of status, power, and legitimacy that flow from office) unless they adopt broader populist, bridging, or catchall strategies. In this context, radical right vote-seeking parties are forced to expand their ideological and social appeals beyond far right antiforeigner cultural protectionism to encompass a broader range of issues and populist appeals, based on vague rhetoric, leadership popularity, and simple slogans largely devoid of substantive policy content, designed to attract a more diverse sector of the electorate. Leadership popularity should be particularly important in this context, for example attracting popular support through charismatic appeals, effective rhetoric, and modern communication skills. Of course radical right parties fighting in majoritarian electoral systems, such as the British National Front and the British National Party, may still decide to focus hard-line anti-immigrant and racist appeals upon narrow segments of the electorate, opting for ideological purity over electoral popularity. But, in this case, the theory predicts that such parties will remain stranded on the fringes of public life, and they may even die out over time, as they will attract too few votes to

TABLE 9.2. *Public Perceptions of Ideological Dispersion in Each Nation*

	Year	Most leftist party		Most rightist party		Difference	Median voter
Australia	1996	3.84	Green Party	6.50	National (Country)	2.66	5.45
Belarus	2001	2.66	Communist Party	5.30	Liberal-Democrat	2.64	5.74
Belgium	1999	3.60	Anders Gaan Leven	7.00	Vlaams Blok	3.40	4.91
Britain	1997	3.90	Labour Party	7.19	Conservative Party	3.29	5.04
Canada	1997	3.40	Bloc Québécois	5.94	Reform Party	2.54	5.36
Czech Rep	1996	0.59	Communist Party	8.93	Civic Democratic	8.34	5.77
Denmark	1998	2.52	Socialist People's Party	8.64	Danish People's Party	6.12	5.56
France	2002	2.30	Workers' Struggle	7.85	Front National	5.55	5.11
Germany	1998	2.40	Party of Democratic Socialism	6.32	CSU Bavaria	3.92	4.29
Hungary	1998	2.93	Socialist Party	7.91	Justice and Life (MIEP)	4.98	4.87
Iceland	1999	2.39	Left Greens	8.41	Independence Party	6.02	5.55
Israel	1996	1.51	Meretz	7.46	Likud	5.95	5.16
Korea	2000	4.21	Democratic Liberal Party	6.56	United Liberal Democrats	2.35	4.89
Lithuania	1997	2.71		8.06	Homeland Union	5.35	5.66
Mexico	1997	2.73	Cardenista Party	6.20	Institutional Revolutionary Party (PRI)	3.47	6.37
Netherlands	1998	2.85	Green Left	7.38	People's Party for Freedom & Democracy	4.53	5.38

Country	Year	Party		Party		Median voter
New Zealand	1996	Alliance	2.67	ACT New Zealand	8.03	5.62
Norway	1997	Socialist Left	2.41	Progress Party	8.30	5.18
Peru	2001	Solucion Popular	4.29	Peru Possible	5.76	5.76
Poland	1997	Democratic Left Alliance	1.69	Solidarity Election Action	8.11	5.60
Portugal	1997	Left Block	1.72	Popular Party	7.72	5.34
Romania	1996	Social Democrats	3.84	National Peasant & Christian Democratic	6.78	6.10
Russia	1999	Communist Party	1.89	Union of Right Forces	8.09	5.15
Slovenia	1996	Social Democrats	3.44	Christian Democrats	6.57	4.94
Spain	1996	United Life	2.26	Partido Popular	7.47	4.55
Sweden	1998	Left Party	1.24	Moderate Rally	9.02	4.96
Switzerland	1999	Green Party	3.00	Swiss People's Party	7.65	5.17
Taiwan	1996	Democratic Progressives	4.44	Nationalist Party	5.80	5.38
Ukraine	1998	Communist Party	1.80	People's Rukh	7.32	5.52
United States	1996					5.64
Mean Majoritarian			3.29			5.34
Mean combined			4.28			5.29
Mean PR			5.18			5.33

Note: The public's perceived location of the six largest parties in each country, and the location of the median voter, on the left-right ideological scale, where 0 = most left and 10 = most right.

Source: Calculated from CSES Module I 1996–2001 for all nations except France, which draws upon Module II.

surmount the higher threshold for elected office characteristic of majoritarian elections. As we shall discuss in the next chapter, radical right parties may make sporadic gains under these circumstances, especially through protest politics in second-order elections such as regional or European contests, but they will fail to consolidate their position.

Evidence for Ideological Competition

Following Cox, a growing body of literature has theorized about the effects of electoral systems on patterns of centrifugal and centripetal party competition, but few have attempted to evaluate the empirical evidence for this relationship across many types of electoral systems. Empirical support for this theory has been found by Dow, however, who compared the location of parties, measured by voter evaluations in national election surveys, in two majoritarian systems (Canada and France) and in two proportional systems (the Netherlands and Israel). The study reported that, as expected, parties were generally located closer to the median voter in majoritarian than PR systems.[13] In majoritarian elections, the radical right parties under comparison (the French Front National and the Canadian Reform parties) remained the furthest away from the median voter, while the winning parties were most centrally located.

To see whether these findings remain robust under different circumstances, the conclusions deserve reexamining in a wider range of national and electoral contexts. Evidence to test these propositions can be derived from the CSES, allowing comparison of party ideological competition in elections held in thirty nations, including both West European and post-Communist societies, as well as majoritarian, combined, and PR electoral systems.[14] In the CSES survey, people in each country were asked to place the six largest parties on a ten-point left-right ideological scale ranging from left (0) to right (10).[15] This data can be used to explore whether the perceived pattern of party competition on this standard scale varied according to the basic type of electoral system. The estimate of degree of left-right party competition is calculated as the difference between the mean position of the most leftist party in each country and the mean position of the most rightist party in each country, as described in Table 9.2. The fact that we are comparing the six largest and most relevant parties in each nation standardizes the comparison and it means that the degree of ideological competition is not merely a reflection of the number of parties elected in each nation, for example the inclusion of more fringe and minor parties in PR systems with low thresholds, such as in Belgium.

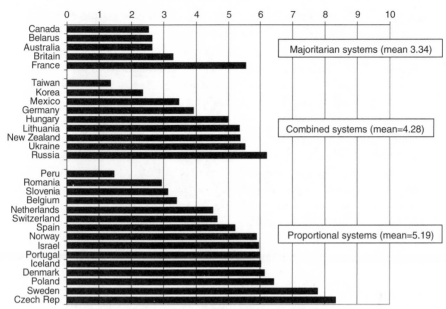

FIGURE 9.2. Public Perceptions of the Maximum Distance in Party Locations on the Ten-Point Left-Right Ideology Scale, Six Largest Parties in Each Nation. The graph shows the maximum distance in the ideological location of the most left-wing and the most right-wing of the six largest parties in each country, on the ten-point left-right ideological scale, as placed by all respondents in each nation. See Table 9.1. *Source:* Calculated from the Comparative Study of Electoral Systems 1996–2001 Module I, with France from CSES Module II.

The results, illustrated visually in Figure 9.2, generally confirm that party competition proves more centrifugal under PR electoral systems and more centripetal under majoritarian systems, with combined electoral systems falling into the middle of the distribution. The ideological distance between the most left and most right party was 3.29 points on the 10-point scale in majoritarian electoral systems, 4.28 points in combined systems, but ranged across 5.18 points in proportional systems. Figure 9.2 shows that not all the countries under comparison fell exactly where predicted; in particular, the Peruvian presidential election, although a proportional system, showed the smallest ideological left-right gap among parties, which probably reflects the clientalistic and personalistic nature of presidential contests in this country.[16] A similar lack of ideological polarization was also evident in Taiwan, using the combined electoral system. By contrast, although using the majoritarian second-ballot electoral system, French party competition displayed considerable polarization between the Workers Struggle on the far left and the Front National on the far right. This pattern may be generated by the second-ballot system, which allows multiple parties to compete in the first-round elections, where people can traditionally express a vote 'with their heart,' before finally casting a ballot 'with their head' for the major center-left and center-right contenders, although further comparisons would be necessary to confirm this pattern.[17] Despite these exceptions, the broad pattern found in most countries does confirm the expectation that the electoral system has 'psychological' effects by influencing the ideological strategies which parties adopt, as well as having mechanical effects which determine the effective number of political parties elected in any country (as documented in Chapter 5). Ideological competition is usually more centripetal under majoritarian rules and more centrifugal under proportional electoral rules.

III RADICAL RIGHT IDEOLOGICAL OR POPULIST APPEALS

So how does the pattern of party competition influence voting behavior? One of the most basic propositions in proximity theories of electoral behavior is that rational voters are expected to maximize their utility by voting for the party closest to their own preferences while shunning parties furthest away.[18] Many accounts focus upon *issue* proximity, on the assumption that voters match their attitudes toward a series of specific public policies, such as on education, health care, and defense, with the policy platforms offered by parties. Yet it is widely recognized that issue voting makes considerable information demands upon citizens when assessing where parties stand on each policy that voters care about. Issue voting also requires judgments about whether parties are likely to deliver upon their promises, based upon their past performance and their record in office, a matter that is particularly difficult to evaluate for new parties. In line with many other accounts, the theory tested here suggests that when deciding how to vote, citizens commonly use a variety of 'cognitive shortcuts' through general left-right ideological cues (understood to represent a running tally of the past performance and an assessment of future actions taken by each party), as effective ways of reducing information demands in each election, while matching general policy preferences, at least in a rough approximation, to the party and candidate choices available.[19] The left-right scale is the most common summary measure for evaluating parties and candidates, widely used in the literature comparing party competition and electoral behavior, so it provides a standard test of how far ideological cues guide voting choices.[20] Evidence for the basic claim about ideological voting can be tested using the CSES, which asked people in each country to place themselves on a ten-point left-right ideological scale ranging from left (0) to right (10).[21] This allows us to analyze whether citizens do indeed support the radical right party if they locate themselves on the far right of the ideological spectrum.

The relative impact of left-right ideology on voting behavior needs to be compared against alternative factors commonly thought to determine support for the radical right. Much of the literature emphasizes the role of populist appeals, which can be regarded as affective orientations based on how far people like a particular party and the party leader, drawing upon general party images and broad rhetorical appeals, but largely devoid of references to substantive policy content or issue positions. Although rarely analyzed with systematic evidence, and with only loose reference to the original Weberian notion of 'charisma,' historical national case studies often claim that 'charismatic' leaders such as Umberto Bossi, Jean-Marie Le Pen, Pauline Hanson, Ross Perot, Mogens Glistrup, Anders Lange, and Pym Fortuyn have played a decisive role through founding and organizing new parties, as well as acting as the figurehead for media attention and controlling the party organization.[22] In some cases, subsequent problems of leadership succession are believed to have undermined support for radical right parties, perhaps best exemplified by the difficulties in establishing a viable Reform Party candidate in the 2000 U.S. presidential election, after Ross Perot retired. Similar problems of continuity were evident in the Danish Progress Party after Mogens Glistrup was imprisoned for tax fraud. One Nation faced a parallel sharp fall in the Australian polls after Pauline Hanson was convicted of electoral irregularities. Leadership effects are also exemplified in cases when new leaders such as Jörg Haider and Christoph Blocher have risen to power within the internal hierarchy of established parties. Both Haider and Blocher moved their parties sharply hard right, especially on race and immigration, thereby driving out more moderate factions. Following the change of leadership, the substantial rise registered in party support for the Austrian Freiheitliche Partei Österreichs after 1986, and for the Swiss Schweizerische Volkspartei after 1999, certainly suggests that the leaders' role may have been decisive, although it remains unclear whether this surge was due to their personal appeal among the public or their ideological shift in party policy and rhetoric.[23] The strategic agency theory suggests that populist appeals by leaders will be particularly important in generating support for radical right parties within majoritarian electoral

TABLE 9.3. *Hypotheses about the Impact of Electoral Systems on Radical Right Support*

	Type of electoral system		
	PR	Combined	Majoritarian
Ideological location (respondent's position on 10-point left-right scale)	Stronger	Moderate	Weaker
Affective party popularity (10-point like/dislike scale)	Weaker	Moderate	Stronger
Exemplar cases	Norway Switzerland	Hungary Russia	Canada France

systems, for example for Ross Perot's Reform Party and for the Canadian Reform/Alliance/Conservative Party.

Radical right voters may also be swayed by other affective considerations, in particular by their general sense of partisan attachment. The classic Michigan model of voting behavior gives primacy to the importance of an affective sense of party identification as one of the core factors driving electoral support.[24] Party identification, regarded as a long-standing anchor for voting behavior, is seen in this account as the best single predictor of the vote, modified by changing circumstances, such as economic conditions and the personality of the leaders, that influence short-run and medium-term electoral forces. A substantial literature suggests that strong loyalties have gradually eroded over the years through partisan dealignment in many established democracies.[25] Nevertheless, partisan identities may continue to play an important role in voting choice, especially when considering whether to support fringe and minor parties which have no record in government and which stand little chance of actually implementing any policy proposals in office.

The institutional context, particularly the electoral system, is therefore expected to influence the relative importance of ideological cues and populist appeals. This generates certain testable propositions, summarized in Table 9.3. In proportional representation electoral systems, minor radical right parties are expected to target core supporters through advocating strong ideological appeals on core issues and values. Hence, in this context, it is predicted that in PR systems (exemplified here by Denmark and

Switzerland), votes cast for radical right parties will be strongly predicted by the perceived ideological proximity of citizens to parties. By contrast, in majoritarian electoral systems (exemplified by Canada and France), radical right parties are expected to emphasize more diffuse populist appeals, so that votes cast for these parties will be more strongly predicted by party popularity. The ideological profile of radical right supporters in combined (otherwise known as 'mixed' or 'dual') electoral systems, which incorporate elements from both PR and majoritarian systems, is predicted to fall into an intermediate position.

Based on these considerations, the regression models presented in Table 9.3 first examine which factors prove to be the strongest predictors of voting choices for radical right parties in the pooled sample of thirteen nations with a relevant radical right party contained in the CSES. The models compare left-right ideology, affective orientations toward leaders, general party popularity, and partisan identification on voting for the radical right. Using a series of standard ten-point scales, respondents in each country were asked to locate their own position on the left-right ideological spectrum, as well as to indicate how far they liked the party leader and the party in general.[26] This allows us to analyze whether leadership popularity lagged behind, or led, overall levels of party popularity. The survey also monitored the direction and strength of partisan identification, measured by the party that respondents felt closest toward.[27] The multivariate models control for most of the factors already established as important in previous chapters, notably the demographic and social characteristics of radical right voters, as well as their greater disaffection with government. Omission of factors already found to predict support for the radical right may result in misspecified models that systematically overstate the importance of ideological values.[28] Replication of the logit (binomial logistic regression) models already used with the ESS also allows us to double-check the robustness and reliability of some of the core findings, although identical results would not be expected given some important methodological differences in each survey.[29]

Table 9.4 demonstrates the results in logit models predicting voting for relevant radical right parties in the pooled CSES thirteen-nation sample of countries containing a relevant radical right party in national legislative elections. Model A enters the social and demographic factors, and political disaffection, where radical right support proved to be greatest among men, younger voters, ethnic majorities, and the less educated, as well as those least satisfied with the democratic process. These results generally

TABLE 9.4. *Ideological and Partisan Attitudes and the Radical Right Vote, Pooled CSES Thirteen-Nation Sample*

	Model A: social background and political trust			Model B: social background, political trust, and partisan attitudes		
	B	Std. error	Sig.	B	Std. error	Sig.
(Constant)	−1.86			−9.169		
Social background and political trust						
Age (in years)	−.008	.003	***	.000	.004	N/s
Sex (male = 1, female = 0)	.483	.098	***	.199	.151	N/s
Ethnic majority (ethnic majority = 1, else = 0)	1.06	.112	***	.742	.164	***
Education (highest level attained on a 3-point scale from low to high)	−.161	.066	**	.586	.106	***
Salariat (professional and managerial employees)	−.030	.122	N/s	−.203	.183	N/s
Petite bourgeoisie (self-employed)	.244	.160	N/s	−.013	.250	N/s
Skilled manual working class	.136	.145	N/s	−.323	.228	N/s
Unskilled manual working class	.304	.178	N/s	.266	.288	N/s
Currently unemployed (1)	−.048	.279	N/s	−.761	.416	N/s
Satisfaction with democratic process (4-point scale)	−.286	.056	***	.073	.088	N/s
Partisan attitudes						
Ideological left-right self-placement (10-point scale)				.064	.030	**
Liking of radical right party leader (10-point scale)				.156	.039	***
Liking of radical right party (10-point scale)				.466	.043	***
Partisan identification (feels closest to a radical right party)				3.04	.165	***
Nagelkerke R²	.064			.668		
Percentage correctly predicted	91%			96%		

Note: The table presents the results of binomial logit regression analysis models where the dependent variable is whether the respondent reported voting for the relevant radical right party in each country in the pooled thirteen-nation CSES sample. The table includes the unstandardized beta coefficients (B), the standard errors, and their significance,. See note for Table 6.1. Ethnicity is defined by the linguistic majority in each country (1), or the linguistic minority (0), based on the primary language spoken at home. For the construction of the ideological and attitudinal scales, all standardized to ten points, see text. The countries include the thirteen nations with a relevant radical right party in legislative elections contained in the CSES (Belgium, Canada, the Czech Republic, Denmark, Hungary, Israel, New Zealand, Norway, Poland, Romania, Russia, Slovenia, and Switzerland).

Sig .001 = ***; Sig .01 = **; Sig .05 = *.

Source: Comparative Study of Electoral Systems (CSES) Module 1 1996–2001.

reflected the demographic profile of radical right voters found earlier in Chapters 6 and 7, with replication lending greater confidence to the results derived from two independent surveys. The Goldthorpe-Heath measure of social class showed a similar pattern to that found earlier, with support for the radical right slightly lower among the salariat while being strongest among the petite bourgeoisie and the unskilled working class, although the beta coefficients failed to prove statistically significant. Model A also explained little variance in radical right voting. Further exploration of the data suggested that this difference in the results was probably due to the inclusion of a broader range of nations contained in the pooled sample in the CSES survey, including post-Communist societies such as Poland, Russia, Hungary, and the Czech Republic, with a distinctive class structure and historical traditions.

Model B maintained these demographic, socioeconomic, and attitudinal factors as controls, and then added the additional indicators of the respondent's ideological position, affective orientations toward parties and party leaders, and partisan identification. The model was tested and confirmed to be free of problems of multicollinearity. The results of Model B indicate that, even with prior controls, the measures of left-right ideology, leadership popularity, party popularity, and partisan identification all proved significant predictors of voting for the radical right. Moreover once these factors were entered, most of the social and demographic characteristics (with the exception of ethnicity and education) became insignificant. The overall fit of the model improved dramatically (indicated by the final Nagelkerke R^2 of .668), confirming that political attitudes predicted support for the radical right far more strongly than social characteristics. The results suggest that social background does affect the propensity to vote for these parties, and the effect works *indirectly*, through shaping political ideology and affective orientations toward the radical right.

The Impact of the Electoral System on Party Competition and Voting Behavior

But does the electoral system also influence this process, so that populist appeals are stronger predictors of radical right support in majoritarian systems while ideological cues prove more important in PR systems, as theorized earlier? This claim can be most clearly illustrated by analyzing voting behavior in four case studies in France, Canada, Norway, and Switzerland, selected to represent comparable affluent postindustrial societies and established democracies, and all containing a relevant radical right party, but varying in their electoral systems.

We can compare support for the Reform Party in the 1997 Canadian election and votes for the Front National in the 2002 French presidential election, both of which exemplify majoritarian electoral systems.[30] Canadian parliamentary elections are fought using single-member plurality districts (first-past-the-post), requiring that the winning candidate gain a simple plurality of votes in each riding. The French presidential elections use the second-ballot system ('runoff' elections), where the first round of the contest determines if any candidate gets an absolute majority of votes (50%+). If none do, then the top two candidates with the highest share of the vote go on into the second-round election two weeks later. The 2002 elections were particularly appropriate to test the basis of Front National support; in the first round Jean-Marie Le Pen unexpectedly came second, with 17% of the vote, his best ever result, shocking commentators and generating massive waves of street protests by those who had been expecting that the second round would be a traditional left-right contest between Jacques Chirac and Lionel Jospin, the Parti Socialiste candidate and French premier, who won only 16.2% of the vote.[31] The case studies also allow us to examine further the important differences we have already noted between Canada and France in the degree of party ideological competition.

These contests are compared with support for radical right parties in two European countries which exemplify PR systems with far lower effective thresholds. The Norwegian Fremskrittspartiet almost tripled its vote, from 6.3% in 1993 to 15.3% in the 1997 parliamentary election, led by Carl I. Hagen. One critical factor which seems to have played a role is the salience of the issue of immigration in the election, which was linked by the Progress Party to problems of juvenile delinquency, unemployment, and dependence on social security, along with a broader antitax movement. In the 1999 election the Swiss Schweizerische Volkspartei also saw a substantial advance in voting support, from 14.9% in 1995 to 23.3%, under the more radical ultranationalist, anti-EU, and isolationist rhetoric of their leader, the billionaire industrialist Christoph Blocher.[32] Both the Norwegian and Swiss elections are highly proportional in their ratio of votes to seats (the Rose standardized version of the Loosemore-Hanby index of proportionality is 95% and 93% respectively). Norway employs closed party lists for the 165 members of the Storting, a 4% legal threshold, and a Sainte-Laguë formula. Switzerland elects 200 members to the Federal Assembly using the d'Hondt formula of votes to seats, panachage lists, and no formal legal minimal voting threshold.[33] The societies also differ substantially in the nature of their electoral cleavages, with Norway relatively homogeneous and divided primarily by a traditional class cleavage, as well as an urban-rural pattern, while Switzerland exemplifies a deeply plural society strongly divided by language, region, and class.

The result of the logit (binomial logistic regression) analysis are presented in Table 9.5, which first entered the standard social characteristics and satisfaction with democracy measures as controls. The models then entered the respondent's left-right self-placement on the ten-point scale (as an indicator of their ideological position) and the scale measuring affective orientations toward radical right parties (as an indicator of populist appeal).[34] The models in Table 9.4 demonstrate that affective party popularity proved significant in all systems, suggesting that populist appeals generating a positive affective orientation toward the radical right represent an important part of their support. By contrast, political ideology proved a significant predictor of voting for the radical right only in the two countries using proportional representation electoral systems, when generating support for the Norwegian Fremskrittspartiet and the Swiss Schweizerische Volkspartei. Moreover, the ideological cues were not significant predictors of radical right voting in the cases of the Canadian Reform Party and the French Front National, in elections held under majoritarian rules. Of course the number of case studies remains limited; in particular, ideally it would have been desirable to test these patterns in a broader range of countries using majoritarian electoral systems. One important reason why few such nations currently contain a relevant radical right party is due to the 'mechanical' effects of electoral systems that were already noted. But despite these limitations, the results of the selected cases are consistent with the basic theory that the type of electoral rules has certain 'psychological' effects by influencing the choice of party ideological strategy, and that, in turn, the appeals that radical right parties emphasize shape patterns of voting behavior. Populism appears to play an important role in all the case studies, with a very strong association with radical right voting behavior, but ideological cues are also relatively strong in Norway and Switzerland, yet insignificant in the cases using majoritarian electoral systems. Overall the full models in each country, containing social background, political trust, and the measures of ideology and party popularity, successfully explained a considerable amount of the variance in radical right voting (as measured by the Nagelkerke R^2, ranging from 47% of the variance in France and Switzerland to 61% in Canada).

TABLE 9.5. The Ideological Basis of Radical Right Votes, Selected Cases

| | Majoritarian electoral systems | | | | | | PR electoral systems | | | | | |
| | Canada 1997 (Reform Party) | | | France 2002 (Front National) | | | Norway 1997 (Progress Party) | | | Switzerland 1999 (People's Party) | | |
	B	Std. error	Sig.	B	Std. error	Sig.	B	Std. error	Sig.	B	Std. error	Sig.
(Constant)	-5.96	1.03		-7.09	1.18		-8.24	1.79		-8.44	.764	
Model A: Controls for social background and trust												
Age (years)	.024	.007	***	.024	.011	*	.008	.007	N/s	.015	.006	***
Sex (male = 1)	.399	.225	N/s	.723	.369	*	.314	.236	N/s	.393	.185	*
Ethnicity[a]	1.33	.433	***	.592	.233	**	-.534	1.45	N/s	2.01	.330	***
Education (3-category scale)	-.031	.198	N/s				-.117	.112	N/s	.117	.112	N/s
Currently unemployed (yes = 1)	-.119	.602	N/s				-2.33	1.44	N/s	-2.33	1.44	N/s
Satisfaction with democracy (4-point scale)	-.393	.165	**	-.365	.212	N/s	-.176	.174	N/s	-.093	.153	N/s
Model B: Ideology and party popularity with prior controls												
Left-right ideological self-placement (10-pt scale)	-.050	.066	N/s	-.009	.075	N/s	.206	.065	***	.142	.052	***
Like the radical right party (10-point scale)	.761	.057	***	.596	.067	***	.797	.066	***	.552	.046	***
Model A: Nagelkerke R^2	.169			.089			.024			.121		
Model B: Nagelkerke R^2	.613			.470			.517			.477		
Model B: Percentage correctly predicted	88%			95%			92%			88%		
Number of cases per nation	817			913			1,537			1,219		

Note: The table presents the results of binomial logit analysis models where the dependent variable is whether the respondent reported voting for the relevant radical right party in each country. See note for Table 6.1. Ethnicity is defined by the linguistic majority in each country (1), or the linguistic minority (o), based on the primary language spoken at home. Note that since self-employment was not included in Module II of the CSES, the Goldthorpe-Heath class classification could not be constructed, so this was dropped from the analysis for consistent comparison across the countries.

Sources: Canada, Norway, and Switzerland – The Comparative Study of Electoral Systems, Module I 1996–2001. France – The Comparative Study of Electoral Systems, Module II 2001–2005.

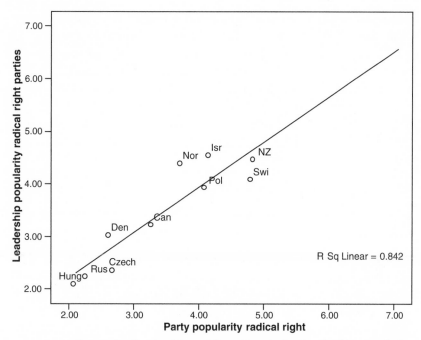

FIGURE 9.3. Comparing Leadership and Party Popularity. Leadership popularity and party popularity for the six largest parties were both estimated by respondents in each country using ten-point scales, ranging from dislike (o) to like (10). *Source:* Calculated from the Comparative Study of Electoral Systems 1996–2001.

Among specific factors, many accounts emphasize that leadership plays a particularly important role in radical right popularity, where studies stress the importance of figures such as Haider, Le Pen, and Zhirinovsky in generating support for their parties. The analysis of the survey evidence available in the CSES showed that leadership and party popularity were closely associated in each country; the strong correlation (R = .804) is illustrated in Figure 9.3. The leader was slightly ahead of levels of party popularity in a few countries, notably in Israel, as well as in the Fremskrittspartiet in Norway, the latter perhaps because the leader's long-standing control was such that it was sometimes described as 'Hagen's party.'[35] By contrast, despite his high profile and long-standing role, support for Christoph Blocher fell slightly behind the general popularity of the Swiss People's Party. From this cross-sectional evidence, however, it remains difficult to determine any independent effect from party leaders per se. Clearly contingent factors will play a role in any particular election, such as the media coverage which the parties receive, the appeal of specific party leaders, or the salience of immigration on the issue agenda. Specific events will also help to flesh out explanations of specific results, exemplified by the assassination of Pym Fortuyn before polling day, the unexpected success of Le Pen in coming second ahead of Jospin in May 2002, and the merger of the Reform/Alliance/Conservative parties in Canada. But a large part of the reason why people vote for the radical right can be explained fairly successfully by similar factors to those which also explain support for other types of parties, namely the ideological location of parties and voters (within institutional contexts) and the affective partisan orientations of voters, as well as the usual sociodemographic cleavages in the electorate.

CONCLUSIONS

Previous supply-side accounts suggest that variations in the success of the radical right can be attributed in large part to the ideological position of the mainstream parties and the opportunities this provides for the radical right. The argument developed in this study suggest that party competition is indeed an important aspect of the explanation for radical right success, but that what is more important is how far the ideological location of radical right parties works within the context of electoral rules and the distribution of public opinion. The core thesis of this book is that the broader institutional context, particularly the electoral rules, affects the electoral strategies that radical right parties adopt to maximize their appeal, and hence that the role of ideological cues and populist appeals vary in generating voting support for these parties. This account emphasizes the role of electoral incentives for spatial patterns of party competition. Three conclusions can be drawn from the available expert and mass survey evidence considered in this chapter.

The analysis based on a comparison of how the electorate perceived the ideological position of parties in thirty nations supports the thesis that party competition is clustered more closely around the median voter in most majoritarian systems, while being dispersed more centrifugally across the whole ideological spectrum from far left to far right in most PR systems. This provides consistent support for the institutionally constrained proximity model of party behavior presented in this study.

It is more difficult to test the proximity model of voting behavior for the radical right. Nevertheless the available evidence in the CSES survey in the pooled thirteen-nation models indicates that both ideological and populist appeals are part of the explanation for the attraction of radical right parties; indeed once these factors were entered into the pooled-sample models, ideological values and affective orientations toward parties reduced the significance of almost all of the social-demographic variables.

Lastly the illustrative case studies of Canada, France, Switzerland, and Norway serve to support the broader claim that the electoral system also plays a role in party strategies and voting behavior; while ideology and partisanship are both important in predicting voting support for the Swiss People's Party and the Norwegian Progress Party, only the indicators of partisanship (not ideology) proved significant in the elections concerning the Canadian Reform Party and the French Front National, held under majoritarian rules.

The theory that we have presented concerning the incentives facing vote-maximizing parties therefore goes some way further down the path of explaining the success of the radical right in some countries and not others. Electoral rules are understood to generate certain important mechanical and psychological effects. First, if challengers do not believe that they stand any chance of being elected in majoritarian systems, the existence of strong electoral thresholds may deter any radical right activists from channeling their energies into political parties; instead they may prefer to mobilize through other organizations, such as social movements and interest groups. If activists do decide to challenge elections through working within party organizations, the mechanical effects of the higher vote thresholds found in majoritarian electoral systems mean that most will fail to gain elected office, with the status, visibility, and resources that entails. Without such resources, radical right parties remain poorly institutionalized extraparliamentary bodies which have problems in maintaining any continuity, becoming subject to internal party factionalization and fragmentation. And if they fight elections, over a succession of elections, majoritarian systems are likely to generate rational vote-maximizing incentives for successful radical right parties to focus upon populist strategies and more moderate ideological appeals, which are necessary for them to get elected.

What we have not yet had a chance to consider are the conditions for radical right parties not just to make sporadic gains but also to sustain their success over a series of elections, and in particular how far organizational development and consolidation are necessary. To consider these issues, the next chapter goes on to compare a series of case studies, including

Britain, where the radical right have failed to make headway despite secular dealignment; the Netherlands and the United States, where there have been occasional 'deviating' elections with temporary sudden advances but equally sudden falls; and Austria, France, and Canada, where radical right parties have consolidated their position after experiencing an initial breakthrough.

10

Consolidating Party Organizations

Previous chapters suggest that party strategy when emphasizing ideological or populist appeals plays a vital role in determining the electoral fortunes of the contemporary radical right, within institutional constraints. Yet the cross-national survey evidence considered so far, while essential for constructing a picture of the factors associated with individual-level voting behavior and the outcome of specific contests, cannot demonstrate the conditions necessary for sustained radical right success over a series of elections. Fringe and minor electoral parties often remain fragile and unstable organizations, vulnerable to unexpected shocks caused by internal organizational splits, difficult leadership transitions, factional rivalries, or sudden scandals. The history of the radical right is littered with short-lived flash parties, exemplified by the Poujadist movement in France, the Reform Party in the United States, and Lijst Pym Fortuyn in the Netherlands. Such parties can surge into the headlines on a tidal wave of public protest, to the consternation of many commentators, gaining seats in 'deviating' elections, but they can equally suddenly fall back into obscurity when circumstances change. Without ballast, they bob in the wake of government and opposition popularity. Minor parties can also experience a precipitate rise and an equally sudden decline. The Freiheitliche Partei Österreichs became part of the ÖVP coalition government in spring 2000, for example, with the support of one in four voters, but their share of the popular vote plummeted to just 10% four years later. Many reasons probably contributed toward the decline in FPÖ fortunes, including organizational difficulties illustrated by public conflict between the conservative nationalist wing and the more pragmatic faction within the parliamentary party, and problems of ineffective communications by the party leader.[1]

By contrast, minor parties which have developed effective party organizations and forged more enduring roots among activists can be expected to prove more resilient to sudden fluctuations of electoral fortunes. They may experience a breakthrough into minor party status in a 'critical' election, and then manage to consolidate and build upon this success in subsequent contests. In these circumstances, certain radical right parties have proved more durable. The Alleanza Nationale, for example, repackaged in 1994 as the Movimento Sociale Italiano, was first founded almost six decades ago. Le Pen's Front National has survived turbulent electoral peaks and troughs in a long series of elections for thirty years, as has the Fremskrittspartiet in Norway. The question is whether many of the parties under comparison have built and consolidated effective party organizations to maintain them through gains and losses.

To consider these issues, Section I in this chapter develops a theoretical framework based on classifying types of elections based on the strength of party-voter alignments. Section II then applies this framework by comparing contests where the radical right have, and have not, steadily advanced into power over successive contests. The chapter compares six case studies which are selected from among established democracies and affluent postindustrial economies and which demonstrate party competition within both majoritarian electoral systems and adversarial democracies (including contests in Britain, Canada, and the United States) and also within PR elections and consensus democracies (exemplified by elections in Austria and the Netherlands).[2] The case-study examples illustrate the conditions facilitating persistent success among the radical right. Admittedly the evidence about the importance of party organizations remains less systematic than in several earlier chapters, as we lack much reliable comparative data on matters such as party membership and financial resources. Nevertheless this dimension remains an important part of the theoretical framework for explaining radical right success and some of the cross-national contrasts can be illustrated from the cases.

The evidence presented here suggests that, by themselves, trends in partisan dealignment fail to account satisfactorily for radical right success; many commentators highlight Britain, for example, as a country exemplifying secular dealignment, with steadily weakening party loyalties and class identities, but, despite a few limited and sporadic victories, the National Front, BNP, and UKIP currently remain marginal forces on the periphery of the political system. Yet a loosening of traditional voter linkages with the mainstream parties does facilitate intermittent cases of deviating elections, exemplified by the meteoric rise of LPF popularity in the May 2002 election in the Netherlands and by Perot's Reform Party vote in the 1992 U.S. presidential election. More importantly, the occasional 'critical' election represents an enduring breakthrough for radical right parties, and a long-term realignment in traditional patterns of party competition. This process is exemplified by breakthroughs for radical right parties which subsequently consolidated, notably the success of the FN in the 1984 European elections in France, the sudden shift in FPÖ support during the 1986 Austrian election, and the watershed for the Reform Party in the 1993 Canadian election. The conclusion builds on this framework to consider the conditions under which the radical right can consolidate its rise and how we should interpret the occasional 'flash' success.

I A FRAMEWORK FOR CLASSIFYING ELECTIONS AND PARTY COMPETITION

To understand the conditions under which radical right parties can experience a sudden electoral breakthrough, and the conditions facilitating a longer-term process of consolidation in their fortunes, elections can be classified into distinct categories. The fivefold typology employed here as a heuristic framework distinguishes among maintaining alignments, secular dealignments, deviating dealignments, secular realignments, and critical realignments.[3] These types of election each have important consequences for the radical right and also more broadly for party systems, understood here as the stable and enduring pattern of interaction and competition among political parties in any country. Particular parties can and do experience fluctuating electoral fortunes in each contest, but the party system represents the broader and longer-lasting features of competition in government and in the electorate among all parties which persist over a series of elections.[4] The conceptual framework helps to interpret the results of specific elections and the way that these have, or have not, altered the long-term fortunes of radical right parties and enduring patterns of party competition.

(i) Maintaining Alignments

The prospects for any advance by new radical right challengers are theorized to be least favorable in elections characterized as maintaining alignments which essentially reflect the status quo in the party system. In such contests, no strong issues, events, or major shifts in public policy deflect citizens from expressing their habitual electoral preferences, and each party typically mobilizes its 'normal base' of support. This concept requires splitting the actual vote cast for a party into two parts: a 'normal' or baseline vote to be expected from a group, based on its behavior over successive elections in the past, and the current deviation from that norm, due to the immediate circumstances of the specific election. This concept draws upon the traditional 'Michigan' model originally developed in *The American Voter* (1960), whereby most voters are perceived to be psychologically attached to parties for long periods of time, perhaps for their lifetime, through developing stable social and partisan alignments.[5] During the 1960s and early 1970s, partisan identification was found to be closely related to voting choice in the United States and in many other established democracies which had developed a series of national election surveys, such as Britain, France, and Norway.[6]

Maintaining elections are characterised by electoral flux more than flow; a few waverers shift between parties, leaving the balance of power largely unchanged. In these contests, the underlying party system persists largely unaltered; they rarely produce much incumbency turnover, let alone changes of government, allowing minimal opportunities for new parties to challenge the status quo. The conventional wisdom, accepted during the 1960s and 1970s, assumed that most elections fell into this category and as a result party systems were largely 'frozen' in established democracies, so that outsiders had few realistic prospects of entering parliament, let alone government. Lipset and Rokkan's classic account regarded the pattern of party competition as highly stable, predictable, and unchanging after the initial expansion of the mass franchise in European democracies, based on enduring links which parties forged with core social groups, leaving minimal room for new challengers: "The party systems of the 1960s reflect, with few but significant exceptions, the cleavage structures of the 1920s."[7] Maintaining elections generate minimal shocks to disturb the status quo in parliament and in government, effectively eliminating new challengers. As a result, maintaining elections provide the fewest opportunities for either incremental or stepped gains in the electoral fortunes of new radical right parties, or for other insurgent parties such as the Greens or nationalists, as the traditional mainstream parties consolidate and maintain their usual share of the vote.

(ii) Secular Dealigning Elections

Secular dealigning elections are characterized by loosening bonds linking voters with mainstream parties. In these elections, the traditional party system in each country may persist through institutional inertia, and indeed the government in power may be returned to office, as in maintaining contests, but nevertheless beneath the ice the underlying conditions of electoral support become destabilized, less predictable, and potentially more fluid. This expands the opportunities for fringe or minor radical right parties to expand their share of the vote, at least on a temporary basis, from citizens dissatisfied with the mainstream status quo or unhappy with the government.

With secular dealignment, the ability of social and partisan identities to predict voting behavior is gradually weakened in a steady series of incremental steps over successive contests, like glaciers eroding rock. During the early 1960s, most voters in established democracies were regarded as largely stable in their voting choices, due to enduring social identities and long-term party loyalties which framed attitudes toward voting choices. This stability was attributed to a cohesive socialization process reinforcing social cues and party identification acquired within the family, school, work group, and social milieu. Lipset and Rokkan suggested that patterns of party politics reflected the main social class, religious, and center-periphery cleavages in the European electorate. Since the early 1970s, there is considerable evidence that changes in the workforce and process of secularization have gradually worn away some of the most important class and religious identities which used to anchor voters to parties over successive elections, so that today many contests are expected to fall into the dealignment category.[8] Such elections are expected to expand the opportunities for radical right challengers to gradually improve their share of the vote over a series of contests. But any support they gather is expected to prove conditional upon specific contingent factors – such as the appeal of individual leaders, the policy issues they emphasize, the effectiveness of their campaign organization and political communications, and their general party image, as well as the popularity of other parties.

(iii) Deviating Elections

Secular and deviating cases of dealignment are closely related, but they differ in a specific election primarily in the pace and durability of electoral change. The long-term process of dealignment can also be expected to facilitate occasional *deviating* elections, characterized by a temporary rapid reversal in the 'normal' share of the vote for major parties, but one which proves highly transient in subsequent contests. The change can be best understood as one of 'trendless fluctuations' or 'impulse-decay,' where a temporary shift is not sustained, leaving no lasting imprint on the party system. Such contests are characterized by dramatic negative protests against the governing parties, for example concerning a series of highly publicized ministerial scandals or a dramatic failure of government policy, which cause dissatisfied supporters to defect temporarily to minor parties, only to return home again in the next contest. 'Second-order' mid-term contests are particularly prone to fall into this category where voters register a temporary mid-term kick against the party or parties in power in local or regional elections, by-elections, and elections to the European Parliament, without the risk of causing the government to fall.[9] In deviating cases the breakdown of traditional party-voter linkages is more sudden, dramatic, and sharp, for example due to institutional reforms to the electoral system, or decisive events transforming the political agenda, such as the impact of the end of the Cold War on foreign policy and security issues. In such contests, we expect that the radical right fringe and minor parties and candidates can suddenly surge in popularity, unexpectedly gaining votes and seats, but that this proves transitory as they fail to consolidate their gains. Deviating elections, where radical right support proves ephemeral, while dramatic, usually have few long-term consequences for the party system.

(iv) Secular Realigning Elections

By contrast, secular realigning elections generate an evolutionary and cumulative *strengthening* in a new party system, meaning an enduring pattern of party competition in government and the electorate which persists over a series of elections. The idea of realignment has attracted a substantial literature, and the utility of this notion as a way of distinguishing distinct periods in the history of American party politics continues to be debated.[10] For V. O. Key, the American party system was thought to display a stable equilibrium for long periods of time; over successive maintaining elections, the pattern of voting by Southerners, African-Americans, or Italian immigrants was regarded as largely predictable. But in the exceptional cases of realigning elections, the American party system was thought to experience an abrupt but enduring change, with long-term consequences for patterns of party competition, for party identification in the electorate, and for governance and public policy, which persisted over a long series of contests.[11] The potential impact of realigning elections is most evident where radical right parties have made a consistent and sustained series of advances at multiple levels over successive contests, including in local and regional councils, the European Parliament, and national parliaments, thereby gaining greater status, power, and resources. The impact of any sudden growth in radical right voting support can be expected to prove more enduring if the party use this as a springboard to nurture a grassroots mass movement, if they win seats in a range of local, regional, and national bodies, and if they expand their membership and activist base, consolidate their party organization, and accumulate financial resources.

Secular realignment is a familiar model in political sociology, giving primacy to broad sociodemographic developments which gradually alter the structural basis of the population, workforce, and community. These processes are exemplified by patterns of generational turnover, where the young gradually replace older cohorts in the electorate; by significant population migrations within or across national borders, such as the influx of Latin American Hispanics seeking work in California, Texas, and New Mexico; by processes of secularization reducing religiosity in most postindustrial societies; and by long-term socioeconomic trends, notably the decline of the manufacturing industry and the expansion of the service sector economy. Their impact upon voting behavior is exemplified by the evolution of the modern gender gap in many affluent nations, where younger generations of women have gradually moved leftward, and also by the erosion of churchgoing habits, the lower salience of religious values, and the weakening links connecting the church to Christian Democratic parties.[12] Long-term patterns of party support can also be gradually transformed by the enfranchisement of new groups of voters, for example the 1964 U.S. Civil Rights Act expanding voting opportunities for African-Americans, and the impact of the reduction in the qualifying age of the franchise on voting turnout. The secular realignment model is understood to produce an incremental, durable, and persistent strengthening in the long-term contours of party support. In this context, any electoral gains made by the radical right are expected gradually to consolidate and institutionalize over a series of contests. Voter-party bonds may strengthen, for example if voters develop habitual preferences for radical right parties, or if an initial breakthrough gives the party access to public funding, media visibility, and the resources and legitimacy that derive from elected office, so that they strengthen campaign organizations and build a core grassroots base of party activists and loyalists who will stick with them through good times and bad.

(v) Critical Elections

Certain exceptional contests, however, can be understood to represent *critical elections*, characterized by abrupt, significant, and durable realignments in the electorate with major consequences for the long-term party order. While *secular* realignments produce a gradual shift in the electorate over successive elections, with the more or less continuous creation of new party-voter linkages and the decay of the old, by contrast *critical* elections generate a more rapid realignment of the party system in government and in the mass electorate. Such contests have a significant impact, not just by altering the electoral fortunes of a single party, but also by generating an enduring shift in general patterns of party competition and in the dominant policy agenda of successive governments. In this sense, the pendulum of party competition ratchets decisively in a new direction. The periods before, and after, these contests can be regarded, rightly, as distinct historical eras. While every contest sees some electoral flux back and forth between parties, lasting transformations of the party order occur rarely. V. O. Key identified critical elections as those "in which more or less profound readjustments occur in the relations of power within the community, and in which new and durable electoral groupings are formed."[13] Critical elections move the party system from equilibrium to a new level, which subsequently stabilizes and consolidates, in a model of punctured equilibrium. Maintaining elections remain the norm, due to a process of dynamic equilibrium, but the occasional experience of a profound external 'shock' can produce stepped change, before maintaining elections again set in producing another period of institutional stasis and party-voter alignments.

The standard exemplar of this phenomenon in the American literature is the 1928–1932 American presidential elections, which saw the assembly of Roosevelt's New Deal coalition, securing Democratic control of the White House for a quarter century and still evident in faded form today.[14] Experience of the Great Depression was thought to reinforce cross-cutting issue cleavages which subsequently consolidated around fundamentally different visions of the role of government in society presented by Democrats and Republicans. Other historical examples include the 1924 and 1945 general elections in Britain, and probably the 1997 Labour landslide as well, as watersheds where the party order changed at

Westminster, and changed decisively.[15] Contemporary illustrations also include the 1993 Canadian election, which saw the meltdown of the Progressive Conservative governing party, the rise of Reform, and widening regional cleavages in party politics; the 1994 Italian election, witnessing the disintegration of the long-dominant Italian Christian Democrats; and the 1993 New Zealand general election held under the Mixed Member Proportional electoral system, which produced a dramatic fragmentation of the traditional two-party system. Critical elections are often attributed to ideological causes and specific events, notably the emergence of new, salient, polarizing issues which cross-cut traditional left-right ideological cleavages, or the growing irrelevance of old divisions, scrambling and reassembling the familiar landscape of party competition. As V. O. Key noted: "Only events with widespread and powerful impact or issues touching deep emotions produce abrupt changes."[16] But, as the New Zealand case shows, fundamental reforms to the electoral system can also generate these changes. In critical elections, radical right parties have not just achieved a short-term victory, for example based on a temporary protest vote, but they have managed to consolidate their support and alter patterns of competition in the party system within each country. Through substantial parliamentary gains, these parties have an opportunity to improve their resources and status, institutionalize their organization, and consolidate processes of leadership transitions, and thereby sustain popular success over a further series of contests.

II EVIDENCE AND CASES

The insights provided by this fivefold typology can prove most valuable when interpreting the outcome of specific elections and the implications of the results for the radical right, in particular when judging whether any sudden breakthrough which they experience is likely to be a relatively transient shock to the party system (classified as a deviating election), or a more enduring change in the traditional party system (if regarded as a critical election). It often remains difficult or even impossible for contemporary commentators to make any satisfactory classification immediately after any specific contest but, with the benefits of hindsight and the insights derived from analysis of a series of national election surveys, contests can be classified more reliably based on subsequent developments over a series of elections. In considering how best to classify and interpret elections using this typology, this study uses a series of indicators.

TABLE 10.1. *Selected Election Case Studies Illustrating the Typology*

Secular dealignment	Deviating elections	Critical realigning elections
UK National Front and British National Party	Dutch Lijst Pym Fortuyn (LPF) (2002)	Austrian Freiheitlíche Partei Öesterreichs (FPÖ) (1986)
	U.S. Reform Party (1992–96)	French Front National (FN) (1984) Canadian Reform Party (1993)

In particular, the most important evidence concerns any changes in party identification over successive elections; maintaining elections see little change in the strength of these attachments, whereas weakening party identification suggests dealignment, and strengthening identification suggests a realignment process. The degree and persistence of electoral change are also important indicators, along with any major shifts in ideological competition. In particular, elections which involve a major breakthrough by the radical right are interpreted here as a critical realignment only if they fulfill certain strict conditions, namely: (i) if any sudden surge in the share of votes or seats won by a radical right party is consolidated and sustained over a series of subsequent elections; (ii) if the party strengthens its support among core identifiers; and also (iii) if other parties respond to the advance of the radical right by changing their ideological position and shifting further rightward. The typology can be illustrated by considering six cases, selected to compare radical right parties seeking office under different electoral rules, as shown in Table 10.1.

The Progressive Weakening of Partisan Attachments

The long-term erosion of social and party identities in electoral behavior, and the growth of dealignment, have now been established by a large body of evidence in many established democracies.[17] The most comprehensive recent comparison by Dalton and Wattenberg collected data from the series of National Election Studies and Eurobarometer (EB) surveys conducted in advanced industrialized democracies. The study reported that the proportion of the electorate willing to express a party identification fell significantly over time in thirteen out of nineteen postindustrial societies and the erosion of 'strong' party identifiers who felt very close to a party was even more widespread and consistent cross-nationally.[18] To update

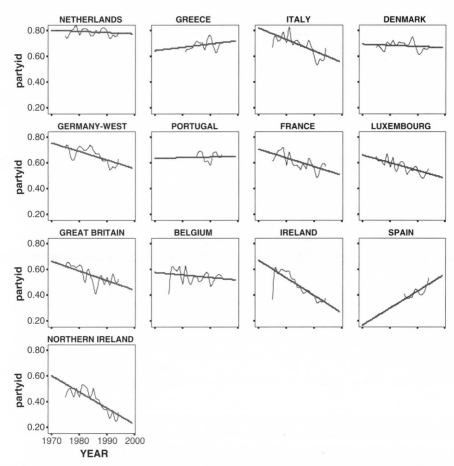

FIGURE 10.1. Trends in Party Identification, EU 1970–1999. Q: "Do you consider yourself to be close to any particular party? <If yes> Do you consider yourself to be very close, fairly close, or merely a sympathizer?" % 'Yes.' The proportion 'yes,' from 1970 to 1999, and the regression line summarizing the trend. *Source:* The Mannheim Eurobarometer Trend File, 1970–1999.

this analysis, and to replicate earlier work by Schmitt and Holmberg,[19] patterns of partisan attachments can be compared in thirteen societies based on the Eurobarometer. The Mannheim Eurobarometer Trend File has integrated these biannual surveys on a consistent basis from 1970 to 1999. The Mannheim data facilitates analysis of the trends in the proportion of all party identifiers (Figure 10.1), while the regression lines summarize the direction of the trends and their significance across the series (in Table 10.2). The results clearly illustrate and further confirm

TABLE 10.2. *Trends in Party Identification, EU 1970–1999*

	All partisan identifiers			Strong partisan identifiers		
	B	Std. error	Sig.	B	Std. error	Sig.
France	−.007	.000	.000	−.035	.003	.000
Belgium	−.002	.000	.000	−.038	.003	.000
Netherlands	−.001	.000	.008	−.039	.003	.000
West Germany	−.007	.000	.000	−.027	.003	.000
Italy	−.009	.000	.000	−.021	.002	.000
Luxembourg	−.006	.001	.000	−.027	.005	.000
Denmark	−.001	.000	.031	−.034	.003	.000
Ireland	−.014	.000	.000	.011	.004	.003
Britain	−.008	.000	.000	.029	.003	.000
Northern Ireland	−.013	.001	.000	.016	.008	.050
Greece	.003	.001	.000	−.039	.004	.000
Spain	.013	.001	.000	.049	.012	.000
Portugal	.001	.001	.646	−.072	.015	.000

Note: Binomial logistic (logit) regression analysis of the effect of year on party identification as the dependent variable, coded as a dummy variable. Q: "Do you consider yourself to be close to any particular party? <If yes> Do you consider yourself to be very close, fairly close, or merely a sympathizer?" 'All' % 'Yes.' 'Strong' identifiers are 'very close.'
Source: The Mannheim Eurobarometer Trend File, 1970–1999.

the steep erosion of party identification found in seven of the thirteen European societies under comparison, plus the more gentle subsidence of party identities occurring in another three societies. The only exceptions, although they are important ones, are the newer Mediterranean democracies, which experience a slight growth in the proportion of party identifiers over a shorter time period, a statistically significant pattern in Greece and Spain (although not Portugal). It seems plausible that the particular historical experience of autocracy and third-wave democracy in these countries may have maintained or even strengthened party loyalties, although unfortunately the difference in time periods of the available comparisons based on EB surveys makes it difficult to test this proposition with any certainty. A significant decline is also observed for the proportion of 'strong' party identifiers in nine European societies under comparison, although not in Ireland, Spain, and (contrary to some national election study data) Britain.

Dispute in the literature continues to surround the interpretation of these trends; as Figure 10.2 illustrates, the magnitude, pace, and precise timing of partisan dealignment are far from identical in every country. The idea of party identification may also have less meaning in European

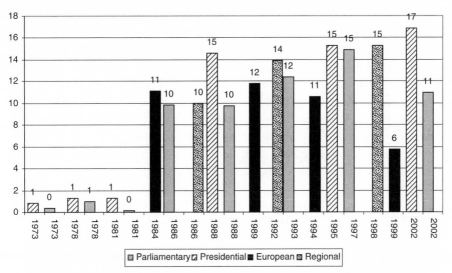

FIGURE 10.2. Trends in Voting Support for the Front National, France 1973–2002. The percentage share of the vote won by the Front National, including the first-round vote in second-ballot elections. *Sources:* Thomas T. Mackie and Richard Rose. 1991. *The International Almanac of Electoral History.* Washington, DC: CQ Press; Tom Mackie and Richard Rose. 1997. *A Decade of Election Results: Updating the International Almanac.* Studies in Public Policy. Glasgow: University of Strathclyde; *Elections around the World.* www.electionworld.org.

parliamentary democracies, where this measure often tends to fluctuate consistently with voting choice, rather than acting as a long-term stable 'home' anchoring loyalists over successive elections.[20] Indeed the limited panel survey election data which is available in the United States also throws doubt on the validity of the basic 'anchoring' proposition, even in America.[21] Yet at the same time, despite these serious doubts, alternative indicators, including measures of public confidence and trust in parties, also indicate growing skepticism about political parties as institutions in many established democracies.[22]

Moreover the picture painted by the survey data is supported by other important aggregate indicators of system-level electoral change in these countries, which is consistent with the thesis of partisan dealignment (although theoretically these indicators could always rest upon other causes, such as the impact of top-down shifts in party strategies or electoral reform). This includes evidence of declining party membership, growing electoral volatility, the greater fragmentation of party systems, more split-ticket voting, the later timing of electoral decisions, and increasingly leader-centered campaigns.[23] For example, Dalton, McAllister, and Wattenberg compared twenty-one advanced industrial democracies, and found that party fragmentation increased during the last four decades in two-thirds of the countries, measured by the effective number of parliamentary parties which existed in the 1950s compared with the 1990s.[24] An alternative measure of system-level change is the share of the vote won by 'new' parties in Western Europe, defined as those which began to contest elections no earlier than 1960. Mair found that the proportion grew steadily decade by decade: new parties won 3.9% of the vote during the 1960s, 9.7% during the 1970s, 15.3% during the 1980s, and 23.7% during the 1990s.[25] Total electoral volatility at aggregate level can be measured using the Pedersen index, summarizing the aggregate electoral gains of all winning parties in a given election.[26] A comparison of fifteen Western European nations found that volatility stayed fairly steady from the 1950s until the 1980s, in the range of 7.9 to 8.8%, but during the last decade this index rose sharply to 12.6%.[27]

What are the implications for the radical right? Any long-term weakening of the bonds anchoring voters to parties and growing electoral volatility expands the opportunities for newer challengers to mobilize support and (within institutional constraints) to break through into elected office. More voters become up for grabs on a contingent basis, which could plausibly lead toward more short-term support for radical right parties based on the factors already seen as important in earlier chapters, notably disaffection with the government and the mainstream opposition, combined with the particular ideological strategies and signature issues they adopt. The process of secular dealignment in many established democracies since the 1970s, as well as weak party-voter alignments in newer democracies, could therefore be an important part of the underlying conditions generating openings for new challenger radical right parties. Certainly the few exceptional cases where partisan alignments have not deteriorated – Portugal, Spain, and Greece – are also ones where radical right parties currently remain extremely marginal.

Nevertheless this common claim needs certain important qualifications. By undermining established party systems, the process of electoral dealignment can benefit any challenger parties and independent candidates from across the political spectrum, not just the radical right. Therefore elections characterized by secular dealignment should perhaps be understood as representing a necessary but *not* a sufficient condition facilitating the advance of the radical right; what matters is how far challenger parties take advantage of the greater permeability provided by this context in crafting their electoral appeals and ideological strategies. There is nothing automatic about partisan dealignment causing the rise of the right. Moreover, dealignment implies that any electoral gains made by radical right parties are based upon contingent factors – whether disaffection with government, the popularity of leaders such as Haider and Le Pen, or the salience of the issues of cultural protectionism – so under these conditions these parties remain equally vulnerable to sudden voting losses in subsequent contests. Support remains conditional and temporary, rather than enduring and loyalist.

SECULAR DEALIGNING ELECTIONS: BRITAIN

Social and partisan dealignment is a long-term process which has occurred in most established democracies, whereas, as we have seen, the radical right demonstrates a highly varied electoral performance in these countries. Despite the overall pattern, there is, in fact, only a poor fit at macro level between the countries which have witnessed the most successful advance of the radical right and those which have seen the greatest fall in party loyalties. Table 10.2 shows that some of the clearest evidence for partisan dealignment since the early 1970s can been found in Ireland, West Germany, and Britain, for example, all countries where radical right parties have failed to establish a serious and sustained challenge.[28] By contrast, the proportion of partisan identifiers did not fall so sharply in Denmark and Belgium, both countries where radical right parties have established a very successful and enduring presence in parliament. In fact, there are numerous examples of countries where radical right-wing parties have failed to make any sustained impact over a long series of contests, despite substantial evidence of dealignment in the mass electorate, including the failure of the National Front in Britain and in Francophone Belgium, as well as the Republikaner Party in Germany (despite some minor fluctuations in support for this party during the early 1990s after unification). The reason is that partisan loyalties are only *one* important legal barrier to new parties, and their erosion is insufficient to facilitate the rise of the radical right if there are prior institutional constraints, derived from majoritarian elections or barriers to ballot access.

The British NF and BNP

This pattern is perhaps best illustrated by the British case, where both the National Front and the British National Party have failed to break through in successive elections, despite substantial evidence for social and party dealignment in the British electorate, as well as the growth of a strongly multicultural society profoundly transformed by patterns of ethnic and religious diversity, and the erosion of national borders caused by membership of the European Union, all conditions which might be considered conducive to the advance of the radical right.

The National Front party was formed in 1967 in Britain following the merger of the Racial Preservation Society, the British National Party, and the League of Empire Loyalists. The NF made repeated attempts to win Westminster seats during the 1970s, fielding 10 parliamentary candidates in the 1970 general election, 54 in February 1974, 90 in October 1974, and 303 in 1979. Yet at the peak of their popularity, during the mid-1970s, the party achieved a negligible share of the nationwide vote (less than 1%). The NF had became engaged in violent scuffles in mass street demonstrations, actively opposed by the Anti-Nazi League and the Labour Party, so their image became indelibly associated with extremist skinhead and Union-Jack-wearing football-hooligan gangs of young men. The liberal consensus in British mainstream party politics agreed not to play the race card, although in January 1978 (in the run-up to the 1979 general election) Mrs. Thatcher came out with a widely publicized television comment in which she claimed that she understood the fears of the British people of being "swamped by people with a different culture." This coded message about Conservative policy toward immigration, and a shift rightward symbolized by Thatcherism, coupled with the steep vote threshold required at Westminster first-past-the-post elections, constituted an insurmountable barrier for the NF. The party had a poor result in the 1979 general election, despite contesting almost half the available seats nationwide.[29] After 1979, the NF split into contending factions, and disappeared as an effective force in national politics, although persisting on the ultrafringe of public life.[30] The new Conservative government introduced the British Nationality Act in 1981, slightly tightening the definition of citizenship and introducing new registration requirements, although this was arguably influenced by the 1981 Brixton riots, and the instinctively populist strain of the party represented by Enoch Powell, as much as by any perceived electoral threat from the NF. Conservative immigration policy was however diluted by the traditional paternalism of the Tory wets in cabinet, led by the Home Secretary, Willie Whitelaw.[31]

The extremist fringe of the public transferred their energies from the National Front to the breakaway British National Party, formed in 1983. Yet this party also failed to achieve more than a negligible share of the vote at Westminster elections; in 2001, for example, the BNP contested 34 out of 659 UK parliamentary seats, achieving 3.7% of the vote in these constituencies.[32] They gain disproportionate campaign publicity among journalists and commentators and perform best at local level, in northern councils like Burnley and Oldham with substantial Asian populations, although there remain fewer than two dozen NF councillors out of almost twenty-two thousand seats in Britain.[33] In the June 2004 local government elections in England and Wales, for example, the party fielded a record number of local candidates (309), had a controversial party political broadcast shown on national TV, and hosted a high profile visit by Jean-Marie Le Pen. Nevertheless, with an average 16.1% of the vote in the wards they fought, the party picked up only four additional council seats, making in the total only twenty-one BNP councillors nationwide.[34]

In the simultaneous British elections to the European Parliament, held under PR rules, the BNP won 808,000 votes (4.9%), an increase, but no seats. The protest vote in these contests mainly benefited the anti-EU UK Independent Party, which doubled its share of the vote to 16.1%, returning a dozen MEPs. A single-issue right-wing party which shares hostility toward Brussels, UKIP advocates British withdrawal from the European Union, but without the overt racist baggage and violent skinhead image which characterize the NF and BNP. UKIP performed well in the European contests, using regional party list PR, but it proved difficult for them to repeat this performance in the 2004 general election, with a broader political agenda, with leadership splits, and with the higher vote thresholds found in single-member plurality districts for Westminster.[35] Long-term processes of secular dealignment facilitate the growth of minor parties, and the conditions should be ripe for radical right parties in Britain, given widespread public hostility toward the entry of asylum seekers and political refugees, as well as pervasive anti-EU sentiments and illiberal attitudes toward Britain's ethnic minorities.[36] Nevertheless the growth of the NF and BNP has been curtailed so far by their extremist image, their narrow, single-issue agenda, and the substantial vote thresholds facing parties contesting the single-member plurality districts, used to date in local council and Westminster elections.

DEVIATING ELECTIONS: THE NETHERLANDS AND THE UNITED STATES

Secular dealignment also facilitates deviating elections, where radical right contenders can occasionally achieve temporary popularity as flash parties, experiencing sudden surges in popular support and short-term seat gains, but then failing to consolidate these advances, with support abruptly melting away in subsequent contests. This pattern was exemplified in earlier decades by the 1959 French election, where a temporary surge in popularity by the Poujadists caused shock waves in the political establishment, as well as by the 1969 American presidential election, where George Wallace's American Independent Party gathered support as a southern backlash against attempts at racial integration, civil rights, and the expansion of the welfare state. Deviating elections are also evident more recently by Perot's success as a third-party challenger in the 1992 and 1996 presidential elections, by Pauline Hanson's One Nation party's prominence on an openly racist anti–Aboriginal-rights platform in the 1999 state elections in Queensland, Australia, by Ny Demokrati's temporary gain of twenty-five seats in the 1991 Swedish election,[37] and most dramatically by Lijst Pym Fortuyn's stunning performance to become the main opposition party on their first attempt in the May 2002 Dutch general election. These contests were widely regarded by contemporary commentators as symbolizing a cataclysmic breakdown of established party systems, but in fact these proved, with the benefit of hindsight, to be strictly temporary phenomena. Deviating elections provide dramatic media headlines, attracting considerable popular and academic attention, but they fail to overturn enduring patterns of party competition.

The Dutch Elections in May 2002 and Lijst Pym Fortuyn

The May 2002 general election in the Netherlands provides a classic illustration of a deviating case. Pym Fortuyn began organizing his party in February 2002, after he was removed as head of the candidate list for the Leefbar Nederland for making controversial statements. A flamboyant personality and strong debater who was an openly gay publicist and former professor, Fortuyn proved a controversial politician who attracted a diverse group of candidates, most without any political experience. The party platform promised the standard radical right policies, including tougher action against immigrants who did not assimilate into Dutch culture, stronger measures against crime, and less government bureaucracy, as well as some moderate social policies reducing teacher shortages in schools and shortening hospital waiting lists. The immigration issue caused heated debates all over the Netherlands. Fortuyn was accused of being a far right racist, an accusation he vehemently denied, and he distanced himself from Le Pen and Haider. He did not advocate deporting immigrants already in the country, nor closing all borders, though he did propose setting an immigration quota that prohibited Muslims from entering the country. In addition, he favored revoking the article of the Dutch constitution which prohibited discrimination. The assassination of Fortuyn by an animal rights activist, Volkert van der Graaf, on 6 May 2002, just nine days before the Dutch general election, led to a sudden surge of support for the Lijst Pym Fortuyn. The party, founded just three months earlier, caused an electoral earthquake by gaining 17% of the national vote and 26 out of 150 members of Parliament, making them the second largest in Parliament.

After a period of negotiations, the party entered coalition government with the Christen Democratisch Appèl (CDA) and the Volkspartij voor Vrijheid en Democratie (VVD), with the cabinet led by Prime Minister Jan Peter Balkenende. Studies suggest that the electoral success of LPF was due to the popularity of Fortuyn among those who had cynical attitudes toward government or who were dissatisfied with the performance of the incumbent government, as well as by attitudes relating to asylum seekers and the integration of foreigners in the country.[38] A critical precondition for their rise was the exceptionally low vote thresholds in the PR nationwide electoral system used in the Netherlands, where any party requires only 0.67% of the national share of the vote to win a parliamentary seat. Yet the sudden LPF advance proved transient; in the months following the election, the recently established party was beset by power struggles between various factions. The news media provided extensive coverage of continuous bickering and scandals within the LPF party as a whole, within their parliament faction, between LPF ministers and high-ranking government officials, and between their officials and the press. Party officials came and went. Moreover, the Balkenende cabinet proved highly unstable, afflicted by the resignation of a series of ministers, including two appointed by the LPF. The party fell apart, without its founder and leader, prior experience of government, and a coherent program. The administration lasted only eighty-six days, the shortest-lived Dutch cabinet in the postwar period. Their most notable decisions were supporting the United States invasion of Iraq and approving EU expansion plans. Lacking experienced political leaders and internally divided, in the January 2003 Tweede Kaamer election which followed the government's collapse the LPF vote faded to just 5.7% (see Table 10.3). Reduced to only eight MPs, the party lost two-thirds of their parliamentary representatives.

Commentators suggest that the populist 'outsider' appeal of the LPF also contributed toward their initial surge, but they lost this advantage

TABLE 10.3. *The Share of the Vote in National Legislative Elections for Relevant Radical Right Electoral Parties in Established Democracies, 1948–2004*

	Canada Ref	Austria VdU/FPÖ	Switzerland SVP	France FN	Norway FrP	Italy MSI/AN	Netherlands LPF	Denmark DF	NZ NZFP	Belgium VlB	Italy LN	Denmark FP	Australia ON
1948						2.0							
1949		11.7											
1950													
1951													
1952													
1953		11.0				5.8							
1954													
1955													
1956		6.5											
1957													
1958						4.8							
1959		7.7											
1960													
1961													
1962		7.1											
1963						5.1							
1964													
1965			11.4										
1966		5.4											
1967			11.0										
1968						4.4							
1969													
1970		5.5											

236

Year										
1971									5.5	
1972								11.0		
1973	15.9				8.7	5.0				
1974									5.4	
1975	13.6				6.1			9.9		
1976										
1977	14.6					1.9				
1978			1.4				0.3	11.6	6.1	
1979	11.0				5.3					
1980										
1981	8.9		1.1			4.5	0.2			
1982										
1983					6.8			11.1	5.0	
1984	3.6		1.4							
1985						3.7	10.0		9.7	
1986										
1987	4.8		1.9		5.9		9.7	11.0		
1988	9.0									2.1
1989						13.0				
1990	6.4		6.6						16.6	
1991					5.4			11.9		
1992		8.7[a]					12.4			18.7
1993				8.4	13.5	6.3				
1994	8.4	8.4							22.6	
1995	6.4		7.8					14.9	21.9	
1996		10.1		13.4	15.7					

(continued)

TABLE 10.3 (continued)

	Canada Ref	Austria VdU/FPÖ	Switzerland SVP	France FN	Norway FrP	Italy MSI/AN	Netherlands LPF	Denmark DF	NZ NZFP	Belgium VlB	Italy LN	Denmark FP	Australia ON
1997	19.4			14.9	15.3								
1998		26.9						7.4				2.4	8.4
1999			23.3						4.3	9.9			
2000	25.5												
2001				11.3	14.7	12.0		12.0			3.9	0.6	4.3
2002		10.0					17.0		10.4				
2003			26.6							11.6			
2004							5.7						
MEAN 1948+	16.4	10.9	14.0	8.1	8.1	7.3	11.4	9.7	9.1	5.2	7.8	9.1	6.4
MEAN 1990+	21.2	19.6	19.2	12.9	12.1	11.7	11.4	9.7	9.1	9.0	7.8	3.9	6.4

Note: Relevant electoral parties are defined as those winning on average at least 3% of the vote in successive elections to the lower house of the national legislature held since 1990. Radical right parties are defined as those with a mean combined score on the Lubbers expert judgment scales of 9.0 or more out of 10.

[a] The 1992 result was for the Lega Lombarda, the predecessor of the Lega Nord.

Sources: Thomas T. Mackie and Richard Rose. 1991. The International Almanac of Electoral History. Washington, DC: CQ Press; Tom Mackie and Richard Rose. 1997. A Decade of Election Results: Updating the International Almanac. Studies in Public Policy. Glasgow: University of Strathclyde; Elections around the World www.electionworld.org.

once they became part of the coalition government. This parallels the erosion of support for the FPÖ after they entered into coalition government in Austria, so this may represent a classic dilemma facing populist antiestablishment parties, undermining their long-term success in government.[39] The contests which followed in the June 2004 elections to the European Parliament saw no LPF members elected, and their long-term prospects as a viable force in Dutch politics must remain in doubt, despite continuing disaffection with mainstream party politics in the Netherlands. The initial success of this party in May 2002 exemplifies deviating elections which generate a short, sharp, shock to the party system, representing dramatic events for headline writers, but without lasting consequences for long-term patterns of party competition. Their meteoric rise and fall, and the subsequent period of political instability and upheaval, did have consequences, however, for the Netherlands, as constitutional reform arose on the political agenda, with debate about electoral reform designed to strength linkages between representatives and constituents.[40]

Perot's Reform Party and the 1992 U.S. Presidential Election

Also in this category, H. Ross Perot's candidacy in the United States, and the subsequent fragmentation of the Reform Party, provides insights into the reasons why American independent candidates and third parties have had so little success.[41] It can be argued that Perot had little in common with the virulently anti-immigrant racist appeal typical of radical right parties such as the Vlaams Blok, FN, or FPÖ, and indeed the Reform Party could be regarded as more center-right than many others in this study, as well as being a one-man show rather than an organized mass-based party. Nevertheless Perot emphasized many classically populist, antiestablishment, and 'outsider' themes in his campaign, adopting folksy appeals and simplistic slogans designed to attract 'the little man,' and focusing mainly upon the need to reduce the size of government and levels of taxation, with the anti-NAFTA theme tapped into fears of 'foreigners' stripping away American jobs and companies.[42]

In the early primary season for the Clinton-Bush 1992 presidential election, Ross Perot was a guest on CNN's *Larry King Live* when he first declared that he would run for president if citizens would get him nominated on the ballots in all fifty states. This triggered a remarkable outpouring of volunteer activism, especially among those most negative toward government institutions and the major party candidates; for example supporters from every state started collecting the necessary nomination petitions to get Perot into the race, while over one million people were estimated to have called the 800 telephone number asking Ross Perot to be their presidential candidate.[43] The campaign suffered, however, from the candidate's erratic behavior; in mid-July, despite success in state petitions, Perot suddenly withdrew from the contest, shocking his volunteer activists; then in early September, after the last petitions were validated, Perot did a volte-face and stepped in again by announcing his official candidacy. By the fall, his support stood at around 5–7% in the opinion polls and he was included in all the presidential debates, as well as airing thirty-minute 'info-mercials.' On polling day, Perot eventually won one-fifth of the popular vote across the country, with the support of almost 20 million Americans, a remarkable figure, easily the best result for a third-party candidate in postwar American politics. As Table 10.4 illustrates, the closest equivalent was the 9.9 million votes cast for George Wallace in 1968 and the 5.7 million that John Anderson won in 1980. Perot's support was especially strong, not surprisingly, among those dissatisfied with the major party candidates, a pattern similar to that also found in earlier elections for Wallace and Anderson.[44]

As a result of this performance, Perot qualified for $29.5 million in matching public campaign funds during the 1996 Clinton-Dole presidential election, in return for accepting spending limits on private funds. Nevertheless, in this contest he was excluded from the official presidential debates, and public satisfaction with the economic performance of President Clinton reduced Perot's support to 9% of the popular vote (8 million). The following year, the National Reform Party was created as a more independent organization, with an elected executive and a membership convention. Their greatest success was the election of Jesse Ventura, who ran under the Reform Party banner in 1998 as Governor of Minnesota. In the run-up to the 2000 presidential elections, however, the nascent party organization fell apart, with factions and the executive divided by internal squabbles about whether the party should move further right, before they eventually adopted Pat Buchanan as the official nominee. Many third-party and independent candidates contest American elections but they have minimal success, in large part because of the complex legal procedures for gaining ballot access in American states, discussed earlier, designed as protectionist cartel arrangements to deter challengers, coupled with the exceptionally high costs of campaigning, and the vote threshold required in the majoritarian electoral college. The permeability of the primary nomination process in the major parties also

TABLE 10.4. *Vote Cast for Leading Minority Party Candidates for President: United States 1940–2000*

Election	Candidate	Party	Vote (000's)
1992	H. Ross Perot	Independent	19,742
1968	George Wallace	American Independent.	9,906
1996	H. Ross Perot	Reform Party	8,085
1980	John Anderson	Independent	5,720
2000	Ralph Nader	Green	2,883
1948	Strom Thurmond	States' Rights	1,176
1948	Henry Wallace	Progressive	1,157
1972	John Schmitz	American	1,099
1980	Ed Clark	Libertarian	921
1976	Eugene McCarthy	Independent	757
1996	Ralph Nader	Green	685
2000	Pat Buchanan	Reform	449
1988	Ron Paul	Libertarian	432
1992	Andre Marrou	Libertarian	292
1984	David Bergland	Libertarian	228
1988	Lenora B. Fulani	New Alliance	217
1976	Roger McBride	Libertarian	173
1952	Vincent Hallinan	Progressive	140
1940	Norman Thomas	Socialist	116
1956	T. Coleman Andrews	States' Rights	111
1944	Norman Thomas	Socialist	79
1972	Benjamin Spock	People's	79
1984	Lyndon H. LaRouche.	Independent	79
1944	Claude Watson	Prohibition	75
1952	Stuart Hamblen	Prohibition	73
1940	Roger Babson	Prohibition	59
1968	Henning Blomen	Socialist Labor	53
1960	Eric Hass	Socialist Labor	48
1960	Rutherford Decker	Prohibition	46
1964	Eric Hass	Socialist Labor	45
1956	Eric Hass	Socialist Labor	44
1964	Clifton DeBerry	Socialist Workers	33

Sources: Congressional Quarterly, Washington, DC, *America at the Polls, 1920–1996,* 1997; *America Votes,* biennial.

deters candidates from pursuing more independent paths. For all these reasons, the 1992 and 1996 presidential elections proved to be deviating contests for the Reform Party; in 2000, Buchanan won less than half a million votes. In 2004 the Reform Party moved in a radically different direction by officially endorsing Ralph Nader, the consumer advocate and independent candidate, facilitating his entry on the ballot in Florida and other states.

CRITICAL ELECTIONS: FRANCE, AUSTRIA, AND CANADA

Three cases exemplify critical elections, generating durable changes in party competition in each nation, include the surge in support for Le Pen's Front National, registered in the 1984 European elections in France; the advance by the Freiheitliche Partei Öesterreichs in the 1986 parliamentary elections in Austria; and the decisive improvement in Reform Party fortunes in the 1993 Canadian general election. The Austrian case involved PR elections and a consociational or consensus democracy, but Canada illustrates that such decisive changes can also occur in majoritarian elections and adversarial democracies.

The 1984 European Election and Le Pen's Front National

Jean-Marie Le Pen's Front National has been a persistent presence in French politics, attracting around one-fifth of the French electorate in different contests during the last fifteen years, after an initial breakthrough or critical election occurring in the mid-1980s. The party was founded by Jean-Marie Le Pen in 1972 but during the first decade the FN achieved a negligible share of the national vote, receiving less than 1% of the first-round vote in parliamentary elections in 1978 and 1981 (see Table 10.3 and Figure 10.2).[45] Le Pen failed to become a presidential candidate in 1981, after he could not gather the 500 sponsorship signatures needed to qualify, and the party won a miserable 0.18% of the vote in the parliamentary elections that year. In the following years the party made some modest gains in second-order elections, including at cantonal and municipal levels as well as in by-elections, raising its visibility, with Le Pen appearing on French national TV for the first time.

The critical election which catapulted the NF from fringe into minor party status was the 1984 contest for the European Parliament.[46] Held under PR rules, with Le Pen heading the party list of eighty-one candidates, this campaign represented a decisive historical breakthrough. FN won one-fifth (11%) of the vote, electing ten MEPs, with particularly strong support concentrated in Paris, Lyon, Alsace, and the Marseilles areas.[47] The lower vote barriers under PR, combined with the opportunity to cast a temporary mid-term protest vote in a second-order contest against the Mitterrand Socialist government, allowed the Front National to gain credibility as a force in national politics. Their success led to a growing number of party members and local deputies. The European elections gave the party momentum which sustained it at roughly the same level with the support of about one-fifth of the French electorate in the 1986 parliamentary elections, in which Mitterrand had introduced PR temporarily in an attempt to divide the French right. Although shortly afterwards the electoral system reverted back again to the second-ballot majoritarian system, in an attempt to put the FN genie back in the bottle, by then Le Pen was a force on the national political stage.[48] The shift in rules failed to dampen the FN share of the first-ballot vote in the 1988 parliamentary contests, which was fairly stable (9.7%), but support rose to 14.4% in the first round of the presidential elections that year.

As shown in Figure 10.2, subsequent contests saw FN voting support fluctuating from the low of 6% in the 1999 European elections, immediately after a damaging split in the party, to a peak of 16.9% in the first round of the May 2002 presidential elections. The latter caused a minor political earthquake, jolting French voters out of electoral apathy, when Le Pen came out just ahead of the Socialist Prime Minister, Lionel Jospin. Although Le Pen secured 17.7% of the vote in the second round, party support fell back to 11% just a month later in the June 2002 elections for the National Assembly. After their initial electoral breakthrough in the early 1980s, the Front National have become a persistent presence in French politics. The party have developed their organization and membership, consolidated the loyalty of core party supporters, fielded candidates with growing success at regional, national, and European levels (gaining patronage and negotiating governing coalitions with the center-right in five of the twenty-two regions), gained resources from generous campaign funding laws and from commercial and investment income, and have arguably influenced the national political agenda by raising the salience of the issue of immigration, forcing the major parties in France to respond to this agenda.[49]

The 1986 Austrian Election and the Freiheitliche Partei Österreichs (FPÖ)

Critical elections which benefited the radical right are also exemplified by the 1986 Austrian parliamentary elections. The Verband der Unabhangigen (League of Independents) was formed in 1949, and subsequently renamed the Freiheitliche Partei Österreichs or Austrian Freedom Party (FPÖ) in 1956. The party was led by a group dissatisfied with the predominance of the conservative Österreichische Volkspartei (Austrian People's Party, or ÖVP) and the socialist Sozialdemokratische Partei Österreichs (SPÖ). Anton Reinthaller, the original chairman of the FPÖ, focused attention on opposition to Marxism and pride in the country's past, arguing that all Austrians should see themselves as part of a greater German cultural community, attracting many ex-Nazis and army veterans. Reinthaller died two years after founding the party, and was succeeded by an ex-SS officer, Friedrich Peter. Aware that their connection to nationalism was tarnished by the connection to their working with the Nazis after the Anschluss, the FPÖ aimed to modernize by developing liberalism. Throughout the 1960s and 1970s support for the party stalled at around 5–7% of the vote, with the division of government spoils divided between the Social Democrats and People's Party, except for a short period in 1983 when the FPÖ joined the SPÖ governing coalition.

The FPÖ's turning point was the surge in popularity which occurred in 1986 when their leader, Norbert Steger, left office and was replaced by Jörg Haider, a man who became the public face of the FPÖ.[50] When Haider took over the leadership, the party share of the vote almost doubled, from 5% in 1983 to 9.7% in 1986. The young and dapper Haider moved the FPÖ sharply toward the radical right, based on an anti-immigrant and anti-EU platform, and populist exploitation of government disaffection, as well as displaying some neo-Nazi sympathies in his language and rhetoric.[51] For example, the platform of the FPÖ favors strict enforcement of existing immigration laws. All potential immigrants, they feel, should be required to prove that they have jobs and accommodation. They also believe in actively searching out and deporting all illegal immigrants in Austria, deporting legal immigrants guilty of any crime, and mandating all aliens carry state-issued identification. The new name chosen officially in 1995, Die Freiheitlichen (the Freedom Movement), dropped all party references in the title. The 1990 election saw the FPÖ share of the vote leap from 9.7% to 16.6%, with their seats rising from eighteen to thirty-three. Nor was this simply a one-off deviating case; instead, they consolidated this advance and even rose further to take one-fifth of the vote in the next two general elections, before advancing to take one-quarter of the vote in 1999, winning fifty-two members of Parliament, and thus tying in second place, equal to the ÖVP (see Table 10.3).

This result led to the entry of the FPÖ into the Austrian government, in coalition with the mainstream conservative ÖVP of Chancellor Wolfgang Schuessel. This step provoked immediate outrage with mass demonstrations at home and, for a few months, a diplomatic boycott by Austria's partners in the European Union and the withdrawal of the U.S. Ambassador. To avoid major political sanctions, and to keep the FPÖ in power, Haider stepped down and Herbert Haupt, the new party leader, became the Austrian Vice Chancellor. Haider continued to remain a strong influence within the party. The entry of the FPÖ into the governing coalition reflected a major break with traditional patterns of government formation and alternation in Austria, producing a fundamental shift in the options for cross-party cooperation and competition within the legislature. Following divisions within the party and instability in the leadership, support for the FPÖ subsequently fell sharply to just 10% in the 2002 general election, leading some commentators to suggest that radical right parties may experience serious problems in sustaining their appeal as 'outsiders' once they enter governing coalitions.[52] Public divisions within rival wings of the FPÖ appear to have damaged their credibility, and critics argue that their leadership has been ineffective. The party may also have been hurt by a broader shift in the Austrian public policy issue agenda, shifting priorities from problems of immigration to rising concern about the economy, unemployment, and social security. The entry of the FPÖ into coalition government also probably undermined their antiestablishment image. Nevertheless, despite falling party popularity reported in the opinion polls, in March 2004 Haider was reelected as Governor of Carinthia, his home province, slightly increasing his share of the vote. The future of the party remains to be determined by subsequent contests, so it would be foolhardy to predict their role in Austrian party politics. Compared with their previous performance, however, the 1986 election represents a watershed contest which changed the credibility, status, and influence of the FPÖ, leading toward their later victories and their entry into government.

The 1993 Canadian Election and the Reform Party

Breakthrough contests are not confined to PR electoral systems; the Canadian case also illustrates how these events can occur among parties with support concentrated in a strong regional base even in majoritarian systems of first past the post. The geographic distribution of voting support is vital for success within single-member districts. The Canadian Reform Party was formed in 1987 by Preston Manning as a populist neoconservative party reflecting alienation with the established party system, and also a reaction by the western states against the rise of nationalist demands by the Bloc Québecois (BQ) in Francophone Canada.[53]

Like other parties under comparison, the Reform Party shared a populist style and certain concerns about the issues of multiculturalism and out-group threats to 'nativism,' although these issues combined with more traditional free market economic philosophy, where they were close to the 'old-right' Progressive Conservatives, by emphasizing the need for re-trenchment of the Canadian welfare state and reductions in income tax. The party promised a new kind of politics, rejecting pan-Canadian accom-modation, interest group pluralism, and the recognition of special minor-ity rights. Reform contested the 1988 general election but they won only 2.1 percent of the vote and no seats. The 1993 election is widely regarded, rightly, as the equivalent of an electoral earthquake in Canadian party pol-itics. The election saw the meltdown of the Progressive Conservatives; the party which had been in government saw their seats decimated from 169 to just 2. The beneficiaries were the Bloc Québecois and Reform, both new challengers intent on remaking the Canadian party system. Support for Reform jumped from 2.1% to 18.7% of the national vote, with support concentrated in Ontario and western English-speaking provinces, return-ing 52 MPs, in third place just behind the Bloc Québecois' 54. The result was initially regarded as a temporary protest vote against government and a regional reaction against BQ, but Reform consolidated their position in subsequent contests, winning 19.4% and 60 MPs in the 1997 general election, with support concentrated in the western states.[54] Repackaged under the label of the Canada Reform Conservative Alliance (Alliance for short), in the attempt to expand out from their regional base, the party won 25.5% of the vote and 66 MPs in the November 2000 general election.

Reform/Alliance subsequently merged with the Progressive Conserva-tives on 15 October 2003, to become the new Conservative Party of Canada under Stephen Harper's leadership. The merger occurred too close to the June 2004 general election to allow development and publication of an official party platform laying out detailed policy proposals, but their declaration of general principles, agreed at merger and available on their website, emphasized the older conservative tradition in Canada, characterized by fairly vague platitudes but also expressing tolerance of multiculturalism combined with free market economics. Yet at the same time, even after the election, the position of the party remains ambiguous; certain campaign comments and candidate speeches seemed to indicate a hard-line stance against abortion rights and gay marriage, which may indicate a strong strand of social conservatism within the new party. The situation still appears to be in flux so that at this point in time the party still has important elements of the old radical right, such as some Reform activists running the 2004 campaign, although the party leader appears to recognize that this is not where the party's ideal target voters lie. Some coming from the old centrist Progressive Conservative tradition saw the merger of the two parties as a hostile takeover by the Alliance. The former PC leader and prime minister, Joe Clark, actually left the new party and campaigned for Liberal candidates, albeit not for the party as a whole. Several other former MPs also defected and ran as Liberals. Yet there are also elements of the PC party remaining in the party – mainly from Atlantic Canada – although whether they will be heard in a parliamentary caucus dominated by westerners from the Reform movement remains to be seen.[55] Compared with the Alliance in 2000, surveys suggest that people were much less likely to name the new party when asked if any federal party was 'just too extreme.'[56] After the election, the Conservatives became the official opposition, with ninety-nine MPs and 29.6% of the vote, facing a minority Liberal-NDP administration, and the prospects of another possible general election in the foreseeable future. This result was an achievement and yet their vote share was less than the combined vote for the Alliance and the Progressive Conservatives in 2000, despite public fury with the Liberals. The new party is in transition and it remains to be seen whether the party leadership and parliamentary party adopt more moderate appeals, in the attempt to maximize their support, necessary under majoritarian rules if they are ever to attain government, or whether Reform activists will pull the party in a more radical direction.

CONCLUSIONS

Understanding the rise of the radical right promises to provide general insights into processes of electoral change and party competition, including the facilitating conditions and campaign strategies that could, in principle, allow any minor party to expand their base, whatever their ideological persuasion. The process of partisan dealignment is widely regarded as integral to the fragmentation of party systems, with weakening psychological anchors to mainstream parties allowing newer challengers to emerge. The evidence considered in this chapter relies upon selected case studies, a less reliable process of comparison than the cross-national survey data used in earlier parts of the book, although specific illustrations also facilitate more contextual description of the conditions leading toward radical right success.

The evidence we have considered suggests that, by itself, secular dealignment fails to account for radical right success. A loosening of traditional voter-party linkages does facilitate intermittent cases of deviating elections. More importantly, the occasional critical election represents an enduring breakthrough for the radical right and a long-term shift in national patterns of party competition. The examples which have been described show that the breakthrough of the radical right has occurred in specific contests under many different conditions; in both majoritarian and proportional electoral systems, in Anglo-American democracies such as Canada as well as in Western Europe, in adversarial as well as consensus democracies. The most important distinction shown in this chapter is the contrast between *dealigning elections*, where the radical right have failed to register any substantial and sustained advance (exemplified by the NF and BNP in Britain); *deviating elections*, where they have made some sudden progress which has subsequently receded (shown by the Reform Party in the United States and by the Lijst Pym Fortuyn in the Netherlands); and *critical elections*, where parties such as the French FN, Austrian FPÖ, and Canadian Reform have made an initial breakthrough which they then solidified in a series of subsequent contests, altering patterns of party competition on an enduring basis across the political system, and thereby generating processes of partisan realignment.

Proportional electoral systems with low thresholds, combined with partisan dealignment and disaffection with the mainstream alternatives, facilitate breakthroughs by minor party challengers, as in the Austrian and French cases. But even under the most favorable conditions, there are no simple guarantees that radical right parties can maintain and build upon any initial breakthrough to consolidate their support on a long-term basis, as shown by the rise and equally rapid downfall of Lijst Pym Fortuyn. Some contextual conditions are beyond each party's control, but the cases strongly suggest that at least part of the answer for long-term success lies in their own hands. The shift rightward that occurred under Haider's leadership in the FPÖ, a long-established party in Austria, generated a strong improvement in their fortunes. There are also many cases, notably Perot's Reform Party, which show how organizational failures, notably disputes about leadership succession, ideological splits, and internal fractionalization, have proved deeply damaging for new and poorly institutionalized parties, causing public support to dissipate rapidly. What remains to be considered in the concluding chapter is whether the advance of new radical right challengers has caused other parties to respond by also moving rightward, for example on issues of immigration and race relations, and what consequences the rise of these parties has had on broader processes of representative democracy and the public policy agenda.

PART V

CONSEQUENCES

Assessing the Rise of the Radical Right and Its Consequences

After summarizing and integrating the key findings of the previous chapters, this conclusion considers their broader implications for party competition and for democracy, including whether there is any 'contagion of the right,' with other parties responding to their success. The results from the study may help to dispel certain common fallacies, while also emphasizing some overlooked factors leading to radical right success. To recap the argument, the advance of new challenger parties is open to multiple interpretations, and demand-side, supply-side, and institutional perspectives can be found in the literature seeking to explain the rise of the radical right. Let us summarize the evidence presented throughout the book, then consider some of the consequences of this phenomenon.

THE INSTITUTIONAL STRUCTURE OF OPPORTUNITIES

From Duverger onwards, the classic literature on electoral systems suggested that these rules have an important mechanical impact upon the number of parties elected to office, with the implication that minor and fringe parties, including the radical right, have more opportunities to gain seats under proportional representation than under majoritarian systems. More recently this conventional wisdom has been questioned by studies which have suggested that electoral systems play little role in the success of the radical right.[1] Indeed it is true that there are examples where these parties have advanced within majoritarian systems (such as in Canada) as well as under PR (illustrated by the Netherlands, Norway, Belgium, and Switzerland). Nevertheless, the balance of evidence indicates that in general rules do matter. The study considered the institutional structure of opportunities that minor parties face in the nomination, campaign, and election stages of the pursuit of elected office.

The conclusion from Chapter 4 was that nomination rules probably contribute toward the electoral success of minor radical right parties. Case studies suggest that the legal requirements governing party registration and ballot access play an important role in limiting opportunities for radical right parties under four main conditions: where the nomination process for ballot access proves cumbersome and burdensome for minor parties (as in the United States); where these parties fall foul of civil law, notably race relations legislation governing hate speech (as in Belgium and the Netherlands), or campaign finance regulations (as in Australia and Denmark); where constitutional provisions and court decisions ban extremist or antidemocratic parties (exemplified by Germany, Chile, and Spain); and in repressive regimes holding manipulated and flawed elections where the ballot access and campaign rules are grossly biased toward the ruling party (illustrated by Belarus). Few liberal democracies ban radical right parties outright, or impose serious limits on the parties or candidates who can be nominated for election, on the grounds that this would interfere with fundamental human rights and civil liberties in free elections. But in a handful of cases – such as in Germany, Spain, and Chile – extremist party organizations that are directly associated with the illegal use of violence, or which condone terrorist tactics, have been forced to disband or occasionally reorganize under new labels. The fragile institutionalization of minor parties means that the fortunes of the radical right remain particularly vulnerable to legal challenges, such as the prosecution of party leaders charged with campaign finance violations, vote-rigging irregularities, or propagating hate speech.

There are many reasons why the legal statutes and formal regulation governing access to campaign media and party funding could serve as a political cartel, reinforcing the power of incumbent parties already in elected office, or alternatively could generate a more level playing field which provides opportunities for minor party challengers. Despite this clear logic, the evidence examined here could find no significant relationship between the available indicators of the formal legal requirements for financial and media access and the national levels of voting support won by the radical right (or more general patterns of party competition). Several important limitations mean that it is advisable to be cautious about drawing any strong positive or negative inferences from the existing evidence, and at best the hypothetical claim must be regarded as essentially 'unproven.' This is a topic deserving of further research, for example historical case studies monitoring developments where the campaign finance rules change to distribute more resources to fringe and minor parties.

The book also examined evidence for the impact of electoral systems, particularly the standard claim that proportional representation with low legal vote thresholds facilitates the election of smaller parties. The results of the comparison presented in Chapter 5 indicate that a revised version of the conventional wisdom is partially correct: electoral systems were found to affect the proportion of seats gained by minor radical right parties, confirming that their representation was facilitated by PR systems with low legal thresholds. Even within the category of PR systems, the existence of high legal vote thresholds also exerts an important mechanical brake on the radical right share of seats. Nevertheless, the evidence suggests an important and overlooked qualification to the standard view: the electoral system works through determining the radical right's share of seats, *not* votes. The effects in this regard can be regarded as mechanical rather than psychological. The institutional context of the electoral system might be expected to influence popular support for minor parties, with majoritarian systems having a psychological effect by depressing the vote share for fringe and minor radical right parties, where voters switch to more viable parties for strategic or tactical reasons. Yet this turns out not to be the case after all. It remains unclear why the 'wasted vote' thesis fails, but given the proximity theory of voting, probably the main reason is that radical right supporters are located too far away from other contenders across the ideological spectrum for them to switch to their second-preference choice for tactical or strategic considerations.

The impact of the electoral system upon seats can be illustrated by a few examples. Under majoritarian elections, for example, the previous chapter showed how the Front National emerged from the fringe in the mid-1980s, boosted by the 1984 European elections held under PR, but after the rules reverted back to the majoritarian runoff system, its subsequent role in the French parliament has remained marginal. The last legislative elections in France, in June 2002, saw the FN receive the support of about 11.3% of the electorate, yet they failed to win a single seat in the National Assembly, due to the second-ballot electoral system. By contrast, after gaining a similar share of the national vote (11–12%) in the most recent general elections, under PR the Vlaams Blok constitute one-tenth of the members of the Belgian Parliament, while Alleanza Nazionale hold ministerial office in Berlusconi's cabinet. Politically, winning seats, *not* votes, is vital for power, since parliamentary representation provides the radical right with legitimacy, resources, and patronage which can be leveraged, with luck and skill, into further advances. Through winning office, minor parties gain access to a public platform on the national stage, allowing them to propagate their views, influence debates, and mobilize popular support via the national news media, not just gain sporadic bursts of publicity during occasional election campaigns.

At the same time, certain important qualifications to these conclusions should be noted. In particular, the evidence about the impact of electoral systems remains limited, and the direction of causality in this relationship cannot be determined from cross-sectional evidence alone, particularly in newer democracies. What this means is that it is not possible to say for certain whether majoritarian electoral systems penalize and thereby discourage extremist parties from competing, or, alternatively, whether newer democracies containing multiple parties dispersed widely across the political spectrum are more likely to adopt PR rules in their electoral laws and constitutions. What can be said more confidently, however, is that in established democracies with relatively stable electoral systems over successive decades, or even for centuries, in the long term it seems plausible that the rules of the game (adopted for whatever reason) will probably constrain *subsequent* patterns of party competition. In Britain, for example, the system of plurality single-member districts has persisted in elections for the House of Commons since the Great Reform Act of 1832, with the exception of a few dual-member seats which were finally abolished in 1948. This system has greatly limited the opportunities for fringe and minor parties like the National Front and BNP to challenge Labour and Conservative predominance at Westminster, despite growing patterns of partisan dealignment and occasional surges of popular support for minor challengers like the UK Independence Party in second-order parliamentary by-elections and European elections. Where electoral rules have persisted unchanged for many decades, they influence how radical right minor parties respond strategically to the structure of opportunities they face. 'Before' and 'after' cases also confirm the impact of rules. For example, when electoral reforms were introduced by the Blair government, changing the system used in European elections from first-past-the-post to regional party list PR, this improved the subsequent performance of fringe parties, including the BNP and the UK Independence Party.

THE SOCIAL BASIS OF SUPPORT AND A 'NEW SOCIAL CLEAVAGE'
IN THE ELECTORATE?

The institutional context of the nomination and election process therefore shapes the opportunities facing radical right parties. As discussed in Chapter 6, structural explanations commonly relate patterns of party support to the major social cleavages in the electorate. Interpretations of the nature of the social base of the radical right differ, with classic accounts of European fascism emphasizing their strength among the petite bourgeoisie displaced by organized labor and big business, and new cleavage theories emphasizing support among the socially disadvantaged in affluent postindustrial societies, while accounts of partisan disadvantage suggest that social identities have generally weakened in their ability to structure voting choices. Where parties are based upon distinct social sectors, then Lipset and Rokkan suggest that they can forge enduring ties with these groups, representing their interests and concerns in the political system. Where such ties have weakened, through social and partisan dealignment, then we would expect greater electoral volatility and more potential for protest voting. What do the results of the survey analysis suggest about the social base of support for the radical right?

As we have seen, the systematic evidence supporting the new social cleavage thesis remains limited, at best. The social class profile of the radical right electorate presented in Chapter 6, including multiple indicators of social inequality, suggests that they are disproportionately overrepresented both among the petite bourgeoisie – self-employed professionals, own-account technicians, and small merchants – *and* among the skilled and unskilled working class. The survey evidence presented in Chapter 6 throws doubt on the claim that support for the radical right in all countries is disproportionately based upon its appeal to a new social cleavage or underclass of low-skilled and low-qualified workers in inner-city areas, or that its voting support is strongest among those with direct experience of unemployment or poverty. This cross-class coalition means that we should look skeptically upon the idea that the rise of the radical right is purely a phenomenon of the politics of resentment among the underclass of low-skilled and low-qualified workers in inner-city areas, or that it can be attributed in any mechanical fashion to growing levels of unemployment and job insecurity in Europe. The socioeconomic profile is more complex than popular stereotypes suggest. At the same time the traditional gender gap has persisted, with these parties drawing disproportionate support from men. Although the pooled analysis suggests some common patterns, the results disaggregated by nation show considerable variations in the social profile of radical right voters. As shown in Chapter 8, radical right voters are significantly more likely to believe that immigrants take jobs away from workers, just as they are also more likely to express instrumental racist sentiments concerning the cultural or general economic threat of immigrants. But this pattern reflects the attitudes of

radical right voters rather than their direct experience, for example of unemployment. It could be that alternative, more sensitive, survey measures
could capture any direct linkages between perceptions of job insecurity,
hostility to immigrants, and support for the radical right, but the available
evidence from the ESS fails to support this thesis.

THE POLITICS OF RESENTMENT?

Another common perspective regards rising support for the radical right
as indicative of widespread protest against the status quo, anger at the
choices offered by mainstream parties, and hence an indicator of broader
public disaffection in democratic societies. The politics of resentment thesis is pervasive in the literature, tapping into the older traditional explaining the propensity of authoritarian personalities to support European fascism.[2] This argument is not necessarily antithetical to the 'new
cleavage' thesis, as these accounts can be combined where political disaffection is concentrated among disadvantaged social sectors. Nevertheless
the explanation remains logically distinct.

The evidence presented in Chapter 7 confirms that those who cast their
ballots for the radical right are indeed less trusting of a range of political institutions in representative democracy. Studies also suggest that a
gradual erosion of institutional confidence has occurred among the public during recent decades in many established democracies, especially a
decline of political trust toward parties and parliaments.[3] This process
should have expanded the constituency of those who are potentially sympathetic toward the expression of antiestablishment sentiments. The evidence presented here therefore does support the politics of resentment
thesis to some extent, but we should not exaggerate either the strength
or the consistency of the indicators. Certain important points need to be
borne in mind before concluding that any erosion of institutional trust in
contemporary democracies can be blamed for the rise of the radical right.

First, growing mistrust of representative institutions is widespread
throughout contemporary democracies, so it is difficult to use this explanation to account for the substantial variations in the electoral fortunes
of the radical right, such as the contrasts between Norway and Sweden,
or Italy and Spain, as well as differences in their performance within
countries, such as the popularity of the Front National in Francophone
Belgium and the Vlaams Blok in Wallonian Belgium, or how well the
Canadian Reform/Alliance/Conservative Party performed in Quebec and
the western states.

In addition, popular journalistic explanations often claim that public disillusionment with politics and dissatisfaction with government has fueled the ascendancy of the radical right. Yet the interpretation of the direction of causality in this relationship remains open to question. Citizens disenchanted with mainstream parties, and alienated from the political system, may indeed gravitate toward supporting the radical right as the party best able to articulate these concerns. Alternatively, the exclusion of radical right parties from power, coupled with the populist antiestablishment rhetoric of their leaders, could plausibly encourage mistrust of political institutions amongst their followers.[4] Chapter 7 established cross-national variations in positive or negative evaluations of government performance among radical right supporters, which were related to whether radical right parties are either included or excluded from power.[5] Where these parties become part of governing coalitions, or where conservative governments rise to power which are closely sympathetic to their aims, then radical right supporters in these nations prove more positive toward government. Where radical right parties are excluded, then, not surprisingly, this encourages mistrust of the responsiveness and performance of government among their supporters. In practice, with cross-sectional survey evidence, it is difficult to disentangle the direction of causality in the relationship between trust and radical right voting. In practice, some interaction effects are probably at the heart of this pattern, rather than the simple one-way relationship often assumed, and analysis of time series, multiwave panel surveys, or experimental data is probably necessary to resolve this issue.

THE GROWING SALIENCE OF CULTURAL PROTECTIONISM?

Another common sociological explanation for the rise of the radical right, indeed the conventional wisdom, focuses upon the spread of multiculturalism and more ethnically diverse societies found today in postindustrial nations. This process is driven by many factors associated with processes of globalization, notably by patterns of long-term social change and population migration, the growth of refugees and asylum seekers fleeing armed conflict and failed states, and more permeable national borders and open labor markets. Many accounts assume that a public backlash against these trends has triggered the popular success of leaders such as Le Pen and Haider who articulate these concerns. In this view, the radical right can be regarded as a single-issue party, especially where mainstream parties and liberal elites in the European Union and Anglo-American democracies have failed to respond to any public resentment and growing hostility directed against 'foreigners' and 'outsiders' by setting stricter limits on immigration and asylum seekers.[6]

The evidence analyzed in Chapter 8 suggests that, contra the standard account, no significant relationship existed at *aggregate* level between the national share of the vote cast for radical right parties and a wide range of indicators of ethnic diversity in a country, whether measured by estimated official rates of refugees and asylum seekers, the proportion of nonnationals and noncitizens living in a country, or public opinion toward immigration. Parties such as the Vlaams Blok, the FPÖ, and the Front National have consistently emphasized racist rhetoric, antiforeigner diatribes, and the theme of cultural protectionism as the leitmotif recurring throughout leadership speeches and at the heart of their election campaigns. Other policies which they advocate, such as restrictions on welfare services or the need for strong law and order, are also often coded implicitly within a racist frame. As a result, the electoral success of these parties is often interpreted to signify a public backlash directed against ethnic minorities in the countries where they do well. But, in fact, the relationship proves more complicated. At the same time, at *individual* level, anti-immigrant and anti-refugee attitudes, as well as general support for cultural protectionism, *do* predict who will vote for the radical right. Their electoral support was typically stronger among people who believed that immigrants are an economic threat, by taking away jobs or depressing wages, that the nation's culture was undermined by foreigners, or that there should be restrictive policies toward refugees. These attitudes remained significant even after applying the standard battery of prior social controls. This pattern was found consistently in many, although not all, of the eight countries in the European Social Survey with a relevant right party. By contrast, attitudes concerning economic policies, such as government policy toward income inequality or the role of trade unions, failed to prove a significant predictor in many nations, although admittedly the full range of economic attitudes toward the role of markets and the state were only poorly gauged in this particular survey.

The apparent mismatch in the results found at both these levels can be accounted for by the well-known ecological fallacy, which suggests that patterns found in public opinion at national level do not necessarily hold at individual level, and also by the individual fallacy, which implies that patterns established at individual level cannot necessarily be assumed to reflect public opinion at national level.[7] Minor radical right parties gain the support of a minority of the electorate, even in countries such as Switzerland, where they are strongest, and this minority is strongly skewed in terms of the normal distribution of public opinion; hence it is misleading to generalize on the basis of the attitudes held by radical right supporters to the general state of public opinion existing in the countries where the radical right performs well. The minority most hostile toward immigration, ethnic diversity, and multiculturalism are indeed most likely to vote for the radical right, as many others have reported. But this does not mean that the popularity or success of the radical right in a country indicates the balance of public opinion toward cultural protectionism, immigration, or race relations within that nation. It may simply mean that public opinion is sharply polarized around these issues and values, not that the median voter favors cultural protectionism.

IDEOLOGICAL APPEALS

On this basis, we can conclude that sociological theories of structural change only take us so far. What needs to be considered is not just how social conditions might facilitate attitudes conducive toward the rise of the radical right, but, even more importantly, how parties respond to public demands when crafting their strategic ideological and value appeals, targeting voters, and building their local and national organizations. Supply-side explanations emphasize these factors, strongly influenced by the Kitschelt thesis that the central ideological location of mainstream parties, for example a liberal elite consensus emphasizing tolerance of refugees and asylum seekers, can maximize opportunities on the far right of the political spectrum for newer insurgents. Yet the comparison of the ideological location of the mainstream center-left and center-right parties in sixteen countries, presented in Chapter 9, failed to support the claim that the radical right advanced most successfully where the left-right gap was smallest. Nor was there strong support for the van der Brug variant of this argument, claiming that it is the ideological position of the mainstream right-wing party which is critical for maximizing opportunities for the radical right.

The argument developed in this book suggests that the broader context constrains party locations across the ideological spectrum. This claim builds on the observation in Chapter 5 that under PR electoral systems with low thresholds, minor parties can gain elected office by winning a relatively modest share of the popular vote. Under these rules, minor parties have a strategic incentive to win seats by adopting 'bonding' strategies which they can use to mobilize and activate niche cleavages within the electorate. Using such strategies, the radical right typically stress the signature issues of cultural protectionism which distinguish these parties most clearly from their mainstream competitors on the center-right and center-left. By contrast, in majoritarian electoral systems, with higher effective electoral thresholds, minor parties will fail to surmount the hurdles to elected office (and thus the rewards of status, power, money, and legitimacy that flow from office) unless they adopt broader populist or catchall appeals by emphasizing a wider range of values, based on vague rhetoric and simple slogans largely devoid of substantive policy content.

The evidence in Chapter 9, based on comparing the perceived ideological location of parties in thirty nations, confirms the idea that party competition is usually more centripetal in majoritarian systems while being dispersed more centrifugally across the whole ideological spectrum from far left to far right in PR systems. The survey evidence also suggests that both ideological values and affective orientations toward parties were important predictors of voting for the radical right in the multivariate analysis of the pooled sample, drawing upon all thirteen nations where these factors could be compared. These attitudes reduced the significance of almost all of the social-demographic variables in the model. But to take account of the institutional context, the analysis was broken down into more detailed case studies, comparing voting behavior in Canada and France (exemplifying majoritarian electoral systems) with Norway and Switzerland (illustrating proportional systems). The multivariate models analyzed the relative impact of left-right ideological location and populist orientations (liking for the far right party) on casting a vote for the radical right in each election, including a battery of prior social and attitudinal controls. The results confirmed that in Switzerland and Norway, using proportional party list electoral systems, both ideology and partisanship played a significant role in shaping the appeal of the radical right. But in the countries using majoritarian electoral systems, in both Canada and France, only populist appeals (*not* ideological proximity) proved significant predictors of radical right votes. It would have been useful to explore the basis of the radical right vote in more countries using majoritarian systems, such as the background and attitudes of BNP supporters in Britain or One Nation in Australia, but there were too few radical right voters contained in the standard election surveys in these countries to facilitate analysis. Given these limitations, the case-study comparison cannot be regarded as definitive, but the results are consistent with the theory that electoral rules shape radical right party strategies and electoral appeals.

ORGANIZATIONAL CONSOLIDATION

The factors leading to an initial surge in support for the radical right are not necessarily sufficient to sustain their advance, as shown by the sudden rise and fall of flash parties. Parties which have developed effective organizations – building up financial campaign resources, institutionalizing party rules, encouraging internal party discipline and cohesion, and fostering a grassroots base – are more likely to endure through good electoral times and bad. Minor challengers and insurgents are also likely to have more difficulties in mobilizing support where mainstream parties have established and maintained enduring partisan attachments in the mass electorate. The case studies discussed in Chapter 10 serve to illustrate the broader conditions under which radical right parties have, and have not, consolidated their advance in successive elections. Britain exemplifies a country which has experienced processes of social and partisan dealignment, but where the National Front and British National Party have consistently failed to surmount other institutional barriers to gain entry at Westminster. Yet dealignment can also facilitate occasional deviating elections; examples include the Netherlands, where the Lijst Pym Fortuyn had sudden success in May 2002, only to fall equally sharply within two years, as well as the short-term breakthrough that Ross Perot's Reform Party enjoyed in the 1992 and 1996 U.S. presidential elections. By contrast, critical elections involve an enduring shift in patterns of party competition, exemplified by the 1984 European elections in France, where Jean-Marie Le Pen's Front National, which had enjoyed poor fortunes for a decade, experienced a major breakthrough from fringe to minor party status, a position which proved durable in subsequent contests; the 1986 Austrian election representing a decisive contest as Jörg Haider moved the Austrian Freedom Party from the margins to mainstream; and the 1993 Canadian elections marking the initial breakthrough for the Reform Party, subsequently sustained as the Alliance and then Conservative Party.

THE CONSEQUENCES FOR PARTY COMPETITION
IN REPRESENTATIVE DEMOCRACIES

The broader implications of this study may also help us to understand the potential impact of radical right parties on the institutions of representative democracy. Many commentators have expressed considerable concern about the advance of the radical right, on the assumption that this development poses substantial threats to government stability, the public policy agenda, and indeed the fundamental health of representative democracies.[8] But are these anxieties actually justified? In particular, here we can consider whether there is good evidence supporting the 'contagion of the right' thesis, which suggests that the advance of the radical right has caused mainstream parties to become more socially conservative on issues of immigration and race relations, for example by encouraging governments to adopt more restrictive policies toward asylum seekers and political refugees.

Many commentators suggest that radical right parties have probably had their greatest influence by raising public concern about their signature issues, especially those of race relations, immigration policy, welfare reform, and law and order, thereby tugging moderate parties toward the extreme right.[9] In France, for example, Schain suggests that the center-right parties, the Rassemblement pour la République and Union pour la Démocratic Française, adopted the Front National anti-immigrant rhetoric after 1986, in the attempt to preempt Le Pen's support.[10] Along similar lines, Pettigrew argues that Austria implemented more restrictive policies toward refugees after the FPÖ entered coalition government with the ÖVP.[11] In spring 2004, the Dutch government legislated to remove tens of thousands of failed asylum seekers, a measure that seems to have been influenced by Lijst Pyim Fortuyn's electoral success. The New Zealand First party have long adopted a hard-line position over race relations, critiquing the Treaty of Waitangi safeguarding Maori rights. Following their example, in January 2004 Don Brash, the leader of the main right-wing opposition Nationalist Party, gave a speech echoing their rhetoric and playing the race card over Maori rights, generating a surge of popular Nationalist support in the polls.

Of course these developments in public policy might have occurred anyway, as governments responded to global patterns of population migration, growing multiculturalism in modern societies, and the shifting tide of public opinion on these issues. In recent years, many EU states have tightened immigration policies, even where these parties remain weak. Yet the growth of the radical right could plausibly have played an important role in this process through challenging the liberal consensus among mainstream governing parties, altering public discourse, expanding the issue space to draw mainstream parties rightwards, heightening the salience and polarization of the issue of immigration on the policy agenda, and legitimating policies founded upon racism and intolerance.[12] Some of the most systematic evidence supporting this thesis was developed by Harmel and Svasand, who compared the content analysis evidence of party manifestos in Norway and Denmark. In these countries, the policy platforms for the moderate Conservative parties have moved rightward since the early 1970s, and this shift can be interpreted as a response to the electoral challenge posed by the success of the Progress parties on their extreme flank.[13]

Building upon this approach, we can use the time-series data provided by the Manifesto Research Group (MRG) to see whether critical elections in France, Canada, Switzerland, and Austria, which saw considerable vote and/or seat gains by a radical right party, were consistently associated with a subsequent rightward ideological shift in the policy platforms offered by mainstream parties. The Manifesto Research Group/Comparative Manifesto Project has used content analysis to code party platforms published from 1945 to 1998 in twenty-five nations, facilitating comparison of party policy programs within a common framework across many Western democracies.[14] Party platforms, manifestos, and election programs provide an important source of information about party priorities and values. They represent authoritative documents, given considerable prominence in election campaigns, which have been widely used in the literature to gauge the relative distance or proximity of parties. The records of parties in government are also commonly evaluated against the manifesto promises they made before coming into power, and studies suggest that many policy pledges are indeed often implemented through legislation, spending budgets, or administrative decisions.[15] The content analysis coding scheme developed by the MRG uses fifty-seven categories of issues, measuring the proportion of manifesto sentences devoted to topics such as law and order, free enterprise, and the expansion of social services, assuming that the amount of attention in the manifesto reflects the relative priority which each party gives to each issue. A summary left-right scale is then developed among a subgroup of twenty-six items, calculated simply by subtracting the sum of 'left' percentages from 'right' percentages. The 'left' coding includes statements about issues which typify social democratic or socialist principles, such as the expansion of social services and education, positive references to labor groups and trade unions, and favorable mentions of economic planning and nationalization. The 'right' reflects priorities such as policies favoring free enterprise, law and order, and the military. The position of the radical right can be compared against the location of other parties in each election based on the overall left-right summary scale. It should be noted that the MRG scale represents the attempt to develop a generic left-right ideological scale, focused heavily upon classic issues of the role of the state versus the free market economy, rather than

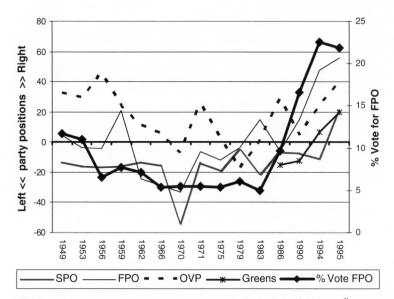

FIGURE 11.1. Austrian Party Competition and Support for the FPÖ, 1949–1995. The estimated left-wing or right-wing party positions are derived from the Manifesto Research Group coding of party platforms. *Source*: The Manifesto Research Group.

the issues of immigration and race relations, which are more properly the distinctive territory of the radical right. Nevertheless, it is one of the best available measures which facilitates time-series analysis of party locations since 1945. The 'contagion of the right' thesis suggests that after a national election where a radical right party registers a sharp gain in their share of votes and/or seats, then in subsequent elections other mainstream parties in the same country who may feel threatened will respond (particularly parties on the center-right) by moving their own position further rightwards. This thesis can be tested in cases where a critical election occurred and where the MRG project coded the platforms of radical right parties, including the sudden rise of the Reform Party in the 1993 Canadian election, the Front National in the 1984 French election, the FPÖ in the 1986 Austrian election, and the Progress Party in the 1989 Norwegian election.

Austria

The trends in the Austrian case, presented in Figure 11.1, illustrate these patterns. The graph displays the steadily eroding voting support for the

Freedom Party from the mid-1950s until 1983, then the sharp surge in the share of the vote won by the FPÖ in successive elections from 1983 to 1994, before a slight fall to 1995 (the latest date available for the Austrian manifesto data in the MRG project). The figure also illustrates the right-wards shift in this party in 1986, after Haider took over the leadership, which continued in successive elections to 1995. The graph also shows the way that, after a short time-lag, other Austrian parties also followed suit by moving their own position rightward, including the shift evident in the ÖVP, the SPÖ, and even the Greens. Now this evidence does not and cannot demonstrate that the electoral success of the FPÖ *produced* a 'follow-my-leader' effect. Indeed all the Austrian parties (including the FPÖ) could have been moving rightward simultaneously during the early nineties, due to many independent external factors. The fall of the Berlin Wall, the end of the Cold War, and conflict in the Balkans, for example, could have altered foreign policy and security priorities on Austria's borders during this era. The influx of refugees, asylum seekers, and migrant labor from southeastern Asia and post-Communist Europe (especially Bosnia and Albania) could have heightened social tensions and renewed attempts to strengthen national borders. The Austrian welfare state could have been facing growing pressures in this period due to many social trends common in modern European societies, such as rising health-care costs, rising unemployment, the breakdown of the traditional family unit, and the growing size of the elderly population. But at the same time the rightward shift evident in the policy platforms of the other major parties in Austria during the early 1990s could also be plausibly explained as their attempt to curtail the growing electoral success of the FPÖ, follow-ing recognition that the public's zone of acquiescence had moved right on issues of cultural protectionism.

One way to confirm the interpretation with greater confidence is to see whether there are consistent patterns for a 'contagion of the right' which occur in other countries, where the timing of changes in party competi-tion can be attributed to the electoral popularity of radical right parties. Examination of trends in party competition in Norway, illustrated in Fig-ure 11.2, show that Austria was not simply an exceptional case; instead similar patterns can also be detected where the sharp rise in support for the FrP between 1985 (3.7% of the vote) and 1989 (13.0%) was followed by a rightward shift among all the other major party platforms between 1989 and 1993. We cannot establish whether it was the rise of the radical right vote in 1989 Norwegian election which caused a subsequent shift rightward among center-right parties, since again many other exogenous

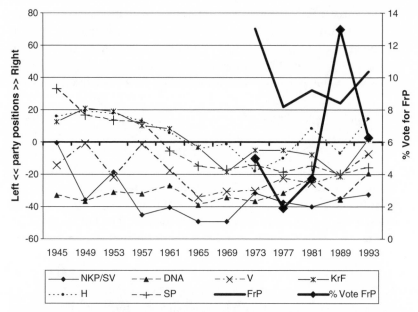

FIGURE 11.2. Norwegian Party Competition and Support for the FrP, 1945–1993. The estimated left-wing or right-wing party positions are derived from the Manifesto Research Group coding of party platforms. *Source*: The Manifesto Research Group.

factors may have generated this pattern. The fact that the Austrian and Norwegian changes in party competition occurred during roughly the same period (between 1989 and 1993 in Norway and between 1986 and 1995 in Austria) means that this pattern could possibly be dismissed as the result of a broader cultural shift in the political zeitgeist. Indeed the timing of such a shift could plausibly be regarded as a *cause* of growing support for the radical right, rather than the result of their rise in popularity. But in each case the timing was certainly coincident with the argument that the initial popular surge of radical right support in one national contest triggered a rightward shift to occur in the ideological position and the public policies adopted by the other major parties in subsequent contests.

Yet there are good reasons to be cautious about assuming that this is a general pattern which holds across diverse nations and electoral systems. In particular, the comparison of trends in party competition in both France and Canada, in contests held under majoritarian rules, shows mixed patterns, or no consistent evidence supporting a 'contagion of the right' thesis

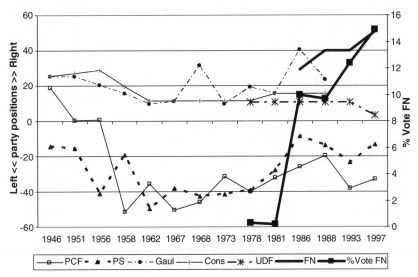

FIGURE 11.3. French Party Competition and Support for the Front National, 1946–1997. The estimated left-wing or right-wing party positions are derived from the Manifesto Research Group coding of party platforms. *Source*: The Manifesto Research Group.

in these countries (see Figures 11.3 and 11.4). In France, the graph shows that the Front National moved ahead in the mid-1980s (notably with their breakthrough in the 1984 European elections), but Figure 11.3 indicates no apparent subsequent rightward shift among other parties in this country. In Canada, as well, the sudden emergence of Reform in 1993 as a serious force in parliamentary politics was not followed by a subsequent rightward shift by other parties, possibly because of the simultaneous meltdown of the Progressive Conservatives as the major opposition party, along with the regional pattern of party competition in this country. The evidence from the comparative manifesto data remains impressionistic and limited, in both the countries and the time period. But the four-nation comparison of trends allows us to conclude that a 'contagion of the right' effect was probably apparent in Norway and Austria, both exemplifying consensus democracies using proportional representation electoral systems, but this pattern was not apparent in Canada and France, using majoritarian rules.

To summarize, this book has only sketched out certain features leading toward the success of the radical right. There are many avenues for further research which are opened by this study, and further cross-national survey

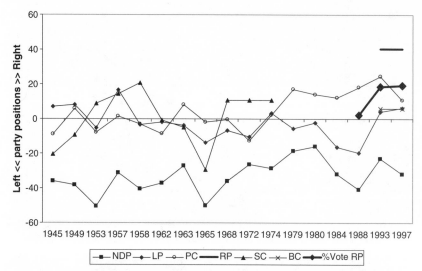

FIGURE 11.4. Canadian Party Competition and Support for the Reform Party, 1945–1997. The estimated left-wing or right-wing party positions are derived from the Manifesto Research Group coding of party platforms. *Sources:* The Manifesto Research Group.

analysis would allow us to explore the consistency of these patterns in far greater depth and across a wider range of societies. It would also be invaluable to examine the nature of the party organizational structures used by the radical right and to analyze the background and attitudes of their grassroots membership, where they have developed such a base. This study has also been unable to analyze the type of campaign coverage these parties receive in the news media, which is likely to be an important part of their success if they receive disproportionate attention relative to their size. Further work is necessary to document the legislative activities and policy priorities of the radical right once they enter elected office and whether they do have problems in reconciling their 'antipolitics' message with their role in power. The impact of their leadership, including their rhetoric and style, would provide important insights into the popularity of the radical right, along with studies of the communication networks linking these parties with broader social movements and diverse groups on the extreme right. In short, a broad and diverse research agenda could build upon and expand some of the initial propositions outlined in this account, providing further insights into this phenomenon.

We can conclude that rather than one-level 'demand,' or even two-level 'supply and demand' models, more comprehensive accounts can be enriched by considering the interaction of supply and demand within a broader institutional context. The book theorizes that the institutional context governing the nomination, campaigning, and election process is critical to the electoral fortunes of fringe and minor parties, notably the use of low threshold PR electoral systems. The most important political attitudes are the existence of widespread political disaffection and processes of partisan dealignment, both of which weaken the anchors of habitual voting choices, coupled with the rising salience of the values of cultural protectionism and antiglobalization. These factors are not confined to explaining the rise of the radical right per se; instead, they can potentially function to benefit other minor parties across the political spectrum. The survey evidence in this account also throws serious doubt on the thesis that support for the radical right is disproportionately based upon their appeal to a new social cleavage or underclass of low-skilled and low-qualified workers in inner-city areas, or to those with direct experience of unemployment or poverty. While common as a popular stereotype, in fact the class basis of support for the radical right remains mixed, drawing upon the petite bourgeoisie as well as traditional working class. There is also no automatic and direct relationship between rates of immigration, asylum seekers, and refugees in a country and the radical right share of votes or seats in that nation.

Within this context, how far radical right parties are capable of responding to popular demands remains critical for their electoral success.[16] And this is not a purely contingent phenomenon. Their ideological values and organizational development are particularly important in determining whether radical right parties remain marginalized at the periphery of the political system (such as the BNP), or whether they become significant political actors influencing the policy agenda, gaining elected office, and even entering government ministries (such as the FPÖ). Their rise depends heavily upon how far their own strategic ideological appeals work within the constraints set by the electoral system and the distribution of public opinion.[17] Under PR systems with low thresholds, radical right parties can be successfully elected by adopting more extreme ideological appeals based on emphasizing their signature issues of cultural protectionism. By contrast, under majoritarian systems with higher thresholds, radical right parties need to adopt more populist strategies to succeed. And where they rise, the process of building, institutionalizing, and consolidating party organizations is critical for the enduring success of the radical right, including developing formal procedures governing leadership succession and organizational structures, mobilizing a grassroots base of supporters and loyalists, and maintaining party discipline within the legislature. Parties which fail to institutionalize can occasionally surge in support in certain deviating elections, but if they fail to consolidate their success, they remain vulnerable to equally sudden collapse. The lessons of this study have important implications, not just for the success of the radical right, but also for patterns of party competition across political systems, for the future public policy agenda on issues of social tolerance, race relations, and multiculturalism, and thus for the underlying health of contemporary democracies.

Notes

Chapter 1: Understanding the Rise of the Radical Right

1. For comparative overviews see, for example, Paul Hainsworth. Ed. 1992. *The Extreme Right in Europe and the USA*. New York: St. Martin's Press; Peter H. Merkl and Leonard Weinberg. Eds. 1993. *Encounters with the Contemporary Radical Right*. Boulder, CO: Westview Press; Hans-Georg Betz. 1994. *Radical Rightwing Populism in Western Europe*. New York: St. Martin's Press; Herbert Kitschelt, with Anthony J. McGann. 1995. *The Radical Right in Western Europe: A Comparative Analysis*. Ann Arbor: University of Michigan; Luciano Cheles, Ronnie Ferguson, and Michalina Vaughan. Eds. 1995. *The Far Right in Western and Eastern Europe*. New York: Longman; Peter H. Merkl and L. Weinberg. Eds. 1997. *The Revival of Right-Wing Extremism in the Nineties*. London: Frank Cass; Hans-Georg Betz and Stefan Immerfall. Eds. 1998. *The New Politics of the Right: Neo-Populist Parties and Movements in Established Democracies*. New York: St Martin's Press; Paul Hainsworth. Ed. 2000. *The Politics of the Extreme Right: From the Margins to the Mainstream*. London: Pinter; Rachel Gibson. 2002. *The Growth of Anti-Immigrant Parties in Western Europe*. Lewiston, NY: Edwin Mellen Press; Martin Schain, Aristide Zolberg, and Patrick Hossay. Eds. 2002. *Shadows over Europe: The Development and Impact of the Extreme Right in Western Europe*. Houndmills: Palgrave Macmillan; Piero Ignazi. 2003. *Extreme Right Parties in Western Europe*. New York: Oxford University Press; Elisabeth Carter. 2005. *The Extreme Right in Western Europe: Success or Failure?* Manchester: Manchester University Press.
2. For the expectation that a worldwide 'liberal revolution' would supersede the attractions of authoritarianism, see, for example, the argument presented by Francis Fukuyama. 1992. *The End of History and the Last Man*. London: Hamish Hamilton.
3. The Canadian Reform Party, although showing considerable continuity, has relaunched its organization occasionally in recent years. The party became the Canada Reform Conservative Alliance (or Alliance for short) in the 2000

Canadian election, and subsequently merged with the Progressive Conservatives in October 2003 to become the Conservative Party of Canada. See Chapter 10 for a fuller discussion.

4. See Paul G. Lewis. 2000. *Political Parties in Post-Communist Eastern Europe*. London: Routledge; Paul G. Lewis. 2001. *Party Development and Democratic Change in Post-Communist Europe: The First Decade*. London: Frank Cass.

5. For a critical literature review, see Christopher T. Husbands. 2002. 'How to tame the dragon.' In *Shadows over Europe: The Development and Impact of the Extreme Right in Western Europe*, ed. Martin Schain, Aristide Zolberg, and Patrick Hossay. Houndmills: Palgrave Macmillan, chapter 3.

6. For early classics see, for example, Seymour Martin Lipset. 1955. 'The sources of the radical right.' In *The New American Right*, ed. Daniel Bell. New York: Criterion Books; Seymour Martin Lipset. 1960. *Political Man: The Social Basis of Politics*. New York: Doubleday; Theodor W. Adorno, Else Fraenkel-Brunswick, David J. Levinson, and R. Nevitt Sanford. 1950. *The Authoritarian Personality*. New York: Harper and Row; Daniel Bell. Ed. 1955. *The New American Right*. New York: Criterion Books.

7. Jens Rydgren. 2002. 'Radical right populism in Sweden: Still a failure, but for how long?' *Scandinavian Political Studies* 25 (1): 27–56.

8. The 'supply' and 'demand' distinction is developed by Roger Eatwell. 2003. 'Ten theories of the extreme right.' In *Right-Wing Extremism in the Twenty-First Century*, ed. Peter Merkl and Leonard Weinberg. London: Frank Cass.

9. This perspective is common throughout the literature but it is perhaps best exemplified by Hans-Georg Betz. 1994. *Radical Rightwing Populism in Western Europe*. New York: St. Martin's Press.

10. One of the clearest theoretical arguments along these lines is developed in Herbert Kitschelt. 1994. *The Transformation of European Social Democracy*. Cambridge: Cambridge University Press.

11. Theodor W. Adorno, Else Fraenkel-Brunswick, David J. Levinson, and R. Nevitt Sanford. 1950. *The Authoritarian Personality*. New York: Harper and Row. For a discussion of the history and impact of this theory, see Martin Roiser and Carla Willig. 2002. 'The strange death of the authoritarian personality: Fifty years of psychological and political debate.' *History of the Human Sciences* 15 (4): 71–96.

12. See Hans-Georg Betz. 1994. *Radical Rightwing Populism in Western Europe*. New York: St. Martin's Press.

13. The class basis of radical right voters is explored in Chapter 6.

14. For a systematic analysis of this pattern, see Marcel Lubbers and Peer Scheepers. 2000. 'Individual and contextual characteristics of the German extreme right-wing vote in the 1990s: A test of complementary theories.' *European Journal of Political Research* 38 (1): 63–94.

15. For this argument, see Pia Knigge. 1998. 'The ecological correlates of right-wing extremism in Western Europe.' *European Journal of Political Research* 34: 249–279.

16. Estimates of the flow of refugee populations are provided by the United Nations High Commissioner for Refugees (UNHCR). 2002 *statistics on asylum seekers, refugees and others of concern to UNHCR*. <u>www.unhcr.ch</u>, table 1.2.

17. For this argument see Piero Ignazi. 1992. 'The silent counter-revolution: Hypotheses on the emergence of extreme right-wing parties in Europe.' *European Journal of Political Research* 22 (1): 3–34; Piero Ignazi. 2003. *Extreme Right Parties in Western Europe.* New York: Oxford University Press.

18. Ronald Inglehart. 1977. *The Silent Revolution: Changing Values and Political Styles among Western Publics.* Princeton: Princeton University Press; Ronald Inglehart. 1997. *Modernization and Postmodernization: Cultural, Economic and Political Change in Forty-Three Societies.* Princeton: Princeton University Press.

19. See Nonna Mayer and P. Perrineau. 1992. 'Why do they vote for Le Pen?' *European Journal of Political Research* 22 (1): 123–141; Hans-Georg Betz. 1994. *Radical Rightwing Populism in Western Europe.* New York: St. Martin's Press.

20. For an overview of the evidence of disaffection with political institutions and with mainstream parties in advanced industrialized democracies, see Russell J. Dalton and Martin P. Wattenberg. Eds. 2000. *Parties without Partisans: Political Change in Advanced Industrial Democracies.* Oxford: Oxford University Press; Russell J. Dalton. 2004. *Democratic Challenges: Democratic Choices.* Oxford: Oxford University Press.

21. See the discussion of this issue in Christopher J. Anderson and Christine A. Guillory. 1997. 'Political institutions and satisfaction with democracy.' *American Political Science Review* 91 (1): 66–81.

22. Russell J. Dalton, Scott Flanagan, and Paul Allen Beck. Eds. 1984. *Electoral Change in Advanced Industrial Democracies: Realignment or Dealignment?* Princeton: Princeton University Press; Russell J. Dalton and Martin Wattenberg. Eds. 2001. *Parties without Partisans.* New York: Oxford University Press.

23. See, for example, Elisabeth Carter. 2005. *The Extreme Right in Western Europe: Success or Failure?* Manchester: Manchester University Press.

24. Herbert Kitschelt, with Anthony J. McGann. 1995. *The Radical Right in Western Europe: A Comparative Analysis.* Ann Arbor: University of Michigan. For a critical discussion of the historical evidence supporting this thesis, see the conclusion of Piero Ignazi. 2003. *Extreme Right Parties in Western Europe.* New York: Oxford University Press.

25. Wouter van der Brug, Meindert Fennema, and Jean Tillie. 2005. 'Why some anti-immigrant parties fail and others succeed: A two-step model of aggregate electoral support.' *Comparative Political Studies* forthcoming.

26. Elisabeth Carter. 2005. *The Extreme Right in Western Europe: Success or Failure?* Manchester: Manchester University Press, chapter 4.

27. Martin Schain. 1987. 'The National Front in France and the constitution of political legitimacy.' *West European Politics* 10 (2): 229–252.

28. Maurice Duverger. 1954. *Political Parties, Their Organization and Activity in the Modern State.* New York: Wiley; Arend Lijphart. 2001. 'The pros and cons – but mainly pros – of consensus democracy.' *Acta Politica* 35: 363–398; R. B. Andeweg. 2001. 'Lijphart v. Lijphart: The cons. of consensus democracy in homogeneous societies.' *Acta Politica* 36: 117–128.

29. For a discussion of the distinction between the 'mechanical' and 'psycholog-
    ical' aspects see André Blais and R. Kenneth Carty. 1991. 'The psychological
    impact of electoral laws – Measuring Duverger's elusive factor.' *British Jour-
    nal of Political Science* 21 (1): 79–93.
30. For a discussion of the concept of 'political opportunity structure,' see W. A.
    Gamson. 1975. *The Strategy of Social Protest*. Homewood: Dorsey Press;
    Sidney Tarrow. 1994. *Power in Movement*. Cambridge: Cambridge Univer-
    sity Press; Sidney Tarrow. 1991. 'Collective action and political opportunity
    structure in waves of mobilization – Some theoretical perspectives.' *Kolner
    Zeitschrift Fur Soziologie Und Sozialpsychologie* 43 (4): 647–670.
31. Ruud Koopmans. 1996. 'Explaining the rise of racist and extreme right
    violence in Western Europe: Grievances or opportunities?' *European Jour-
    nal of Political Research* 30: 185–216; Ruud Koopmans and Paul Statham.
    Eds. 2000. *Challenging Immigration and Ethnic Relations Politics: Compar-
    ative European Perspectives*. Oxford: Oxford University Press, introduction;
    Wouter van der Brug, Meindert Fennema, and Jean Tillie. 2005. 'Why some
    anti-immigrant parties fail and others succeed: A two-step model of aggregate
    electoral support.' *Comparative Political Studies* forthcoming.
32. Ruud Koopmans. 1999. 'Political. Opportunity. Structure. Some splitting to
    balance the lumping.' *Sociological Forum* 14(1): 93–105.
33. We put aside, for the moment, any consideration of 'informal' electoral rules,
    which can be understood as those widely shared tacit social norms and con-
    ventions governing electoral behavior enforced by social sanction within any
    particular culture. These are more properly understood as 'social norms'
    rather than informal institutions. This definition also excludes more ambigu-
    ous cases, such as party rulebooks that are enforced by internal committees
    within particular party organizations rather than by court of law, although
    there is a gray dividing line, as these cases may be relevant for legal redress.
    For a discussion of the meaning of 'rules' see J. M. Carey. 1999. 'Parchment,
    equilibria, and institutions.' *Comparative Political Studies* 33 (6–7): 735–761.
    See also Pippa Norris. 2004. *Electoral Engineering*. Cambridge: Cambridge
    University Press.
34. For the previous development of this theory, see Pippa Norris. 2004. *Electoral
    Engineering*. Cambridge: Cambridge University Press.
35. For alternative rational choice accounts of political extremism, see Albert
    Breton, Gianluigi Galeotti, Pierre Salmon, and Ronald Wintrobe. 2002.
    Eds. *Political Extremism and Rationality*. Cambridge: Cambridge University
    Press.
36. The 'proximity model' is also known as the 'least-distance' model. This
    model is adopted for the study, rather than the alternative Rabinowitz and
    McDonald directional model, in part because of the absence of suitable is-
    sue scales in the datasets under comparison. George Rabinowitz and Stuart
    Elaine MacDonald. 1989. 'A directional theory of voting.' *American Polit-
    ical Science Review* 83: 93–121. For a discussion and comparison of these
    models, and the extensive literature flowing from these theories, see Samuel
    Merrill III and Bernard Grofman. 1999. *A Unified Theory of Voting: Di-
    rectional and Proximity Spatial Models*. Cambridge: Cambridge University
    Press.

37. The classic argument is presented in Anthony Downs. 1957. *An Economic Theory of Democracy*. New York: Harper and Row. See also James M. Enelow and Melvin Hinich. Eds. 1984. *The Spatial Theory of Voting*. New York: Cambridge University Press. The modified version of the theory presented here has been influenced by the account developed by James A. Stimson. 1991. *Public Opinion in America: Moods, Cycles and Swings*. Boulder, CO: Westview Press, as well as by work on party competition under different electoral rules, notably Gary Cox. 1990. 'Centripetal and centrifugal incentives in electoral systems.' *American Journal of Political Science* 34: 903–935.

38. See, for example, the trends in attitudes toward gender equality, women's roles, and sexual liberalization, documented in Ronald Inglehart and Pippa Norris. 2003. *Rising Tide: Gender Equality and Cultural Change Worldwide*. Cambridge: Cambridge University Press.

39. Benjamin I. Page and Robert Y. Shapiro. 1992. *The Rational Public: Fifty Years of Trends in Americans' Policy Preferences*. Chicago: University of Chicago Press. See also William G. Mayer. 1992. *The Changing American Mind: How and Why American Public Opinion Changes between 1960 and 1988*. Michigan: University of Michigan Press; Christopher Wlezien. 1995. 'The public as thermostat: Dynamics of preferences for spending.' *American Journal of Political Science* 39 (4): 981–1000.

40. Pippa Norris and Joni Lovenduski. 2004. 'Why parties fail to learn: Electoral defeat, selective perception and British party politics.' *Party Politics* 10 (1): 85–104.

41. David Held, Anthony McGrew, David Goldblatt, and Jonathan Perraton. 1999. *Global Transformations: Politics, Economics and Culture*. Stanford, CA: Stanford University Press; Paul Hirst and G. Thompson. 1996. *Globalization in Question: The International Economy and the Possibilities of Governance*. Cambridge: Polity; Joseph Nye and John Donahue. Eds. 2002. *Governance in a Globalizing World*. Washington, DC: Brookings Institution Press.

42. Maurice Duverger. 1954. *Political Parties, Their Organization and Activity in the Modern State*. New York: Wiley; Douglas W. Rae. 1971. *The Political Consequences of Electoral Laws*. Rev. ed. New Haven: Yale University Press; William H. Riker. 1976. 'The number of political parties: A reexamination of Duverger's Law.' *Comparative Politics* 9: 93–106; William H. Riker. 1982. 'The two-party system and Duverger's Law: An essay on the history of political science.' *American Political Science Review* 76: 753–766; William H. Riker. 1986. 'Duverger's Law Revisited.' In *Electoral Laws and Their Political Consequences*, ed. Bernard Grofman and Arend Lijphart. New York: Agathon Press; Arend Lijphart, 1994. *Electoral Systems and Party Systems*. Oxford: Oxford University Press.

43. For a similar argument, see C. L. Carter. 2002. 'Proportional representation and the fortunes of right-wing extremist parties.' *West European Politics* 25 (3): 125–146; Elisabeth Carter. 2005. *The Extreme Right in Western Europe: Success or Failure?* Manchester: Manchester University Press.

44. Gary Cox. 1990. 'Centripetal and centrifugal incentives in electoral systems.' *American Journal of Political Science* 34: 903–935.

45. The distinction between 'bridging' and 'bonding' parties is derived from the literature on social capital, as originally applied to social groups and associations. See Robert D. Putnam. 2002. *Democracies in Flux*. New York: Oxford University Press, p. 11. The term 'bridging party' is similar to the use of the term 'catch-all' developed by Kirchheimer, except that these concepts carry different normative baggage. See Otto Kirchheimer. 1966. 'The transformation of Western European party systems.' In *Political Parties and Political Development*, ed. J. La Palombara and M. Weiner. Princeton, NJ: Princeton University Press.

46. Herbert Kitschelt, with Anthony J. McGann. 1995. *The Radical Right in Western Europe: A Comparative Analysis*. Ann Arbor: University of Michigan; Wouter van der Brug, Meindert Fennema, and Jean Tillie. 2005. 'Why some anti-immigrant parties fail and others succeed: A two-step model of aggregate electoral support.' *Comparative Political Studies* forthcoming.

47. See the discussion in Arend Lijphart. 1994. *Electoral Systems and Party Systems*. Oxford: Oxford University Press.

48. See David Robertson. 1976. *A Theory of Party Competition*. London: Wiley; Ian Budge, David Robertson, and Derek Hearl. Eds. 1987. *Ideology, Strategy and Party Change: Spatial Analysis of Postwar Election Programmes in Nineteen Democracies*. Cambridge: Cambridge University Press; Ian Budge, Hans-Dieter Klingemann, Andrew Volkens, Judith Bara, and Eric Tanenbaum. 2001. *Mapping Policy Preferences*. Oxford: Oxford University Press.

49. See Jan Kleinnijenhuis and Paul Pennings. 2001. 'Measurement of party positions on the basis of party programs, media coverage and voter perceptions.' In *Estimating the Policy Position of Political Actors*, ed. Michael Laver. London: Routledge.

50. David P. Fan. 1988. *Predictions of Public Opinion from the Mass Media: Computer Content Analysis and Mathematical Modeling*. New York: Greenwood.

51. For previous expert surveys, see Francis G. Castles and Peter Mair. 1984. 'Left-right political scales: Some 'expert' judgments.' *European Journal of Political Research* 12 (1): 73–88; John Huber and Ronald Inglehart. 1995. 'Expert interpretations of party space and party locations in forty-two societies.' *Party Politics* 1 (January): 73–111. This book draws mainly upon the most recent survey, conducted in 2000 by Marcel Lubbers, for which we are much indebted. Details of the data, methodology, and codebook are available from Marcel Lubbers [principal investigator]. 2000. *Expert Judgment Survey of Western European Political Parties 2000* [machine readable data-set]. Nijmegen, the Netherlands: NWO, Department of Sociology, University of Nijmegen. For a discussion of the pros and cons of this approach, see Ian Budge. 2000. 'Expert judgments of party policy positions: Uses and limitations in political research.' *European Journal of Political Research* 37 (1): 103–113.

52. See, for example, Hans-Georg Betz. 2002. 'The divergent paths of the FPÖ and the *Lega Nord*.' In *Shadows over Europe: The Development and Impact of the Extreme Right in Western Europe*, ed. Martin Schain, Aristide Zolberg, and Patrick Hossay. Houndmills: Palgrave Macmillan.

53. See Patrick Hossay. 2002. 'Why Flanders?' In *Shadows over Europe: The Development and Impact of the Extreme Right in Western Europe*, ed. Martin Schain, Aristide Zolberg, and Patrick Hossay. Houndmills: Palgrave Macmillan.

54. Tor Bjørklund and Jørgen Goul Andersen. 'Anti-immigration parties in Denmark and Norway.' In *Shadows over Europe: The Development and Impact of the Extreme Right in Western Europe*, ed. Martin Schain, Aristide Zolberg, and Patrick Hossay. Houndmills: Palgrave Macmillan.

Chapter 2: Classifying the Radical Right

1. This book draws mainly upon the most recent expert survey, conducted in 2000 by Marcel Lubbers, for which we are much indebted. Details of the data, methodology, and codebook are available from Marcel Lubbers [principal investigator]. 2000. *Expert Judgment Survey of Western European Political Parties 2000* [machine readable dataset]. Nijmegen, the Netherlands: NWO, Department of Sociology, University of Nijmegen.

2. For a discussion of the most different and most similar approaches to comparative politics, see Todd Landman. 2000. *Issues and Methods in Comparative Politics*. London: Routledge, chapter 2.

3. For more details of the European Social Survey, including the questionnaire and methodology, see http://naticento2.uuhost.uk.uu. net/index.htm. Data for an initial twenty countries, along with comprehensive documentation, is accessible at http://ess.nsd.uib.no. It is anticipated that subsequent releases will include data from two more countries which participated in Round One, namely France and Turkey. The survey is funded via the European Commission's fifth Framework Program, with supplementary funds from the European Science Foundation, which also sponsored the development of the study over a number of years. I am most grateful to the European Commission and the ESF for their support for this project, and to the work of the ESS Central Coordinating Team, led by Roger Jowell, for making this survey data available.

4. The CSES dataset also includes an election survey in Hong Kong, but this was dropped to facilitate consistent comparison across independent nation-states. The dataset used in this study is based on the 31 July 2002 release of Module 1, with the exception of France which was derived from the early release of Module II of the CSES. Full details are available at www.umich.edu/˜nes/cses. I am most grateful to the CSES secretariat, and all the partner national election survey organizations, for making this dataset available.

5. Although use of the term 'transitional democracies' may be misleading. See Thomas Carothers. 2002. 'The End of the Transition Paradigm.' *Journal of Democracy* 13 (1): 5–21.

6. See Adam Przeworski, Michael E. Alvarez, Jose Antonio Cheibub, and Fernando Limongi. 2000. *Democracy and Development: Political Institutions and Well-Being in the World, 1950–1990*. New York: Cambridge University Press. For the World Bank indicators of good governance see Daniel Kaufmann, Aart Kraay, and M. Mastruzzi. May 2003. *Governance*

Matters III: Governance Indicators 1996–2002. http://www.worldbank.org/ wbi/governance/pubs/govmatters3.html. For the 'democratic audit' approach, see International IDEA www.IDEA.int.

7. See also Geraldo L. Munck and Jay Verkuilen. 2002. 'Conceptualizing and measuring democracy – Evaluating alternative indices.' *Comparative Political Studies* 35 (1): 5–34.

8. See, in particular, Ronald Inglehart and Pippa Norris. 2003. *Rising Tide: Gender Equality and Cultural Change around the World.* New York: Cambridge University Press.

9. Societies are defined based on the annual ratings provided by Freedom House since 1972. *The level of freedom* is classified according to the combined mean score for political rights and civil liberties in Freedom House's 1972–2000 annual surveys *Freedom of the World.* www.freedomhouse.org.

10. For a discussion see, for example, Peter Mair and Cas Mudde. 1998. 'The party family and its study.' *Annual Review of Political Science* 1: 211–229; Meindert Fennema. 1997. 'Some conceptual issues and problems in the comparison of anti-immigrant parties in Western Europe.' *Party Politics* 3:473–92.

11. Cas Mudde. 2000. *The Ideology of the Extreme Right.* New York: St. Martin's Press.

12. Simon Hix. 2002. 'Parties at the European level.' In *Political Parties in Advanced Industrial Democracies*, ed. Paul Webb, David Farrell, and Ian Holliday. Oxford: Oxford University Press, table 10.5.

13. For example, in the EP Lega Nord is affiliated with the Regionalist parties and European Radical Alliance Group.

14. Sabrina P. Ramet. Ed. 1999. *The Radical Right in Central and Eastern Europe since 1989.* Pennsylvania: The University of Pennsylvania Press, p. 24.

15. See, for example, Kenneth Hoover and Raymond Plant. 1989. *Conservative Capitalism in Britain and the United States.* New York: Routledge; Desmond S. King. 1987. *The New Right: Politics, Markets and Citizenship.* Chicago: Dorsey Press.

16. Herbert Kitschelt, with Anthony J. McGann. 1995. *The Radical Right in Western Europe: A Comparative Analysis.* Ann Arbor: University of Michigan Press, pp. 27–42.

17. Michael Cox and Martin Durham. 'The politics of anger: The extreme right in the United States.' In *The Politics of the Extreme Right*, ed. Paul Hainsworth. London: Pinter.

18. Daniel Bell. Ed. [1963] 2001. *The Radical Right.* New York: Transaction Books. See also Seymour Martin Lipset. 1978. *The Politics of Unreason: Rightwing Extremism in America 1790–1977.* 2d ed. Chicago: University of Chicago Press; Richard Hofstedter. 1967. *The Paranoid Style in American Politics.* New York: Vintage Books.

19. Peter Mair and Cas Mudde. 1998. 'The party family and its study.' *Annual Review of Political Science* 1: 211–229.

20. For previous expert surveys, see Francis G. Castles and Peter Mair. 1984. 'Left-right political scales: Some "expert" judgments.' *European Journal of Political Research* 12 (1): 73–88; Michael Laver and W. Ben Hunt. 1992. *Policy and Party Competition.* New York: Routledge; John Huber and Ronald

Inglehart. 1995. 'Expert interpretations of party space and party locations in forty-two societies.' *Party Politics* 1 (January): 73–111. For a discussion of the pros and cons of this approach, see Myunghee Kim and Michael D. Mc-Donald. 2002. 'Cross-national comparability of party left-right positions.' Southern Political Science Association Annual Meeting, November, Savannah, Georgia; Ian Budge. 2000. 'Expert judgments of party policy positions: Uses and limitations in political research.' *European Journal of Political Research* 37 (1): 103–113.

21. Michael Coppedge. 'A classification of Latin American political parties.' Kellogg Institute, University of Notre Dame Working Paper 244, November 1997.

22. The Alleanza Nazionale, in particular, is not always consistently classified as part of the radical right family in all studies.

23. Sabrina P. Ramet. Ed. 1999. *The Radical Right in Central and Eastern Europe since 1989.* University Park: Pennsylvania State University Press; Michael Coppedge. 'A classification of Latin American political parties.' Kellogg Institute, University of Notre Dame Working Paper 244, November 1997.

24. Notably by Arthur S. Banks, Thomas C. Mueller, and William R. Overstreet. 2003. *Political Handbook of the World, 2000–2002.* Binghamton, NY: CSA Publications; and also Jan-Erik Lane, David McKay, and Kenneth Newton. Eds. 1997. *Political Data Handbook.* 2d ed. Oxford: Oxford University Press.

25. *Parliamentary* parties are defined in a similar way as those that win seats in the lower house of the national legislature. *Fringe parliamentary parties* win less than 2.9% of seats, while by contrast *relevant parliamentary parties* gain 3.0% or more.

26. Thomas T. Mackie and Richard Rose. 1991. *The International Almanac of Electoral History.* Washington, DC: CQ Press; Tom Mackie and Richard Rose. 1997. *A Decade of Election Results: Updating the International Almanac.* Studies in Public Policy. Glasgow: University of Strathclyde; Richard Rose, Neil Munro, and Tom Mackie. 1998. *Elections in Central and Eastern Europe since 1990.* Studies in Public Policy 300. Glasgow: University of Strathclyde; Elections around the World www.electionworld.org.

27. Giovanni Sartori. 1976. *Parties and Party Systems: A Framework for Analysis.* New York: Cambridge University Press.

Chapter 3: Comparing Parties

1. Seymour Martin Lipset and Stein Rokkan. 1967. *Party Systems and Voter Alignments.* New York: Free Press. See also Richard Rose and Derek W. Urwin. 1970. 'Persistence and change in Western party systems since 1945.' *Political Studies* 18 (3): 287–319. Rose and Urwin concluded: "The electoral strength of most parties in Western nations since the war had changed very little from election to election, from decade to decade, or within the lifespan of a generation," p. 318.

2. Mogens N. Pedersen. 1979. 'The dynamics of European party systems: Changing patterns of electoral volatility.' *European Journal of Political*

Research 7: 1–26. For the argument that the electoral changes were largely within, rather than across, the major blocks, see Stephano Bartolini and Peter Mair. 1990. *Identity, Competition, and Electoral Availability: The Stabilization of European Electorates, 1885–1985.* Cambridge: Cambridge University Press; Peter Mair. 1997. *Party System Change: Approaches and Interpretations.* Clarendon Press: Oxford.

3. The sources, discussed in the previous chapter, include Arthur S. Banks and Thomas C. Mueller. 1999. *Political Handbook of the World, 1999.* Binghamton, NY: CSA Publications; Arthur S. Banks, Thomas C. Mueller, and William R. Overstreet. 2003. *Political Handbook of the World, 2000–2002.* Binghamton, NY: CSA Publications.

4. Stanley Hoffman. 1956. *Le Mouvement Poujade.* Paris: A. Colin.

5. Martin Schain. 1987. 'The National Front in France and the Construction of Political Legitimacy.' *West European Politics* 10 (2): 229–252; Subrata Mitra. 1988. 'The National Front in France – A Single-Issue Movement?' *West European Politics* 11 (2): 47–64; E. G. DeClair. 1999. *Politics on the Fringe: The People, Policies, and Organization of the French National Front.* Durham, NC: Duke University Press; John W. P. Veugelers. 2000. 'Right-wing extremism in contemporary France: A "silent counterrevolution"?' *Sociological Quarterly* 41 (1): 19–40; Peter Davis. 2002. *The Extreme Right in France, 1789 to the Present: From De Maistre to Le Pen.* London: Routledge.

6. D. S. Bell and Byron Criddle. 2002. 'Presidentialism restored: The French elections of April–May and June 2002.' *Parliamentary Affairs* 55 (4): 643–650; Arnauld Miguet. 2002. 'The French elections of 2002: After the earthquake, the deluge.' *West European Politics* 25 (4): 207–220.

7. Joop van Holsteyn and Josje M. den Ridder. 2003. 'In the eye of the beholder: The perception of the List Pim Fortuyn and the parliamentary elections of May 2002.' *Acta Politica* 38 (1): 69–88; Joop van Holsteyn. 2003. 'A new kid on the block: Pim Fortuyn and the Dutch parliamentary election of May 2002.' In *British Elections and Parties Review*, ed. Colin Rallings et al. London: Frank Cass, pp. 29–46; Joop van Holsteyn and G. A. Irwin. 2003. 'Never a dull moment: Pim Fortuyn and the Dutch parliamentary election of 2002.' *West European Politics* 26 (2): 41–66.

8. Marc Swyngedouw. 2000. 'Belgium: Explaining the relationship between Vlaams Blok and the city of Antwerp.' In *The Politics of the Extreme Right*, ed. Paul Hainsworth. London: Pinter.

9. Marc Swyngedouw and G. Ivaldi. 2001. 'The extreme right utopia in Belgium and France: The ideology of the Flemish *Vlaams Blok* and the French *Front National*.' *West European Politics* 24 (3): 1–22; M. Breuning and J. T. Ishiyama. 1998. 'The rhetoric of nationalism: Rhetorical strategies of the *Volksunie* and *Vlaams Blok* in Belgium, 1991–1995.' *Political Communication* 15 (1): 5–26.

10. Christopher T. Husbands. 1992. 'Belgium: Flemish legions on the march.' In *The Extreme Rights in Europe and the USA*, ed. Paul Hainsworth. New York: St. Martin's Press; Jack Billiet and Hans de Witte. 1995. 'Attitudinal dispositions to vote for a "new" extreme right-wing party: The case of "Vlaams Blok."' *European Journal of Political Research* 27 (2): 181–202.

11. Wolfgang C. Müller. 2000. 'The Austrian election of October 1999: A shift to the right.' *West European Politics* 23 (3): 191–200.
12. Lothar Höbelt. 2003. *Defiant populist: Jörg Haider and the Politics of Austria.* Purdue: Purdue University Press; Ruth Woder and Anton Pelinska. Eds. 2002. *The Haider Phenomenon in Austria.* New Brunswick: Transaction Publishers; Wolfgang C. Müller. 2000. *Elections and the Dynamics of the Austrian Party System since 1986.* Vienna: Zentrum für angewandte Politikforschung; Wolfgang C. Müller. 2002. 'Evil or the "engine of democracy"? Populism and party competition in Austria.' In *Populism in Western Democracies*, ed. Yves Mény and Yves Surel. Houndmills: Palgrave Macmillan, pp. 155–175; Wolfgang C. Müller. 2000. 'Wahlen und die Dynamik des österreichischen Parteiensystems seit 1986.' In *Das österreichische Wahlverhalten*, ed. Fritz Plasser, Peter A. Ulram, and Franz Sommer. Vienna: Signum, pp. 13–54; Wolfgang C. Müller. 2004. 'The parliamentary election in Austria, November 2002.' *Electoral Studies* 23 (2): 346–353.
13. A. Ladner. 2001. 'Swiss political parties: Between persistence and change.' *West European Politics*. 24 (2): 123ff.
14. Hanspeter Kriesi. 1998. *Le système politique suisse.* Paris: Economica; Urs Altermatt and Hanspeter Kriesi. Eds. 1995. *Rechtsextremismus in der Schweiz: Organisationen und Radikalisierung in den 1980er und 1990er Jahren.* Zürich: Neue Zürcher Zeitung.
15. Richard Stöss. 1988. 'The problem of rightwing extremism in West Germany.' In *Right Extremism in Western Europe*, ed. Klaus von Beyme. London: Frank Cass.
16. Richard Stöss. 1988. 'The problem of rightwing extremism in West Germany.' In *Right Extremism in Western Europe*, ed. Klaus von Beyme. London: Frank Cass; Marcel Lubbers and Peers Scheepers. 2001. 'Explaining the trend in extreme right-wing voting: Germany 1989–1998.' *European Sociological Review* 17 (4): 431–449; Susann Backer. 2000. 'Right-wing extremism in unified Germany.' In *The Extreme Rights in Europe and the USA*, ed. Paul Hainsworth. New York: St. Martin's Press.
17. Franco Ferraresi. 1996. *Threats to Democracy: The Radical Right in Italy after the War.* Princeton, N.J.: Princeton University Press, 1996.
18. Roberto Chiarini. 1995. 'The Italian far right: The search for legitimacy.' In *The Far Right in Western and Eastern Europe*, ed. Luciano Cheles, Ronnie Ferguson, and Michalina Vaughan. New York: Longman, pp. 19–45; Piero Ignazi. 1993. 'The Changing Profile of the Italian Social Movement.' In *Encounters with the Contemporary Radical Right*, ed. Peter H. Merkl and Leonard Weinberg. Oxford: Westview Press, pp. 75–94; Tom Gallagher. 2000. 'The Italian far right in the 1990s.' In *The Extreme Rights in Europe and the USA*, ed. Paul Hainsworth. New York: St. Martin's Press.
19. Thomas W. Gold. 2003. *The Lega Nord and Contemporary Politics in Italy.* New York: Palgrave Macmillan; Anna Bull and Mark Gilbert. 2001. *The Lega Nord and the Northern Question in Italian Politics.* New York: Palgrave Macmillan.
20. Piero Ignazi. 2003. *Extreme Right Parties in Western Europe.* Oxford: Oxford University Press, p. 61.

21. Sheelagh Ellwood. 1995. 'The extreme right in Spain: A dying species?' In *The Far Right in Western and Eastern Europe*, ed. Luciano Cheles, Ronnie Ferguson, and Michalina Vaughan. New York: Longman; P. Chibber and M. Torcal. 1997. 'Elite strategy, social cleavages, and party systems in a new democracy – Spain.' *Comparative Political Studies* 30 (1): 27–54.

22. Antonio Costa Pinto. 1995. 'The radical right in contemporary Portugal.' In *The Far Right in Western and Eastern Europe*, ed. Luciano Cheles, Ronnie Ferguson, and Michalina Vaughan. New York: Longman.

23. Lars Svåsand. 1998. 'Scandinavian Right-Wing Radicalism.' In *The New Politics of the Right: Neo-Populist Parties and Movements in Established Democracies*. New York: St. Martin's Press, pp. 77–94.

24. Jens Rydgren. 2004. 'Explaining the emergence of radical right-wing populist parties: The case of Denmark.' *West European Politics* 27 (3): 474–502.

25. For details of their website, see http://www.danskfolkeparti.dk/.

26. Christopher J. Anderson. 1996. 'Economics, politics, and foreigners: Populist party support in Denmark and Norway.' *Electoral Studies* 15 (4): 497–511.

27. W. M. Downs. 2001. 'Pariahs in their midst: Belgian and Norwegian parties react to extremist threats.' *West European Politics* 24 (3): 23–42; Robert Harmel and Lars Svåsand. 1997. 'The influence of new parties on old parties' platforms: The cases of the progress parties and conservative parties of Denmark and Norway.' *Party Politics* 3 (3): 315–340.

28. Jens Rydgren. 2002. 'Radical right populism in Sweden: Still a failure, but for how long?' *Scandinavian Political Studies* 25 (1): 27–56.

29. The ultramarginal right-wing parties in Finland include the Isänmaallinen Kansallis Liitto (IKL – Patriotic National Alliance), launched in April 1993, and the older Poujadist Finnish Rural Party/True Finns Party. See Kyösti Pekonen. Ed. 1999. *The New Radical Right in Finland*. Helsinki: The Finnish Political Science Association.

30. The 'preferential' voting system used for the Australian House of Representatives, where electors cast rank-ordered ballots, is also known as the Alternative Voting System. Of the thirty-nine federal elections held in Australia since 1901, only eight have produced non–major party support above 10% in the first-preference vote. See Ian McAllister. 2002. 'Political parties in Australia: Party stability in a utilitarian society.' In *Political Parties in Advanced Industrial Democracies*, ed. Paul Webb, David Farrell, and Ian Holliday. Oxford: Oxford University Press.

31. Carol Johnson. 1998. 'Pauline Hanson and One Nation.' In *The New Politics of the Right*, eds Hans-Georg Bens and Stefan Immerfall. New York: St. Martin's Press; S. Jackman. 1998. 'Pauline Hanson, the mainstream and political elites: The place of race in Australian political ideology.' *Australian Journal of Political Science* 33 (2): 167–186; I. E. Deutchman. 2000. 'Pauline Hanson and the rise and fall of the radical right in Australia.' *Patterns of Prejudice* 34 (1): 49–62; D. Ben-Moshe. 2001. 'One Nation and the Australian far right.' *Patterns of Prejudice* 35 (3): 24–40; Rachel Gibson, Ian McAllister, and T. Swenson. 2002. 'The politics of race and immigration in Australia: One Nation voting in the 1998 election.' *Ethnic and Racial Studies* 25 (5): 823–844; Anthony Mughan, Clive Bean, and Ian McAllister. 2003. 'Economic

globalization, job insecurity and the populist reaction.' *Electoral Studies* 22: 617–633. In the October federal elections, One Nation polled 1.15% of the first-preference nationwide vote in the House of Representatives, and 1.9% in the Senate, far less successful than the 6.94% and 7.54% won respectively by the Greens, another minor party. See the Australian Election Commission http://vtr.aec.gov.au/NationalTotal-12246.htm.

32. Jack Vowles. 2002. 'Parties and society in New Zealand,' table 14.3. In *Political Parties in Advanced Industrial Democracies*, ed. Paul Webb, David Farrell, and Ian Holliday. Oxford: Oxford University Press.

33. Jonathan Boston, Stephen Levine, Elizabeth McLeay, and Nigel S. Roberts. 1996. *New Zealand under MMP: A New Politics?* Auckland: Auckland University Press; Jack Vowles, Peter Aimer, Susan Banducci, and Jeffrey Karp. 1998. *Voters' Victory? New Zealand's First Election under Proportional Representation*. Auckland: Auckland University Press; Raymond Miller. 1998. 'New Zealand First.' In *The New Politics of the Right*, ed. Hans-Georg Betz and Stefan Immerfall. New York: St. Martin's Press; D. Denemark and Shaun Bowler. 2002. 'Minor parties and protest votes in Australia and New Zealand: Locating populist politics.' *Electoral Studies* 21(1): 47–67. Another new right-wing party is ACT New Zealand, but their party program emphasizes libertarian principles governing the market and immigration policies as well, so that they do not qualify for the radical right as such.

34. L. S. Tossutti. 1996. 'From communitarian protest towards institutionalization – The evolution of "hybrid" parties in Canada and Italy.' *Party Politics* 2 (4): 435–454; Neil Nevitt, Andre Blais, Elisabeth Gidengil, Richard Johnston, and Henry Brady. 1998. 'The populist right in Canada: The rise of the Reform party of Canada.' In *The New Politics of the Right*, ed. Hans-Georg Betz and Stefan Immerfall. New York: St. Martin's Press; Harold D. Clarke, Alan Kornberg, F. Ellis, and J. Rapkin. 2000. 'Not for fame or fortune – A note on membership and activity in the Canadian Reform Party.' *Party Politics* 6 (1): 75–93; Lawrence Mayer, Erol Kaymak, and Jeff W. Justice. 2000. 'Populism and the triumph of the politics of identity: The transformation of the Canadian party system.' *Nationalism and Ethnic Politics* 6 (1): 72–102.

35. I am indebted to Lynda Erickson, Larry LeDuc, Elisabeth Gidengil, and André Blais for these observations, made in personal communications with the author.

36. Richard C. Thurlow. 2000. *Fascism in Britain: From Oswald Mosley's Blackshirts to the National Front*. Stroud: Sutton; Martin Walker. 1977. *The National Front*. London: Fontana/Collins; Christopher T. Husbands. 1988. 'Extreme right-wing politics in Great Britain: The recent marginalization of the National Front.' In *Right-Wing Extremism in Western Europe*, ed. Klaus von Beyme. 1988. London: Frank Cass.

37. Overall, in total the BNP won 47,000 votes or 0.2% of the national vote in the May 2001 UK general election. *The British Parliamentary Constituency Database 1992–2001*.

38. See the UKIP official party website: http://www.ukip.org/index.php?menu=fivefreedoms&page=fivefreedoms3.

39. Peter John, Helen Margetts, and Stuart Weir. 2004. 'The Rise of the BNP and UKIP: Public Opinion and Voting in the 2004 European Elections.' Paper presented at the EPOP annual conference, Nuffield College, Oxford, September 2004.

40. For details, see John Curtice and Michael Steed. 2001. 'Appendix 2: An analysis of the results.' In *The British General Election of 2001*, David Butler and Dennis Kavanagh. London: Macmillan; Andrew Pierce. 2001. 'Medical white coat has replaced the white suit.' In *The Times Guide to the House of Commons*. London: Times Books.

41. See Michael Cox and Martin Durham. 'The politics of anger: The extreme right in the United States.' In *The Politics of the Extreme Right*, ed. Paul Hainsworth. London: Pinter; Jeffrey Kaplan and Leonard Weinberg. 1998. *The Emergence of a Euro-American Right*. New Brunswick, NJ: University of Rutgers Press; Betty Dobratz and Stephanie L. Shanks-Meile. 2000. *The White Separatist Movement in the United States: White Power, White Pride!* Baltimore: Johns Hopkins University Press; Carol Swain and Russ Nieli. Eds. 2003. *Contemporary Voices of White Nationalism in America*. Cambridge: Cambridge University Press.

42. Stephen Rosenstone, R. L. Behr, and E. H. Lazarus. 1996. *Third Parties in America*. Princeton: Princeton University Press.

43. Richard Gunther and Larry Diamond. 2003. 'Species of political parties: A new typology.' *Party Politics* 9 (2): 167–199.

44. See Herbert Kitschelt. 1992. 'The formation of party systems in East Central Europe.' *Politics and Society* 20 (March): 7–50; Herbert Kitschelt, Zdenka Mansfeldova, Radoslaw Markowski, and Gabor Toka. 1999. *Post-Communist Party Systems*. Cambridge: Cambridge University Press; William L. Miller, Stephen White, and Paul Heywood. 1998. *Values and Political Change in Post-Communist Europe*. New York: St. Martin's Press.

45. Paul G. Lewis. 2000. *Political Parties in Post-Communist Eastern Europe*. London: Routledge; Paul G. Lewis. 2001. *Party Development and Democratic Change in Post-Communist Europe: The First Decade*. London: Frank Cass.

46. Sabrina P. Ramet. Ed. 1999. *The Radical Right in Central and Eastern Europe since 1989*. University Park: Pennsylvania State University Press.

47. Further reference information about all these parties can be found in Arthur S. Banks, Thomas C. Muller, and William R. Overstreet. Eds. 2002. *Political Handbook of the World 2000–2002*. Binghamton, NY: CSA Publications.

48. Robert Jackson Alexander. Ed. 1988. *Political Parties of the Americas: Canada, Latin America, and the West Indies*, 2 vols. Westport, CT: Greenwood Press; Robert H. Dix. 1989. 'Cleavage structures and party systems in Latin America.' *Comparative Politics* (October): 23–37. Charles D. Ameringer. Ed. 1992. *Political Parties of the Americas: 1980s to 1990s*. Westport, CT: Greenwood Press; Mark P. Jones. 1994. 'Presidential election laws and multipartyism in Latin America.' *Political Research Quarterly* 47: 41–57; Scott Mainwaring and Timothy Scully. 1995. *Building Democratic Institutions: Party Systems in Latin America*. Stanford, CA: Stanford

University Press; Michael Coppedge. 1998. 'The dynamic diversity of Latin American party systems.' *Party Politics* 4 (4): 547–568.

49. R. Meneguello. 1995. 'Electoral behaviour in Brazil: The 1994 presidential elections.' *International Social Science Journal* 47 (4): 627.

50. Scott Mainwaring. 1997. 'Multi-partism, robust federalism, and presidentialism in Brazil.' In *Presidentialism and Democracy in Latin America*, ed. Scott Mainwaring and Matthew Soberg Shugart. New York: Cambridge University Press; Mathew Soberg Shugart and John Carey. 1992. *Presidents and Assemblies: Constitutional Design and Electoral Dynamics*. Cambridge: Cambridge University Press; Octavio Amorim Neto and Fabio Santos. 2001. 'The executive connection: Presidentially defined factions and party discipline in Brazil.' *Dados-Revista De Ciencias Sociais* 44 (2): 291–321; Scott Mainwaring. 1999. *Rethinking Party Systems in the Third Wave of Democratization: The Case of Brazil*. Stanford: Stanford University Press.

51. Carlos Pereira and Lucio Rennó. 2001. 'What are re-elected legislators all about? Local and national political and institutional dynamics in the 1998 elections to the Brazilian House of Representatives.' *Dados-Revista De Ciencias Sociais* 44 (2): 323–362; Carlos Ranulfo and Felix de Melo. 2000. 'Parties and party migration in the chamber of deputies.' *Dados* 43 (2).

52. Torcuato DiTella. 1965. 'Populism and Reform in Latin America.' In Claudio Véliz, ed., *Obstacles to Change in Latin America*. Oxford: Oxford University Press, pp. 47–74; A. E. van Niekerk. 1974. *Populism and Political Development in Latin America*. Rotterdam: Universitaire Pers Rotterdam; Michael L. Conniff. Ed. 1982. *Latin American Populism in Comparative Perspective*. Albuquerque, NM: University of New Mexico Press.

53. Michael Coppedge. 1997. 'A classification of Latin American party systems.' Working paper 244, Kellogg Center, University of Notre Dame; Michael Coppedge. 1998. 'The dynamic diversity of Latin American party systems.' *Party Politics* 4 (4): 547–568. Unfortunately the distinction between the religious right and the secular right dimensions in the Coppedge typology makes it difficult to compare the ratings directly with parallel expert ratings of parties in Western Europe.

54. For example, from the country entries contained in Arthur S. Banks, Thomas C. Muller, and William R. Overstreet. Eds. 2002. *Political Handbook of the World 2000–2002*. Binghamton, NY: CSA Publications.

55. John Fuh-Sheng Hsieh and David Newman. Eds. 2002. *How Asia Votes*. Chatham, NJ: Chatham House, p. 121.

56. John Fuh-Sheng Hsieh and David Newman. Eds. 2002. *How Asia Votes*, Chatham, NJ: Chatham House, pp. 38–39.

57. Kenneth Wald and S. Shye. 1995. 'Religious influence in electoral behavior: The role of institutional and social forces in Israel.' *Journal of Politics* 57 (2): 495–507; Asher Arian and Michael Shamir. 2001. 'Candidates, parties and blocs: Israel in the 1990s.' *Party Politics* 7 (6): 689–710; D. Peretz, R. Kook, and G. Doron. 2003. 'Knesset election 2003: Why Likud regained its political domination and Labor continued to fade out.' *Middle East Journal* 57 (4): 588–603; Ehud Sprinzak. 1993. 'The Israeli radical right: History, culture

and politics.' In *Encounters with the Contemporary Radical Right*, ed. Peter H. Merkl and Leonard Weinberg. Boulder, CO: Westview Press.

58. Ami Pedahzur and A. Perliger. 2004. 'An alternative approach for defining the boundaries of "party families": Examples from the Israeli extreme right-wing party scene.' *Australian Journal of Political Science* 39 (2): 285–305; Shai Bermanis, Daphna Canetti-Nisim, and Ami Pedahzur. 2004. 'Religious fundamentalism and the extreme right-wing camp in Israel.' *Patterns of Prejudice* 38 (2): 159–176.

59. R. Heinisch. 2003. 'Success in opposition – Failure in government: Explaining the performance of right-wing populist parties in public office.' *West European Politics* 26 (3): 91–130.

60. Peter Davis. 2002. *The Extreme Right in France, 1789 to the Present: From De Maistre to Le Pen.* London: Routledge; Seymour Martin Lipset. 1960. *Political Man.* New York: Doubleday, pp. 154–163.

61. See, for example, Herbert Kitschelt, with Anthony J. McGann. 1995. *The Radical Right in Western Europe: A Comparative Analysis.* Ann Arbor: University of Michigan.

62. Wouter van der Brug and Meindert Fennema. 2003. 'Protest or mainstream? How the European anti-immigrant parties developed into two separate groups by 1999.' *European Journal of Political Research* 42: 55–76.

63. See, for example, Roger Eatwell. 1994. 'Why are fascism and racism reviving in Western Europe?' *Political Quarterly* 65 (3): 313–325; Roger Eatwell. 2000. 'The Rebirth of the "Extreme Right" in Western Europe?' *Parliamentary Affairs* 53: 407–425.

64. R. Witte. 1995. 'Racist violence in Western Europe.' *New Community* 21: 489–500.

65. R. Koopmans. 1995. *A Burning Question: Explaining the Rise of Racist and Extreme Right Violence in Western Europe.* Berlin: WZB.

Chapter 4: Ballot Access and Campaign Finance

1. See Richard S. Katz. 1997. 'Districting: Apportionment and gerrymanders.' In *Democracy and Elections* (Oxford: Oxford University Press).

2. For the argument that many established democracies have been moving toward a cartelized party system, see Richard S. Katz and Peter Mair. 1995. 'Changing models of party organization and party democracy: The emergence of the cartel party.' *Party Politics* 1: 5–28.

3. See André Blais and R. Kenneth Carty. 1991. 'The psychological impact of electoral laws – Measuring Duverger's elusive factor.' *British Journal of Political Science* 21 (1): 79–93; Ken Benoit. 2002. 'The endogeneity problem in electoral studies: A critical re-examination of Duverger's mechanical effect.' *Electoral Studies* 21 (1): 35–46; Pippa Norris. 2004. *Electoral Engineering.* New York: Cambridge University Press.

4. For a discussion, see J. M. Carey. 'Parchment, equilibria, and institutions.' *Comparative Political Studies* 33 (6–7): 735–761.

5. Election Process Information Collection (EPIC). 2004. 'Registration requirements for parties running in national elections.' http://epicproject.org/ace/compepic/en/PC01.

6. See Shaun Bowler, Elisabeth Carter, and David M. Farrell. 2003. 'Changing party access to elections.' In *Democracy Transformed?* ed. Bruce Cain, Russell Dalton and Susan Scarrow. Oxford: Oxford University Press; Louis Massicotte, André Blais, and Antoine Yoshinaka. *Establishing the Rules of the Game*. Toronto: University of Toronto Press, table 2.1.

7. See Steve Rosenstone, R. L. Behr, and E. H. Lazarus. 1996. *Third Parties in America*. 2d ed. Princeton: Princeton University Press, chapter 2; Michael Lewisbeck and P. Squire. 1995. 'The politics of institutional choice: Presidential ballot access for third parties in the United States.' *British Journal of Political Science* 25: 419–427.

8. Carol Johnson. 1998. 'Pauline Hanson and One Nation.' In *The New Politics of the Right*, ed. Hans-Georg Betz and Stefan Immerfall. New York: St. Martin's Press; S. Jackman. 1998. 'Pauline Hanson, the mainstream and political elites: The place of race in Australian political ideology.' *Australian Journal of Political Science* 33 (2): 167–186.

9. Tor Bjørklund and Jørgen Goul Andersen. 2002. 'Anti-immigration parties in Denmark and Norway: The Progress Party and the Danish People's Party.' In *Shadows over Europe*, ed. Martin Schain, Aristide Zolberg, and Patrick Hossay. Houndmills: Palgrave Macmillan.

10. Meindert Fennema. 2000. 'Legal repression of extreme-right parties and racial discrimination.' In *Challenging Immigration and Ethnic Relations Politics*, ed. Ruud Koopmans and Paul Statham. Oxford: Oxford University Press.

11. Christopher T. Husbands. 1995. 'Militant neo-Nazism in the Federal Republic of Germany in the 1990s.' In *The Far Right in Western and Eastern Europe*, ed. Luciano Cheles, Ronnie Ferguson, and Michalina Vaughan. New York: Longman.

12. Elena A. Korosteleva, Colin W. Lawson, and R. Marsh. 2003. *Contemporary Belarus: Between Democracy and Dictatorship*. London: Routledge; S. Navumava. 2004. 'Parties without power: Harmless thorns in the side of the autocracy.' *Osteuropa* 54 (2): 31–6.

13. Human Rights Watch. *World Report 2001*. http://www.hrw.org/wr2k1/europe/belarus.html; Human Rights Watch. *World Report 2002*. http://www.hrw.or/europe4.html.

14. Timothy Colton and Michael McCaul. 2003. *Popular Choice and Managed Democracy: The Russian Elections of 1999 and 2000*. Washington, DC: Brookings Institution Press.

15. Maurice Duverger. 1954. *Political Parties, Their Organization and Activity in the Modern State*. New York: Wiley.

16. For a study of these factors, see Shaun Bowler, Elisabeth Carter, and David M. Farrell. 2003. 'Changing party access to elections.' In *Democracy Transformed?* ed. Bruce Cain, Russell Dalton, and Susan Scarrow. Oxford: Oxford University Press. For an application of these factors to the radical right, see Elisabeth Carter. 2005. *The Extreme Right in Western Europe: Success or Failure?* Manchester: Manchester University Press, chapter 5.

17. Richard Katz and Peter Mair. Eds. 1994. *How Parties Organize: Change and Adaptation in Party Organizations in Western Democracies*. London: Sage, table 1.1; Peter Mair and Ingrid van Biezen. 2001. 'Party membership in

twenty European democracies 1980–2000.' *Party Politics* 7 (1): 7–21; Susan
Scarrow. 2001. 'Parties without members?' In *Parties without Partisans*, ed.
Russell J. Dalton and Martin Wattenberg. New York: Oxford University
Press; Pippa Norris. 2002. *Democratic Phoenix*. New York: Cambridge University Press, chapter 6.

18. For comparative studies, see Herbert E. Alexander and Rei Shiratori. Eds.
    1994. *Comparative Political Finance among the Democracies*. Boulder, CO:
    Westview Press; Arthur B. Gunlicks. Ed. 1993. *Campaign and Party Finance
    in North America and Western Europe*. Boulder, CO: Westview Press; Karl-
    Heinz Nassmacher. Ed. 2001. *Foundations for Democracy*. Baden-Baden:
    Nomos; International IDEA. 2003. *Funding of Political Parties and Election
    Campaigns*. Stockholm: International IDEA.

19. Peter Mair. 1997. *Party System Change*. Oxford: Oxford University Press,
    chapter 5 (with Richard S. Katz), p. 106. See the debate surrounding the
    notion of party cartels in Richard S. Katz and Peter Mair. 1995. 'Changing models of party organization and party democracy: The emergence of
    the cartel party.' *Party Politics* 1: 5–28; Ruud Koole. 1996. 'Cadre, catch-
    all or cartel? A comment on the notion of the cartel party.' *Party Politics* 2 (4): 507–523; Richard S. Katz and Peter Mair. 1996. 'Cadre, catch-
    all or cartel? A rejoinder.' *Party Politics* 2 (4): 525–534; L. Helms. 2001.
    'The cartel party thesis and its critics.' *Politische Vierteljahresschrift* 42 (4): 698–708.

20. International IDEA. 2003. *Funding of Political Parties and Election Campaigns*. Stockholm: International IDEA.

21. Information was not classified by the IDEA handbook for six nations under
    comparison: Belarus, Greece, the Republic of Korea, Luxembourg, Slovenia,
    and Taiwan.

22. Ellen Mickiewicz. 1999. *Changing Channels: Television and the Struggle for
    Power in Russia*. Durham, NC: Duke University Press.

23. Shaun Bowler, Elisabth Carter, and David M. Farrell. 2003. 'Changing party
    access to elections.' In *Democracy Transformed?* ed. Bruce Cain, Russell
    Dalton, and Susan Scarrow. Oxford: Oxford University Press.

Chapter 5: Electoral Systems

1. Given limitations of space, this chapter will set aside the impact of partisan
   bias arising from any malapportionment or gerrymandering of constituency
   boundaries, which could also disadvantage minor parties. This is an important but complex topic. See Richard S. Katz. 1997. 'Districting: Apportionment and gerrymanders.' In *Democracy and Elections*. Oxford: Oxford
   University Press.

2. Jackman and Volpert conclude: "Electoral disproportionality (through the
   mechanism of thresholds) increasingly dampens support for the extreme right
   as the number of parliamentary parties expands. At the same time, multi-
   partyism increasingly fosters parties of the extreme right with rising electoral proportionality," p. 516. See Robert W. Jackman and Karin Volpert.
   1996. 'Conditions favouring parties of the extreme right in Western Europe.'

British Journal of Political Science 264: 501–522. Others, however, critique this assumption. For example, after reanalyzing Jackman and Volpert's dataset, Golder concludes: "There is no evidence that (*national*) electoral thresholds actually influence extreme right parties at all" (my parenthesis), p. 8. See Matt Golder. 2003. 'Electoral institutions, unemployment and extreme right parties: A correction.' *British Journal of Political Science* 33 (3): 525–534. See also Elisabeth Carter. 2002. 'Proportional representation and the fortunes of right-wing extremist parties.' *West European Politics* 25 (3): 125–146; Matt Golder. 2003 'Explaining variation in the electoral success of extreme right parties in Western Europe.' *Comparative Political Studies* 36 (4): 432–466; Elisabeth Carter. 2004. 'Does PR promote political extremism? Evidence from the West European parties of the extreme right.' *Representation* 40 (2): 82–100.

3. Piero Ignazi. 2003. *Extreme Right Parties in Western Europe.* Oxford: Oxford University Press, p. 205. See also Robert W. Jackman and Karin Volpert. 1996. 'Conditions favouring parties of the extreme right in Western Europe.' *British Journal of Political Science* 264: 501–522.

4. Douglas W. Rae. 1971. *The Political Consequences of Electoral Laws.* Rev. ed. New Haven: Yale University Press.

5. Maurice Duverger. 1954. *Political Parties, Their Organization and Activity in the Modern State.* New York: Wiley.

6. Maurice Duverger. 1986. 'Duverger's Law: Forty years later.' In *Electoral Laws and Their Political Consequences*, ed. Bernard Grofman and Arend Lijphart. New York: Agathon Press.

7. Douglas W. Rae. 1971. *The Political Consequences of Electoral Laws.* Rev. ed. New Haven: Yale University Press; William H. Riker. 1976. 'The number of political parties: A reexamination of Duverger's Law.' *Comparative Politics* 9: 93–106; William H. Riker. 1982. 'The two-party system and Duverger's Law: An essay on the history of political science.' *American Political Science Review* 76: 753–766; William H. Riker. 1986. 'Duverger's Law revisited.' In *Electoral Laws and Their Political Consequences*, ed. Bernard Grofman and Arend Lijphart. New York: Agathon Press; Arend Lijphart, 1994. *Electoral Systems and Party Systems.* Oxford: Oxford University Press; Rein Taagepera. 1999. 'The number of parties as a function of heterogeneity and electoral system.' *Comparative Political Studies* 32 (5): 531–548; Patrick Dunleavy and Françoise Boucek. 2003. 'Constructing the number of parties.' *Party Politics* 9 (3): 291–315.

8. Arendt Lijphart. 1994. *Electoral Systems and Party Systems: A Study of Twenty-Seven Democracies, 1945–1990.* Oxford: Oxford University Press. See also Richard S. Katz. 1997. *Democracy and Elections.* New York/Oxford: Oxford University Press.

9. Pippa Norris. 2004. *Electoral Engineering.* New York: Cambridge University Press, chapter 4.

10. Similar patterns were found when the analysis was confined to the thirty-seven nations classified worldwide by the Freedom House Gastil index as 'older' or 'newer' democracies. In these countries, the mean number of parliamentary parties was 7.4 in majoritarian systems and 10.2 in PR systems.

The mean effective number of relevant parties was 3.0 in majoritarian systems and 5.5 in PR systems.

11. See the discussion in Arend Lijphart. 2001. 'The pros and cons – but mainly pros – of consensus democracy.' *Acta Politica* 35:363–398; R. B. Andeweg. 2001. 'Lijphart v. Lijphart: The cons of consensus democracy in homogeneous societies.' *Acta Politica* 36: 117–128.

12. Richard S. Katz. 1997. *Democracy and Elections*. New York/Oxford: Oxford University Press, p. 154. See also tables 10.4 and 10.5. See also David M. Farrell. 2001. *Electoral Systems: A Comparative Introduction*. London: Palgrave, pp. 199–200.

13. Paul Hainsworth. 2004. 'The extreme right in France: The rise and rise of Jean-Marie Le Pen's Front National.' *Representation* 40 (2): 101–114.

14. Jack Vowles, Peter Aimer, Susan Banducci, and Jeffrey Karp. 1998. *Voters' Victory? New Zealand's First Election under Proportional Representation*. Auckland: Auckland University Press; Jack Vowles. 1995. 'The politics of electoral reform in New Zealand.' *International Political Science Review* 16 (1): 95–116; D. Denemark and Shaun Bowler. 2002. 'Minor parties and protest votes in Australia and New Zealand: Locating populist politics.' *Electoral Studies* 21 (1): 47–67.

15. See Herbert Kitschelt, with Anthony J. McGann. 1995. *The Radical Right in Western Europe: A Comparative Analysis*. Ann Arbor: University of Michigan Press, table 2.4, p. 60.

16. Elisabeth Carter. 2002. 'Proportional representation and the fortunes of right-wing extremist parties.' *West European Politics* 25 (3): 125–146; Elisabeth Carter. 2004. 'Does PR promote political extremism? Evidence from the West European parties of the extreme right.' *Representation* 40 (2): 82–100; Elisabeth Carter. 2005. *The Extreme Right in Western Europe: Success or Failure?* Manchester: Manchester University Press. It should be noted that both Kitschelt and Carter limited their comparison to examining the evidence for the effect of the major type of electoral systems on the radical right share of *voting* support, rather than seats.

17. Maurice Duverger. 1954. *Political Parties, Their Organization and Activity in the Modern State*. New York: Wiley, p. 226.

18. For a detailed discussion, see Gary W. Cox. 1997. *Making Votes Count*. New York/Cambridge: Cambridge University Press.

19. It can be argued that a further distinction needs to be drawn between majority and plurality elections, given the higher effective electoral threshold used in the former. Nevertheless the classification used in this study is more parsimonious, the ballot structure used for plurality and majoritarian elections is similar (casting a vote for a single candidate), and it reflects the standard typology used in the literature.

20. Geoffrey Evans, John Curtice, and Pippa Norris. 1998. 'New Labour, New Tactical Voting?' In *British Elections and Parties Review*, ed. Charles Pattie et al. London: Frank Cass, pp. 65–79.

21. A. Schuessler. 2000. *A Logic of Expressive Choice*. Princeton: Princeton University Press.

22. Calculated simply by dividing the percentage of votes won by radical right parties into their percentage of seats.

23. Support for this relationship has been found by Matt Golder. 2003. 'Explaining variation in the success of extreme right parties in Western Europe.' *Comparative Political Studies* 36 (4): 432–466; Kenneth Wald and S. Shye. 1995. 'Religious influence in electoral-behavior: The role of institutional and social forces in Israel.' *Journal of Politics* 57 (2): 495–507.

24. Richard Stöss. 1988. 'The problem of rightwing extremism in West Germany.' In *Right Extremism in Western Europe*, ed. Klaus von Beyme. London: Frank Cass.

25. Dieter Nohlen. 2001. 'Threshold of exclusion.' In *The Encyclopedia of Electoral Systems*, ed. Richard Rose. Washington, DC: CQ Press.

26. Lijphart estimates the effective threshold as the mean of the threshold of representation and exclusion. It is calculated as $50\%/(M+1) + 50\%/2M$, where M is the district magnitude. See Arendt Lijphart. 1994. *Electoral Systems and Party Systems: A Study of Twenty-Seven Democracies, 1945–1990*. Oxford: Oxford University Press, pp. 25–56.

27. See Arendt Lijphart. 1994. *Electoral Systems and Party Systems: A Study of Twenty-Seven Democracies, 1945–1990*. Oxford: Oxford University Press. See also Rein Taagepera and Matthew Soberg Shugart. 1989. *Seats and Votes: The Effects and Determinants of Electoral Systems*. New Haven: Yale University Press; Rein Taagepera. 1998. 'Effective magnitude and effective threshold.' *Electoral Studies* 17 (4): 393–404; Rein Taagepera. 2002. 'Nationwide threshold of representation.' *Electoral Studies* 21 (3): 383–401.

28. Arendt Lijphart. 1994. *Electoral Systems and Party Systems: A Study of Twenty-Seven Democracies, 1945–1990*. Oxford: Oxford University Press, p. 141.

29. Marc Hooghe and K. Pelleriaux. 1998. 'Compulsory voting in Belgium: An application of the Lijphart thesis.' *Electoral Studies* 17 (4): 419–424; Leuvan De Winter and J. Ackaert. 1998. 'Compulsory voting in Belgium: A reply to Hooghe and Pelleriaux.' *Electoral Studies* 17 (4): 425–428.

30. Wolfgang Hirczy. 1994. 'The impact of mandatory voting laws on turnout: A quasi experimental approach.' *Electoral Studies* 13(1): 64–76; Arend Lijphart. 1997. 'Unequal participation: Democracies' unresolved dilemma.' *American Political Science Review* 91: 1–14; Mark Franklin. 1999. 'Electoral engineering and cross-national turnout differences: What role for compulsory voting?' *British Journal of Political Science* 29 (1): 205–216; Wolfgang Hirczy. 2001. 'Compulsory voting.' In *The International Encyclopedia of Elections*, ed. Richard Rose. Washington, DC: CQ Press.

31. Ian McAllister. 1986. 'Compulsory voting, turnout and party advantage in Australia.' *Politics* 21(1): 89–93.

32. Pippa Norris. 2001. 'Apathetic landslide: The 2001 British general election.' In *Britain Votes, 2001*, ed. Pippa Norris. Oxford: Oxford University Press.

33. Pippa Norris. 2004. *Electoral Engineering*. New York: Cambridge University Press, chapter 4.

Chapter 6: The 'New Cleavage' Thesis: The Social Basis of Right-Wing Support

1. Note that performance-based theories of political economy are discussed in detail in later chapters. These are distinct from the sociological accounts focusing upon secular trends, as political economists emphasize the impact of more specific developments in government policy performance on radical right support, notably surges in immigration, refugees, and asylum seekers, combined with rates of unemployment and job insecurity among poorer sectors. See Chapter 8 for details and also Terri E. Givens. 2002. 'The role of socioeconomic variables in the success of radical right parties.' In *Shadows over Europe*, ed. Martin Schain, Aristide Zolberg, and Patrick Hossay. Houndmills: Palgrave Macmillan; Matt Golder. 2003. 'Explaining variations in the success of extreme right parties in Western Europe.' *Comparative Political Studies* 36 (4): 432–466.

2. Exemplified by Seymour Martin Lipset. 1960. *Political Man: The Social Basis of Politics*. New York: Doubleday; Daniel Bell. Ed. *The Radical Right*. 3rd ed. New Brunswick, NJ: Transaction Publisher (first published in 1955 as *The New American Right*, subsequently expanded in the 2d ed. in 1963).

3. Hans-Georg Betz. 1994. *Radical Rightwing Populism in Western Europe*. New York: St Martin's Press, chapters 1 and 5; Piero Ignazi. 2003. *Extreme Right Parties in Western Europe*. New York: Oxford University Press. See also Herbert Kitschelt with Anthony J. McGann. 1995. *The Radical Right in Western Europe: A Comparative Analysis*. Ann Arbor: University of Michigan, table 2.11; J. G. Anderson and T. Bjorkland. 1990. 'Structural changes and new cleavages: The Progress Parties in Denmark and Norway.' *Acta Sociologica* 33 (3): 195–217.

4. For example, Betz collects together many separate studies from the literature, but each uses slightly different measures and definitions of occupational class and education. See Hans-Georg Betz. 1994. *Radical Rightwing Populism in Western Europe*. New York: St. Martin's Press, chapter 5.

5. Seymour Martin Lipset and Stein Rokkan. 1967. *Party Systems and Voter Alignments*. New York: Free Press.

6. For some of the key classics in this literature, see Daniel Lerner. 1958. *The Passing of Traditional Society: Modernizing the Middle East*. New York: Free Press; Walt W. Rostow. 1952. *The Process of Economic Growth*. New York: Norton; Walt W. Rostow. 1960. *The Stages of Economic Growth*. Cambridge: Cambridge University Press; Daniel Bell. 1999. *The Coming of Post-Industrial Society: A Venture in Social Forecasting*. New York: Basic Books.

7. Seymour Martin Lipset. 1960. *Political Man: The Social Basis of Politics*. New York: Doubleday, chapters 4 and 5 and p. 175. See also Daniel Bell. Ed. *The Radical Right*. 3rd ed. New Brunswick, NJ: Transaction Publisher (first published in 1955 as *The New American Right*, subsequently expanded in the 2d ed. in 1963); W. Sauer. 1967. 'National Socialism: Totalitarianism or fascism?' *American Historical Review* 73 (4): 404–424.

8. Juan Linz. 1976. 'Some notes toward a comparative study of fascism in sociological historical perspective.' In *Fascism: A Reader's Guide*, ed. Walter Laquer. Berkeley: University of California Press; Detlef

Mühlberger. 1987. *The Social Basis of European Fascist Movements*. London: Croom Helm.

9. Cas Mudde. 2000. *The Ideology of the Extreme Right*. New York: St. Martin's Press.

10. Piero Ignazi. 2003. *Extreme Right Parties in Western Europe*. New York: Oxford University Press, p. 218.

11. See, for example, G. Esping-Anderson. 1990. *The Three Worlds of Welfare Capitalism*. Princeton, NJ: Princeton University Press; Paul Pierson. 1998. 'Irresistible forces, immovable objects: Post-industrial welfare states confront permanent austerity.' *Journal of European Public Policy* 5: 539–560; G. Esping-Andersen. 1999. *The Social Foundations of Post-industrial Economies*, Oxford University Press.

12. Indeed the relative lack of class dealignment in Swedish party politics has been suggested as one reason why the radical right has failed to make much headway in this nation. See Jens Rydgren. 2002. 'Radical right populism in Sweden: Still a failure, but for how long?' *Scandinavian Political Studies* 25 (1): 27–56; Jens Rydgren. 2003. 'Meso-level reasons for racism and xenophobia: Some converging and diverging effects of radical right populism in France and Sweden.' *European Journal of Social Theory* 6 (1): 45–68.

13. Hans-Georg Betz. 1994. *Radical Rightwing Populism in Western Europe*. New York: St. Martin's Press.

14. Seymour Martin Lipset. 1960. *Political Man: The Social Basis of Politics*. New York: Doubleday; Hans-Georg Betz. 1994. *Radical Rightwing Populism in Western Europe*. New York: St. Martin's Press; Marcel Lubbers, Mérove Gijsberts, and Peer Scheepers, 2002. 'Extreme right-wing voting in Western Europe.' *European Journal of Political Research* 41 (3): 345–378, table 4.

15. Marcel Lubbers, Mérove Gijsberts, and Peer Scheepers, 2002. 'Extreme right-wing voting in Western Europe.' *European Journal of Political Research* 41 (3): 345–378. See also Marcel Lubbers and Peers Scheepers. 2001. 'Explaining the trend in extreme right-wing voting: Germany 1989–1998.' *European Sociological Review* 17 (4): 431–449. Knigge also reported a negative relationship between national levels of unemployment and voting support for extreme right parties. Pia Knigge. 1998. 'The ecological correlates of right-wing extremism in Western Europe.' *European Journal of Political Research* 34: 249–79.

16. Terri E. Givens. 2004. 'The radical right gender gap.' *Comparative Political Studies* 37 (1): 30–54.

17. Oskar Niedermayer. 1990. 'Sozialstruktur, politische Orientierungen und die Uterstutzung extrem rechter Parteien in Westeuropa.' *Zeitschrift fur Parlamentsfragen* 21 (4): 564–582; Herbert Kitschelt with Anthony J. McGann. 1995. *The Radical Right in Western Europe: A Comparative Analysis*. Ann Arbor: University of Michigan, table 2.11.

18. Robert W. Jackman and Karin Volpert. 1996. 'Conditions favouring parties of the extreme right in Western Europe.' *British Journal of Political Science* 264: 501–522.

19. Terri E. Givens. 2002. 'The role of socioeconomic variables in the success of radical right parties.' In *Shadows over Europe*, ed. Martin Schain, Aristide Zolberg, and Patrick Hossay. Houndmills: Palgrave Macmillan.

20. Robert W. Jackman and Karin Volpert. 1996. 'Conditions favouring parties of the extreme right in Western Europe.' *British Journal of Political Science* 264: 501–522; Matt Golder. 2003. 'Explaining variations in the success of extreme right parties in Western Europe.' *Comparative Political Studies* 36 (4): 432–466.

21. Wouter van der Brug, Meindert Fennema, and Jean Tillie. 2000. 'Anti-immigrant parties in Europe: Ideological or protest vote?' *European Journal of Political Research* 37 (1): 77–102; Wouter van der Brug and Meindert Fennema. 2003. 'Protest or mainstream? How the European anti-immigrant parties developed into two separate groups by 1999.' *European Journal of Political Research* 42: 55–76.

22. Michael Lewis-Beck and G. E. Mitchell. 1993. 'French electoral theory: The National Front test.' *Electoral Studies* 12 (2): 112–127; John W. P. Veugelers. 1997. 'Social cleavage and the revival of far right parties: The case of France's National Front.' *Acta Sociologica* 40 (1): 31–49; Subrata Mitra. 1988. 'The National Front in France: A Single-Issue Movement?' *West European Politics* 11 (2): 47–64.

23. Ivor Crewe, Jim Alt, and Bo Sarlvik. 1977. 'Partisan dealignment in Britain 1964–1974.' *British Journal of Political Science* 7: 129–90; Norman Nie, Sidney Verba, and John Petrocik. 1976. *The Changing American Voter.* Cambridge, MA: Harvard University Press; Ivor Crewe and David Denver. Eds. 1985. *Electoral Change in Western Democracies: Patterns and Sources of Electoral Volatility.* New York: St. Martin's Press; Mark Franklin, Tom Mackie, Henry Valen, et al. 1992. *Electoral Change: Responses to Evolving Social and Attitudinal Structures in Western Countries.* Cambridge: Cambridge University Press; Russell J. Dalton, Scott Flanagan, and Paul Allen Beck. Eds. 1984. *Electoral Change in Advanced Industrial Democracies: Realignment or Dealignment?* Princeton: Princeton University Press; Mark Franklin 1985. *The Decline of Class Voting in Britain: Changes in the Basis of Electoral Choice, 1964–1983.* Oxford: Clarendon Press; Jeff Manza and Clem Brooks. 1999. *Social Cleavages and Political Change: Voter Alignments and U.S. Party Coalitions.* New York: Oxford University Press; Terry Nichols Clark and Seymour Martin Lipset. Eds. 2001. *The Breakdown of Class Politics.* Baltimore: Johns Hopkins University Press.

24. Russell J. Dalton and Martin P. Wattenberg. Eds. 2001. *Parties without Partisans: Political Change in Advanced Industrial Democracies.* New York: Oxford University Press. For a discussion of the trends, see chapter 2.

25. Russell J. Dalton and Martin P. Wattenberg. Eds. 2001. *Parties without Partisans: Political Change in Advanced Industrial Democracies.* New York: Oxford University Press. For a discussion of the consequences, see chapter 3.

26. Anthony Heath, Roger Jowell, and John Curtice. 1985. *How Britain Votes.* Oxford: Pergamon; John H. Goldthorpe. 1980. *Social Mobility and Class Structure in Modern Britain.* Oxford: Clarendon Press.

27. The Lubbers et al. study used data derived from the 1994 Eurobarometer European Election Study and the 1998 International Social Survey Program. See Marcel Lubbers, Mérove Gijsberts, and Peer Scheepers. 2002. 'Extreme right-wing voting in Western Europe.' *European Journal of Political Research* 41 (3): 345–378.

28. Wouter van der Brug, Meindert Fennema and Jean Tillie. 2000. 'Anti-immigrant parties in Europe: Ideological or protest vote?' *European Journal of Political Research* 37 (1): 77–102.

29. Piero Ignazi. 2003. *Extreme Right Parties in Western Europe.* New York: Oxford University Press. See table 6.2. See also Max Riedisperger. 1992. 'Heil Haider! The revitalization of the Austrian Freedom Party since 1986.' *Politics and Society in Germany, Austria and Switzerland* 4 (3): 18–47.

30. Hans-Georg Betz. 2002. 'The divergent paths of the FPO and the Lega Nord.' In *Shadows over Europe*, ed. Martin Schain, Aristide Zolberg, and Patrick Hossay. Houndmills: Palgrave Macmillan, p. 76.

31. See, for example, Robert W. Jackman and Karin Volpert. 1996. 'Conditions favouring parties of the extreme right in Western Europe.' *British Journal of Political Science* 264: 501–522.

32. Herbert L. G. Tingsten, 1937. *Political Behavior: Studies in Election Statistics.* London: P. S. King, pp. 37–65.

33. Seymour M. Lipset and Stein Rokkan. 1967. *Party Systems and Voter Alignments.* New York: Free Press.

34. Maurice Duverger. 1955. *The Political Role of Women.* Paris: UNESCO, pp. 65–66; Seymour M. Lipset. 1960. *Political Man: The Social Bases of Politics.* Garden City, NY: Doubleday, p. 143; Angus Campbell, Philip Converse, Warren Miller, and Donald Stokes. 1960. *The American Voter.* New York: Wiley, p. 493.

35. Seymour M. Lipset. 1960. *Political Man: The Social Bases of Politics.* Garden City, NY: Doubleday, p. 260; Jean Blondel. 1970. *Votes, Parties and Leaders.* London: Penguin, pp. 55–56.

36. For a critical summary of the assumptions in the early literature, however, see Murray Goot and Elizabeth Reid. 1984. 'Women: If not apolitical, then conservative.' In *Women and the Public Sphere*, ed. Janet Siltanen and Michelle Stanworth. London: Hutchinson.

37. Seymour M. Lipset. 1960. *Political Man: The Social Bases of Politics.* Garden City, N.Y: Doubleday; Terri E. Givens. 2004. 'The radical right gender gap.' *Comparative Political Studies* 37 (1): 30–54.

38. Ola Listhaug, Arthur H. Miller, and Henry Vallen. 1985. 'The gender gap in Norwegian voting behavior.' *Scandinavian Political Studies* 83: 187–206; Maria Oskarson. 1995. 'Gender gaps in Nordic voting behavior.' In *Women in Nordic Politics*, ed. Lauri Karvonen and Per Selle. Aldershot: Dartmouth; Lawrence Mayer and Roland E. Smith. 1985. 'Feminism and religiosity: Female electoral behavior in Western Europe'. In *Women and Politics in Western Europe*, ed. Sylvia Bashevkin. London: Frank Cass; David DeVaus and Ian McAllister. 1989. 'The changing politics of women: Gender and political alignments in eleven nations.' *European Journal of Political Research* 17: 241–262; Donley Studlar, Ian McAllister, and Bernadette Hayes. 1998.

'Explaining the gender gap in voting: A cross-national analysis.' *Social Science Quarterly* 79; Clyde Wilcox. 1991. 'The causes and consequences of feminist consciousness among Western European women.' *Comparative Political Studies* 23 (4): 519–545; Lee Ann Banaszak and Eric Plutzer. 1993. 'The social bases of feminism in the European Community.' *Public Opinion Quarterly* 57 (1): 29–53; Lee Ann Banaszak and Eric Plutzer. 1993. 'Contextual determinants of feminist attitudes: National and sub-national influences in Western Europe.' *American Political Science Review* 87 (1): 147–157; Frank L Rusciano. 1992. 'Rethinking the gender gap: The case of West German elections, 1949–87.' *Comparative Politics* 24 (3): 335–57.

39. Pippa Norris and Ronald Inglehart. 2003. *Rising Tide: Gender Equality and Cultural Change Worldwide.* New York: Cambridge University Press.

40. As argued by Matt Golder. 2003. 'Explaining variations in the success of extreme right parties in Western Europe.' *Comparative Political Studies* 36 (4): 432–466.

Chapter 7: 'None of the Above': The Politics of Resentment

1. D. Denemark and Shaun Bowler. 2002. 'Minor parties and protest votes in Australia and New Zealand: Locating populist politics.' *Electoral Studies* 21 (1): 47–67; Colin Rallings and Michael Thrasher. 2000. 'Personality politics and protest voting: The first elections to the Greater London Authority.' *Parliamentary Affairs* 53 (4): 753–764; P. L. Southwell and M. J. Everest. 1998. 'The electoral consequences of alienation: Non-voting and protest voting in the 1992 presidential race.' *Social Science Journal* 35 (1): 43–51. For an American interpretive monograph, see Jean Hardisty. 1999. *Mobilizing Resentment: Conservative Resurgence from the John Birch Society to the Promise Keepers.* Boston: Beacon Press.

2. Hans-Georg Betz. 1994. *Radical Rightwing Populism in Western Europe.* New York: St. Martin's Press, pp. 37–38.

3. For an overview of the evidence of disaffection with political institutions and with mainstream parties in advanced industrialized democracies see Russell J. Dalton and Martin P. Wattenberg. Eds. 2000. *Parties without Partisans: Political Change in Advanced Industrial Democracies.* Oxford: Oxford University Press; Russell J. Dalton. 2004. *Democratic Challenges: Democratic Choices.* Oxford: Oxford University Press.

4. Piero Ignazi. 2003. *Extreme Right Parties in Western Europe.* New York: Oxford University Press, p. 215.

5. Some support is found at aggregate level by Pia Knigge. 1998. 'The ecological correlates of right-wing extremism in Western Europe.' *European Journal of Political Research* 34: 249–279. On the other hand, a more skeptical perspective is provided at individual level by Jack Billiet and H. De Witte. 1995. 'Attitudinal dispositions to vote for a "new" extreme rightwing party: The case of Vlaams Blok.' *European Journal of Political Research* 27 (2): 181–202.

6. Richard Rose. 2000. 'The end of consensus in Austria and Switzerland.' *Journal of Democracy* 11 (2): 26–40.

7. Wouter van der Brug, Meindert Fennema, and Jean Tillie. 2000. 'Anti-immigrant parties in Europe: Ideological or protest vote?' *European Journal of Political Research* 37 (1): 77–102; Wouter van der Brug and Meindert Fennema. 2003. 'Protest or mainstream? How the European anti-immigrant parties developed into two separate groups by 1999.' *European Journal of Political Research* 42: 55–76.

8. Wouter van der Brug and Meindert Fennema. 2003. 'Protest or mainstream? How the European anti-immigrant parties developed into two separate groups by 1999.' *European Journal of Political Research* 42: 55–76. "In the absence of direct indicators of protest voting, our conceptualization of protest voting is necessarily based on circumstantial evidence. The consequence of this is that some conceivable results may not be interpretable without ambiguity. If votes for anti-immigrant parties are largely protest votes, we must find a weaker effect of ideology and party size than for other parties. However, in case we do find such a weaker effect, other explanations may conceivably exist," p. 83. Moreover reliance of the study upon party preferences as the dependent variable (measured by probability to vote scales), rather than voting intentions or reported votes cast, provides another important limitation, as this procedure is likely to underestimate the extent of actual pragmatic voting due to a systematic bias.

9. David Easton. 1975. 'A reassessment of the concept of political support.' *British Journal of Political Science* 5: 435–457.

10. For a fuller discussion, see Pippa Norris. 1998. *Critical Citizens: Global Support for Democratic Governance.* Oxford: Oxford University Press. See also Russell J. Dalton. 2004. *Democratic Challenges: Democratic Choices.* Oxford: Oxford University Press.

11. Joseph Cooper. Ed. 1999. *Congress and the Decline of Public Trust.* Boulder, CO: Westview Press.

12. For a discussion see Kenneth Newton and Pippa Norris. 2000. 'Confidence in public institutions: Faith, culture or performance?' In *Disaffected Democracies: What's Troubling the Trilateral Countries?* ed. Susan Pharr and Robert Putnam. Princeton: Princeton University Press; Kenneth Newton. 2001. 'Trust, social capital, civic society, and democracy.' *International Political Science Review* 22(2): 201–214.

13. The seminal works are Robert D. Putnam. 1993. *Making Democracy Work: Civic Traditions in Modern Italy.* Princeton: Princeton University Press; Robert D. Putnam. 1996. 'The Strange Disappearance of Civic America.' *The American Prospect* 24; Robert D. Putnam. 2000. *Bowling Alone: The Collapse and Revival of American Community.* New York: Simon and Schuster. More recent comparative research is presented in Susan Pharr and Robert Putnam. Eds. 2000. *Disaffected Democracies: What's Troubling the Trilateral Countries?* Princeton: Princeton University Press; Robert D. Putnam. Ed. 2002. *Democracies in Flux.* Oxford: Oxford University Press.

14. For alternative conceptualizations of this concept see Pierre Bourdieu. 1970. *Reproduction in Education, Culture and Society.* London: Sage; James S. Coleman. 1988. 'Social capital in the creation of human capital.' *American*

Journal of Sociology 94: 95–120; James S. Coleman. 1990. *Foundations of Social Theory.* Cambridge: Belknap.

15. Robert D. Putnam. 2000. *Bowling Alone: The Collapse and Revival of American Community.* New York: Simon and Schuster.

16. For comparative work see Jan Willem van Deth. Ed. 1997. *Private Groups and Public Life: Social Participation, Voluntary Associations and Political Involvement in Representative Democracies.* London: Routledge; Jan Willem van Deth and F. Kreuter. 1998. 'Membership of voluntary associations.' In *Comparative Politics: The Problem of Equivalence,* ed. Jan W. van Deth. London: Routledge, pp. 135–155; Kees Aarts. 1995. 'Intermediate organizations and interest representation.' In *Citizens and the State,* ed. Hans-Dieter Klingemann and Dieter Fuchs. Oxford: Oxford University Press; Peter Hall. 1999. 'Social capital in Britain.' *British Journal of Political Science* 29 (3): 417–61. See also William L. Maloney, Graham Smith, and Gerry Stoker. 2000. 'Social capital and associational life.' In *Social Capital: Critical Perspectives,* ed. Stephen Baron, John Field, and Tom Schuller. Oxford: Oxford University Press; Michael Johnston and Roger Jowell. 2001. 'How robust is British civil society?' In *British Social Attitudes: The Eighteenth Report,* ed. Alison Park et al. London: Sage; Pippa Norris. 2002. *Democratic Phoenix: Reinventing Political Activism.* Cambridge: Cambridge University Press.

17. Hans-Georg Betz. 1994. *Radical Rightwing Populism in Western Europe.* New York: St. Martin's Press, p. 41.

18. Marcel Lubbers, Mérove Gijsberts, and Peer Scheepers. 2002. 'Extreme rightwing voting in Western Europe.' *European Journal of Political Research* 41 (3): 345–378.

19. J. Linde and J. Ekman. 2003. 'Satisfaction with democracy: A note on a frequently used indicator in comparative politics.' *European Journal of Political Research* 42 (3): 391–408; D. Canache, J. J. Mondak, and Mitch A. Seligson. 2001. 'Meaning and measurement in cross-national research on satisfaction with democracy.' *Public Opinion Quarterly* 65 (4): 506–528. Jeffrey A. Karp, Susan A. Banducci, and Shaun Bowler. 2003. 'To know it is to love it? Satisfaction with democracy in the European Union.' *Comparative Political Studies* 36 (3): 271–292.

20. Pippa Norris. 1999. 'Institutional explanations for political support.' In *Critical Citizens: Global Support for Democratic Governance,* ed. Pippa Norris. Oxford: Oxford University Press, chapter 11.

21. Christopher J. Anderson. 1995. *Blaming the Government: Citizens and the Economy in Five European Democracies.* New York: M. E. Sharpe; Christopher J. Anderson. 1996. 'Economics, politics, and foreigners: Populist party support in Denmark and Norway.' *Electoral Studies* 15 (4): 497–511; Christopher J. Anderson and Christine A. Guillory. 1997. 'Political institutions and satisfaction with democracy.' *American Political Science Review* 91 (1): 66–81.

22. Pippa Norris. 1998. *Critical Citizens: Global Support for Democratic Governance.* Oxford: Oxford University Press; Russell J. Dalton. 2004. *Democratic Challenges: Democratic Choices.* Oxford: Oxford University Press.

23. See, for example, J. W. Koch. 2003. 'Political cynicism and third party support in American presidential elections.' *American Politics Research* 31 (1): 48–65.

Chapter 8: 'Us and Them': Immigration, Multiculturalism, and Xenophobia

1. Christian Boswell. 2002. *European Migration Policies in Flux: Changing Patterns of Inclusion and Exclusion.* Oxford: Oxford University Press; Sarah Spencer. Ed. 2003. *The Politics of Migration.* Oxford: Blackwell.
2. For a discussion, see Hans-Georg Betz. 1994. *Radical Rightwing Populism in Western Europe.* New York: St. Martin's Press, chapter 3; Roger Karapin. 2002. 'Far right parties and the construction of immigration issues in Germany.' In *Shadows over Europe: The Development and Impact of the Extreme Right in Western Europe*, ed. Martin Schain, Aristide Zolberg, and Patrick Hossay. Houndmills: Palgrave Macmillan; Rachel Gibson, Ian McAllister, and T. Swenson. 2002. 'The politics of race and immigration in Australia: One Nation voting in the 1998 election.' *Ethnic and Racial Studies* 25 (5): 823–844; Cas Mudde. 1999. 'The single-issue party thesis: Extreme right parties and the immigration issue.' *West European Politics* 22 (3): 182–197; R. A. DeAngelis. 2003. 'A rising tide for Jean-Marie, Jorg, and Pauline? Xenophobic populism in comparative perspective.' *Australian Journal of Politics and History* 49 (1): 75–92. The fullest account of this thesis can be found in Rachel Gibson. 2002. *The Growth of Anti-Immigrant Parties in Western Europe.* Lewiston, NY: Edwin Mellen Press; and also Rachel Gibson. 1995. 'Anti-immigrant parties: The roots of their success.' *Current World Leaders* 38 (2): 119–30.
3. C. Boswell. 2000. 'European values and the asylum crisis.' *International Affairs* 76 (3): 537–47.
4. Herbert Kitschelt, with Anthony J. McGann. 1995. *The Radical Right in Western Europe: A Comparative Analysis.* Ann Arbor: University of Michigan Press.
5. See, for example, Jeff Crisp. 2003. 'The closing of the European gates? The new populist parties of Europe.' In *The Politics of Migration*, ed. Sarah Spencer. Oxford: Blackwell; Grete Brochmann and Tomas Hammar. Eds. 1999. *Mechanisms of Immigration Control: A Comparative Analysis of European Regulation Policies.* New York: Berg.
6. Hans-Georg Betz. 1994. *Radical Rightwing Populism in Western Europe.* New York: St. Martin's Press, p. 81.
7. For a discussion, see Thomas F. Pettigrew. 1998. 'Reactions toward the new minorities of Western Europe.' *Annual Review of Sociology* 24:77–103; Rachel Gibson. 2002. *The Growth of Anti-Immigrant Parties in Western Europe.* Lewiston, NY: Edwin Mellen Press.
8. Herbert Kitschelt, with Anthony J. McGann. 1995. *The Radical Right in Western Europe: A Comparative Analysis.* Ann Arbor: University of Michigan Press.
9. Marcel Lubbers, Mérove Gijsberts, and Peer Scheepers. 2002. 'Extreme rightwing voting in Western Europe.' *European Journal of Political Research* 41 (3): 345–378.

10. Matt Golder. 2003. 'Explaining variations in the success of extreme right parties in Western Europe.' *Comparative Political Studies* 36 (4): 432–466.

11. John Salt. 1994. *Europe's International Migrants: Data Sources, Patterns and Trends.* London: HMSO; European Commission. 2004. 'Migration and asylum.' In *Eurostat Yearbook 2004.* Luxembourg: European Commission.

12. See United Nations High Commissioner for Refugees. 2003. *Asylum Applications Lodged in Industrialized Countries: Levels and Trends, 2000–2002.* Geneva: UNHCR. http://www.unhcr.ch/cgi-bin/texis/vtx/statistics.

13. Matt Golder. 2003. 'Explaining variations in the success of extreme right parties in Western Europe.' *Comparative Political Studies* 36 (4): 432–466.

14. Martin Schain. 1987. 'The National Front in France and the Construction of Political Legitimacy.' *West European Politics* 10 (2): 229–252.

15. For a discussion, see Joel S. Fetzer. 2001. *Public Attitudes toward Immigration in the United States, France, and Germany.* Cambridge: Cambridge University Press.

16. Subra Mitra. 1988. 'The National Front in France: A Single-Issue Movement?' *West European Politics* 11 (2): 47–64.

17. For a discussion, see David Held, Anthony McGrew, David Goldblatt, and Jonathan Perraton. 1999. *Global Transformations.* Stanford, CA: University of Stanford Press, chapter 7.

18. The conceptual distinction between 'instrumental' and 'symbolic' forms of anti-immigrant attitudes is derived from Rachel Gibson. 2002. *The Growth of Anti-Immigrant Parties in Western Europe.* Lewiston, NY: Edwin Mellen Press, pp. 74–78. See also the discussion in Lawrence Bobo, James R. Kluegel, and Ryan A. Smith. 1997. 'Laissez-faire racism: The crystallization of a kinder, gentler, anti-black ideology.' In *Racial Attitudes in the 1990s: Continuity and Change,* ed. Steven A. Tuch and Jack K. Martin. Westport, CT: Praeger, pp. 15–41.

19. Herbert Kitschelt, with Anthony J. McGann. 1995. *The Radical Right in Western Europe: A Comparative Analysis.* Ann Arbor: University of Michigan Press.

20. Human Rights Watch. 2002. *We Are Not the Enemy: Hate Crimes against Arabs, Muslims, and Those Perceived to Be Arab or Muslim after September 11.* http://www.hrw.org/reports/2002/usahate/.

21. See the critique by Mitch A. Seligson. 2002. 'The renaissance of political culture or the renaissance of the ecological fallacy?' *Comparative Politics* 34 (3): 273ff. and the reply by Ronald Inglehart and Christopher Welzel. 2003. 'Political culture and democracy – Analyzing cross-level linkages.' *Comparative Politics* 36 (1): 61ff.

Chapter 9: Location, Location, Location: Party Competition

1. Herbert Kitschelt, with Anthony J. McGann. 1995. *The Radical Right in Western Europe: A Comparative Analysis.* Ann Arbor: University of Michigan Press, p. 17.

2. Amit Abedi. 2002. 'Challenges to established parties: The effects of party system features on the electoral fortunes of anti-political-establishment parties.' *European Journal of Political Research* 41 (4): 551–583.

3. Wouter van der Brug, Meindert Fennema, and Jean Tillie. 2005. 'Why some anti-immigrant parties fail and others succeed: A two-step model of aggregate electoral support.' *Comparative Political Studies* forthcoming.

4. Marcel Lubbers, Mérove Gijsberts, and Peer Scheepers. 2002. 'Extreme right-wing voting in Western Europe.' *European Journal of Political Research* 41 (3): 345–378.

5. Piero Ignazi. 2003. *Extreme right parties in Western Europe.* New York: Oxford University Press, p. 208.

6. For a discussion of these issues see Patrick Hossay and Aristide Zolberg. 2002. 'Democracy in peril?' In *Shadows over Europe: The Development and Impact of the Extreme Right in Western Europe*, ed. Martin Schain, Aristide Zolberg, and Patrick Hossay. Houndmills: Palgrave Macmillan.

7. Marcel Lubbers [principal investigator]. 2000. *Expert Judgment Survey of Western European Political Parties 2000* [machine readable dataset]. Nijmegen, the Netherlands: NWO, Department of Sociology, University of Nijmegen.

8. The classic account is presented in Anthony Downs. 1957. *An Economic Theory of Democracy.* New York: Harper and Row. For a discussion of the extensive literature flowing from this account, see, for example, James M. Enelow and Melvin Hinich. Eds. 1984. *The Spatial Theory of Voting.* New York: Cambridge University Press; Samuel Merrill III. 1993. 'Voting behavior under the directional spatial model of electoral competition.' *Public Choice* 77: 739–756; Samuel Merrill III and Bernard Grofman. 1999. *A Unified Theory of Voting: Directional and Proximity Spatial Models.* Cambridge: Cambridge University Press.

9. Anthony Downs. 1957. *An Economic Theory of Democracy.* New York: Harper and Row. The modified version of the theory presented here has been influenced by the account developed by James A. Stimson. 1991. *Public Opinion in America: Moods, Cycles and Swings.* Boulder, CO: Westview Press.

10. See the classic discussion in Donald E. Stokes. 1966. 'Spatial models of party competition.' In *Elections and the Political Order*, ed. Angus Campbell, Philip E. Converse, Warren E. Miller, and Donald E. Stokes. New York: Wiley.

11. Daniel Bell. 1962. *The End of Ideology.* New York: Random House; Otto Kirchheimer. 1966. 'The transformation of Western European party systems.' In *Political Parties and Political Development*, ed. Joseph Lapalombara and Myron Weiner. Princeton: Princeton University Press.

12. See Gary W. Cox. 1987. 'Electoral equilibrium under alternative voting institutions.' *American Journal of Political Science* 31: 82–108; Gary Cox. 1990. 'Centripetal and centrifugal incentives in electoral systems.' *American Journal of Political Science* 34: 903–935; Gary W. Cox. 1997. *Making Votes Count: Strategic Coordination in the World's Electoral Systems.* Cambridge: Cambridge University Press.

13. Jay K. Dow. 2001. 'A comparative spatial analysis of majoritarian and proportional elections.' *Electoral Studies* 20: 109–125.
14. For details about the classification and typology of electoral systems, see Pippa Norris. 2004. *Electoral Engineering*. Cambridge: Cambridge University Press.
15. CSES question A3031: "In politics people sometimes talk of left and right. Where would you place yourself on a scale from 0 to 10 where 0 means the left and 10 means the right?" It should be noted that Module I of the CSES did not include issue scales, so we cannot use this dataset to test the directional theory of voting.
16. Michael Coppedge. 1998. 'The dynamic diversity of Latin American party systems.' *Party Politics* 4 (4): 547–568.
17. Peter Davis. 2002. *The Extreme Right in France, 1789 to the Present: From De Maistre to Le Pen*. London: Routledge.
18. The 'proximity model' based on left-right political ideology, also known as the 'least-distance' model, is adopted for the study. The proximity model of issue voting and the Rabinowitz and McDonald directional model of issue voting were not able to be tested as neither the ESS nor Module I of the CSES incorporated suitable issue voting scales. The directional account suggests that people will vote for a party that is most likely to change policies in a way that will leave them most satisfied, depending upon a neutral point from which to judge the expected direction of change. See George Rabinowitz and Stuart Elaine MacDonald. 1989. 'A directional theory of voting.' *American Political Science Review* 83: 93–121. For a discussion and comparison of these models, and the extensive literature flowing from these theories, see Samuel Merrill III and Bernard Grofman. 1999. *A Unified Theory of Voting: Directional and Proximity Spatial Models*. Cambridge: Cambridge University Press.
19. See, for example, Morris P. Fiorina. 1979. *Retrospective Voting in American National Elections*. New Haven: Yale University Press; Samuel L. Popkin. 1994. *The Reasoning Voter*. Chicago: University of Chicago Press.
20. For a discussion, see Ian Budge and Derek Farlie. 1977. *Voting and Party Competition*. London: Wiley; Ian Budge, David Robertson, and Derek J. Hearl. 1987. *Ideology, Strategy and Party Change: Spatial Analysis of Post-War Election Programmes in Nineteen Democracies*. Cambridge: Cambridge University Press; Hans-Dieter Klingemann, Richard I. Hofferbert, and Ian Budge. 1994. *Parties, Policies and Democracy*. Boulder, CO: Westview; Hee Min Kim and Richard C. Fording. 2003. 'Voter ideology in Western democracies: An update.' *European Journal of Political Research* 42 (1): 95–105.
21. CSES question A3031: "In politics people sometimes talk of left and right. Where would you place yourself on a scale from 0 to 10 where 0 means the left and 10 means the right?" It should be noted that Module I of the CSES did not include issue scales, so we are unable to use this dataset to test the directional theory of voting.
22. See, for example, R. Barraclough. 1998. 'Umberto Bossi: Charisma, personality, and leadership.' *Modern Italy* 3 (2).

23. Max Riedisperge. 1992. 'Heil Haider! The revitalization of the Austrian Free-dom Party since 1986.' *Politics and Society in Germany, Austria and Switzer-land* 4 (3): 18–47; Richard Rose. 2000. 'The end of consensus in Austria and Switzerland.' *Journal of Democracy* 11 (2): 26–40.

24. For the classic accounts see Angus Campbell, Philip Converse, Warren Miller, and Donald Stokes. 1960. *The American Voter.* New York: Wiley; Angus Campbell, Philip Converse, Warren Miller, and Donald Stokes. 1966. *Elec-tions and the Political Order.* New York: Wiley.

25. For cross-national accounts of partisan dealignment, see Russell J. Dalton, Scott Flanagan, and Paul Allen Beck. Eds. 1984. *Electoral Change in Ad-vanced Industrial Democracies: Realignment or Dealignment?* Princeton: Princeton University Press; Russell J. Dalton and Martin Wattenberg. Eds. 2001. *Parties without Partisans.* New York: Oxford University Press.

26. CSES A3020: "I'd like to know what you think about each of our political parties. After I read the name of a political party, please rate it on a scale from 0 to 10, where 0 means you strongly dislike that party and 10 means that you strongly like that party." A3021: "And now, using the same scale, I'd like to ask you how much you like or dislike some political leaders." Note that in some nations up to nine parties were coded on these scales, but the comparison in this study is restricted to the first six parties, defined in terms of those with the greatest share of the vote in the election under comparison, in order to standardize results across all nations.

27. The *direction* of party identification was measured in the CSES by the follow-ing questions: Q: "Do you usually think of yourself as close to any particular political party?" (If 'yes') "Which party is that?" The first party mentioned by the respondent was coded. The *strength* of party identification was measured as well by the following: "Do you feel very close to this party, somewhat close, or not very close?"

28. For a discussion, see James Adams. 2001. 'A theory of spatial competition with biased voters: Party policies viewed temporally and comparatively.' *British Journal of Political Science* 31: 121–158.

29. In particular, the ESS and CSES surveys differed in their detailed occupational codings, and in their classification of self-employment and religion, as well in their timing. It should also be noted that we cannot provide direct comparison with previous chapters concerning attitudes toward cultural protectionism, such as negative feelings toward immigrants and refugees, since these were not monitored in the CSES survey.

30. The data for the French 2002 presidential election are derived from the second module of the CSES, released May 2003.

31. For more details of the French contests, see D. S. Bell and Byron Criddle. 2002. 'Presidentialism restored: The French elections of April–May and June 2002.' *Parliamentary Affairs* 55 (4): 643ff.; Arnauld Miguet. 2002. 'The French elec-tions of 2002: After the earthquake, the deluge.' *West European Politics* 25 (4): 207–220; Yves Bitrin. 2003. *Vote Le Pen et psychologie des foules: 21 avril 2002, "un coup de tonnerre dans un ciel bleu."* Paris: Harmattan; Patrick Cohen and Jean-Marc Salmon. 2003. *21 avril 2002: Contre-enquête sur le choc Le Pen.* Paris: Denoël.

On the Canadian elections, see Elizabeth Gidengil, André Blais, Richard Nadeau, and Neil Nevitte. 1999. 'Making sense of regional voting in the 1997 Canadian federal election: Liberal and Reform support outside Quebec.' *Canadian Journal of Political Science-Revue Canadienne de Science Politique* 32 (2): 247–272.

32. See C. H. Church. 2000. 'The Swiss elections of October 1999: Learning to live in more interesting times.' *West European Politics* 23 (3): 215–230; A. Ladner. 2001. 'Swiss political parties: Between persistence and change.' *West European Politics* 24 (2): 123ff.; Richard Rose. 2000. 'The end of consensus in Austria and Switzerland.' *Journal of Democracy* 11 (2): 26–40; W. M. Downs. 2001. 'Pariahs in their midst: Belgian and Norwegian parties react to extremist threats.' *West European Politics* 24 (3): 23–42.

33. For details, see Pippa Norris. 2004. *Electoral Engineering*. Cambridge: Cambridge University Press, table 2.1.

34. To maintain consistency among the countries under comparison, as the case studies were drawn from module I and II of the CSES, affective orientations toward the party leadership and party identification were dropped from the models, as these were not carried across both modules. Moreover it should be noted that certain socioeconomic and demographic variables were also not consistently coded across all the four case studies, so these items were also dropped from the comparison.

35. Tor Bjørklund and Jørgen Goul Andersen. 2002. 'Anti-immigration parties in Denmark and Norway.' In *Shadows over Europe: The Development and Impact of the Extreme Right in Western Europe*, ed. Martin Schain, Aristide Zolberg, and Patrick Hossay. Houndmills: Palgrave Macmillan.

Chapter 10: Consolidating Party Organizations

1. K. R. Luther. 2003. 'The self-destruction of a right-wing populist party? The Austrian parliamentary election of 2002.' *West European Politics* 26 (2): 136–152. I am also most grateful to personal communications with Fritz Plasser for this information.

2. France is a mixed category: the 1984 and 1986 'critical elections' facilitating the surge in FN support used PR, although these were exceptional and the French usually use the second ballot majoritarian system for parliamentary election. For the main conceptual and institutional differences between 'adversarial' and 'consensus' democracies, see the discussion in Pippa Norris. 2003. *Electoral Engineering: Voting Rules and Political Behavior*. New York: Cambridge University Press, chapter 2.

3. The conceptual framework presented here was first developed to interpret developments in British elections, following Tony Blair's historic landslide in 1997, but the theory can be applied equally, and indeed extended, to clarify developments for the radical right in many countries. See Pippa Norris and Geoffrey Evans. 1999. 'Introduction: Understanding critical elections.' In *Critical Elections: British Voters and Parties in Long-Term Perspective*, ed. Geoffrey Evans and Pippa Norris. London: Sage.

4. See the discussion in Peter Mair. 1997. *Party System Change: Approaches and Interpretations*. Oxford: Oxford University Press; Alan Ware. 1996. *Political Parties and Party Systems*. Oxford: Oxford University Press.

5. Angus Campbell, Philip Converse, Warren E. Miller, and Donald E. Stokes. 1960. *The American Voter*. New York: Wiley; Philip Converse. 1969. 'Of time and partisan stability.' *Comparative Political Studies* 2: 139–71. For more recent work in the Michigan tradition, see Warren Miller and J. Merrill Shanks. 1996. *The New American Voter*. Cambridge: Harvard University Press; Donald P. Green, Bradley Palmquist, and Eric Schickler. 2002. *Partisan Hearts and Minds: Political Parties and the Social Identity of Voters*. New Haven: Yale University Press.

6. For Britain, see David Butler and Donald Stokes. 1974. *Political Change in Britain*. Rev. ed. London: Macmillan. For Norway, see Angus Campbell and Henry Valen. 1961. 'Party identification in Norway and the United States.' *Public Opinion Quarterly* 22: 505–525. For France, see Philip E. Converse and Georges Dupeux. 1962. 'Politicization of the electorate in France and the United States.' *Public Opinion Quarterly* 26: 1–23; Philip E. Converse and Roy Pierce. 1986. *Political Representation in France*. Cambridge: Harvard University Press.

7. Seymour Martin Lipset and Stein Rokkan. 1967. *Party Systems and Voter Alignments*. New York: Free Press, p. 50. See also Robert R. Alford. 1967. 'Class voting in the Anglo-American political systems.' In *Party Systems and Voter Alignments: Cross National Perspectives*, ed. Seymour M. Lipset and Stein Rokkan. New York: Free Press; Richard Rose and Derek W. Urwin. 1970. 'Persistence and change in Western party systems since 1945.' *Political Studies* 18: 287–319; Richard Rose. Ed. 1974. *Electoral Behavior: A Comparative Handbook*. New York: Free Press.

8. Morgens N. Pedersen. 1979. 'The dynamics of European party systems: Changing patterns of electoral volatility.' *European Journal of Political Research* 7:1–26; Ivor Crewe, Jim Alt, and Bo Sarlvik. 1977. 'Partisan dealignment in Britain 1964–1974.' *British Journal of Political Science* 7: 129–90; Norman Nie, Sidney Verba, and John Petrocik. 1976. *The Changing American Voter*. Cambridge: Harvard University Press; Ivor Crewe and David Denver. Eds. 1985. *Electoral Change in Western Democracies: Patterns and Sources of Electoral Volatility*. New York: St. Martin's Press; Mark Franklin et al. 1992. *Electoral Change: Responses to Evolving Social and Attitudinal Structures in Western Countries*. Cambridge: Cambridge University Press; Russell J. Dalton, Scott Flanagan, and Paul Allen Beck. Eds. 1984. *Electoral Change in Advanced Industrial Democracies: Realignment or Dealignment?* Princeton: Princeton University Press; Mark Franklin. 1985. *The Decline of Class Voting in Britain: Changes in the Basis of Electoral Choice, 1964–1983*. Oxford: Clarendon Press; Jeff Manza and Clem Brooks. 1999. *Social Cleavages and Political Change: Voter Alignments and U.S. Party Coalitions*. New York: Oxford University Press; Terry Nichols Clark and Seymour Martin Lipset. Eds. 2001. *The Breakdown of Class Politics*. Baltimore: Johns Hopkins University Press.

9. Karl-Heinz Reif and Herman Schmitt. 1980. 'Second-order national elections: A conceptual framework for the analysis of European election results.' *European Journal of Political Research* 8 (1): 3–44; Karl-Heinz Reif. 1997. 'European elections as member state second-order elections revisited.' *European Journal of Political Research* 31 (1–2): 115–124; Michael Marsh. 1998. 'Testing the second-order election model after four European elections.' *British Journal of Political Science* 28 (4): 591–607.

10. See, for example, David R. Mayhew. 2003. *Partisan Realignments*. New Haven: Yale University Press.

11. V. O. Key. 1959 'Secular realignment and the party system.' *The Journal of Politics* 21 (2): 198–210.

12. Ronald Inglehart and Pippa Norris. 2003. *Rising Tide: Gender Equality and Cultural Change*. New York: Cambridge University Press; Pippa Norris and Ronald Inglehart. 2004. *Sacred and Secular: Religion and Politics Worldwide*. New York: Cambridge University Press.

13. V. O. Key. 1955. 'A theory of critical elections.' *The Journal of Politics* 17: 3–18.

14. Walter Dean Burnham. 1970. *Critical Elections and the Mainsprings of American Politics*. New York: Norton.

15. For a summary of the evidence, see the introduction and conclusion in *Critical Elections: British Voters and Parties in Long-Term Perspective*, ed. Geoffrey Evans and Pippa Norris. 1999 London: Sage.

16. V. O. Key. 1959. 'Secular realignment and the party system.' *The Journal of Politics* 21 (2): 198–210.

17. Russell J. Dalton, Scott Flanagan, and Paul Allen Beck. Eds. 1984. *Electoral Change in Advanced Industrial Democracies: Realignment or Dealignment?* Princeton: Princeton University Press; Ivor Crewe and David Denver. Eds. 1985. *Electoral Change in Western Democracies: Patterns and Sources of Electoral Volatility*. New York: St. Martin's Press; Mark Franklin et al. 1992. *Electoral Change: Responses to Evolving Social and Attitudinal Structures in Western Countries*. Cambridge: Cambridge University Press.

18. Russell J. Dalton. 2000. 'The decline of party identification.' In *Parties without Partisans: Political Change in Advanced Industrial Democracies*, ed. Russell J. Dalton and Martin P. Wattenberg. Oxford: Oxford University Press, chapter 2, table 2.1.

19. Hermann Schmitt and Soren Holmberg. 1995. 'Political parties in decline?' In *Citizens and the State*, ed. Hans-Dieter Klingemann and Dieter Fuchs. Oxford: Oxford University Press;

20. Jacques Thomassen. 1976. 'Party identification as a cross-national concept: Its meaning in the Netherlands.' In *Party Identification and Beyond*, ed. Ian Budge, Ivor Crewe, and Dennis Farlie. London: Wiley; Lawrence LeDuc. 1979. 'The dynamic properties of party identification: A four nation comparison.' *European Journal of Political Research* 9:257–268; Sören Holmberg. 1994. 'Party identification compared across the Atlantic.' In *Elections at Home and Abroad*, ed. M. Kent Jennings and Thomas Mann. Ann Arbor: University of Michigan Press; I. Kabashima and Y. Ishio. 1998. 'The instability of party identification among eligible Japanese voters: A

seven-wave panel study, 1993–6.' *Party Politics* 4 (2): 151–176; E. Schickler and D. P. Green. 1997. 'The stability of party identification in western democracies: Results from eight panel surveys.' *Comparative Political Studies* 30 (4): 450–483; M. Brynin and David Sanders. 1997. 'Party identification, political preferences, and material conditions: Evidence from the British Household Panel Survey, 1991–2.' *Party Politics* 3 (1): 53–77.

21. Richard A. Brody and Lawrence S. Rothenberg. 1988. 'The instability of party identification: An analysis of the 1980 presidential election.' *British Journal of Political Science* 18: 445–465; Donald P. Green, Bradley Palmquist, and Eric Schickler. 2002. *Partisan Hearts and Minds: Political Parties and the Social Identity of Voters*. New Haven: Yale University Press.

22. Russell Dalton. 2004. *Democratic Challenges, Democratic Choices*. Oxford: Oxford University Press; Harold Clarke and Marianne Stewart. 1998. 'The decline of parties in the minds of citizens.' *Annual Review of Political Science* 1: 357–378.

23. Peter Mair and Ingrid van Biezen. 2001. 'Party membership in twenty European democracies 1980–2000.' *Party Politics* 7 (1): 7–22; Susan Scarrow. 2001. 'Parties without members?' In *Parties without Partisans: Political Change in Advanced Industrial Democracies*, ed. Russell J. Dalton and Martin Wattenberg. Oxford: Oxford University Press; Paul Webb, David Farrell, and Ian Holiday. Eds. 2002. *Political Parties in Advanced Industrial Democracies*. Oxford: Oxford University Press.

24. Russell J. Dalton, Ian McAllister, and Martin P. Wattenberg. 2000. 'The consequences of party dealignment.' In *Parties without Partisans: Political Change in Advanced Industrial Democracies*, ed. Russell J. Dalton and Martin P. Wattenberg. Oxford: Oxford University Press.

25. Peter Mair. 2002. 'Mass electoral behavior in Western Europe.' In *Comparative Democratic Politics*, ed. Hans Keman. London: Sage, table 6.4. For his earlier analysis, see Stefano Bartolini and Peter Mair. 1990. *Identity, Competition, and Electoral Stability: The Stabilization of European Electorates 1885–1985*. Cambridge: Cambridge University Press.

26. Mogens Pedersen. 1979. 'The dynamics of European party systems: Changing patterns of electoral volatility.' *European Journal of Political Research* 7 (1): 1–26.

27. Peter Mair. 2002. 'Mass electoral behavior in Western Europe.' In *Comparative Democratic Politics*, ed. Hans Keman. London: Sage, table 6.3.

28. Russell J. Dalton. 2000. 'The decline of party identification.' In *Parties without Partisans: Political Change in Advanced Industrial Democracies*, ed. Russell J. Dalton and Martin P. Wattenberg. Oxford: Oxford University Press, chapter 2, table 2.1.

29. Richard C. Thurlow. 2000. *Fascism in Britain: From Oswald Mosley's Blackshirts to the National Front*. Stroud: Sutton; Martin Walker. 1977. *The National Front*. London: Fontana/Collins; Christopher T. Husbands. 1988. 'Extreme right-wing politics in Great Britain: The recent marginalization of the National Front.' In *Right-Wing Extremism in Western Europe*, ed. Klaus von Beyme. 1988. London: Frank Cass.

30. See, for example, the NF website: http://www.natfront.com/.

31. Ian R. G. Spencer. 1997. *British Immigration Policy since 1939*. London: Routledge; Hugo Young. 1989. *One of Us: A Biography of Margaret Thatcher*. London: Macmillan, p. 137.
32. In the May 2001 UK general election, the BNP won 47,000 votes in total, or 0.2% of the national vote. *The British Parliamentary Constituency Database 1992–2001*.
33. Catherine Fieschi. 2004. *The Resistible Rise of the BNP*. Fabian Society pamphlet. London: Fabian Society. http://www.fabian-society. org.uk/documents/ViewADocument.asp?ID=83&CatID=52.
34. *Local Elections 2004*. Research Paper 04/49. London: House of Commons.
35. For the argument the UKIP could potentially mobilize greater support in subsequent general elections, see Peter John, Helen Margetts, and Stuart Weir. 2004. 'The rise of the BNP and UKIP: Public opinion and voting in the 2004 European elections.' Paper presented at the EPOP annual conference, Nuffield College, Oxford, September 2004.
36. Erik Bleich. 2003. *Race Politics in Britain and France: Ideas and Policymaking since the 1960s*. Cambridge: Cambridge University Press.
37. Nick Aylott. 1995. 'Back to the future: The 1994 Swedish election.' *Party Politics* 1 (3): 419–429; Jens Rydgren. 2002. 'Radical right populism in Sweden: Still a failure, but for how long?' *Scandinavian Political Studies* 25 (1): 27–56.
38. Joop van Holsteyn and Josje M. den Ridder. 2003. 'In the eye of the beholder: The perception of the List Pim Fortuyn and the Parliamentary Elections of May 2002.' *Acta Politica* 38 (1): 69–88; Joop van Holsteyn. 2003. 'A new kid on the block: Pim Fortuyn and the Dutch Parliamentary Election of May 2002.' In *British Elections and Parties Review*, ed. Colin Rallings et al. London: Frank Cass, pp. 29–46; Joop van Holsteyn and G. A. Irwin. 2003. 'Never a dull moment: Pim Fortuyn and the Dutch Parliamentary Election of 2002.' *West European Politics* 26 (2): 41–66; Wouter van der Brug. 2003. 'How the LPF fueled discontent: Empirical tests of explanations of LPF support.' *Acta Politica* 38 (1): 89–106.
39. R. Heinisch. 2003. 'Success in opposition – failure in government: Explaining the performance of right-wing populist parties in public office.' *West European Politics* 26 (3): 91–130.
40. R. B. Andeweg. 2004. 'Parliamentary democracy in the Netherlands.' *Parliamentary Affairs* 57 (3): 568–580.
41. Steven Rosenstone, R. L. Behr, and E. H. Lazarus. 1996. *Third Parties in America*. Princeton: Princeton University Press; Ted G. Jelen. *Ross for Boss: The Perot Phenomenon and Beyond*. Albany: SUNY Press.
42. John Zaller. 1995. 'The rise and fall of candidate Perot: The outsider versus the political-system.' *Political Communication* 12 (1): 97–123.
43. J. A. McCann, R. B. Rapoport, and W. J. Stone. 1999. 'Heeding the call: An assessment of mobilization into H. Ross Perot's 1992 presidential campaign.' *American Journal of Political Science* 43 (1): 1–28.
44. Paul R. Abramson, John H. Aldrich, P. Paolino, and D. W. Rohde. 2000. 'Challenges to the American two-party system: Evidence from the 1968, 1980, 1992, and 1996 presidential elections.' *Political Research Quarterly* 53 (3):

495–522; John Zaller. 1995. 'The rise and fall of candidate Perot: The outsider versus the political-system.' *Political Communication* 12 (1): 97–123.

45. Martin A. Schain. 1987. 'The National Front in France and the construction of political legitimacy.' *West European Politics* 10 (2): 229–252; Subrata Mitra. 1988. 'The National Front in France: A single-issue movement?' *West European Politics* 11 (2): 47–64; E. G. DeClair. 1999. *Politics on the Fringe: The People, Policies, and Organization of the French National Front.* Durham, NC: Duke University Press; John W. P. Veugelers. 2000. 'Right-wing extremism in contemporary France: A "silent counterrevolution"?' *Sociological Quarterly* 41 (1): 19–40; Peter Davis. 2002. *The Extreme Right in France, 1789 to the Present: From De Maistre to Le Pen.* London: Routledge.

46. Pierre Martin. 1998. 'Qui vote pour le Front National français?' In *L'Extrême Droite en France et en Belgique.* Brussels: Editions Complexe.

47. Pascal Perrineau. 1997. *Le Symptôme Le Pen.* Paris: Fayard.

48. Patricia L. Southwell. 1997. 'Fairness, governability, and legitimacy: The debate over electoral systems in France.' *Journal of Political and Military Sociology* 25:163–185.

49. Martin A. Schain. 2002. 'The impact of the French National Front on the French political system.' In *Shadows over Europe*, ed. Martin A. Schain, Aristide Zolberg, and Patrick Hossay. Houndmills: Palgrave Macmillan. For details of estimated party membership and party finance, see Andrew Knapp. 2002. 'France: Never a golden age.' In *Political Parties in Advanced Industrial Democracies*, ed. Paul Webb, David Farrell, and Ian Holliday. Oxford: Oxford University Press, tables 5.8 and 5.9.

50. Lothar Höbelt. 2003. *Defiant Populist: Jörg Haider and the Politics of Austria.* Purdue: Purdue University Press; Melanie A. Sully. 1997. *The Haider Phenomenon.* New York: Columbia University Press; Wolfgang C. Müller. 2000. *Elections and the Dynamics of the Austrian Party System since 1986.* Vienna: Zentrum für angewandte Politikforschung; Wolfgang C. Müller. 2002. 'Evil or the "Engine of Democracy"? Populism and party competition in Austria.' In *Populism in Western Democracies*, ed. Yves Mény and Yves Surel. Houndmills: Palgrave Macmillan, pp. 155–175; Wolfgang C. Müller, 2000. 'Wahlen und die Dynamik des österreichischen Parteiensystems seit 1986.' In *Das österreichische Wahlverhalten*, ed. Fritz Plasser, Peter A. Ulram, and Franz Sommer. Vienna: Signum. pp. 13–54.

51. For example, FPÖ posters in an election campaign warned of *Ueberfremdung* – a word last used by the Nazis to describe the country being "overrun with foreigners."

52. R. Heinisch. 2003. 'Success in opposition – failure in government: Explaining the performance of right-wing populist parties in public office.' *West European Politics* 26 (3): 91–130.

53. L. S. Tossutti. 1996. 'From communitarian protest towards institutionalization: The evolution of "hybrid" parties in Canada and Italy.' *Party Politics* 2 (4): 435–454; Neil Nevitt, Andre Blais, Elisabeth Gidengil, Richard Johnston, and Henry Brady. 1998. 'The populist right in Canada: The rise of the Reform Party of Canada.' In *The New Politics of the Right*, ed. Hans-Georg Betz and Stefan Immerfall. New York: St. Martin's Press; Harold D. Clarke,

Alan Kornberg, F. Ellis, and J. Rapkin. 2000. 'Not for fame or fortune: A note on membership and activity in the Canadian Reform Party.' *Party Politics* 6 (1): 75–93; Lawrence Mayer, Erol Kaymak, and Jeff W. Justice. 2000. 'Populism and the triumph of the politics of identity: The transformation of the Canadian party system.' *Nationalism and Ethnic Politics* 6(1): 72–102.

54. Elisabeth Gidengil, André Blais, Richard Nadeau, and Neil Nevitte. 1999. 'Making sense of regional voting in the 1997 Canadian federal election: Liberal and Reform support outside Quebec.' *Canadian Journal of Political Science–Revue Canadienne de Science Politique* 32 (2): 247–272.

55. I am indebted to Lynda Erickson, Larry LeDuc, and André Blais for these observations, made in personal communications with the author.

56. I am indebted to Elisabeth Gidengil for this observation, made in a personal communication with the author.

Chapter 11: Assessing the Rise of the Radical Right and Its Consequences

1. Herbert Kitschelt, with Anthony J. McGann. 1995. *The Radical Right in Western Europe: A Comparative Analysis*. Ann Arbor: University of Michigan Press; Elisabeth Carter. 2002. 'Proportional representation and the fortunes of right-wing extremist parties.' *West European Politics* 25 (3): 125–146; Elisabeth Carter. 2004. 'Does PR promote political extremism? Evidence from the West European parties of the extreme right.' *Representation* 40 (2): 82–100.

2. This claim is most clearly articulated by Hans-Georg Betz. 1994. *Radical Rightwing Populism in Western Europe*. New York: St. Martin's Press. For the U.S. case, see Jean Hardisty. 1999. *Mobilizing Resentment: Conservative Resurgence from John Birch to the Promise Keepers*. Boston: Beacon Press. The most systematic survey analysis evidence is presented in Wouter van der Brug and Meindert Fennema. 2003. 'Protest or mainstream? How the European anti-immigrant parties developed into two separate groups by 1999.' *European Journal of Political Research* 42: 55–76.

3. Pippa Norris. 1998. *Critical Citizens: Global Support for Democratic Governance*. Oxford: Oxford University Press; Russell J. Dalton. 2004. *Democratic Challenges: Democratic Choices*. Oxford: Oxford University Press.

4. See, for example, J. W. Koch. 2003. 'Political cynicism and third party support in American presidential elections.' *American Politics Research* 31 (1): 48–65.

5. A similar interpretation of the general causes of satisfaction with government is presented in Christopher J. Anderson. 1995. *Blaming the Government: Citizens and the Economy in Five European Democracies*. New York: M. E. Sharpe; Christopher J. Anderson and Christine A. Guillory. 1997. 'Political institutions and satisfaction with democracy.' *American Political Science Review* 91 (1): 66–81.

6. See, for example, Rachel Gibson. 2002. *The Growth of Anti-Immigrant Parties in Western Europe*. Lewiston, NY: Edwin Mellen Press.

7. For a debate about these issues, see M. A. Seligson. 2002. 'The renaissance of political culture or the renaissance of the ecological fallacy?' *Comparative*

Politics 34 (3): 273–285; Ronald Inglehart and Christopher Welzel. 2003. 'Political culture and democracy: Analyzing cross-level linkages.' *Comparative Politics* 36 (1): 61–70.

8. See Patrick Hossay and Aristide Zolberg. 2002. 'Democracy in peril?' In *Shadows over Europe: The Development and Impact of the Extreme Right in Western Europe*, ed. Martin Schain, Aristide Zolberg, and Patrick Hossay. Houndmills: Palgrave Macmillan, chapter 13.

9. Tim Bale. 2003. 'Cinderella and her ugly sisters: The mainstream and extreme right in Europe's bi-polarizing party systems.' *West European Politics* 26 (3): 67–90.

10. Martin Schain. 1987. 'The National Front in France and the Construction of Political Legitimacy.' *West European Politics* 10 (2): 229–252.

11. Thomas F. Pettigrew. 1998. 'Reactions toward the new minorities of Western Europe.' *Annual Review of Sociology* 24: 77–103.

12. Ruud Koopmans and Paul Statham. Eds. 2000. *Challenging Immigration and Ethnic Relations Politics: Comparative European Perspectives.* Oxford: Oxford University Press. See also the comparison of Germany and Italy on this issue in Ted Perlmutter. 2002. 'The politics of restriction.' In *Shadows over Europe: The Development and Impact of the Extreme Right in Western Europe*, ed. Martin Schain, Aristide Zolberg, and Patrick Hossay. Houndmills: Palgrave Macmillan.

13. Robert Harmel and Lars Svasand. 1997. 'The influence of new parties on old parties' platforms: The cases of the progress parties and conservative parties of Denmark and Norway.' *Party Politics* 3 (3): 315–340; W. M. Downs. 2001. 'Pariahs in their midst: Belgian and Norwegian parties react to extremist threats.' *West European Politics* 24 (3): 23–42.

14. See David Robertson. 1976. *A Theory of Party Competition.* London: Wiley; Ian Budge, David Robertson, and Derek Hearl. Eds. 1987. *Ideology, Strategy and Party Change: Spatial Analysis of Postwar Election Programmes in Nineteen Democracies.* Cambridge: Cambridge University Press; Ian Budge, Hans-Dieter Klingemann, Andrew Volkens, Judith Bara, and Eric Tanenbaum. 2001. *Mapping Policy Preferences.* Oxford: Oxford University Press.

15. See, for example, Richard Rose. 1974. *The Problem of Party Government.* London: Macmillan; Hans-Dieter Klingemann, Richard Hofferbert, and Ian Budge. 1994. *Parties, Policies and Democracy.* Boulder, CO: Westview Press.

16. In this regard, the approach adopted by this book builds upon, but also adapts, earlier work developed by Herbert Kitschelt, with Anthony J. McGann. 1995. *The Radical Right in Western Europe: A Comparative Analysis.* Ann Arbor: University of Michigan Press.

17. This aspect of the theory draws heavily upon earlier work developed by the author, as applied to this particular context. See Pippa Norris. 2004. *Electoral Engineering.* New York: Cambridge University Press.

Select Bibliography

Aarts, Kees, Stuart Elaine MacDonald, and George Rabinowitz. 1999. 'Issues and party competition in the Netherlands.' *Comparative Political Studies* 32 (1): 63–99.

Abedi, Amir. 2002. 'Challenges to established parties: The effects of party system features on the electoral fortunes of anti-political-establishment parties.' *European Journal of Political Research* 41 (4): 551–583.

Achen, Christopher H., and W. Phillips Shively. 1995. *Cross-Level Inference*. Chicago: University of Chicago Press.

Adams, James. 2001. 'A theory of spatial competition with biased voters: Party policies viewed temporally and comparatively.' *British Journal of Political Science* 31: 121–158.

Adorno, Theodore W., Else Fraenkel-Brunswick, David J. Levinson, and R. Nevitt Sanford. 1950. *The Authoritarian Personality*. New York: Harper and Row.

Aldrich, John H. 1995. *Why Parties? The Origin and Transformation of Party Politics in America*. Chicago: University of Chicago Press.

Alexander, Robert Jackson. 1957. *Communism in Latin America*. New Brunswick, NJ: Rutgers University Press.

Alexander, Robert Jackson. Ed. 1988. *Political Parties of the Americas: Canada, Latin America, and the West Indies*, 2 vols. Westport, CT: Greenwood Press.

Alford, Robert R. 1967. 'Class voting in the Anglo-American political systems.' In *Party Systems and Voter Alignments: Cross National Perspectives*, ed. Seymour M. Lipset and Stein Rokkan. New York: Free Press.

Allport, Gordon W. 1954. *The Nature of Prejudice*. London: Addison-Wesley.

Almond, Gabriel A., and Sidney Verba. 1963. *The Civic Culture: Political Attitudes and Democracy in Five Nations*. Princeton: Princeton University Press.

Ameringer, Charles D. Ed. 1992. *Political Parties of the Americas: 1980s to 1990s*. Westport, CT: Greenwood Press.

Ames, Barry. 1995. 'Electoral strategy under open-list proportional representation.' *American Journal of Political Science* 39 (2): 406–433.

Anderson, Christopher J. 1995. *Blaming the Government: Citizens and the Economy in Five European Democracies*. New York: M. E. Sharpe.

Anderson, Christopher J. 1996. 'Economics, politics, and foreigners: Populist party support in Denmark and Norway.' *Electoral Studies* 15 (4): 497–511.

Anderson, Christopher J., and Christine A. Guillory. 1997. 'Political institutions and satisfaction with democracy.' *American Political Science Review* 91 (1): 66–81.

Andeweg, R. B. 2001. 'Lijphart v. Lijphart: The "cons" of consensus democracy in homogeneous societies.' *Acta Politica* 36: 117–128.

Arian, Asher, and Michael Shamir. 2001. 'Candidates, parties and blocs: Israel in the 1990s.' *Party Politics* 7 (6): 689–710.

Arnold, Edwards J. Ed. 2000. *The Development of the Radical Right in France: From Boulanger to Le Pen*. Basingstoke: Macmillan.

Atkin, Nicholas, and Frank Tallett. 2003. *The Right in France: From Revolution to Le Pen*. London: I. B. Tauris.

Austen-Smith, David, and Jeffrey S. Banks. 1988. 'Elections, coalitions, and legislative outcomes.' *American Political Science Review* 82: 405–422.

Austen-Smith, David, and Jeffrey S. Banks. 1990. 'Stable governments and the allocation of policy portfolios.' *American Political Science Review* 84: 891–906.

Aylott, Nick. 1995. 'Back to the future: The 1994 Swedish election.' *Party Politics* 1 (3): 419–429.

Bale, Tim, 2003. 'Cinderella and her ugly sisters: The mainstream and extreme right in Europe's bipolarizing party systems.' *West European Politics* 26 (3): 67–90.

Banks, Arthur S., and Thomas C. Mueller. 1999. *Political Handbook of the World, 1999*. Binghamton, NY: CSA Publications.

Banks, Arthur S., Thomas C. Mueller, and William R. Overstreet. 2003. *Political Handbook of the World, 2000–2002*. Binghamton, NY: CSA Publications.

Barnes, Samuel, and Max Kaase. 1979. *Political Action: Mass Participation in Five Western Democracies*. Beverly Hills: Sage.

Barnes, Samuel, and Janos Simon. Eds. 1998. *The Post-Communist Citizen*. Budapest, Hungary: Erasmus Foundation.

Bartle, John. 1998. 'Left-right position matters, but does social class? Causal models of the 1992 British general election.' *British Journal of Political Science* 28: 501–529.

Bartolini, Stephano, and Peter Mair. 1990. *Identity, Competition, and Electoral Availability: The Stabilization of European Electorates, 1885–1985*. Cambridge: Cambridge University Press.

Bayle, Marc. 1995. *Le Front national: Ca n'arrive pas qu'aux autres*. Toulon: Plein Sud.

Bell, D. S., and Byron Criddle. 2002. 'Presidentialism restored: The French elections of April–May and June 2002.' *Parliamentary Affairs* 55 (4): 643ff.

Bell, Daniel. Ed. [1995/1963] 2001. *The Radical Right*. New York: Transaction Books.

Ben-Moshe, D. 2001. 'One Nation and the Australian far right.' *Patterns of Prejudice* 35 (3): 24–40.

Benoit, Ken. 2001. 'District magnitude, electoral formula, and the number of parties.' *European Journal of Political Research* 39 (2): 203–224.

Benoit, Ken. 2002. 'The endogeneity problem in electoral studies: A critical re-examination of Duverger's mechanical effect.' *Electoral Studies* 21 (1): 35–46.

Berelson, Bernard, Paul F. Lazarsfeld, and W. N. McPhee, 1954. *Voting*. Chicago: University of Chicago Press.

Berglund, Sten, and Jan A. Dellenbrant. 1994. *The New Democracies in Eastern Europe: Party Systems and Political Cleavages*. Aldershot: Edward Elgar.

Bermanis, Shai, Daphna Canetti-Nisim, and Ami Pedahzur. 2004. 'Religious fundamentalism and the extreme right-wing camp in Israel.' *Patterns of Prejudice* 38 (2): 159–176.

Betz, Hans-Georg. 1994. *Radicalism and Right-Wing Populism in Western Europe*. New York: St. Martin's Press.

Betz, Hans-Georg, and Stefan Immerfall. Eds. 1998. *The New Politics of the Right: Neo-Populist Parties and Movements in Established Democracies*. New York: St. Martin's Press.

Beyme, Klaus von. Ed. 1988. *Right-Wing Extremism in Western Europe*. London: Frank Cass.

Bielasiak, Jack. 2002. 'The institutionalization of electoral and party systems in post-communist states.' *Comparative Politics* 34 (2): 189.

Billiet, Jack. 1995. 'Church involvement, ethnocentrism, and voting for a radical right-wing party: Diverging behavioral outcomes of equal attitudinal dispositions.' *Sociology of Religion* 56 (3): 303–326.

Billiet, Jack, and Hans de Witte. 1995. 'Attitudinal dispositions to vote for a "new" extreme right-wing party: The case of "Vlaams Blok."' *European Journal of Political Research* 27 (2): 181–202.

Bitrin, Yves. 2003. *Vote Le Pen et psychologie des foules: 21 avril 2002, "un coup de tonnerre dans un ciel bleu."* Paris: Harmattan.

Bjørklund, Tor, and Jørgen Goul Andersen. 2002. 'Anti-immigration parties in Denmark and Norway.' In *Shadows over Europe: The Development and Impact of the Extreme Right in Western Europe*, ed. Martin Schain, Aristide Zolberg, and Patrick Hossay. Houndmills: Palgrave Macmillan.

Bleich, Erik. 2003. *Race Politics in Britain and France: Ideas and Policymaking since the 1960s*. Cambridge: Cambridge University Press.

Bohrer, R. E., A. C. Pacek, and B. Radcliff. 2000. 'Electoral participation, ideology, and party politics in post-communist Europe.' *Journal of Politics* 62 (4): 1161–1172.

Borre, Ole. 1984. 'Critical electoral change in Scandinavia.' In *Electoral Change in Advanced Industrial Democracies: Realignment or Dealignment?* ed. Russell J. Dalton, Scott C. Flanigan, and Paul Allen Beck. Princeton: Princeton University Press.

Bowler, Shaun, and D. J. Lanoue. 1992. 'Strategic and protest voting for third parties: The case of the Canadian NDP.' *Western Political Quarterly* 45 (2): 485–499.

Braun, Aurel, and Stephen Scheinberg. 1997. *The Extreme Right: Freedom and Security at Risk*. Boulder, CO: Westview Press.

Bresson, Gilles, and Christian Lionet. 1994. *Le Pen: Biographie*. Paris: Seuil.

Breuning, M., and J. T. Ishiyama. 1998. 'The rhetoric of nationalism: Rhetorical strategies of the *Volksunie* and *Vlaams Blok* in Belgium, 1991–1995.' *Political Communication* 15 (1): 5–26.

Broughton, David, and Mark Donovan. Eds. 1999. *Changing Party Systems in Western Europe*. London: Pinter.

Bryk, A. S., and S. W. Raudenbush. 1992. *Hierarchical Linear Models*. Newbury Park, CA: Sage.

Budge, Ian. 2000. 'Expert judgments of party policy positions: Uses and limitations in political research.' *European Journal of Political Research* 37 (1): 103–113.

Budge, Ian, Ivor Crewe, and Dennis Farlie. Eds. 1976. *Party Identification and Beyond*. New York: Wiley.

Budge, Ian, and Dennis J. Farlie. 1983. *Explaining and Predicting Elections: Issue Effects and Party Strategies in Twenty-Three Democracies*. London: Allen and Unwin.

Budge, Ian, and Richard I. Hofferbert. 1990. 'Mandates and policy outputs: U.S. party platforms and federal expenditures.' *American Political Science Review* 84: 111–131.

Budge, Ian, Hans-Dieter Klingemann, Andrew Volkens, Judith Bara, and Eric Tanenbaum. 2001. *Mapping Policy Preferences*. Oxford: Oxford University Press.

Budge, Ian, and Michael J. Laver. Eds. 1992. *Party Policy and Government Coalitions*. Basingstoke: Macmillan.

Budge, Ian, David Robertson, and Derek Hearl. Eds. 1987. *Ideology, Strategy and Party Change: Spatial Analysis of Postwar Election Programmes in Nineteen Democracies*. Cambridge: Cambridge University Press.

Burgess, K., and Stephen Levitsky. 2003. 'Explaining populist party adaptation in Latin America: Environmental and organizational determinants of party change in Argentina, Mexico, Peru, and Venezuela.' *Comparative Political Studies* 36 (8): 881–911.

Burnham, Walter Dean. 1970. *Critical Elections and the Mainsprings of American Politics*. New York: Norton.

Cambadélis, Jean-Christophe, and Eric Osmond. 1998. *La France blafarde: Une histoire politique de l'extrême droite*. Paris: Plon.

Campbell, Angus, Philip Converse, Warren Miller, and Donald Stokes. 1960. *The American Voter*. New York: Wiley.

Campbell, Angus, Philip Converse, Warren Miller, and Donald Stokes. 1966. *Elections and the Political Order*. New York: Wiley.

Canache, D., J. J. Mondak, and M. A. Seligson. 2001. 'Meaning and measurement in cross-national research on satisfaction with democracy.' *Public Opinion Quarterly* 65 (4): 506–528.

Carothers, Thomas. 2002. 'The end of the transition paradigm.' *Journal of Democracy* 13 (1): 5–21.

Carstairs, Andrew McLaren. 1980. *A Short History of Electoral Systems in Western Europe*. London: Allen and Unwin.

Carter, Elisabeth. 2002. 'Proportional representation and the fortunes of right-wing extremist parties.' *West European Politics* 25 (3): 125–146.

Carter, Elisabeth. 2004. 'Does PR promote political extremism? Evidence from the West European parties of the extreme right.' *Representation* 40 (2): 82–100.

Carter, Elisabeth. 2005. *The Extreme Right in Western Europe: Success or Failure?* Manchester: Manchester University Press.

Castles, Francis G., and Peter Mair. 1984. 'Left-Right political scales: Some "expert" judgments.' *European Journal of Political Research* 12 (1): 73–88.

Cesarani, David, and Mary Fulbrook. Eds. 1996. *Citizenship, Nationality and Migration in Europe*. London: Routledge.

Chapin, Wesley D. 1992. 'Explaining the electoral success of the new right: The German case.' *West European Politics* 20 (2): 53–72.

Chebel d'Appollonia, Ariane. 1996. *L'extrême-droite en France: De Maurras à Le Pen*. Bruxelles: Editions Complexe.

Cheles, Luciano, Ronnie Ferguson, and Michalina Vaughan. 1995. *The Far Right in Western and Eastern Europe*. New York: Longman.

Chibber P., and M. Torcal. 1997. 'Elite strategy, social cleavages, and party systems in a new democracy – Spain.' *Comparative Political Studies* 30 (1): 27–54.

Clark, Terry Nichols, and Seymour Martin Lipset. Eds. 2001. *The Breakdown of Class Politics*. Baltimore: Johns Hopkins University Press.

Clarke, Harold D., Alan Kornberg, F. Ellis, and J. Rapkin. 2000. 'Not for fame or fortune: A note on membership and activity in the Canadian Reform Party.' *Party Politics* 6 (1): 75–93.

Clarke, Harold, and Marianne Stewart. 1998. 'The decline of parties in the minds of citizens.' *Annual Review of Political Science* 1: 357–378.

Cohen, Patrick, and Jean-Marc Salmon. 2003. *21 avril 2002: Contre-enquête sur le choc Le Pen*. Paris: Denoël.

Conniff, Michael L. Ed. 1982. *Latin American Populism in Comparative Perspective*. Albuquerque: University of New Mexico Press.

Converse, Philip E., 1964. 'The nature of belief systems in mass publics.' In *Ideology and Discontent*, ed. David Apter. New York: Free Press.

Converse, Philip E. 1969. 'Of time and partisan stability.' *Comparative Political Studies* 2: 139–171.

Converse, Philip E., 1970. 'Attitudes vs. non-attitudes: The continuation of a dialogue.' In *The Quantitative Analysis of Social Problems*, ed. E. R. Tufte. Reading, MA: Addison-Wesley.

Coppedge, M. 1997. 'District magnitude, economic performance, and party-system fragmentation in five Latin American countries.' *Comparative Political Studies* 30 (2): 156–185.

Coppedge, M. 1998. 'The dynamic diversity of Latin American party systems.' *Party Politics* 4 (4): 547–568.

Cox, Gary W. 1987. *The Efficient Secret: The Cabinet and the Development of Political Parties in Victorian England*. Cambridge: Cambridge University Press.

Cox, Gary W. 1987. 'Electoral equilibrium under alternative voting institutions.' *American Journal of Political Science* 31: 82–108.

Cox, Gary W. 1990. 'Centripetal and centrifugal incentives in electoral systems.' *American Journal of Political Science* 34: 903–935.

Cox, Gary W. 1997. *Making Votes Count: Strategic Coordination in the World's Electoral Systems.* Cambridge: Cambridge University Press.

Crewe, Ivor, and David Denver. Eds. 1985. *Electoral Change in Western Democracies: Patterns and Sources of Electoral Volatility.* New York: St. Martin's Press.

Crothers, Lane. 2003. *Rage on the Right: The American Militia Movement from Ruby Ridge to Homeland Security.* Lanham, MD: Rowman and Littlefield.

Dalton, Russell J. 1999. 'Political support in advanced industrial democracies.' In *Critical Citizens: Global Support for Democratic Governance,* ed. Pippa Norris. Oxford: Oxford University Press.

Dalton, Russell J. 2000. 'Citizen attitudes and political behavior.' *Comparative Political Studies.* 33 (6–7): 912–940.

Dalton, Russell J. 2002. *Citizen Politics.* 3rd ed. Chatham, NJ: Chatham House.

Dalton, Russell J. 2004. *Democratic Challenges: Democratic Choices.* Oxford: Oxford University Press.

Dalton, Russell J., Scott Flanagan, and Paul Allen Beck. Eds. 1984. *Electoral Change in Advanced Industrial Democracies: Realignment or Dealignment?* Princeton: Princeton University Press.

Dalton, Russell J., and Martin Wattenberg. Eds. 2001. *Parties without Partisans.* New York: Oxford University Press.

D'Amato, Gianni. 2003. 'Origins of right-wing extremism: A programmatic approach for social research in Switzerland.' *Schweizerische Zeitschrift fur Politikwissenschaft* 9 (2): 89–106.

Darmon, Michaël, and Romain Rosso. 1998. *L'après Le Pen: Enquête dans les coulisses du Front national.* Paris: Seuil.

Davis, Peter. 2002. *The Extreme Right in France, 1789 to the Present: From De Maistre to Le Pen.* London: Routledge.

Day, Alan J., Richard German, and John Campbell. 2002. *Political Parties of the World.* 5th ed. London: John Harper.

DeAngelis, Richard A. 2003. 'A rising tide for Jean-Marie, Jorg, and Pauline? Xenophobic populism in comparative perspective.' *Australian Journal of Politics and History* 49 (1): 75–92.

DeClair, E. G. 1999. *Politics on the Fringe: The People, Policies, and Organization of the French National Front.* Durham, NC: Duke University Press.

Delury, George. Ed. 1983. *World Encyclopedia of Political Systems and Parties.* New York: Facts on File.

De Mesquita, E. B. 2000. 'Strategic and non-policy voting: A coalitional analysis of Israeli electoral reform.' *Comparative Politics* 33 (1): 63ff.

Denemark, D., and Shaun Bowler. 2002. 'Minor parties and protest votes in Australia and New Zealand: Locating populist politics.' *Electoral Studie* 21 (1): 47–67.

Deutchman, I. E. 2000. 'Pauline Hanson and the rise and fall of the radical right in Australia.' *Patterns of Prejudice* 34 (1): 49–62.

De Winter, Leuvan, and J. Ackaert. 1998. 'Compulsory voting in Belgium: A reply to Hooghe and Pelleriaux.' *Electoral Studies* 17 (4): 425–428.

Diamond, Larry, and Juan J. Linz. 1989. 'Introduction: Politics, society, and democracy in Latin America.' In *Democracy in Developing Countries*, vol. 4, *Latin America*, ed. Larry Diamond, Juan J. Linz, and Seymour Martin Lipset. Boulder, CO: Lynne Rienner.

Di Tella, Torcuato. 1965. 'Populism and reform in Latin America.' In *Obstacles to Change in Latin America*, ed. Claudio Véliz. Oxford: Oxford University Press.

Dix, Robert H. 1989. 'Cleavage structures and party systems in Latin America.' *Comparative Politics* (October): 23–37.

Dominguez, Jorge I., and James A. McCann. 1996. *Democratizing Mexico: Public Opinion and Electoral Choices*. Baltimore: Johns Hopkins University Press.

Dow, Jay K. 2001. 'A comparative spatial analysis of majoritarian and proportional elections.' *Electoral Studies* 20: 109–125.

Downs, Anthony. 1957. *An Economic Theory of Democracy*. New York: Harper and Row.

Downs, W. M. 2001. 'Pariahs in their midst: Belgian and Norwegian parties react to extremist threats.' *West European Politics* 24 (3): 23–42.

Durand, Géraud. 1996. *Enquête au coeur du Front national*. Paris: J. Grancher.

Duverger, Maurice. 1954. *Political Parties, Their Organization and Activity in the Modern State*. New York: Wiley.

Duverger, Maurice. 1986. 'Duverger's Law: Forty years later.' In *Electoral Laws and Their Political Consequences*, ed. Bernard Grofman and Arend Lijphart. New York: Agathon Press.

Eatwell, Roger. 1994. 'Why are fascism and racism reviving in Western Europe?' *Political Quarterly* 65 (3): 313–325.

Eatwell, Roger. 1997. 'Toward a new model of the rise of the extreme right.' *German Politics* 6 (3):166–184.

Eatwell, Roger. 1998. 'The dynamics of right-wing electoral breakthrough.' *Patterns of Prejudice* 32 (3): 3–31.

Eatwell, Roger. 2000. 'The rebirth of the "extreme right" in Western Europe?' *Parliamentary Affairs* 53: 407–425.

Eatwell, Roger. 2002. 'The rebirth of right-wing charisma? The cases of Jean-Marie Le Pen and Vladimir Zhirinovsky.' *Totalitarian Movements and Political Religions* 3 (3): 1–24.

Eatwell, Roger. 2003. 'Ten theories of the extreme right.' In *Right-Wing Extremism in the Twenty-First Century*, ed. Peter Merkl and Leonard Weinberg. London: Frank Cass.

Eatwell, Roger. 2004. 'Charisma and the revival of the European extreme right.' In *Movements of Exclusion: Radical Right-Wing Populism*, ed. Jens Rydgren. New York: Nova Science Publishers.

Eatwell, Roger, and Cas Mudde. Eds. 2004. *Western Democracies and the New Extreme Right Challenge*. London: Routledge.

Eijk, Cees van der, Mark Franklin, et al. 1996. *Choosing Europe? The European Electorate and National Politics in the Face of the Union*. Ann Arbor: University of Michigan Press.

Eldersveld, Samuel James. 1982. *Political Parties in American Society*. New York: Basic Books.

Enelow, J., and M. Hinich. Eds. 1984. *The Spatial Theory of Voting*. New York: Cambridge University Press.

Epstein, Leon. 1980. *Political Parties in Western Democracies*. New Brunswick, NJ: Transaction Books.

Esping-Anderson, G. 1990. *The Three Worlds of Welfare Capitalism*. Princeton: Princeton University Press.

Esping-Andersen, G. 1999. *The Social Foundations of Post-industrial Economies*. Oxford: Oxford University Press.

Eulau, Heinz, and Michael S. Lewis-Beck. Eds. 1985. *Economic Conditions and Electoral Outcomes: The United States and Western Europe*. New York: Agathon Press.

Evans, Geoffrey. 1999. *The Decline of Class Politics?* Oxford: Oxford University Press.

Evans, Geoffrey. 2000. 'The continued significance of class voting.' *Annual Review of Political Science* 3: 401–417.

Evans, Geoffrey, and Pippa Norris. Eds. 1999. *Critical Elections: British Parties and Voters in Long-Term Perspective*. London: Sage.

Fennema, Meindert. 1997. 'Some conceptual issues and problems in the comparison of anti-immigrant parties in Western Europe.' *Party Politics* 3: 473–492.

Fennema, Meindert. 2000. 'Legal repression of extreme-right parties and racial discrimination.' In *Challenging Immigration and Ethnic Relations Politics*, ed. Ruud Koopmans and Paul Statham. Oxford: Oxford University Press.

Ferber, Abby L. Ed. 2004. *Home-Grown Hate: Gender and Organized Racism*. New York: Routledge.

Fieschi, Catherine. 2000. 'The far right in the context of the European Union.' *Parliamentary Affairs* 54: 3.

Fieschi, Catherine. 2004. *Fascism, Populism and the Fifth Republic: In the Shadow of Democracy*. Manchester: Manchester University Press.

Fieschi, Catherine, J. Shields, and R. Woods. 1996. 'Extreme right-wing parties in Europe.' In *Political Parties and the European Union*, ed. J. Gaffney. London: Routledge.

Franklin, Mark. 1985. *The Decline of Class Voting in Britain: Changes in the Basis of Electoral Choice, 1964–1983*. Oxford: Clarendon Press.

Franklin, Mark, Tom Mackie, Henry Valen, et al. 1992. *Electoral Change: Responses to Evolving Social and Attitudinal Structures in Western Countries*. Cambridge: Cambridge University Press.

Fukuyama, Francis. 1992. *The End of History and the Last Man*. London: Hamish Hamilton.

Gallagher, Michael. 1992. 'Comparing proportional representation electoral systems: Quotas, thresholds, paradoxes, and majorities.' *British Journal of Political Science* 22: 469–496.

Gallego, Ferran. 2002. *Por qué Le Pen?* Barcelona: Ediciones de Intervención Cultural.

Gibson, Rachel. 1995. 'Anti-immigrant parties: The roots of their success.' *Current World Leaders* 38 (2): 119–130.

Gibson, Rachel. 2002. *The Growth of Anti-Immigrant Parties in Western Europe*. Lewiston, NY: Edwin Mellen Press.

Gibson, Rachel, Ian McAllister, and T. Swenson. 2002. 'The politics of race and immigration in Australia: One Nation voting in the 1998 Election.' *Ethnic and Racial Studies* 25 (5): 823–844.

Gidengil, Elisabeth, André Blais, Richard Nadeau, and Neil Nevitte. 1999. 'Making sense of regional voting in the 1997 Canadian federal election: Liberal and Reform support outside Quebec.' *Canadian Journal of Political Science – Revue Canadienne de Science Politique* 32 (2): 247–272.

Gidengil, Elisabeth, André Blais, Neil Nevitte, and Richard Nadeau. 2001. 'The correlates and consequences of anti-partyism in the 1997 Canadian election.' *Party Politics* 7 (4): 491–513.

Givens, Terri E. 2004. 'The radical right gender gap.' *Comparative Political Studies* 37 (1): 30–54.

Golder Matthew. 2003. 'Explaining variation in the success of extreme right parties in Western Europe.' *Comparative Political Studies* 36 (4): 432–466.

Goldstein, Harvey. 1995. *Multilevel Statistical Models.* 3rd ed. New York: Halstead Press.

Golsan, Richard J. Ed. 1995. *Fascism's Return: Scandal, Revision and Ideology since 1980.* Lincoln: University of Nebraska Press.

Grendstad, G. 2003. 'Reconsidering Nordic party space.' *Scandinavian Political Studies* 26 (3): 193–217.

Guilledoux, Frédéric-Joël. 2004. *Le Pen en Provence.* Paris: Fayard.

Gunther, Richard, and Larry Diamond. 2003. 'Species of political parties: A new typology.' *Party Politics* 9 (2): 167–199.

Hainsworth, Paul. Ed. 1992. *The Extreme Right in Europe and the USA.* New York: St. Martin's Press.

Hainsworth, Paul. Ed. 2000. *The Politics of the Extreme Right: From the Margins to the Mainstream.* London: Pinter.

Hardisty, Jean. 1999. *Mobilizing Resentment: Conservative Resurgence from John Birch to the Promise Keepers.* Boston: Beacon Press.

Harmel, Robert, and Kenneth Janda. 1994. 'An integrated theory of party goals and party change.' *Journal of Theoretical Politics* 6: 259–287.

Harmel, Robert, and Lars Svasand. 1997. 'The influence of new parties on old parties' platforms: The cases of the progress parties and conservative parties of Denmark and Norway.' *Party Politics* 3 (3): 315–340.

Hazan, Reuven Y. 1997. 'Three levels of election in Israel: The 1996 party, parliamentary and prime ministerial elections.' *Representation* 34 (3/4): 240–249.

Hazan, Reuvan Y., and Abraham Diskin. 2000. 'The 1999 Knesset and prime ministerial elections in Israel.' *Electoral Studies* 19 (4): 628–637.

Heinisch, R. 2003. 'Success in opposition – failure in government: Explaining the performance of right-wing populist parties in public office.' *West European Politics* 26 (3): 91–130.

Hirschman, Albert O. 1970. *Exit, Voice and Loyalty.* Cambridge: Harvard University Press.

Hoffman, Stanley. 1956. *Le Mouvement Poujade.* Paris: A. Colin.

Hofstedter, Richard. 1967. *The Paranoid Style in American Politics.* New York: Vintage Books.

Holmberg, Sören. 1994. 'Party identification compared across the Atlantic.' In *Elections at Home and Abroad*, ed. M. Kent Jennings and Thomas Mann. Ann Arbor: University of Michigan Press.

Holsteyn, Joop van. 2003. 'A new kid on the block: Pim Fortuyn and the Dutch Parliamentary Election of May 2002.' In: *British Elections and Parties Review*, ed. Colin Rallings et al. London: Frank Cass.

Holsteyn, Joop van, and G. A. Irwin. 2003. 'Never a dull moment: Pim Fortuyn and the Dutch Parliamentary Election of 2002.' *West European Politics* 26 (2): 41–66.

Holsteyn, Joop van, and Josje M. den Ridder. 2003. 'In the eye of the beholder: The perception of the List Pim Fortuyn and the Parliamentary Elections of May 2002.' *Acta Politica* 38 (1): 69–88.

Hooghe, Marc, and K. Pelleriaux. 1998. 'Compulsory voting in Belgium: An application of the Lijphart thesis.' *Electoral Studies* 17 (4): 419–424.

Huber, John, and Ronald Inglehart. 1995. 'Expert interpretations of party space and party locations in forty-two societies.' *Party Politics* 1: 73–111.

Huntington, Samuel P. 1968. *Political Order in Changing Societies*. New Haven: Yale University Press.

Huntington, Samuel P. 1993. *The Third Wave: Democratization in the Late Twentieth Century*. Norman: University of Oklahoma Press.

Husbands, Christopher T. 1988. 'The dynamic of racial exclusion and expulsion: Racist policy in Western Europe.' *European Journal of Political Research* 16: 688–700.

Husbands, Christopher T. 1989. *Racist Political Movements in Western Europe*. London: Routledge.

Husbands, Christopher T. 1992. 'The other face of 1992: The extreme-right explosion in Western Europe.' *Parliamentary Affairs* 45: 267–284.

Ignazi, Piero. 1992. 'The silent counter-revolution: Hypotheses on the emergence of extreme right-wing parties in Europe.' *European Journal of Political Research* 22 (1): 3–34.

Ignazi, Piero. 1993. 'The changing profile of the Italian social movement.' In *Encounters with the Contemporary Radical Right*, ed. Peter H. Merkl and Leonard Weinberg. Oxford: Westview Press.

Ignazi, Piero. 2003. *Extreme right parties in Western Europe*. New York: Oxford University Press.

Inglehart, Ronald. 1977. *The Silent Revolution: Changing Values and Political Styles among Western Publics*. Princeton: Princeton University Press.

Inglehart, Ronald. 1990. *Culture Shift in Advanced Industrial Society*. Princeton: Princeton University Press.

Inglehart, Ronald. 1997. *Modernization and Postmodernization: Cultural, Economic and Political Change in Forty-Three Societies*. Princeton: Princeton University Press.

Inglehart, Ronald, and Pippa Norris. 2003. *Rising Tide: Gender Equality and Cultural Change around the World*. Cambridge: Cambridge University Press.

International IDEA. 2004. *Handbook on Funding of Political Parties and Election Campaigns*. Stockholm: International IDEA.

Jackman, Robert W., and Karin Volpert. 1996. 'Conditions favouring parties of the extreme right in Western Europe.' *British Journal of Political Science* 264: 501–522.

Jackman, S. 1998. 'Pauline Hanson, the mainstream and political elites: The place of race in Australian political ideology.' *Australian Journal of Political Science* 33 (2): 167–186.

Janda, Kenneth. 1993. 'Comparative political parties: Research and theories.' In *Political Science: The State of the Discipline II*, ed. Ada W. Finifter. Washington, DC: American Political Science Association.

Janda, Kenneth, Robert Harmel, C. Edens, and P. Goff. 1995. 'Changes in party identity: Evidence from party manifestos.' *Party Politics* 1: 171–196.

Jelen, Ted Gerard, and Clyde Wilcox. Eds. 2002. *Religion and Politics in Comparative Perspective*. New York: Cambridge University Press.

Jenssen, A. T. 1999. 'All that is solid melts into air: Party identification in Norway.' *Scandinavian Political Studies* 22 (1): 1–27.

Jesse, Eckhard. 2003. 'The performance of the PDS and the right-wing parties at the Bundestag Election 2002.' *Zeitschrift fur Politik* 50 (1): 17–36.

Kang, W. T. 2004. 'Protest voting and abstention under plurality rule elections: An alternative public choice approach.' *Journal of Theoretical Politics* 16 (1): 79–102.

Karapin, Roger. 1998. 'Radical-right and neo-fascist political parties in Western Europe.' *Comparative Politics* 30 (2): 213–234.

Karp, Jeffrey A., Susan A. Banducci, and Shaun Bowler. 2003. 'To know it is to love it? Satisfaction with democracy in the European Union.' *Comparative Political Studies* 36 (3): 271–292.

Katz, Richard S. 1997. *Democracy and Elections*. Oxford: Oxford University Press.

Katz, Richard S., and Peter Mair. 1992. 'The membership of political parties in European democracies, 1960–1990.' *European Journal of Political Research* 22: 329–45.

Katz, Richard S. and Peter Mair. 1995. 'Changing models of party organization and party democracy: The emergence of the cartel party.' *Party Politics* 1 (1): 5–28.

Katz, Richard S., and Peter Mair. 1996. 'Cadre, catch-all or cartel? A rejoinder.' *Party Politics* 2 (4): 525–534.

Katz, Richard S., and Peter Mair. Eds. 1992. *Party Organizations: A Data Handbook on Party Organizations in Western Democracies, 1960–1990*. London: Sage.

Katz, Richard S., and Peter Mair. Eds. 1994. *How Parties Organize: Change and Adaptation in Party Organizations in Western Democracies*. London: Sage.

Keman, Hans. Ed. 2002. *Comparative Democratic Politics*. London: Sage.

Key, V. O., Jr. 1949. *Southern Politics in State and Nation*. New York: Vintage.

Key, V. O., Jr. 1964. *Politics, Parties, and Pressure Groups*. 5th ed. New York: Crowell.

Kim, H., and R. C. Fording. 2001. 'Does tactical voting matter? The political impact of tactical voting in recent British elections.' *Comparative Political Studies* 34 (3): 294–311.

Kinder, Donald R., and David O. Sears. 1981. 'Prejudice and politics: Symbolic racism vs. racial threats to the good life.' *Journal of Personality and Social Psychology* 40: 414–431.

King, Anthony. Ed. 2002. *Leaders' Personalities and the Outcomes of Democratic Elections.* Oxford: Oxford University Press.

Kirchheimer, Otto. 1966. 'The transformation of Western European party systems.' In *Political Parties and Political Development*, ed. J. La Palombara and M. Weiner. Princeton: Princeton University Press.

Kitschelt, Herbert. 1988. 'Organization and strategy of Belgian and West European parties: A new dynamic of party politics in Western Europe?' *Comparative Politics* 20: 127–154.

Kitschelt, Herbert. 1989. *The Logics of Party Formation: Ecological Politics in Belgium and West Germany.* Ithaca, NY: Cornell University Press.

Kitschelt, Herbert. 1992. 'The formation of party systems in East Central Europe.' *Politics and Society* 20 (March): 7–50.

Kitschelt, Herbert. 1993. 'Class structure and Social-Democratic party strategy.' *British Journal of Political Science* 23 (3): 299–337.

Kitschelt, Herbert. 1994. *The Transformation of European Social Democracy.* Cambridge: Cambridge University Press.

Kitschelt, Herbert. 1995. 'Formation of party cleavages in post-communist democracies: Theoretical propositions.' *Party Politics* 1 (4): 447–472.

Kitschelt, Herbert. 2000. 'Linkages between citizens and politicians in democratic polities.' *Comparative Political Studies* 33 (6–7): 845–879.

Kitschelt, Herbert, Zdenka Mansfeldova, Radoslaw Markowski, and Gabor Toka. 1999. *Post-Communist Party Systems.* Cambridge: Cambridge University Press.

Kitschelt, Herbert, with Anthony J. McGann. 1995. *The Radical Right in Western Europe: A Comparative Analysis.* Ann Arbor: University of Michigan Press.

Klingemann, Hans-Dieter. 1979. 'Measuring ideological conceptualizations.' In *Political Action*, ed. Samuel Barnes, Max Kaase, et al. Beverly Hills: Sage.

Klingemann, Hans-Dieter. 1995. 'Party positions and voter orientations.' In *Citizens and the State*, ed. Hans-Dieter Klingemann and Dieter Fuchs. Oxford: Oxford University Press.

Klingemann, Hans-Dieter, and Dieter Fuchs. Eds. 1995. *Citizens and the State.* Oxford: Oxford University Press.

Klingemann, Hans-Dieter, Richard Hofferbert, and Ian Budge. 1994. *Parties, Policies and Democracy.* Boulder, CO: Westview Press.

Knapp, Andrew. 1987. 'Proportional but bipolar: France's electoral system in 1986.' *West European Politics* 10 (1): 89–114.

Knigge, Pia. 1998. 'The ecological correlates of right-wing extremism in Western Europe.' *European Journal of Political Research* 34: 249–279.

Koopmans, Ruud. 1996. 'Explaining the rise of racist and extreme right violence in Western Europe: Grievances or opportunities?' *European Journal of Political Research* 30: 185–216.

Koopmans, Ruud. 1999. 'Political. Opportunity. Structure. Some splitting to balance the lumping.' *Sociological Forum* 14 (1): 93–105.

Koopmans, Ruud, and Paul Statham. Eds. 2000. *Challenging Immigration and Ethnic Relations Politics: Comparative European Perspectives*. Oxford: Oxford University Press.

Laakso, M., and Rein Taagepera. 1979. 'Effective number of parties: A measure with application to Western Europe.' *Comparative Political Studies* 12: 3–27.

Ladner, A. 2001. 'Swiss political parties: Between persistence and change.' *West European Politics* 24 (2): 123–+.

Landman, Todd. 2000. *Issues and Methods in Comparative Politics*. London: Routledge.

Lane, Jan-Erik, David McKay, and Kenneth Newton. Eds. 1997. *Political Data Handbook*. 2nd ed. Oxford: Oxford University Press.

Laver, Michael, and Ian Budge. 1992. *Party Policy and Government Coalitions*. Houndmills: Macmillan.

Laver, Michael, and W. Ben Hunt. 1992. *Policy and Party Competition*. New York: Routledge.

Laver, Michael, and Norman Schofield. 1990. *Multiparty Government: The Politics of Coalition in Europe*. Oxford: Oxford University Press.

Laver, Michael, and Kenneth A. Shepsle. 1996. *Making and Breaking Governments: Cabinets and Legislatures in Parliamentary Democracies*. Cambridge: Cambridge University Press.

Lawson, Kay. 1980. *Political Parties and Linkage: A Comparative Perspective*. New Haven: Yale University Press.

Lazarsfeld, Paul F., Bernard Berelson, and H. Gaudet. 1948. *The People's Choice*. New York: Columbia University Press.

LeDuc, Lawrence. 1979. 'The dynamic properties of party identification: A four nation comparison.' *European Journal of Political Research* 9: 257–268.

LeDuc, Lawrence, Richard G. Niemi, and Pippa Norris, Eds. 1996. *Comparing Democracies: Elections and Voting in Global Perspective*. Thousand Oaks, CA: Sage.

LeDuc, Lawrence, Richard Niemi, and Pippa Norris. Eds. 2002. *Comparing Democracies 2: New Challenges in the Study of Elections and Voting*. Thousand Oaks, CA: Sage.

LeVine, Robert A., and Campbell, Donald T. 1972. *Ethnocentrism: Theories of Conflict, Ethnic Attitudes and Group Behavior*. New York: Columbia University Press.

Lewis, Paul G. 2000. *Political Parties in Post-Communist Eastern Europe*. London: Routledge.

Lewis, Paul G. 2001. *Party Development and Democratic Change in Post-Communist Europe: The First Decade*. London: Frank Cass.

Lewis-Beck, Michael S. 1988. *Economics and Elections: The Major Western Democracies*. Ann Arbor: University of Michigan Press.

Lewis-Beck, Michael S., and Glenn E. Mitchell. 1993. 'French electoral theory: The National Front test.' *Electoral Studies* 12: 112–127.

Lewis-Beck, Michael S., and M. Stegmaier. 2000. 'Economic determinants of electoral outcomes.' *Annual Review of Political Science* 3: 183–219.

Lijphart, Arend. 1979. 'Religion vs. linguistic vs. class voting.' *American Political Science Review* 65: 686.

Lijphart, Arend. 1980. 'Language, religion, class, and party choice: Belgium, Canada, Switzerland, and South Africa compared.' In *Electoral Participation: A Comparative Analysis*, ed. Richard Rose. Beverly Hills: Sage.

Lijphart, Arend. 1984. *Democracies: Patterns of Majoritarian and Consensus Government in Twenty-One Countries*. New Haven: Yale University Press.

Lijphart, Arend. 1994. *Electoral Systems and Party Systems: A Study of Twenty-Seven Democracies 1945–1990*. New York: Oxford University Press.

Lijphart, Arend. 1999. *Patterns of Democracy: Government Forms and Performance in Thirty-Six Countries*. New Haven: Yale University Press.

Lijphart, Arend. 2001. 'The pros and cons – but mainly pros – of consensus democracy.' *Acta Politica*. 35: 363–398.

Linde, J., and J. Ekman. 2003. 'Satisfaction with democracy: A note on a frequently used indicator in comparative politics.' *European Journal of Political Research* 42 (3): 391–408.

Lipset, Seymour Martin. 1955. 'The sources of the radical right.' In *The New American Right*, ed. Daniel Bell. New York: Criterion Books.

Lipset, Seymour Martin. 1960. *Political Man: The Social Basis of Politics*. New York: Doubleday.

Lipset, Seymour Martin, and Earl Raab. 1978. *The Politics of Unreason: Rightwing extremism in America 1790–1977*. 2nd ed. Chicago: University of Chicago Press.

Lipset, Seymour Martin, and Stein Rokkan. 1967. *Party Systems and Voter Alignments*. New York: Free Press.

Lubbers, Marcel [Principal investigator]. 2000. *Expert Judgment Survey of Western-European Political Parties 2000* [machine readable dataset]. Nijmegen, the Netherlands: NWO, Department of Sociology, University of Nijmegen.

Lubbers, Marcel, Mérove Gijsberts, and Peer Scheepers, 2002. 'Extreme right-wing voting in Western Europe.' *European Journal of Political Research* 41 (3): 345–378.

Lubbers, Marcel, and Peer Scheepers. 2000. 'Individual and contextual characteristics of the German extreme right-wing vote in the 1990s: A test of complementary theories.' *European Journal of Political Research* 38 (1): 63–94.

Lubbers, Marcel, and Peers Scheepers. 2001. 'Explaining the trend in extreme right-wing voting: Germany 1989–1998.' *European Sociological Review* 17 (4): 431–449.

Luther, K. R. 2003. 'The self-destruction of a right-wing populist party? The Austrian parliamentary election of 2002.' *West European Politics* 26 (2): 136–152.

MacDonald, Stuart Elaine, Ola Listhaug, and George Rabinowitz. 1991. 'Issues and party support in multiparty systems.' *American Political Science Review* 85 (4): 1107–1131.

Mackie, Thomas J. 1989, 1990, 1991. 'Report National Elections'. *European Journal of Political Research* 17 (4), 19 (4), 21 (4).

Mackie, Thomas J., and Richard Rose. 1991. *The International Almanac of Electoral History*. London: Macmillan.

Mackie, Thomas J., and Richard Rose. 1991. *The International Almanac of Electoral History*. 3rd ed. Washington, DC: Congressional Quarterly Press.

Mackie, Thomas J., and Richard Rose. 1997. *A Decade of Election Results: Updating the International Almanac*. Glasgow: Centre for the Study of Public Policy, University of Strathclyde.

Maguire, Maria. 1983. 'Is there still persistence? Electoral change in Western Europe, 1948–1979.' In *Western European Party Systems: Continuity and Change*, ed. Hans Daalder and Peter Mair. Beverly Hills: Sage.

Mainwaring, Scott, and Timothy R. Scully. Eds. 1995. *Building Democratic Institutions: Party Systems in Latin America*. Stanford, CA: Stanford University Press.

Mainwaring, Scott, and Timothy R. Scully. 1995. 'Introduction: Party systems in Latin America.' In *Building Democratic Institutions: Party Systems in Latin America*, ed. Mainwaring and Scully. Stanford, CA: Stanford University Press.

Mair, Peter. 1983. 'Adaptation and control: Towards an understanding of party and party system change.' In *Western European Party Systems: Continuity and Change*, ed. Hans Daalder and Peter Mair. Beverly Hills: Sage.

Mair, Peter. 1993. 'Myths of electoral change and the survival of traditional parties.' *European Journal of Political Research* 24: 121–133.

Mair, Peter. 1997. *Party System Change*. Oxford: Oxford University Press.

Mair, Peter. 2000. 'The limited impact of Europe on national party systems.' *West European Politics* 23 (4): 27ff.

Mair, Peter. 2001. 'In the aggregate: Mass electoral behaviour in Western Europe, 1950–2000.' In *Comparative Democracy*, ed. Hans Keman. London: Sage.

Mair, Peter. 2001. 'Party membership in twenty European democracies 1980–2000.' *Party Politics* 7 (1): 5–22.

Mair, Peter, and Francis Castles. 1997. 'Reflections: Revisiting expert judgments.' *European Journal of Political Research* 31 (1–2): 150–157.

Mair, Peter, and Cas Mudde. 1998. 'The party family and its study.' *Annual Review of Political Science* 1: 211–229.

Manza, Jeff, and Clem Brooks. 1999. *Social Cleavages and Political Change: Voter Alignments and U.S. Party Coalitions*. New York: Oxford University Press.

March, James, and Johan Olsen. 1989. *Rediscovering Institutions: The Organizational Basis of Politics*. New York: Free Press.

Marcus, Jonathan. 1995. *The National Front and French Politics: The Resistible Rise of Jean-Marie Le Pen*. New York: New York University Press.

Maréchal, Yann, and Nicolas Gauthier. 2001. *Le Pen*. Paris: Editions Objectif France.

Marsh, Alan. 1977. *Protest and Political Consciousness*. Beverly Hills: Sage.

Marsh, Alan. 1990. *Political Action in Europe and the USA*. London: Macmillan.

Marsh, Michael. 1998. 'Testing the second-order election model after four European elections.' *British Journal of Political Science* 28 (4): 591–607.

Mason, William M., G. M. Wong, and Barbara Entwistle. 1983. 'Contextual analysis through the Multilevel Linear Model.' *Sociological Methodology* 3: 72–103.

Massicotte, Louis, André Blais, and Antoine Yoshinaka. 2004. *Establishing the Rules of the Game*. Toronto: University of Toronto Press.

Mayer, Lawrence C., Erol Kaymak, and Jeff W. Justice. 2000. 'Populism and the triumph of the politics of identity: The transformation of the Canadian party system.' *Nationalism and Ethnic Politics.* 6 (1): 72–102.

Mayer, Nonna. 2002. *Ces Français qui votent Le Pen.* Paris: Flammarion.

Mayer, Nonna, and P. Perrineau. 1992. 'Why do they vote for Le Pen?' *European Journal of Political Research* 22 (1): 123–141.

Mayhew, David R. 1986. *Placing Parties in American Politics: Organization, Electoral Settings, and Government Activity in the Twentieth Century.* Princeton: Princeton University Press.

Mayhew, David R. 2002. *Electoral Realignments: A Critique of the American Genre.* New Haven: Yale University Press.

McConahay, J. B., and J. C. Hough. 1976. 'Symbolic racism.' *Journal of Social Issues* 32: 23–45.

McDonald, Ronald H., and J. Mark Ruhl. 1989. *Party Politics and Elections in Latin America.* Boulder, CO: Westview Press.

McKenzie, Robert T., 1955. *British Political Parties.* New York: St. Martin's Press.

Mény, Yves, and Yves Surel. Eds. 2002. *Democracies and the Populist Challenge.* Houndmills: Palgrave Macmillan.

Merkl, Peter H., and Leonard Weinberg. Eds. 1993. *Encounters with the Contemporary Radical Right.* Boulder, CO: Westview Press.

Merkl, Peter H., and Leonard Weinberg, Eds. 1997. *The Revival of Right-Wing Extremism in the Nineties.* London: Frank Cass.

Merkl, Peter, and Leonard Weinberg. 2003. Eds. *Right-Wing Extremism in the Twenty-First Century.* London: Frank Cass.

Merrill, Samuel III, and James Adam. 'Centifugal incentives in multi-candidate elections.' *Journal of Theoretical Politics* 14 (3): 275–300.

Merrill, Samuel III, and Bernard Grofman. 1999. *A Unified Theory of Voting: Directional and Proximity Spatial Models.* Cambridge: Cambridge University Press.

Miguet, Arnauld. 2002. 'The French elections of 2002: After the earthquake, the deluge.' *West European Politics* 25 (4): 207–220.

Miller, Arthur H. 2000. 'The development of party identification in post-Soviet societies.' *American Journal of Political Science* 44 (4): 667–686.

Miller, Warren E. 1991. 'Party identification, realignment, and party voting: Back to the basics.' *American Political Science Review* 85 (2): 557–568.

Miller, Warren E., and J. Merrill Shanks. 1996. *The New American Voter.* Cambridge: Harvard University Press.

Miller, William L., Stephen White, and Paul Heywood. 1998. *Values and Political Change in Post-Communist Europe.* New York: St. Martin's Press.

Minkenberg, Michael. 2002. 'The radical right in post-socialist central and eastern Europe: Comparative observations and interpretations.' *East European Politics and Societies* 16 (2): 335–362.

Minkenberg, Michael. 2003. 'The West European radical right as a collective actor: Modeling the impact of cultural and structural variables on party formation and movement mobilization.' *Comparative European Politics* 1 (2): 149–170.

Mitra, Subrata. 1988. 'The National Front in France: A single-issue movement?' *West European Politics* 11 (2): 47–64.

Morlino, Leonardo. 1998. *Democracy between Consolidation and Crisis: Parties, Groups, and Citizens in Southern Europe.* Oxford: Oxford University Press.

Moser, Robert G. 1999. 'Electoral systems and the number of parties in post-communist states.' *World Politics* 51 (3): 359.

Moser, Robert G. 2001. *Unexpected Outcomes: Electoral Systems, Political Parties and Representation in Russia.* Pittsburgh: University of Pittsburgh Press.

Mudde, Cas. 1996. 'The paradox of the anti-party party: Insights from the extreme right.' *Party Politics* 2 (2): 265–276.

Mudde, Cas. 1999. 'The single-issue party thesis: Extreme right parties and the immigration issue.' *West European Politics.* 22 (3): 182–197.

Mudde, Cas. 2000. *The Ideology of the Extreme Right.* New York: St. Martin's Press.

Mughan, Anthony, Clive Bean, and Ian McAllister. 2003. 'Economic globalization, job insecurity and the populist reaction.' *Electoral Studies* 22 (4): 617–633.

Mughan, Anthony, and David Lacy. 2002. 'Economic performance, job insecurity and electoral choice.' *British Journal of Political Science* 32 (3): 513–533.

Müller, Wolfgang C. 2000. 'The Austrian election of October 1999: A shift to the right.' *West European Politics* 23 (3): 191–200.

Müller, Wolfgang C. 2000. 'Wahlen und die Dynamik des österreichischen Parteiensystems seit 1986.' In *Das österreichische Wahlverhalten,* ed. Fritz Plasser, Peter A. Ulram, and Franz Sommer. Vienna: Signum.

Müller, Wolfgang C. 2004. 'The parliamentary election in Austria, November 2002.' *Electoral Studies* 23 (2): 346–353.

Muller-Rommel, Ferdinand, and Geoffrey Pridham. Eds. 1991. *Small Parties in Western Europe.* London: Sage.

Neto, Octavio Amorim, and Gary Cox. 1997. 'Electoral institutions, cleavage structures and the number of parties.' *American Journal of Political Science* 41 (1): 149–174.

Nie, Norman, Sidney Verba, and John Petricik. 1976. *The Changing American Voter.* Cambridge: Harvard University Press.

Niekerk, A. E. van. 1974. *Populism and Political Development in Latin America.* Rotterdam: Universitaire Pers Rotterdam.

Nielsen, H. J. 1999. 'The Danish election 1998.' *Scandinavian Political Studies* 22 (1): 67–81.

Nieuwbeerta, Paul. 1995. *The Democratic Class Struggle in Twenty Countries 1945–90.* Amsterdam: Thesis Publishers.

Nieuwbeerta, Paul, and Nan Dirk de Graaf. 1999. 'Traditional class voting in twenty postwar societies.' In *The End of Class Politics?* ed. Geoffrey Evans. Oxford: Oxford University Press.

Nohlen, Dieter. 1996. *Elections and Electoral Systems.* Delhi: Macmillan.

Norpoth, Helmut, Michael S. Lewis-Beck, and Jean-Dominique Lafay. Eds. 1991. *Economics and Politics: The Calculus of Support.* Ann Arbor: University of Michigan Press.

Norris, Pippa. 1996. *Electoral Change since 1945.* Oxford: Blackwell.

Norris, Pippa. 1998. *Critical Citizens: Global Support for Democratic Governance.* Oxford: Oxford University Press.

Norris, Pippa. 2000. *A Virtuous Circle: Political Communication in Post-Industrial Democracies*. New York: Cambridge University Press.

Norris, Pippa. 2001. *Digital Divide: Civic Engagement, Information Poverty and the Internet Worldwide*. New York: Cambridge University Press.

Norris, Pippa. 2002. *Democratic Phoenix: Political Activism Worldwide*. New York: Cambridge University Press.

Norris, Pippa. 2004. *Electoral Engineering: Voting Rules and Political Behavior*. New York: Cambridge University Press.

Norris, Pippa. Ed. 1999. *Critical Citizens: Global Support for Democratic Governance*. Oxford: Oxford University Press.

Norris, Pippa. Ed. 2001. *Britain Votes 2001*. Oxford: Oxford University Press.

Norris, Pippa, and Ronald Inglehart. 2003. *Rising Tide: Gender Equality and Cultural Change Worldwide*. New York: Cambridge University Press.

Norris, Pippa, and Ronald Inglehart. 2004. *Sacred and Secular: Religion and Politics Worldwide*. New York: Cambridge University Press.

Norris, Pippa, and Joni Lovenduski. 2004. 'Why parties fail to learn: Electoral defeat, selective perception and British party politics.' *Party Politics* 10 (1): 85–104.

North, Douglas, C. 1990. *Institutions, Institutional Change, and Economic Performance*. Cambridge: Cambridge University Press.

Olzak, Susan. 1993. *The Dynamics of Ethnic Competition and Conflict*. Stanford, CA: Stanford University Press.

Oppenhuis, Eric. 1995. *Voting Behavior in Europe: A Comparative Analysis of Electoral Participation and Party Choice*. Amsterdam: Het Spinhuis.

Ordeshook, Peter C., and Olga Shvetsova. 1994. 'Ethnic heterogeneity, district magnitude and the number of parties.' *American Journal of Political Science* 38: 100–23.

Pammett, Jon H., and Joan DeBardeleben. Eds. 1998. 'Special issue: Voting and elections in post-Communist states.' *Electoral Studies* 17 (2).

Panebianco, Angelo. 1988. *Political Parties: Organization and Power*. Cambridge: Cambridge University Press.

Pedahzur, Ami. 2003. 'The potential role of "pro-democratic" civil society in responding to extreme right-wing challenges: The case of Brandenburg.' *Contemporary Politics* 9 (1): 63–74.

Pedahzur, Ami, and A. Perliger. 2004. 'An alternative approach for defining the boundaries of "party families": Examples from the Israeli extreme right-wing party scene.' *Australian Journal of Political Science* 39 (2): 285–305.

Pedersen, Mogens N. 1979. 'The dynamics of European party systems: Changing patterns of electoral volatility.' *European Journal of Political Research* 7: 1–26.

Peretz, D., and G. Doron. 1996. 'Israel's 1996 elections: A second political earthquake?' *Middle East Journal* 50 (4): 529–546.

Peretz, D., R. Kook, and G. Doron. 2003. 'Knesset election 2003: Why Likud regained its political domination and Labor continued to fade out.' *Middle East Journal* 57 (4): 588–603.

Perrineau, Pascal. 1997. *Le symptome Le Pen: Radiographie des électeurs du Front national*. Paris: Fayard.

Pettigrew, Thomas F. 1998. 'Reactions toward the new minorities of Western Europe.' *Annual Review of Sociology* 24: 77–103.

Pettigrew, Thomas F., and R. W. Meertens. 1995. 'Subtle and blatant prejudice in Western Europe.' *European Journal of Social Psychology* 25: 57–77.

Pierson, Paul. 1998. 'Irresistible forces, immovable objects: Post-industrial welfare states confront permanent austerity.' *Journal of European Public Policy* 5: 539–560.

Pomper, Gerald. 1997. *The Election of 1996*. Chatham, NJ: Chatham House.

Powell, G. Bingham, Jr. 1982. *Contemporary Democracies: Participation, Stability, and Violence*. Cambridge: Harvard University Press.

Powell, G. Bingham, Jr. 2000. *Elections as Instruments of Democracy*. New Haven: Yale University Press.

Pridham, Geoffrey, and Paul G. Lewis. Eds. 1996. *Stabilizing Fragile Democracies: Comparing Party Systems in Southern and Eastern Europe*. London: Routledge.

Przeworski, Adam, Michael E. Alvarez, Jose Antonio Cheibub, and Fernando Limongi. 2000. *Democracy and Development: Political Institutions and Well-Being in the World, 1950–1990*. New York: Cambridge University Press.

Przeworski, Adam, and John Sprague. 1986. *Paper Stones: A History of Electoral Socialism*. Chicago: University of Chicago Press.

Przeworski, Adam, and Henry Teune. 1970. *The Logic of Comparative Social Inquiry*. New York: Wiley–Interscience.

Quillian, Lincoln. 1995. 'Prejudice as a response to perceived group threat: Population composition and anti-immigrant and racial prejudice in Europe.' *American Sociological Review* 60: 586–611.

Rabinowitz, George, and Stuart Elaine Macdonald. 1989. 'A directional theory of issue voting.' *American Political Science Review* 83: 93–121.

Rae, Douglas W. 1971. *The Political Consequences of Electoral Laws*. 2d ed. New Haven: Yale University Press.

Rallings, Colin, and Michael Thrasher. 2000. 'Personality politics and protest voting: The first elections to the Greater London Authority.' *Parliamentary Affairs* 53 (4): 753–764.

Reif, Karl-Heinz. 1997. 'European elections as member state second-order elections revisited.' *European Journal of Political Research* 31 (1–2): 115–124.

Reif, Karl-Heinz, and Herman Schmitt. 1980. 'Second-order national elections: A conceptual framework for the analysis of European election results.' *European Journal of Political Research* 8 (1): 3–44.

Renouvin, Bertrand. 1997. *Une tragédie bien française: Le Front national contre la nation*. Paris: Ramsay.

Reynolds, Andrew, and Ben Reilly. Eds. 1997. *The International IDEA Handbook on Electoral System Design*. Stockholm: IDEA.

Riedisperger, Max. 1992. 'Heil Haider! The revitalization of the Austrian Freedom Party since 1986.' *Politics and Society in Germany, Austria and Switzerland* 4 (3): 18–47.

Riker, William H. 1962. *The Theory of Political Coalitions*. New Haven: Yale University Press.

Riker, William H. 1976. 'The number of political parties: A reexamination of Duverger's Law.' *Comparative Politics* 9: 93–106.

Riker, William H. 1982. 'The two-party system and Duverger's Law: An essay on the history of political science.' *American Political Science Review* 76: 753–766.

Riker, William H. 1986. 'Duverger's Law Revisited.' In *Electoral Laws and Their Political Consequences*, ed. Bernard Grofman and Arend Lijphart. New York: Agathon Press.

Rokkan, Stein. 1970. *Citizens, Elections, Parties; Approaches to the Comparative Study of the Processes of Development*. New York: McKay.

Rose, Richard. 2000. 'The end of consensus in Austria and Switzerland.' *Journal of Democracy* 11 (2): 26–40.

Rose, Richard. Ed. 1974. *Electoral Behavior: A Comparative Handbook*. New York: Free Press.

Rose, Richard. Ed. 2001. *The International Encyclopedia of Elections*. Washington, DC: CQ Press.

Rose, Richard, and Neil Munro. 2002. *Elections without Order: Russia's Challenge to Vladimir Putin*. New York: Cambridge University Press.

Rose, Richard, Neil Munro, and Tom Mackie. 1998. *Elections in Central and Eastern Europe since 1990*. Strathclyde: Center for the Study of Public Policy.

Rose, Richard, and Derek W. Urwin. 1969. 'Social cohesion, political parties and strains in regime.' *Comparative Political Studies* 2: 7–67.

Rose, Richard, and Derek W. Urwin. 1970. 'Persistence and change in Western party systems since 1945.' *Political Studies* 18: 287–319.

Rosenstone, Stephen, R. L. Behr, and E. H. Lazarus. 1996. *Third Parties in America*. 2d ed. Princeton: Princeton University Press.

Rydgren, Jens. 2002. 'Radical right populism in Sweden: Still a failure, but for how long?' *Scandinavian Political Studies* 25 (1): 27–56.

Rydgren, Jens. 2003. 'Meso-level reasons for racism and xenophobia: Some converging and diverging effects of radical right populism in France and Sweden.' *European Journal of Social Theory* 6 (1): 45–68.

Rydgren, Jens. 2004. 'Explaining the emergence of radical right-wing populist parties: The case of Denmark.' *West European Politics* 27 (3): 474–502.

Rydgren, Jens. 2004. *The Populist Challenge: Political Protest and Ethno-Nationalist Mobilization in France*. New York: Berghahn Books.

Sartori, Giovanni. 1966. 'European political parties: The case of polarized pluralism.' In *Political Parties and Political Development*, ed. Joseph LaPalombara and Myron Weiner. Princeton: Princeton University Press.

Sartori, Giovanni. 1976. *Parties and Party Systems: A Framework for Analysis*. New York: Cambridge University Press.

Sartori, Giovanni. 1994. *Comparative Constitutional Engineering: An Inquiry into Structures, Incentives, and Outcomes*. New York: Columbia University Press.

Sawer, Marian. Ed. 2001. *Elections: Full, Free and Fair*. Sydney: Federation Press.

Schain, Martin. 1987. 'The National Front in France and the construction of political legitimacy.' *West European Politics* 10 (2): 229–252.

Schain, Martin, Aristide Zolberg, and Patrick Hossay. Editors. 2002. *Shadows over Europe: The Development and Impact of the Extreme Right in Western Europe*. Houndmills: Palgrave Macmillan.

Schattschneider, E. E. 1942. *Party Government*. New York: Farrar and Rinehart.

Schedler, Andreas. 1996. 'Anti-political-establishment parties.' *Party Politics* 2: 291–312.

Scheepers, P., H. Schmeets, and A. Felling. 1997. 'Fortress Holland? Support for ethnocentric policies among the 1994-electorate of The Netherlands.' *Ethnic and Racial Studies* 20 (1): 145–159.

Schickler E., and D. P. Green. 1997. 'The stability of party identification in Western democracies – Results from eight panel surveys.' *Comparative Political Studies* 30 (4): 450–483.

Schmitt, Herman, and Sören Holmberg. 1995. 'Political parties in decline?' In *Citizens and the State*, ed. Hans-Dieter Klingemann and Dieter Fuchs. Oxford: Oxford University Press.

Schumpeter, Joseph A. 1952. *Capitalism, Socialism and Democracy*. 4th ed. London: Allen and Unwin.

Selle, Per. 1991. 'Membership in party organizations and the problems of decline of parties.' *Comparative Political Studies* 23 (4): 459–477.

Shugart, Matthew Soberg, and Martin P. Wattenberg. Eds. 2001. *Mixed-Member Electoral Systems: The Best of Both Worlds?* Oxford: Oxford University Press.

Simmons, Harvey Gerald. 1995. *The French National Front: The Extremist Challenge to Democracy*. Boulder, CO: Westview Press.

Simmons, Harvey Gerald. 1996. *The French National Front: The Extremist Challenge to Democracy*. 2nd ed. Boulder, CO: Westview Press.

Smith, J. 2002. 'European right-wing: A turn to the right.' *World Today* 58 (6): 7–8.

Snijders, T. A. B., and R. J. Bosker. 1999. *Multilevel Analysis. An Introduction to Basic and Advanced Multilevel Modelling*. London: Sage.

Southwell, Patricia L. 1997. 'Fairness, governability, and legitimacy: The debate over electoral systems in France.' *Journal of Political and Military Sociology* 25: 163–185.

Southwell, Patricia L., and M. J. Everest. 1998. 'The electoral consequences of alienation: Nonvoting and protest voting in the 1992 presidential race.' *Social Science Journal* 35 (1): 43–51.

Stimson, James A. 1991. *Public Opinion in America: Moods, Cycles and Swings*. Boulder, CO: Westview Press.

Stöss, Richard. 1988. 'The problem of rightwing extremism in West Germany.' In *Right Extremism in Western Europe*, ed. Klaus von Beyme. London: Frank Cass.

Strøm, Kaare. 1990. *Minority Government and Majority Rule*. New York: Cambridge University Press.

Studlar, Donley T. 1979. 'Individual socioeconomic attributes and attitudes towards coloured immigrants.' *New Community* 10: 228–52.

Svåsand, Lars. 1998. 'Scandinavian right-wing radicalism.' In *The New Politics of the Right: Neo-Populist Parties and Movements in Established Democracies*. New York: St. Martin's Press.

Swyngedouw, Marc. 1992. 'National elections in Belgium: The breakthrough of the extreme right in Flanders.' *Regional Politics and Policy* 2 (3): 62–75.

Swyngedouw, Marc. 2001. 'The subjective cognitive and affective map of extreme right voters: Using open-ended questions in exit polls.' *Electoral Studies* 20 (2): 217–241.

Swyngedouw, Marc, and G. Ivaldi. 2001. 'The extreme right utopia in Belgium and France: The ideology of the Flemish *Vlaams Blok* and the French *Front National*.' *West European Politics* 24 (3): 1–22.

Taagepera, Rein. 1998. 'Effective magnitude and effective threshold.' *Electoral Studies* 17 (4): 393–404.

Taagepera, Rein. 1999. 'The number of parties as a function of heterogeneity and electoral system.' *Comparative Political Studies* 32 (5): 531–548.

Taagepera, Rein. 2002. 'Nationwide threshold of representation.' *Electoral Studies* 21 (3): 383–401.

Taagepera, Rein, and Bernard Grofman. 1985. 'Rethinking Duverger's Law: Predicting the effective number of parties in plurality and PR systems – parties minus issues equals one.' *European Journal of Political Research* 13: 341–352.

Taagepera, Rein, and Matthew Soberg Shugart. 1989. *Seats and Votes: The Effects and Determinants of Electoral Systems*. New Haven: Yale University Press.

Taggart, Paul. 1995. 'New populist parties in Western Europe.' *West European Politics* 18 (1): 34–51.

Taggart, Paul. 1996. *The New Populism and New Politics: New Protest Parties in Sweden in Comparative Perspective*. London: Macmillan.

Thomassen, Jacques. 1976. 'Party identification as a cross-national concept: Its meaning in the Netherlands.' In *Party Identification and Beyond*, ed. Ian Budge, Ivor Crewe, and Dennis Farlie. London: Wiley.

Thomassen, Jacques. 1994. 'The intellectual history of election studies.' *European Journal of Political Research* 25: 239–245.

Thranhardt, Dietrich. 1995. 'The political uses of xenophobia in England, France and Germany.' *Party Politics* 1: 323–345.

Thurlow, R. 1998. *Fascism in Britain: From Oswald Mosley's Blackshirts to the National Front*. London: I. B. Tauris.

Tossutti, L. S. 2002. 'How transnational factors influence the success of ethnic, religious and regional parties in twenty-one states.' *Party Politics* 8 (1): 51–74.

United Nations High Commissioner for Refugees. 2003. *Asylum Applications Lodged in Industrialized Countries: Levels and Trends, 2000–2002*. Geneva: UNHCR. http://www.unhcr.ch/cgi-bin/texis/vtx/statistics.

van der Brug, Wouter. 1999. 'Voters' perceptions and party dynamics.' *Party Politics* 5 (2): 147–169.

van der Brug, Wouter. 2003. 'How the LPF fueled discontent: Empirical tests of explanations of LPF support.' *Acta Politica* 38 (1): 89–106.

van der Brug, Wouter, and Meindert Fennema. 2003. 'Protest or mainstream? How the European anti-immigrant parties developed into two separate groups by 1999.' *European Journal of Political Research* 42: 55–76.

van der Brug, Wouter, Meindert Fennema, and Jean Tillie. 2000. 'Anti-immigrant parties in Europe: Ideological or protest vote?' *European Journal of Political Research* 37 (1): 77–102.

van der Brug, Wouter, Meindert Fennema, and Jean Tillie. 2005. 'Why some anti-immigrant parties fail and others succeed: A two-step model of aggregate electoral support.' *Comparative Political Studies* forthcoming.

Van Holsteyn, J. J. M., and G. A. Irwin. 2002. 'Never a dull moment: Pim Fortuyn and the Dutch parliamentary election of 2002.' *West European Politics* 26 (2): 41–66.

Veugelers, John W. P. 1997. 'Social cleavage and the revival of far right parties: The case of France's National Front.' *Acta Sociologica* 40 (1): 31–49.

Veugelers, John W. P. 1999. 'A challenge for political sociology: The rise of far right parties in contemporary Western Europe.' *Current Sociology* 47: 78–105.

Veugelers, John W. P. 2000. 'Right-wing extremism in contemporary France: A "silent counterrevolution"?' *Sociological Quarterly* 41 (1): 19–40.

Vowles, Jack. 1995. 'The politics of electoral reform in New Zealand.' *International Political Science Review* 16 (1): 95–116.

Vowles, Jack, Peter Aimer, Susan Banducci, and Jeffrey Karp. 1998. *Voters' Victory? New Zealand's First Election under Proportional Representation.* Auckland: Auckland University Press.

Wald, Kenneth, and S. Shye. 1995. 'Religious influence in electoral behavior: The role of institutional and social forces In Israel.' *Journal of Politics* 57 (2): 495–507.

Walker, Martin. 1977. *The National Front.* London: Fontana/Collins.

Wattenberg, Martin P. 1998. *The Decline of American Political Parties 1952–1996.* Cambridge: Harvard University Press.

Wattenberg, Martin P. 2002. *Where Have All the Voters Gone?* Cambridge: Harvard University Press.

Webb, Paul, David Farrell, and Ian Holliday. Eds. *Political Parties in Advanced Industrial Democracies.* Oxford: Oxford University Press.

White, Stephen, Richard Rose, and Ian McAllister. 1996. *How Russia Votes.* Chatham, NJ: Chatham House.

Whitefield, S. 2002. 'Political cleavages and post-communist politics.' *Annual Review of Political Science* 5: 181–200.

Widfeldt, Andre. 2000. 'Scandinavia: Mixed success for the populist right.' *Parliamentary Affairs* 53 (3): 468–500.

Williams, Edward J. 1967. *Latin American Christian Democratic Parties.* Knoxville: University of Tennessee Press.

Wilson, Frank L. Ed. 1998. *The European Center-Right at the End of the Twentieth Century.* New York: St. Martin's Press.

Wolintz, Steven B. 1979. 'The transformation of Western European party systems revisited.' *West European Politics* 2: 7–8.

Wolintz, Steven B. 1988. *Parties and Party Systems in Liberal Democracies.* London: Routledge.

Zielinski, Jakub. 2002. 'Translating social cleavages into party systems: The significance of new democracies.' *World Politics* 54: 184–211.

Index